THE PICTORIAL GUIDE
TO MODERN HOME KNITTING

A DRESS WITH PLEAT EFFECTS

See pages 246-248 for directions

THE PICTORIAL GUIDE TO MODERN HOME KNITTING

EDITED BY
CATHERINE FRANKS, A.R.C.A.

ODHAMS PRESS LIMITED
LONG ACRE, LONDON, W.C.2

MADE AND PRINTED IN GREAT BRITAIN
BY ODHAMS (WATFORD) LTD., WATFORD

CONTENTS

INTRODUCTION

THIS book has been compiled to contain inside one cover both a textbook, giving instruction in all the principles and processes of the crafts of knitting and crochet, and a book of directions for making many types of attractive garments and useful articles for the home. We are taught at school the basic principles of knitting, i.e., how to cast on and off, how to increase by making a stitch and to decrease by knitting two stitches together, and a few other elementary processes. Then there is a big gap when other processes are not considered until there is the need to work them when copying directions for garments. Printed directions are then followed, row by row, and the worker is not aware that a definite law or principle of shaping has been carried out. In this book the principles and various processes are shown and discussed separately and quite apart from garment making, so that the worker can become familiar with all the ways of shaping and constructing shapes. In some cases directions for making garments are given which incorporate these processes, and by following these instructions the worker cannot fail to understand the principles involved. For instance, after the section on " Mechanical Shaping," directions are given for making a girl's vest, using one of the processes described, and it will be clearly seen how the method used affects the shape of the garment.

The entire scheme of the book has been planned to cover the crafts of knitting and crochet as far as the majority of workers require, and it is so laid out that the principles develop in easy stages, from the very first processes to the most advanced types of work that can possibly be needed by the serious worker.

A need for such a book as this must have been felt by many who, being able to follow instructions well, need to know how to develop their own ideas or experiment with unusual methods. There is now no need to be disappointed because a printed leaflet of instructions does not make up a particularly attractive jumper to suit you. Just follow the simple instructions given on how to adapt existing patterns to your own measures and you will find that it is possible to knit whatever garment you choose.

There are many workers who prefer crochet to knitting, and these people will find all they need to know in the crochet section at the back of the book. Crochet work has been planned out in the same way as the knitting, and all necessary details are fully explained, leading the worker to use ingenuity and giving her the knowledge required for designing her own garments if she so desires.

One of the most important things to become familiar with is the tension of your own work, as the whole craft of both knitting and crochet is built up on this. Do study, most carefully, the pages devoted to tension and the various ways of measuring and adapting it. When the tension of work is known in knitting and crochet it is possible to copy a knitted garment in crochet work and vice versa. A crocheted fabric can be chosen to give a similar effect to the knitted fabric and then the garment can be worked up to the same measurements and shape. Crochet works up a little thicker than knitting, and when copying a knitted design in crochet it may be best to use thinner wool. As an instance of this, a jumper knitted in stocking stitch, or moss stitch, or any of the smooth textures, can be copied in double crochet, or treble stitch for quicker work, in a wool 1-ply thinner. It may be necessary to experiment with a small square of work first, to get the right thickness of hook. On the other hand, in copying crocheted designs in knitting, it is not always necessary to use thicker wool; sometimes it is better to work on needles thicker than the hook.

There are some workers, knitters as well as crocheters, who find it impossible to work from printed directions. For them there is a special section describing how to work from charts and graphs. It is also possible to work from dressmakers' patterns, the shape of each part being copied in either knitting or crochet. Where the paper pattern allows turnings, cut these away, as no turnings will be needed, and it may be an advantage to make each piece of garment about $\frac{1}{4}$ in. smaller each way to allow for the expansion of the fabric when it is pressed.

All the garments given in this book contain some basic process, each one different, so that if all of them are made up a good groundwork knowledge will be gained.

CATHERINE FRANKS.

PART I
EQUIPMENT, HINTS AND PATTERNS

KNITTING TOOLS

Knitters will find that there are other things besides needles and wools necessary for good work. If the tools shown in the accompanying illustration are kept handy, much valuable time will be saved.

A small pair of scissors for cutting ends and opening skeins.

Pencil and paper for jotting down points to be remembered. It is as well to take a note of any alterations made in the pattern so that the worker remembers to make them on both sides of the garment.

An inch tape for comparing the given measures with those required, and for testing proportions as work progresses.

Some safety pins for marking rows. A small pin inserted to mark a row will often save a knitter having to recount whole sections.

A medium sized crochet hook is handy. It has many uses, including the picking up of dropped stitches and the making of narrow edgings round the necks and armholes of lingerie.

Needles, both darning and the special blunt pointed needle for wool, are always required for fastening off ends at the beginning and end of work, and at joins.

Squared paper will be needed by the advanced worker for planning out decreasings, increasings and the working of texture patterns.

A knitting bag for keeping the work clean.

WOOLS

It would be impossible to describe the dozens of different kinds of knitting wools on the market, for they seem to increase every week. Sometimes they are quite new and sometimes they are new varieties of old threads.

The illustration shows specimens of the more common types, and of these there are many more varieties.

1. Fingering. A smooth evenly twisted wool, and one of the oldest varieties. It is warm and wears well, and is used chiefly for jumpers, babies' wear and lingerie. (*a*) The 2-ply is very fine, being used for lacy textures. (*b*) The 3-ply is, perhaps, used more than any other for medium weight garments. (*c*) 4-ply fingering is used chiefly for heavier types of garments; it is strong and gives a close fabric.

2. Double knitting. A very thick thread for skirts and outer wear.

3. Wool string; a new variety. A round, thin thread not unlike macramé string, but softer.

4. Bouclé. An imitation of hand spun wool. It represents one of the pleasanter types of "fancy" wools.

5. Tweed effect wool. When knitted it is hard to tell the fabric from a soft tweed. If too thick, it is difficult to handle.

6. Two-colour effect. An attractive variety; a thick and a thin thread twisted together.

7. Novelty wools. These come in great variety; this one gives a charming misty quality to the texture.

8. Astrakhan. Another new variety which, when knitted, resembles astrakhan fur.

OTHER KINDS OF THREADS

Silks, artificial silks, cottons and various combinations of threads, can be used in knitting garments for summer wear. Some of the pure silks are very lovely, with a dull gloss that gives a rich texture to the fabric. Great care should be taken when laundering garments made from silks and artificial silks, because being so heavy they lose their shape quickly. Do not hang them up to dry, but lay them flat on a dry towel and pull them into shape as they dry.

1. A pure silk thread of the best quality. This will knit into delightful garments; its chief use is for babies' clothes, jumpers and young girls' dresses. Some knitting silks are smooth while others have a crêpe twist.

2. Artificial silk of good quality. A cheap artificial silk is seldom satisfactory. It looks too shiny and does not hang well.

3. Mercerized cotton. This is a pleasant thread to work with, and may be used for table mats, hats and very cool jumpers.

4. Silk and wool mixtures. These threads make up into very attractive lingerie, which wears and washes well.

5. Plain cotton yarn. This can be bought in a great variety of colours, and is a good thread for summer jumpers and children's garments.

WINDING WOOL

There are various devices on the market which may be used with advantage to help the knitter wind her wool. They save a great deal of time, and render the worker independent of outside help. Prices vary considerably, but the cheaper kinds are very efficient, and their prices are within the range of the most moderate purse. Nearly all drapers sell these wool winders.

1

1. A simple wooden holder, consisting of a wooden clamp to fasten to the edge of a table, and a metal rod threaded through four adjustable arms. The knitter who likes to make things for herself could construct a similar holder for quite a small sum. Metal holders working on a similar principle can also be bought.

2

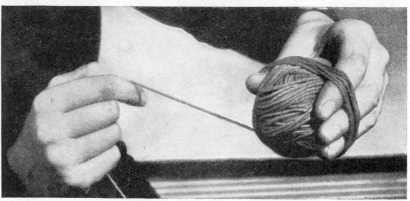

2. Winding the ball. Wool must never be wound tightly. The strands should pass over all four fingers and thumb of one hand, while the other hand guides the wool from the skein. The wool should be allowed to pass through the guiding hand very lightly, so that there is no tautness between the skein and the ball to stretch the wool.

3

3. This useful device winds the ball from the skein on a holder. All that the knitter has to do, is to turn the knob on the top. When work is in progress, the wool passes from this ball to the knitter via the hole in the metal upright at the side, which ensures a smooth working thread.

TAKING CARE OF WOOLS AND NEEDLES

The serious knitter should have a complete set of needles, ranging from the bone and composition types to the finer metal needles. It is so useful to be able to change the size of the needle at will, in order to get fine adjustment in the tension.

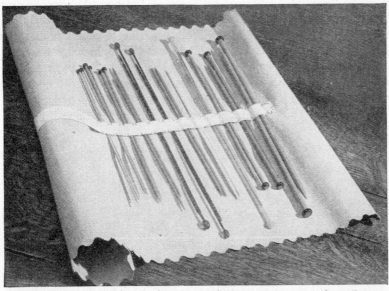

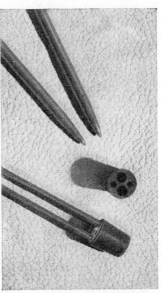

1. A very welcome gift to a knitter would be an entire set of needles in a folder as shown in the illustration. Take a piece of flannel, baize, or American cloth and a length of 1-in. wide elastic. Sew the elastic down the middle of the cloth at intervals of 1 in. for the large needles, gradually lessening for the finer needles; do not forget a pocket for the gauge, inch tape and small scissors.

4. Needle shields. A rubber cup slips over the points of the needles to prevent them working through your knitting bag. A cup can replace a broken knob.

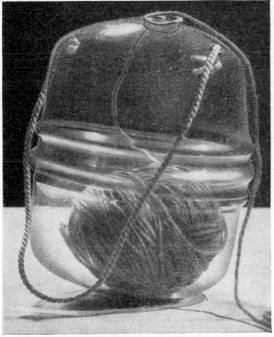

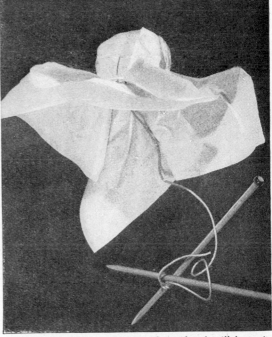

2. If the ball of wool is allowed to roll about the floor or the railway carriage it will soon get soiled. Keep it clean in a holder like this or in any of the many others which can be bought for a few pence.

3. A paper serviette and an elastic band will be quite useful for keeping a ball of wool clean. 2-lb. jam jars are very useful for holding balls of wool, especially when more than one colour is being knitted.

KNITTING NEEDLES

Needle sizes are so finely graded that great care must be taken in their choice. So much depends upon suitable needles being used, as a glance at the pages on comparative tensions and textures will show. Three-ply wool worked with size 11 needles will give a warm, close texture, but if the same wool is worked with size 3 needles, the fabric will be extremely open and it will only be warm if worn under a garment of much closer texture.

There are many different kinds of needles: bone, celluloid, composition, light metal, steel and wood. Some of the newest kinds have a metal core which is covered with either celluloid or composition. This metal centre makes the needles comfortable to hold because they are well balanced in the hand, and will seldom slip out of the work when only holding a few stitches. Who has not had this happen with the heavy-knobbed celluloid needles?

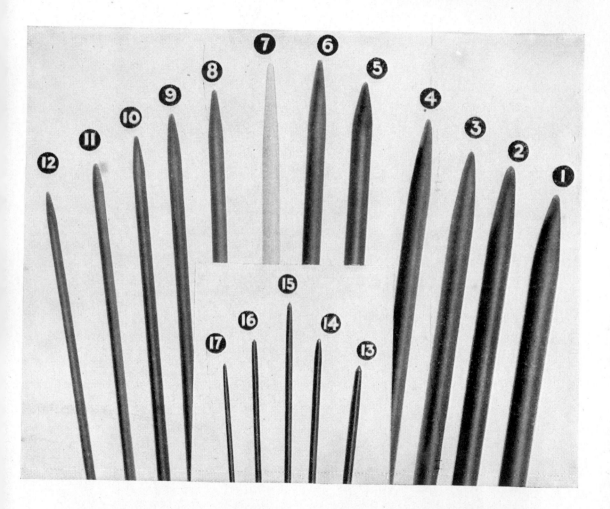

1—12. The larger illustration shows the sizes of needles in general use today. They can be used as a guide when a gauge is not handy. English needles are numbered 1, 2, 3, etc.; the smaller the number, the larger the size. The colour of the needles should, if possible, contrast with the colour of the wool.

13—17. The smaller illustration shows thin steel needles. Metal needles are seldom used because they are so heavy and work is seldom so fine as to require a very thin strong needle. Socks, stockings for children, gloves and strappings for cardigans are about the only pieces of work carried out on steel needles nowadays.

NEEDLE GAUGINGS

Until recently needles were not marked with their numbers and before being used, they had to be tested on a gauge. For those workers who still have these needles and wish to use them here are some hints on using the gauge.

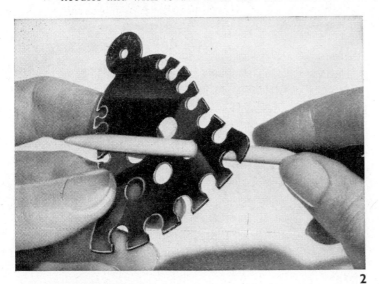

2

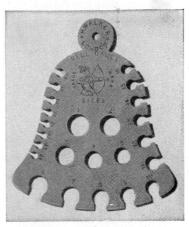

1

3

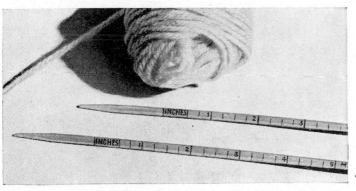

4

1. This is the old-fashioned bell gauge, so called from its shape. Being of metal it is the safest kind to use because it does not expand in hot weather.

The round holes in the middle are for large bone or wood needles; the small holes are for steel needles, and the medium sized holes at the edge are for needles of celluloid and composition.

2. Testing needle sizes. Pass the needle into the holes until the one which takes it tightly is found. Needles may vary by a fraction, but so long as it is impossible to move the needle sideways in the hole, or while it is passing through the slot, as in the case of the holes round the edge of a bell gauge, then it is sure to be the correct size.

3. The modern needle is well marked. Soon, gauges will not be needed.

4. A very useful needle which is another recent acquisition.

ABBREVIATIONS

It is a common practice to use only the first letters of many of the words used in knitting directions. This is done to shorten the directions and to make them easier to read. Where more than one word has the same initial letter it is followed by the second letter, or when there would otherwise be the same letter representing words in both knitting and crochet, then enough of the word is given to show its meaning. Here is a list of the more commonly used abbreviations.

k. = knit (plain).   r. = round.   sl. = slip.
m. = make.   p. = purl.   c. = cable.

st. = stitch or stitches.   ins. = inches.   tog. = together. rep. = repeat. patt. = pattern. g.st. = garter stitch.   st.st. = stocking stitch.
p.s.s.o. = pass the slipped stitch over.
w.r.n. = wool round needle.
w.fd. = wool forward.
dec. = decrease or decreasing.
inc. = increase or increasing.
...... = sign of repetition.
(......) = directions inside brackets are repeated the number of times stated directly after, i.e., (m. 1, k. 1), 3 = repeat 3 times.

USEFUL GADGETS

Gadgets for recording the numbers of decreasings, rows and increasings can be bought at reasonable prices. Alternatively, it is an easy matter to construct simple devices from pieces of strong card.

I. No doubt many knitters are already familiar with this little cylinder which slips on to the end of the needle, and by means of revolving numbers, records the number of rows, etc., as they are worked.

USEFUL GADGETS
continued

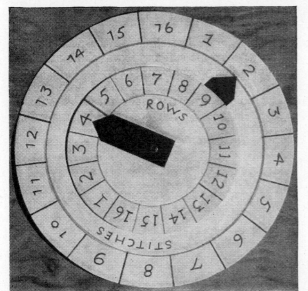

2. To make this wheel for marking the numbers of rows and stitches, cut two circles from a piece of white card; one circle should be 5 ins. in diameter, and the other 3 ins. The two pointers are strips of the same card ½ in. wide by 2¼ ins. and 1¼ ins. long respectively. Mark off each card along the edges as shown and number each section. Punch holes in the centres of the circles and at one end of each pointer. Mitre the other ends of the pointers and clip all the pieces together with a large paper fastener or a very large press stud. The long pointer goes between the two disks and the short one goes on top of the small disk. By moving the pointers round, various numberings can be obtained. The circles and pointers can be coloured in different shades to help to distinguish the two sets of numbers.

2

3

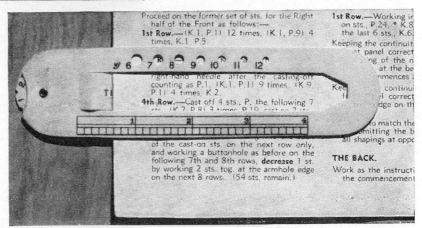

3. A gadget with many uses. It will tell you the size of your needles, measure ribbing bands, record numbers and mark your place on the directions.

4

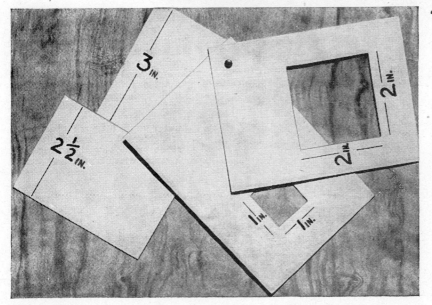

4. From three post cards you can make a very useful set of guides. Cut out a 2-in. square aperture from one card for testing the tension of thick wools; another card with a 1-in. square aperture will measure the tension of finer knitting; and for measuring quickly the depths of ribbings cut another card, like the third one shown here, to mark 2½ and 3 ins.

A FEW HINTS

Tight knitters should try casting on and casting off on needles two sizes larger.

Needles pointed at both ends can now be obtained made of composition; there is no more need to work with heavy steel needles.

Finish the row before putting work away, otherwise the last stitch on the needle will be larger than the rest and it will show as a larger loop when worked.

Very short needles pointed at both ends can be bought specially made for cable stitching. Broken needles can be sharpened for cabling.

1

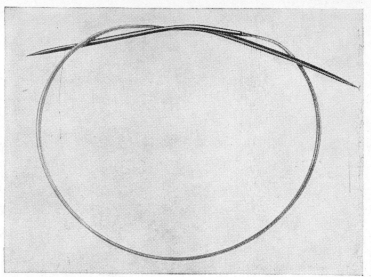

1. A circular needle for knitting tubular garments saves the time spent in changing from one needle to another in the four-needle method. The circular needle is not so practical for a large garment like a skirt or adult's dress, because the weight of the knitting becomes too heavy; it is better to knit a large garment in sections on two needles, seaming them carefully by machine.

2

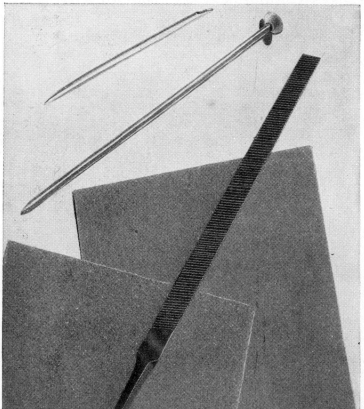

2. Do not throw away a broken needle. If one piece left is of workable length, sharpen the broken end with a fine file, polishing it afterwards with fine sand-paper. The short end will be very useful as a cablestitch needle.

Bent needles need not be discarded either. Steep them in very hot water until they are pliable, then straighten them and set them in shape by allowing them to get cold in water which is as cold as possible.

CASTING ON

There are several methods of casting on stitches and the one used must be carefully chosen to give the best edge to the piece of work on hand. If you knit at a slightly tighter tension than the average worker, it is a good plan to cast on with needles a size larger than those to be used for the rest of the work and to knit the first row with these.

The loose knitter should try casting on and knitting the first row with needles a size smaller to prevent a stretching edge.

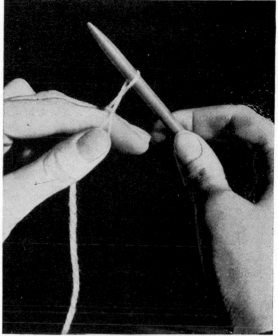

2

2. Take up a needle in the right hand and insert it under the first loop made round the fingers. Pass it over the strand which crosses the loop, then take the needle downwards between the fingers and pull the strand, as a stitch round the needle, through the loop made on the fingers.

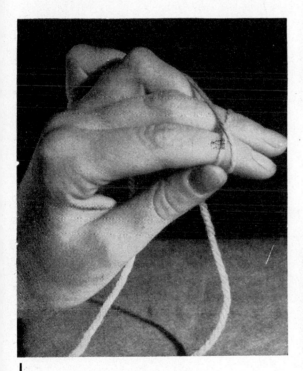

I

1. Hold the end of wool between the thumb and first finger of the left hand, wind it once round the first and second fingers of the same hand and then again, this time taking the wool across the first strand from right to left.

3. Pull the loop tightly to form the first stitch.

3

CASTING ON—METHOD A

This is the usual method and it gives a medium tension to the edge.

The method used when knitting the first row can alter the effect of the cast-on stitches.

1. Take the needle holding the first stitch in the left hand, and take up the free needle in the right hand. Pass the right-hand needle into the stitch from below, and take it behind the left-hand needle. Hold the wool in the right hand and arrange it through the fingers to give the most comfortable tension.

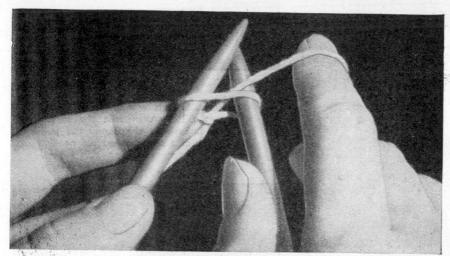

2. Make a loop round the point of the right-hand needle by passing the wool first behind and then in front of the needle.

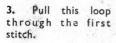

3. Pull this loop through the first stitch.

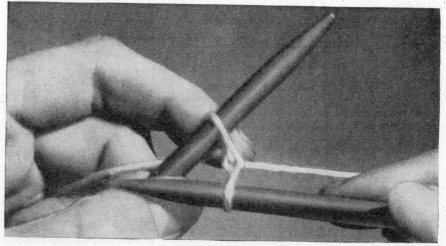

CASTING ON—METHOD A *continued*

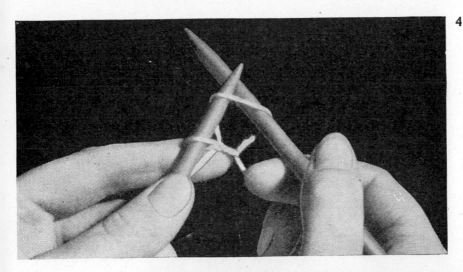

4. Make the second stitch by slipping the left-hand needle through the loop, just made, with an upward movement from below.

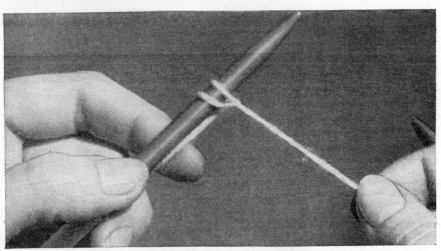

5. Remove the right-hand needle and pull the new stitch fairly tight.

6. This is the edge made with method A.

CASTING ON—METHOD B

An attractive corded edge, suitable for scarves, collars and other edges which must not stretch, will result from this method. Form the first stitch in the usual way, make the second cast-on stitch as for method A, and remove the right-hand needle.

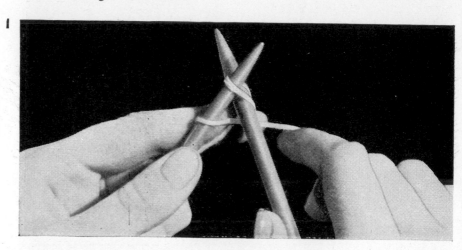

1. Pass the right-hand needle between the two stitches on the left-hand needle. Make a loop round the point of the right-hand needle as in the previous method.

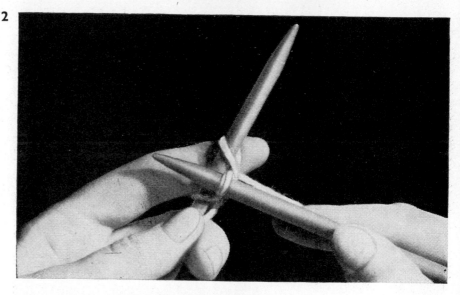

2. Pull the loop through to the front of the work and pass it over the point of the left-hand needle to form the third cast-on stitch. Remove the right-hand needle. Make the fourth stitch by pulling a loop between the second and third stitches and continue in a like manner until enough stitches are on the left-hand needle.

3. A piece of knitting with a corded cast-on edge.

CASTING ON—METHOD C

By this method, an invisible cast-on edge can be made: it is ideal for babies' clothes knitted in fine wool, when method B would result in a line of loops along the edge. It is a good edge when a fringe is to be added.

It is also useful for casting on very thick wool which, with other methods, would give an edge too hard and thick.

Make the first stitch on one needle as described before. Hold this needle in the right hand, instead of the left, and grip the wool in the palm of the left hand.

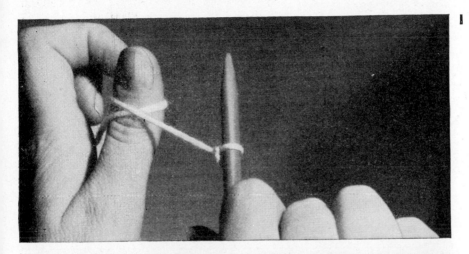

1. Holding the wool taut between the needle and the left hand, make a loop round the thumb of the left hand by passing the thumb in front of, and below, the strand twice, forming a loop in such a way that the strand from the needle crosses above the strand coming from the left hand.

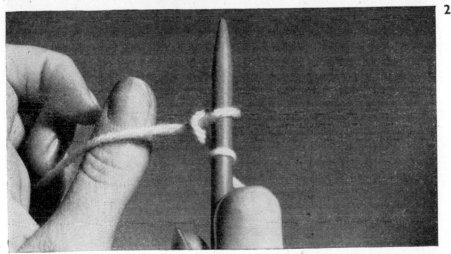

2. Transfer the loop on to the needle by holding the thumb upright and slipping the needle into the loop from below. Pull the loop tight, and repeat for every stitch.

3. These stitches were cast on with the invisible method. There is no definite selvedge, and the edge is very elastic.

CASTING ON FOR THREE NEEDLES

Socks, stockings and gloves are knitted on three needles, and worked in "rounds" continuously without a seam.

The stitches are held on three needles, while a fourth is used for the work. Casting on is done with either method A or B, the total number of stitches being divided among the three needles. As a rule, the stitches are divided equally, but sometimes, as in the case of shaped stockings, one needle has more than a third of the total number, and the remainder are divided between the other two needles.

1

I. When the stitches for one needle have been cast on, make an extra stitch and leave it on the right-hand needle. This becomes the first stitch when the right-hand needle is changed into the left hand; continue casting on the stitches for the second needle and repeat for the third needle.

2

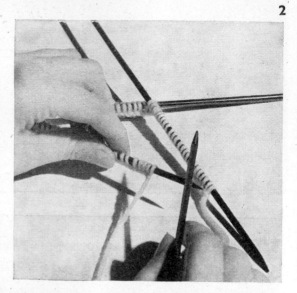

3

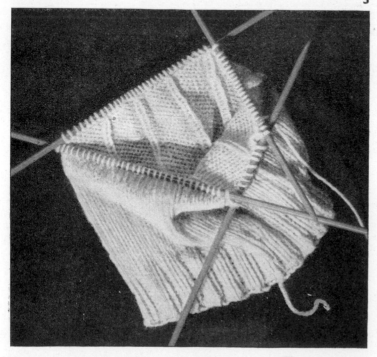

2. Lay all three needles on the table and arrange them to form a triangle, making sure that the cast-on edge does not twist, or it will be impossible to complete the round. The point between the beginning and end of the casting on should be towards the worker. Lift the first needle in the left hand and take up the free needle into the right hand. The wool from the third needle should be arranged round the fingers of the right hand. Knitting is commenced by inserting the fourth needle into the first stitch on the left-hand needle. For methods of work see appropriate pages. It will be quite in order if a short strand is left as a loop between the last cast-on stitch and the first knitted one. This is caused by the weight of the third needle, and after a few rounds have been worked it will disappear.

3. A piece of tubular knitting on three needles; the end of wool marks the beginning of the round.

KNITTING THE FIRST ROW

There are two ways of knitting the first row after casting on. One method gives a tight edge while the other leaves a loose elastic selvedge.

It is very important to choose the one that will give an edge suitable to the work on hand: a sock with too tight an edge can be very uncomfortable.

Underwear like vests must be cast on loosely and the first row must be knitted in the ordinary way to give the maximum amount of stretch. The casting on and knitting of the first row may be done on larger needles. Dresses, jumpers and babies' outer wear should have the first row knitted with the crossed method as a slightly firmer selvedge is required.

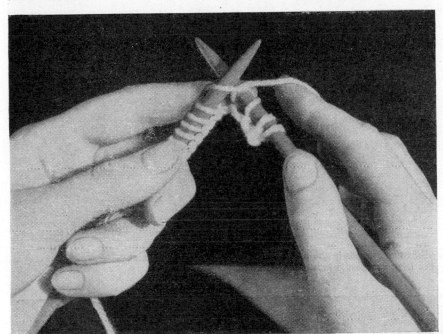

1. Knitting the first row in the ordinary method as a plain knit row. The process is the same as for plain knitting. Some knitters find that if double wool is used for this first row, a much firmer beginning to the work is obtained. This is particularly desired for vests that are not knitted in ribbing, and in other garments that are knitted on comparatively large needles. Before casting on, break off a piece of thread long enough to knit the first row; leave the ends at the beginning and the end of the row long enough to darn into the fabric.

2. A strong edge is given by knitting into the back of each cast-on stitch. It is the same method as for crossed plain knitting and the process will be seen on that page. This method is often used on jumpers where the cast-on edge is stretched a little.

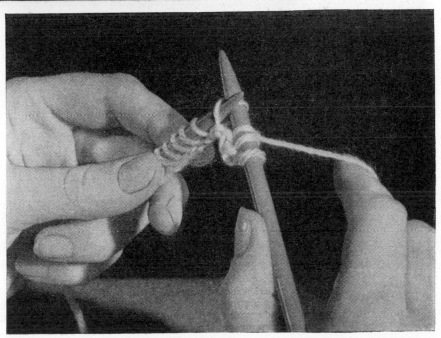

CASTING OFF

To complete the knitting, the last row must be bound off in such a way that the stitches are securely fastened.

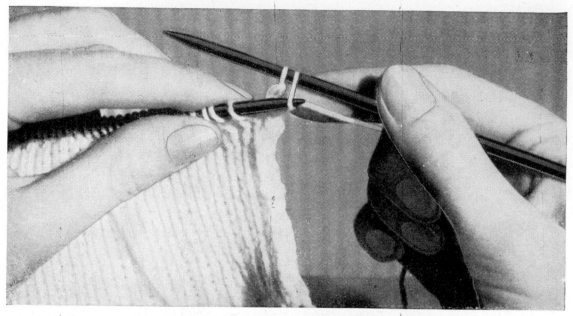

I. Knit two stitches in the usual way (plainwise). Pass the point of the left-hand needle into the first stitch.

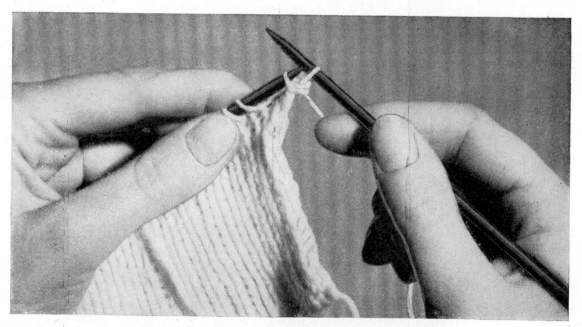

2. Lift up this stitch, pull it towards the left, pass it over the second stitch and off the needle. The cast-off stitch will lie horizontally along the top of the work. Knit a third stitch on to the right-hand needle and pass the second over it and off the needle in the same way as the first. Repeat to the end.

CASTING OFF *continued*

3. Cut the wool leaving enough to darn into the fabric to make the end secure, pull the last stitch through and finish off. When the casting off ends at the end of a seam do not cut the wool short, but leave the thread long enough to sew up the seam. This will save the trouble of fastening on a new piece of wool.

4

4. Stocking stitch cast off on the purl side. This is the neatest way of casting off, as the chain-like edge lies flat on the wrong side of the fabric and it does not appear on the right side at all.

5

5. Stocking stitch cast off on the plain side. Note how the casting off lies on the same side as it is worked. Remember to cast off on the side that best keeps the work neat. Wherever possible cast off the edges of collars, belts and trimmings on the wrong side to prevent the hard ridge curling to the front of the work.

JOINING WOOL

There are two good methods of joining wool threads. The first is by grafting and the second by knitting the two ends together. Both methods are suitable for fine wool, but for very thick wool grafting is preferable. Be sure to unravel sufficient wool to make a strong join.

1.

1. Knitting the two ends together. Finish the old end to within 8 ins. Lay the new thread along the old in such a way that 2 ins. of the new extends beyond the last stitch knitted. Knit the next four stitches with double thread.

2.

2. Now leave the remainder of the old thread hanging on one side of the work, and continue knitting with the new.

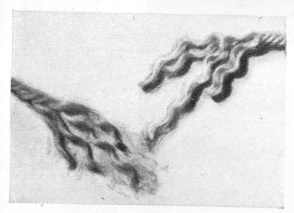

4. Lay the strands of both ends together and dovetailing, roll them all together, copying the twist of the wool as much as possible. This join will be perfectly strong when knitting proceeds.

4

3. Grafting. Cease knitting when there is about 6 ins. more of old thread. Unravel the end of both old and new threads, so that the plies are separated for about 2 ins. Cut these ply ends at uneven lengths.

MEASURING TENSIONS

Many knitting directions tell the worker to what tension the original garment was worked, and every effort should be made to copy that tension.

Every knitter should be familiar with her own tension. In this way she will ensure that her garments will be the correct size, and she will be able to adapt her work to form an exact copy of the original.

Tension can be measured with an inch tape, or a useful guide can be cut out of a post card. If the worker is an extremely tight knitter, her guide will show more stitches to the inch than is required for the work. In this case she will add a number of stitches to make up the correct width. Thus, if the directions state that the original was worked to 9 stitches to the inch, and that the garment will fit a 34-in. bust, and the guide shows that the worker knits to a tension of 10 stitches to the inch when working with the same sized needles and thread, it will be necessary to cast on 17 stitches more, back and front, than are given in the directions.

The same process is applied when the number of rows to the inch varies. If the directions state that there should be 9 rows to the inch and the worker's specimen shows $9\frac{1}{2}$ rows, and the garment must measure 18 ins. in length, then an extra 9 rows will have to be worked to give the correct measurement.

1

1. Place one end of the inch tape along a row in order to count the number of stitches to one inch for fine work, or two inches for coarse knitting. To count the number of rows to a given measure place the tape vertically down the fabric.

If it is difficult to count while the tape is on the knitting, mark the distance with pins and then remove the tape.

2. From a post card, cut out a square hole; this may be either 1 in. or 2 ins. square, according to the size of stitch to be measured.

Knit a 3-in. square of fabric and lightly press it as though it were the finished garment. Place the guide over this piece of knitting and, to count the stitches, arrange it so that one edge of the square hole is parallel to a row of knitting. To count the rows, lay the guide with one edge of the aperture running down a line of stitches.

2

COMPARATIVE TENSIONS

Here are a few photographs of the various tensions made by the more commonly used thicknesses of wools and needles.

Many knitters will like to make their own sampler of tensions by knitting squares and mounting them on to a card, adding notes of the thickness of needles used, and the thickness of the wool.

When a garment is under consideration, its tension can be checked by reference to this chart and if a texture chart, as described on the next page, has been made, the most suitable kind of yarn can be chosen too.

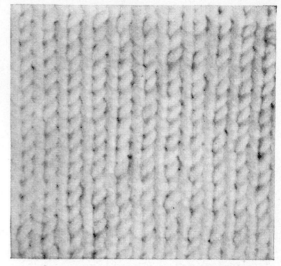

3. 4-ply wool worked on No. 9 needles.

1. 2-ply wool worked on No. 13 needles.

4. 3-ply wool worked on No. 9 needles.

2. 3-ply wool worked on No. 13 needles.

5. Double knitting wool worked on No. 6 needles.

COMPARATIVE TEXTURES

The serious knitter will want to possess a texture chart, for use when considering the kind of yarn to choose for the next piece of work.

Knit up odd scraps of wool left over from other knitting; they must be as varied as possible, because the chart is really a sampler of all the different textures obtainable with different kinds of threads. There should be a square of 2-ply, 3-ply and 4-ply fingering, tweed effect wool, crêpe wool, bouclé, pure silk, artificial silk, cotton and mercerized cotton, and as many other new threads as can be collected.

Paste these specimens on to a card, and label them with the name of the wool and the number of the needle.

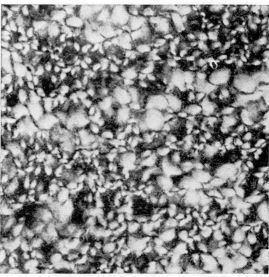

1. Bouclé wool; a pleasant rough surface. An attractive fabric for women's, men's and children's outer wear. Stocking stitch gives the best texture. It is difficult to undo.

3. Novelty wool; gives an attractive "misty" effect. The thread is not so easy to work with as a fingering, but the beauty of the fabric is worth while.

2. Tweed effect wool gives a hard-wearing fabric, closely resembling tweed.

4. Plain cotton; a loose fabric with a hard surface.

SIDE EDGES

The kind of selvedge formed at each side of the knitting is just as important as the kind of tension made by the stitch for the surface of the fabric.

Selvedges can be formed in various ways to suit particular purposes.

When making a large garment like a dress or a costume, do be careful about the selvedges. They must not be looser than the rest of the fabric, or the seam will drop in a bad line at the hem. A selvedge too tight will cause the bottom of the seam to curl up and so give a very bad hem line; also, being tight, the seam will not wear well.

1

2

I. A machine seam selvedge. Four extra stitches are cast on at each side. The inner stitches of these two extra groups are knitted to form purl stitches on the right side of the fabric and the remaining stitches are worked as stocking stitch. This shows the seam ready to be machined. All seam shapings are done inside the purl stitch.

2. When making up, stitch the seam by machine on the wrong side working along the purled stitches, and then press the seam open with a hot iron and a damp cloth, as for a flat seam in dressmaking. This is a very useful seam for coats and dresses. When pressing this seam open take very great care that it is not stretched, so causing the end of the seam to droop and sag inwards.

SIDE EDGES
continued

3. To prevent stocking stitch curling to the back, knit every end but one stitch, to form a purl stitch on the right side. This change of stitch can also be used as a guide when joining a seam by hand. Bring each sewing stitch down to take in the purled stitch and then press the seam carefully, laying it over a padded roller so that only the stitching is touched by the iron.

4. **A seam selvedge;** that is, the kind of edge required for a seam at sides, armholes and sleeves. The knitting is commenced on the first stitch in every row. When making up the garment, join with over-sewing stitch on the wrong side.

5. **Chain edge.** This selvedge is made by slipping all first stitches without knitting them. It is used when the edge will not be seamed. Belts, sides of collars and edges of pockets are chain edged.

3

4

5

PLAIN KNITTING

GARTER STITCH

The fabric formed by all plain knitting, or garter stitch as it is called, is not a decorative one, but is very suitable for scarves, cot blankets, kicking-bags and quickly made shawls.

The five steps needed for each stitch will soon become mechanical, and with practice the worker will make them all as one movement, taking only a fraction of a second for each completed stitch.

Plain knitting is made up of two rows worked on two needles. All the stitches are taken off the left-hand needle and slipped to the back of the work over loops of wool taken up on the right-hand needle. Each successive row forms a ridge on alternate sides of the work.

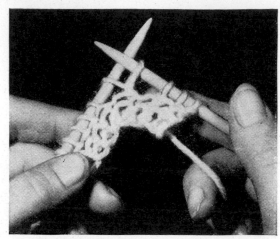

3. Bring the loop thus formed through the stitch.

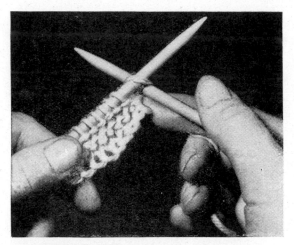

I. Pass the right-hand needle through the first stitch on the left-hand needle, taking it from in front and below. Slip the point behind the left-hand needle

4. Slip the stitch off the left-hand needle and to the back of the work. Pull the new stitch tight enough to be easy to knit in the next row. Repeat to the end of the row and continue knitting plain in every row.

How to work the stitch.

Hold the needles lightly: the one with the stitches in the left hand and the free needle in the right hand. The wool is held to the back, and arranged round the fingers of the right hand in such a way as to give the correct tension.

The tension should be just sufficient to make firm stitches which will move easily along the needle.

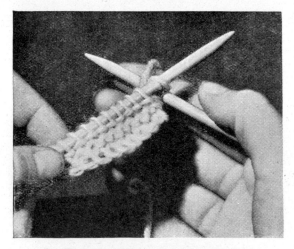

2. Throw the wool round the point of the right-hand needle with a circular movement going first behind and then in front.

PLAIN KNITTING *continued*

5. A piece of garter stitch knitting.

CROSSED OR TWISTED PLAIN KNITTING

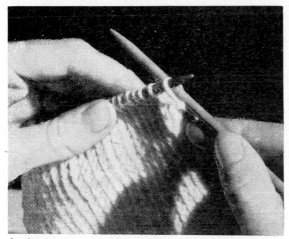

6. Insert the right-hand needle into the back of the first stitch on the left-hand needle.

This stitch is of very ancient origin: historic specimens show that it was in universal use for many centuries for the making of garments knitted in tubular fabric on four, six, or even more needles.

Crossed knitting tends to pull the fabric in the direction of the twist of the stitch. This was not a drawback for circular garments; in fact, it added to their flexibility. But when it became usual to make up garments from flat pieces of knitting sewn together with seams, this diagonal pull was not practicable and so crossed knitting went out of favour and plain knitting as we know it today came into fashion.

How to work the stitch.

Hold the needles and wool as described for ordinary plain knitting.

7. Form a loop round the right-hand needle as for plain knitting, bring the loop through the stitch and slip the stitch off the left-hand needle to the back of the work.

8. It will be seen that the vertical rows of stitches are more clearly marked than in ordinary work; also the stitches are more closely packed.

PURL KNITTING

The movements of knitting purlwise are the reverse of those used for plainwise knitting. The stitch on the left-hand needle is slipped off to the front of the work. If purl stitches are worked in every row the fabric will be identical to that of plain knitting; but, because purling is more difficult it is not used as an alternative. Purl stitches are introduced into plain knitting to give (a) variation, (b) decoration, (c) to form ribbing to make an elastic fabric.

3

1

4

2

How to work the stitch.
The needles are held in the same way as for plain knitting, but the wool is held in front of the work.
1. Slip the point of the right-hand needle through the front of the first stitch on the left-hand needle, passing from above and in front of the left-hand needle.
2. Throw a loop round the point of the right-hand needle, taking the wool over and below the needle.
3. Take this loop through the stitch.
4. Slip the stitch off the left-hand needle and to the front of the work. Pull the stitch to the required tension.

CROSSED PURL STITCHES

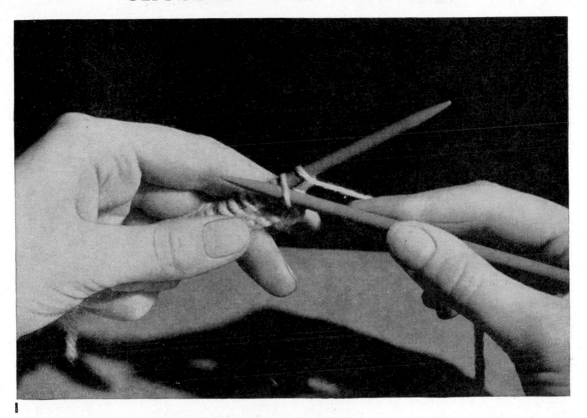

1

2

It is very difficult to work crossed purl in a similar way to crossed plain, i.e., by knitting into the back of the stitch, and so another method has been devised. Besides being easy to work, this method gives a very interesting texture.

Many attractive patterns can be invented using this stitch combined with other stitches, such as blocks or stripes of plain knitting, for the heavier kinds of men's and women's cardigans and sports wear.

1. Hold the wool as for ordinary purl stitch. Miss the first stitch on the left-hand needle and work a purl into the second. Work a purl into the first stitch and take both stitches off the left-hand needle. Continue to the end.

2. This attractive stitch has many uses, it is particularly successful in very thick wool.

PLAIN AND PURL RIBBINGS

Parts of garments which need to cling more tightly than the rest, such as wrists, waists and collars, and entire garments such as vests and sweaters, which need to be made of a very elastic-like fabric, are often knitted in ribbing.

From previous pages it has been seen that plainwise stitches take the loops of wool to the back of the fabric, while purled stitches take the loops to the front.

These backward and forward tendencies pull the fabric together laterally; and if the two stitches are combined on the same piece of work, being used in equal proportions with purl over purl, and plain over plain, half the fabric will be going back and half will be coming forward. The result will be a narrower piece of knitting which will open out and cling to a circumference larger than its own and with little loss to its warmth-giving qualities. Ribbings are often worked on smaller needles.

1

2

3

1. A ribbing of two plain and two purl is the one generally used.
Directions. Cast on a number of stitches divisible by 4 ; the work consists of 4 stitches and 1 row to a pattern.
1st row, k. 2, p. 2 ; repeat to the end of the row.
2nd and every succeeding row is the same as the 1st.

2. For a ribbing of finer texture, work 1 plain and 1 purl. Cast on an even number of stitches.
1st row, k. 1, p. 1; repeat to the end of the row.
2nd and all succeeding rows are the same as the 1st.

3. Sometimes the legs of socks and stockings are knitted with a wide rib, especially for sports wear if the wool is thick. The rib is planned according to the number of stitches in the round (seventy-two is usual), and this illustration shows a type of rib for a seventy-two-stitch round, that is, five plain and one purl continued all round and in every round. Leg shapings are not worked in a ribbed leg because the expansion of the rib gives all the shaping required.

MORE RIBBINGS

Besides the orthodox ribbings described on the previous page, there are semi-decorative kinds and others which give elasticity vertically.

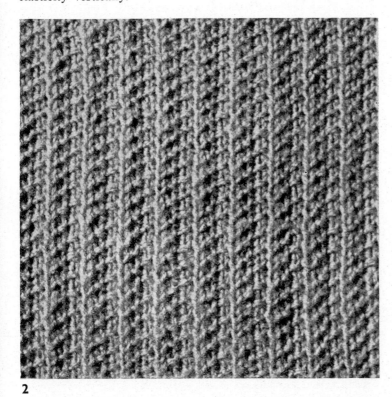

2

I. Here is a very useful ribbing made horizontally and giving a vertical stretch. It is worked with a number of rows of stocking stitch alternating with the same number of purl rows. A very compact fabric results.

Directions. Cast on any number of stitches.

1st row, k.
2nd row, p.
3rd row, k.
4th row, k.
5th row, p.
6th row, k.

Repeat these 6 rows throughout. The fabric will be alike on both sides.

2. A finer type of ribbing, more decorative than the usual rib, although not quite so elastic, is this one made with vertical bands of plain and moss stitch. The plain stitches stand out well from the background of moss stitch. Two stitches and two rows make the pattern.

Directions. Cast on a number of stitches divisible by 3.

1st row, k. 2, p. 1 all along.
2nd row, k. 1, p. 1, k. 1 all along.

Repeat these 2 rows throughout.

I

RIB PATTERNS

The previous pages show how ribbings are worked for an elastic-like effect. The illustrations on this and the two next pages show how they can be used for decorative purposes as well as giving slight elasticity. These groups of plain and purl stitches give a thicker fabric than most other combinations of different stitches.

These ribbings, which are for decoration only, should be pressed with a hot iron and a damp cloth. Ribbings which are used specially for elasticity are not pressed.

1. A fine broken rib. It is made with 2 sts. and 2 rows to a pattern.

Directions.
Cast on an even number of stitches.
1st row, k. 1, p. 1.
2nd row, all plain. Continue to the end.
Rep. these 2 rows throughout.

When pressed lightly on the wrong side, the work has a very pleasing texture; the fabric will be very warm.

2. This is a suitable pattern for sports wear made up in plain wool. 6 sts. and 3 rows make the pattern.

Directions.
Cast on a number of stitches divisible by 6.
1st row, k. 3, p. 3; continue to the end.
2nd row, p.
3rd row, k.
Repeat these 3 rows throughout.

RIB PATTERNS *continued*

3

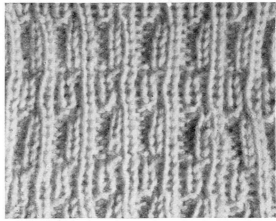

5

4

3. Patterns suitable for the cardigan type of garment, or a skirt, can be made with a broken horizontal ribbing. The one shown here is particularly good for men's pullovers. The pattern is made with 16 sts. and 8 rows.
Directions. Cast on a number of stitches divisible by 16.
1st row, k. 8, p. 8; repeat to the end.
2nd, 3rd and 4th rows are the same as the 1st.
5th row, k. 1, p. 8, k. 7; repeat to the end.
6th row, p. 7, k. 8, * p. 8, k. 8 *; repeat from * to * to the end.
Repeat rows 5 and 6 to complete the pattern. Continue knitting these 8 rows for the work. The raised plain ridge is made by moving the 5th row along 1 st. The ridge comes on alternate sides of the work.

4. Rib principles can be applied to adding decoration to part of a surface only. This photograph shows the back of a coat broken in the middle with lines of purl stitches of unequal length. The coat is knitted with thick wool on thin needles making a close fabric without much stretch and these ribbed lines give a little elasticity in the centre of the garment.

5. Here pattern is made with two different ribs on the one piece of work; the effect is a close and very warm fabric. Commence with 6 rows of 2 plain and 2 purl, then for 4 rows work 1 plain and 1 purl. Repeat these two bands for the work. The best results will be gained with thick wool and fairly fine needles. Many other kinds of ribbed patterns can be made by combining groups in unusual ways. There are so many ribs to choose from that the inventive worker can easily design patterns.

RIB PATTERNS *continued*

Still further effects can be gained by working bands of ribbing alternating with narrower bands of other stitches.

The rib bands may be wide, but the intervening bands should be quite narrow, otherwise the side edges of the garment will go out of shape. The ribbing will take up the width more than will the other pattern.

1. A wide band of two plain and three purl with a strip of moss stitch. There are twelve rows of ribbing and six rows of moss stitch. Press this kind of ribbing lightly to open out the rib just enough to make the surface more interesting.

I

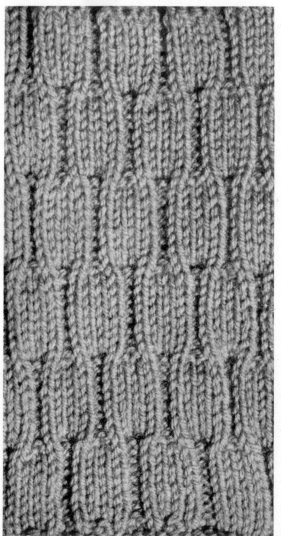

2

2. This curiously twisted pattern is made very simply. It only consists of changing the order of the ribbing. Knit ten rows of four plain and two purl, and then another ten rows of the same rib, arranged so that the two purled stitches are over the two middle stitches in the wide band of plain. This pattern could form the basis of many experiments in stitch designing; the rib could be much wider with a central stitch, or group of stitches, worked purlwise. This would give a spot pattern with a chain line meandering down the fabric and between the spots. Another suggestion is to make the plain rib a little wider in order to leave enough room to work a daisy, in embroidery, in the centre.

PLAIN AND PURL BLOCKS

Texture patterns can be made with blocks of these two stitches. The fabric is only suitable for small figures or for men's pullovers and cardigans: the pattern tends to emphasize the curves of large, or out-size figures. But for small women's size they make very good fabrics.

1. One of the easiest block patterns is this one made up of squares of plain and purl. The pattern is made with 10 sts. and 10 rows.

Directions. Cast on a number of stitches divisible by 10.

1st row, k. 5, p. 5; repeat to the end.
2nd row, p. 5, k. 5; repeat to the end.
3rd row, the same as the 1st.
4th row, the same as the 2nd.
5th row, the same as the 1st.
This completes one-half of the pattern. For the second half the order of work is reversed, thus:
6th row, p. 5, k. 5; repeat to the end.
7th row, k. 5, p. 5; repeat to the end.
8th row, the same as the 6th.
9th row, the same as the 7th.
10th row, the same as the 6th.

Continue working these 10 rows. If multiples of 10 sts. will make the work too wide, the row may end with a half pattern, i.e., the number of stitches will be a multiple of 10 plus 5.

2. An attractive fabric is made by breaking up a plain surface with horizontal and vertical lines of purl stitches. The squares of stocking stitch may be any size desired, small ones are shown here, but larger ones of 2 or 3 ins. are quite suitable for garments in thicker wool.

Directions. Cast on a number of stitches divisible by 7. The first 6 rows are the same, k. 6, p. 1; repeat to the end. **7th row,** all p. Continue these 7 rows for the work. The pattern is made of 7 sts. and 7 rows,

PLAIN AND PURL BLOCKS *continued*

The larger patterns made with blocks, are suitable for skirts, especially those for sports wear. Tweed effect wools should not be worked up in patterned knitting. The "bumpy" nature of their textures will not show the pattern to advantage, so there is no point in taking the extra trouble involved.

1. Although this is purely a block pattern, the texture gives a ribbed effect too. 8 sts. go to a pattern, and as many rows as desired may be worked in the length of the pattern. The purl block commences with 1 purl st., then 2, then 3 and finally 4 in succeeding rows. Continue purling 4 sts. for as far as required and then 3, 2 and 1 purl sts., in that order, at the opposite side of the block to make the upper point. The amount of stocking stitch between may also be varied to suit.

2. A different type of block pattern is this one with six-sided shapes of purl stitches. The shapes can be made to any size desired, but the following directions were used for the piece in the illustration. Cast on a number of stitches divisible by 7. Work the first 6 rows in a ribbing of 1 plain and 6 purl. In the next rows increase the number of stitches that appear as plain on the right side, until all stitches are knitted plain. Then diminish the number of plain until the original one for ribbing is reached. Knit the next 6 rows in ribbing.

3. This pattern, worked in coarse wool, would be very suitable for a skirt.

PLAIN AND PURL ALL-OVER PATTERNS

A stocking stitch ground broken with a purl stitch pattern can be devised to suit any kind of garment or style.

In the seventeenth century very elaborately worked patterns were made with floral designs carried out in purl stitch on a plain background. The work needed great skill. The pattern was drawn on paper and then copied stitch by stitch, entailing close counting of the stitches as they were worked.

The art of this kind of knitting has quite died out. Today, the all-over patterns consist of a stocking stitch background with a small diamond or check pattern in purl stitch.

1. Moss stitch. Perhaps the simplest of all these patterns is the familiar moss stitch, or diamond stitch, as it used to be called. A pleasant broken texture of even warmth is given by the stitch. The pattern is made with 2 sts., plus 1 at the end of the row, and 1 row of work.

Directions. Cast on an odd number of stitches.
1st row, k. 1, p. 1; repeat to the end, k. 1.
Repeat this row for the work.

2. A pleasing variation of moss stitch is the double moss stitch. The work is done with 4 sts., plus 2 at the end of the row, and 1 row of pattern.

Directions. Cast on a number of stitches divisible by 4 plus 2.
1st row, k. 2, p. 2; repeat to the end, k. 2.
Repeat this row for the work.

3. This specimen shows a softly broken ground; groups of 3 purl sts. being worked at regular intervals all the way over the stocking stitch. The pattern is built up on 8 sts. and 8 rows.

Directions. If possible cast on a number of stitches divisible by 8. When this is not possible, take care to arrange the working of the purl stitches in the 5th row so that they come over the middle of the space between two groups of purl stitches in the 1st row.
1st row, k. 5, p. 1, k. 1, p. 1; repeat to the end.
2nd row, p. 1, * k. 1, p. 7 *; repeat from * to * to the end. It will be seen that this row is purl except for a knit stitch between the 2 p. sts. of the previous row.
3rd row, all k.
4th row, all p.
5th row, k. 1, * p. 1, k. 1, p. 1, k. 5 *; repeat from * to * to the end.
6th row, p. with k. 1, between the 2 p. sts. of the previous row.
7th row, k.
8th row, p.
Repeat these 8 rows.

FANCY KNITTING

Many unusual effects can be obtained by combining wools and needles that are not used together as a rule. Only three patterns are shown, but no doubt the worker will like to find out others for herself. Experiment with any odd lengths; sometimes the most interesting results are arrived at by accident.

1. At a casual glance this fabric appears to be very loose: it is very open, but it is not loose. The ridges are quite tightly secured which gives a firmness to the fabric.

Directions. Cast on and work the first row on No. I needles using either 2-ply or 3-ply wool. The rest of the knitting is done in garter stitch with No. 11 and No. I needles used for alternate rows. It is the small needles which tighten the ridge made by the large needles.

1

2

2. This is a very unusual and interesting fabric for scarves and bed jackets. Two thicknesses of wool are used with No. I needles. The specimen was knitted with 2-ply and 4-ply wool; the work is done in garter stitch.

Directions. Cast on and work the first row with both thicknesses of wool. Knit the first stitch in the second row with both wools and then continue with only one, the thicker one for preference. Knit back with the same wool. In the next row knit the first stitch with both wools and continue with the one that was discarded in the second row. Return with the same wool. Continue knitting in this way, knitting each pair of rows with a different wool. Remember to knit the first stitch, when changing the wool, with both thicknesses.

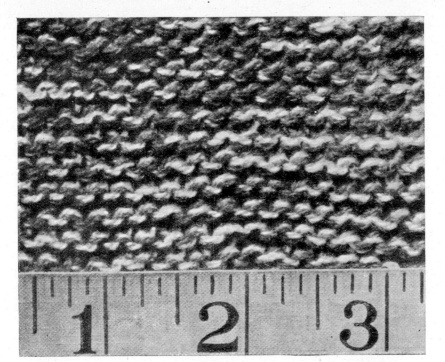

3

FANCY KNITTING

continued

3. Variegated effects can be obtained by knitting with two colours. The wools may be of different colours, or different shades of one colour. When choosing the needles consider the combined thickness of the two wools and work accordingly. Two threads of 2-ply wool will equal 4-ply; 2-ply and 3-p.y together will equal double-knitting wool. The illustration was worked with 2-ply and 3-ply on No. 9 needles.

NOVELTY FABRICS

Wool yarns combined with other kinds of threads make good fabrics for various purposes if they are used intelligently. A fine silk thread worked with wool makes an extremely warm fabric, apart from the decorative possibilities of this combination. For warmth be sure to use pure silk, and not an artificial silk, which has very little warmth indeed.

I. Here is a fine pure silk together with thick wool knitted on No. 9 needles giving a thick close cloth. Instead of the silk being used throughout, it could be worked-in in bands only; in this case it is better to have colour-matching threads.

47

MECHANICAL SHAPINGS

"Mechanical shaping" means the shaping of a garment by changing the size of the needles or the process in knitting.

It does not mean shaping by lessening the number of stitches on the same size of needle: that will be dealt with later.

To be able to produce a perfectly shaped garment, it is very necessary that a good range of needles is at hand, so that the size of the needle can be changed at will, to take in the width, or let out the garment to a slightly larger measurement. On one garment alone one may have to use three sizes of needles. This will be seen in the directions for knitting a shaped vest.

Sleeves will fit very much better if the needles are changed to expand the width gradually to the elbow, and again towards the top. A smartly tailored effect will be given to cardigans and coats if the shaping on various sizes of needles is carefully worked out. In this way, shaping is not only done at the sides, as in a garment cut out of a piece of cloth, but every stitch in the fabric helps to pull in or let out the garment. There should not be more than two sizes difference in the numbers of the needles at each change.

1. This piece of knitting was commenced on No. 7 needles, then No. 9 were used, and at the top the needles were changed again for still finer work on No. 11's.

2. The top of a knitted skirt will fit much better if the needles are changed to about four sizes smaller. There will be no superfluous fullness to dispose of when mounting the petersham band. The skirt top will fit snugly and it will be impossible for it to sag away from the waist.

MECHANICAL SHAPINGS *continued*

Shapings in ribbing can be made by changing the type of rib. For instance, 1 plain and 1 purl can be taken in with 2 plain and 2 purl, which, in turn may be let out with 1 plain and 1 purl.

The waist ribbing of a jumper will not curl up in wear if it is knitted in the three sets of ribbing described on this page.

The illustrations on the previous page show how shapings are done by changing needles, the photographs on this page illustrate shaping worked by changing the stitch.

1

2

1. Stocking stitch can be taken in about one-third of its width with a ribbing of 1 plain and 1 purl. This is suitable for wrist and waist ribbings of jumpers.

2. A much greater reduction is gained with a rib of 2 plain and 2 purl. This is also suitable for reducing a wide rib of 5 plain and 1 purl, such as is worked for socks.

49

A PLAIN SCARF

This little scarf is a practical demonstration of the principles of shaping by mechanical means, which have been illustrated in the two previous pages.

Materials required. I oz. of 4-ply wool in yellow, I oz. of 4-ply wool in brown, a skein of embroidery wool to match both colours (for the cord), and a pair of No. 7 needles.

Directions. Cast on 44 sts. Knit the first row into the backs of the stitches. Knit 88 rows (44 ridges) in garter stitch. Change to a rib of I plain and I purl for the remainder of the wool. Cast off. The rib will have made the neck part much narrower. Repeat in the brown wool; leave enough wool after casting off to sew the two pieces together. Oversew the two halves together with brown wool. Further shaping is done during pressing. Lay the scarf flat on an ironing blanket, put a damp cloth on top and with a hot iron press from the centre back outwards to the end. Push the iron along to stretch the scarf. Take hold of the centre back of the scarf in one hand and pull it as the iron is once more rubbed from the back to the end. This will still further shape the scarf and pull it out to its right length. Make a cord about 7 ins. long with the embroidery wool as described on the page on making cords. Join this into a ring and sew it to one end, when the scarf is put on, the other end will thread through the cord loop.

A SCARF WITH SHAPED ENDS

Many people prefer scarves with shaped ends. This illustration shows one made in tweed effect wool worked in ribbing of 1 plain and 1 purl throughout and without any shaping done when the scarf was pressed.

1. Materials required. 2 ozs. of tweed effect wool and two No. 9 needles.

Directions. Cast on 2 sts.

1st row, k. twice into the first stitch, p. 1.

2nd row, k. 1, p. 1, k. 1.

3rd row, k. twice into the first stitch, k. 1, p. 1.

4th row, k. 1, p. 1, k. 1, p. 1.

Continue in this manner, increasing a stitch at the beginning of the same edge until there are 50 sts. on the needle, all the while keeping to the rib. Work in rib until the scarf measures 33 ins. from the beginning. Decrease the number of stitches by knitting two together at the beginning of every other row, making this shaping come on the opposite side of the scarf to the increased stitches of the first point.

2. Another method of making a pointed end.

Directions. Cast on the number of stitches required for the width.

1st row, k. twice into the first st., k. to the end.

2nd row, k. 2 sts. together, k. to the end. Repeat these two rows throughout. Any kind of stitch suitable for a scarf may be used in this shaping process.

3. The kind of edge gained by knitting twice into the first stitch of every other row.

A LITTLE GIRL'S VEST

This little vest has been simplified so that a schoolgirl can knit it herself. Two ounces of 2-ply wool in any soft pastel shade and a pair of No. 7 needles will be required. The shell edging at the neck and armholes is worked with a medium-sized crochet hook, and is threaded with narrow satin ribbon in a slightly darker shade than the wool.

Directions for working the edging will be found in the crochet section.

Directions.

Cast on 68 sts. using method A, to give the greatest elasticity. Work in a ribbing of 2 plain and 2 purl for 15 ins. To make the front neck, k. 16 sts. in ribbing, cast off 36, and slip the 16 sts. just knitted on to a stitch holder. On the remaining 16 sts. work one shoulder for 6½ ins. Remove the stitches from the holder on to the free needle and put the stitches of the shoulder strap on the holder and break off the wool, leaving an end to darn in. Join the wool to the first stitch of the 16 from the holder by making a loop as for casting on, slip it on the needle holding the stitches and knit the second strap. Let the last row of this second strap end at the inside, that is, at the end nearest to the first strap, and cast on 36 sts. Take the stitches from the holder on to the free needle and knit them in ribbing. There will now be 16 ribbed stitches, 36 cast-on stitches, and then another 16 ribbed stitches on the needle. Continue knitting in rib for the back; make this 1 in. longer than the front, and cast off very loosely so that the edge will stretch as much as the cast-on edge. Sew up the side seams for 14 ins.; do this loosely. Work the edging, thread the ribbon through the holes, and the vest is ready to wear. The finished measurements are: length from shoulder, 19½ ins.

A SHAPED VEST FOR GIRL
OR SMALL WOMEN'S SIZE

A very shapely garment can be made by working parts on needles of different sizes, so that the garment becomes shaped all round instead of at the sides only. It could be called "tailoring" on the needles. In this way a nicely fitting vest is made quickly, and although the directions given here are for a fairly small size, they can be enlarged quite easily by following the hints given on measuring tensions.

The length of this vest when finished is 24 ins. The little sleeves are 3 ins. long.

Four ounces of 3-ply wool; two each of Nos. 7, 9 and 11 needles; a medium-sized crochet hook and a length of ribbon for the neck will be required.

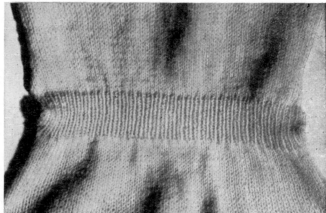

1. A detail of the waist shaping.

2. The sleeve set into the armhole.

2

1

Directions.

Cast on 72 sts. on the No. 7 needles. Remember that the edges must be as elastic as possible and so method A of casting on is used, and the first row of knitting is done in the usual way of making plain stitches. Work 9½ ins. of stocking stitch on the No. 7 needles. Change to No. 9 needles and work 1½ ins. Then change to No. 11 needles and k. for 1 in. Now work 16 rows in ribbing of 1 plain and 1 purl. Work ½ in. of stocking stitch on the 11 needles. Change to No. 9 needles and work a further 1½ ins. Finally change back to the No. 7 needles and k. 4 ins. This brings it to the neck, and let the knitting end on a purl row. K. 21 sts., cast off 30 sts. and place the 21 sts. knitted on a holder. On the remaining 21 sts. work in stocking stitch for 4 ins., ending on a plain row. Cast off 7 sts. at the beginning of the next 3 purl rows, and break off the wool. Knit the second shoulder like the first to complete the front of the vest. Knit the back of the vest like the front, but continue the bodice part for 2 more ins. and the shoulders will be 2 ins. shorter. For the sleeves cast on 60 sts. on the No. 7 needles and work 16 rows in stocking stitch. Change to No. 11 needles and work 11 rows of the same ribbing as at the waist. Cast off loosely on the wrong side. Press lightly on the wrong side, join side, shoulder and sleeve seams and set in the little sleeves using a loose oversewing stitch. Work a suitable edging round the neck, chosen from the pages on crochet, and thread it with ribbon.

A KNITTED COT BLANKET

Cot blankets knitted in a special thick soft wool, are very cosy and light in weight. This one took 8 ozs. of blanket wool, knitted on No. 1 needles, and 4 yds. of satin ribbon $2\frac{1}{2}$ ins. wide.

Directions. Cast on 50 sts. and knit the first row in ordinary plain knitting to give a loose edge.

2nd row, knit the first stitch; when knitting the next stitches wind the wool round the needle twice. Knit the last stitch in the usual way.

3rd row, knit the first stitch, knit the first loop of the next stitch and slip the second loop off the needle, repeat to the end, knit the last stitch.

Continue knitting rows 2 and 3 throughout. Cast off in the usual way. Do not press the blanket. Commence binding the edge at one corner. Lay the ribbon just over the edge, leaving about 1 in. beyond the blanket for joining, and sew with small running stitches placed along the selvedge. Pleat the ribbon at each corner, leaving enough to turn the corner without tightening, join the ends of the ribbon neatly and then hem the opposite selvedge to the other side of the blanket, placing the stitches on top of the running stitches. Press the ribbon lightly. The knitted fabric will make the ribbon cockle a little; this cannot be helped.

A KICKING BAG FOR A YOUNG BABY

Baby can kick to his heart's content if he is popped into one of these cosy bags. The covering cannot be kicked off and baby will not be exposed to draughts.

Any thick wool can be used; it should be hard rather than soft, and the pattern of knitting must be a close one to give a compact fabric.

Materials required. 8 ozs. of double knitting or coarse 4-ply wool. 4 ozs. of one colour and 4 ozs. of another will make a bag of chequered pattern like the one shown here. A pair of No. 6 needles.

Directions. For each square cast on 25 sts., knit in garter stitch for 38 rows and then cast off. Knit eight of these squares in each colour (or sixteen if one colour is used), and join them together with oversewing, using one of the wools or alternating the colours. There are various ways of making up the bag. The back may be a piece of blanket, or another set of squares can be knitted; the outer edges may be bound with ribbon like the cot blanket, or a long narrow strip can be knitted in one of the colours and sewn round after the two layers of the bag have been joined together. To make the blanket back, cut a piece of blanket the same width as the top and 1 in. longer, make a hem along one edge with the extra inch and tack the blanket to the knitted top. Bind both together with ribbon round three sides leaving open the end with the neatened edge of blanket. To make up the bag from two layers of knitted squares, oversew the layers together along three sides and then sew a narrow strip of knitting all round, attaching it to the upper side only at the open end. The edges may be bound with ribbon, binding one edge only at the opening, or the opening may be bound all round.

A BABY'S BODY BELT

These directions are for a baby's body belt for winter wear. For summer, use 2-ply wool, No. 11 needles and work to the same measurements, increasing the number of stitches to 108 and working the number of rows to correspond to the measures of the belt illustrated here.

Measurements. Width at widest, 12 ins.; length, 5½ ins.; length of 2 plain and 2 purl ribbing, 1¼ ins.; length of fine ribbing, 1 in.

Materials. 1 oz. of 4-ply fingering in natural colour; No. 4 and No. 10 needles with points at both ends.

Directions. Cast on 96 sts., that will be 32 on each needle; the belt is made circular. Knit in ribbing of 2 plain and 2 purl for 12 rounds. Then change the ribbing to a wide one of 7 plain and 1 purl for 34 rounds. The fine rib is worked next in 1 plain and 1 purl for 10 rounds. Cast off very loosely. It is essential that the casting on and off is done very loosely; a tight edge at these places will be very uncomfortable for the baby to wear.

REINS AND HARNESS

1. Choose cheap hard wool for these reins and harness.

Measurements. Length of front, 9½ ins.; depth of front, 5 ins.; length of shoulder strap, 13 ins.; length of waist strap, 8 ins.; length of loop, 38 ins., or according to requirements.

Materials required. 2 ozs. of 4-ply wool (cheap quality); a pair of No. 7 needles.

Directions.

The front piece. Cast on 44 sts. Knit 6 rows in moss stitch. Then change the pattern to a central block of stocking stitch with a band of 7 sts. in moss stitch on each side. Knit thus for 21 rows and then change back to all moss stitch for another 6 rows.

Shoulder straps. Knit 7 moss sts., slip these on to a stitch holder and then cast off 30 sts. On the remaining 7 sts. knit in moss stitch for 13 ins., cast off and join to the front piece, or body part, at the bottom of the opposite side. Take the stitches from the holder and knit a second shoulder strap.

The loop. This loop is knitted on 7 sts. in moss stitch as long as is required.

2. This illustration shows how the straps are crossed and sewn at the back.

I

57

A TRIO OF KETTLE HOLDERS

Kettle holders need not be " just a bit of knitting." They can be well thought out pieces of work and as such they will make quite useful presents.

Materials. One hank of double knitting wool will make two holders and one strip for the third; the cheap kinds of wool will be quite suitable. Two No. 3 needles.

Directions for the first holder. Using the double knitting wool cast on 8 sts. and knit plain for 4½ ins. Cast off. Oddments of other kinds of wool can be used up for the side strips, using 4-ply wool singly, or 3-ply wool double, cast on 9 sts. and knit for 4½ ins. Join the strips with oversewing in another colour, make the loop and press.

Directions for the second holder. Cast on 21 sts. in method A. Knit the first 6 rows in moss stitch, commencing straight away in the first row.
7th row, moss stitch 6, k. 9, moss stitch 6.
8th row, moss stitch 6, p. 9, moss stitch 6.
9th row, as the 7th.
10th row, as the 9th.
11th row, as the 8th.
12th row, as the 10th.
Repeat rows 7 to 12 inclusive twice. Knit 6 rows in moss stitch, cast off, make a loop and lightly press.

Directions for the third holder. Cast on 25 sts., using method A. Knit the first 5 rows, working the first row into the backs of the stitches, and slipping all first stitches.
6th row, k. 5, p. 3, k. 9, p. 3, k. 5.
7th row, k. 5, p. 1, k. 3, p. 7, k. 3, p. 1, k. 5.
8th row, k. 7, p. 3, k. 5, p. 3, k. 7.
9th row, k. 5, p. 3, k. 3, p. 3, k. 3, p. 3, k. 5.
10th row, k. 9, p. 3, k. 1, p. 3, k. 9.
11th row, k. 5, p. 5, k. 5, p. 5, k. 5.
12th row, k. 11, p. 3, k. 11.
13th row, k. 5, p. 5, k. 6, k. 3, p. 6, k. 5 (middle row).
Repeat from row 12 back to 1 (in reverse order). Slip all first stitches. Cast off with purlwise stitches to send the chained edge to the far side. Leave an end long enough to make a crochet chain for a loop to hang up the holder.

A PAIR OF BED SOCKS

Bed socks can be very quickly knitted; thick needles and 3-ply wool are used, and the work is done as a flat piece of knitting, which is sewn into a sock shape after it has been pressed. These will fit a foot from size 3 to 6.

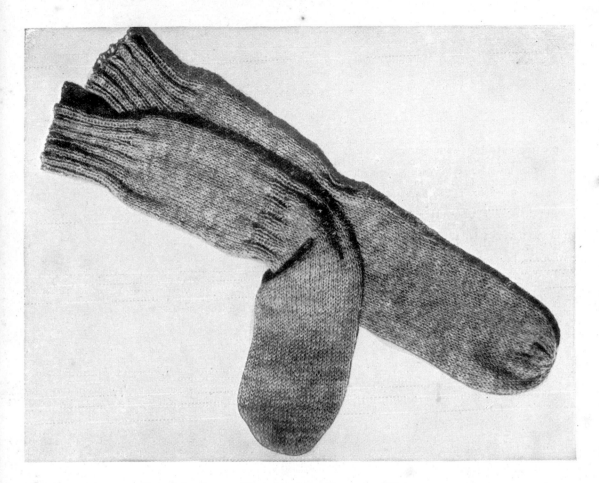

Materials. 2 ozs. of 3-ply wool in white, natural, light grey, or any pastel shade. Two No. 7 needles; short ones will be best.

Directions. Cast on 50 sts. Knit in 2 plain and 2 purl ribbing for $3\frac{1}{4}$ ins. Every odd numbered row will commence and end with 2 plain, and every even numbered row will begin and end with 2 purl. The reason for this will be seen when the sock is made up. Knit in stocking stitch for 6 ins. Change back to the ribbing for $1\frac{1}{4}$ ins. so that this part will grip the ankle. Knit in stocking stitch again for the foot which should be to the end of the wool. Leave an end of wool just long enough to fasten off; that is, about 6 ins. Do not cast off in the usual way; insert the right-hand needle through the first 2 sts. as for knitting two together, make the new stitch and then pull the end of wool through. Repeat to the end so that all the stitches are threaded on to the wool. Pull up the end fairly tightly and fasten off by darning

it in and out of the fabric strongly. Lay the sock flat on an ironing blanket and, with a hot iron and damp cloth, shrink away as much of the superfluous fullness at the toe as possible; this, of course, must be done on the wrong side of the fabric. Keeping the sock on the wrong side sew up the back seam with oversewing stitches, taking up the first stitch of each edge. Thus the 2 plain sts. left on either side of the sewing will show as the rib of 2 plain. Lightly press this seam.

Hints on making. Cast on as shown in method A to give the most elastic edge and commence the ribbing in the first row. Knit rather loosely; these socks will give good practice in handling thin wool on large needles and would be a good exercise for those workers who are tight knitters.

WOOLLY TEA-COSIES

Knitted tea-cosies make attractive and useful presents. All sorts of ideas can be worked out and odd lengths of thick wool used up. The ground can be plain knitting, stocking stitch, moss stitch, or garter stitch, and then decorated with flowers cut from brightly-coloured felt arranged to form a posy and sewn down on to the knitting.

1. This is the outline of one half of a "battlemented" shape, which is a little more decorative than the plain, rounded shape.
Materials required. 3 ozs. thick 4-ply or double knitting wool; a pair of No. 5 needles.
Directions. Cast on 54 sts. and knit 44 rows in double moss stitch which is described elsewhere in this book. Cast off 4 sts. at the beginning of the next 2 rows. K. 4 rows in pattern; repeat these 6 rows 3 more times. Cast off remaining stitches.
To make up the cosy. Work blanket stitch all round both sides of the cosy in embroidery wool of a darker colour. Place both sides together, right sides outside and oversew the loops of the blanket stitching with the same colour, or a contrasting one. A tassel made of wool can be sewn to the middle of the top by which to lift the tea-cosy. The finished size will be about 12 ins. wide and 10 ins. deep.

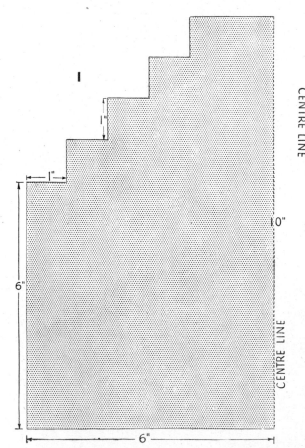

2. For those who prefer the usual rounded shape for a tea-cosy, here is a half diagram and the directions for one.
Materials required. 3 ozs. of double knitting wool; a pair of No. 5 needles.
Directions. Cast on 58 sts. K. 44 rows in any texture or pattern desired. At the beginning of the next 12 rows sl. 1, k. 1, p.s.s.o. On each of the next 14 rows sl. 1, k. 1, p.s.s.o. at the beginning and at the end, k. 2 tog. Cast off the remainder of the stitches.
To make up the cosy. The same method as described for the first cosy may be used; or, as an alternative, the two sides may be sewn together by oversewing with the same wool as was used for the knitting and then a thick cord sewn round the edge. Leave a loop, or group of three smaller loops, to act as a handle. The finished side will be about 13 ins. wide and 11 ins. deep.

LOVERS OF GOOD BOOKS

will be particularly pleased to know that something very special has been planned this year—for the children.

It is a new and original book—the finest of its kind ever published—**"The Mammoth Book of Working Models"**—a volume that will thrill every boy and girl and provide them with countless hours of happy entertainment.

The demand is going to be tremendous, but War emergency restrictions have enforced the necessity of limiting the production of supplies.

That is why this special Opportunity Voucher has been enclosed in order that a copy of "The Mammoth Book of Working Models" can be reserved at once, and so disappointment avoided.

On receipt of the Voucher below the reservation will be entered on our Red Star Priority List—and as soon as copies of the book are available—one will be set aside ready for dispatch to the applicant.

No one should miss getting the children the greatest book of the year —it will make some child thrilled and happy—the Voucher below should be filled in and returned at once !

A Privilege Invoice will then be forwarded, entitling readers to secure this book for the amazingly low privilege price of only 3/9, which includes carriage, packing, insurance, etc. On receipt of Invoice and remittance, the Book will at once be dispatched.

PART II
BASIC SHAPINGS
SHAPING BY CASTING ON

It is very necessary for the knitter to know how to shape edges by casting on and off. The processes are often used in making lingerie and men's underwear, when magyar sleeves are required.

1. Finish knitting at the end where the stitches are to be cast on. Turn the work on to the reverse side and take the needle which holds the stitches into the left hand. With the free needle knit into the first stitch, pull the loop through on the right-hand needle and slip as a new stitch on to the left-hand needle, in the same way as casting on a first row.

2. A number of stitches cast on beyond a piece of knitting. The first row of knitting on these new stitches should be worked into the backs of the cast-on stitches. Generally this kind of shaping will be required for magyar styles, for adding the extra stitches required for the sleeves. The most essential thing to do here is to prevent a hole forming between the last old stitch and the first new one. The hole can be avoided when making the first stitch by knitting twice into the last old stitch and then continuing the casting on in the method chosen. The casting on should be done so that the edge will not tighten the seam. Method A of casting on will probably be the best.

SHAPING BY CASTING OFF

To reduce the number of stitches on a piece of work in a straight line it is necessary to know how to cast off some stitches and leave the remainder to be knitted in the usual way.

I

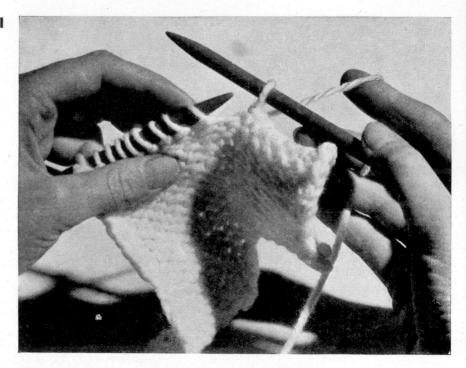

I. Finish knitting at the side where the stitches are to be cast off. Turn the work to the reverse side and take the needle which holds the stitches into the left hand. With the free needle cast off in the usual way. The last stitch left on the right-hand needle will be the first stitch of the knitted row, so be careful not to cast off one stitch too many.

2

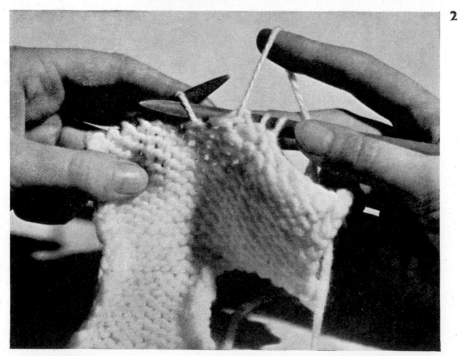

2. Where possible arrange to cast off on a purl row, because the chained cast-off edge will then lie on the wrong side of the work.

A KNITTED TABLE MAT

Knitted table mats are used to prevent plates scratching polished tables; they are not used for hot plates unless a cork mat is slipped under them.

The mat shown here is made of a soft artificial silk. One ball should make a set of four small mats, and a larger one for a dish.

Directions. Using small needles, either No. 11's or No. 13's, cast on 34 sts. and knit the first row into the backs of the stitches. Knit 10 rows of garter stitch, increasing 1 st. at the beginning of each row. Now the centre patterning starts. It is made of square blocks of plain and purl, with a band of garter stitch, 11 sts. wide, on each side. Each block is 6 sts. wide and 6 rows deep. Continue knitting and increasing until two more blocks have been added to the centre pattern. K. the next 36 rows without increasing. To make the knitting narrower, decrease at the beginning of every row until there are two blocks less in the centre pattern. Continue knitting in garter stitch and decreasing, until there are again 34 sts. on the needle. Cast off fairly loosely and add a fringe at the cast-on and cast-off edges.

ZIGZAG PATTERNS

Zigzag patterns are very useful for sports wear and especially for men's pullovers and cardigans. The needles and wool should be chosen to give a close fabric.

1. A vertical zigzag ribbing for a tennis sweater. The pattern is made on 7 sts.
Directions. Cast on a number of stitches divisible by 7.
1st row, k. 4, p. 3; repeat to the end.
2nd row, p. 1, * k. 3, p. 4; repeat to the end. Continue knitting, moving the 3 purled sts. 1 st. to the left on the right side for 7 rows. Then move the purled stitches 1 st. to the left for the same number of rows. Repeat these 14 rows for the rest of the work.

2. This is a horizontal zigzag ribbing. The pattern is made on 14 sts. and 10 rows.
Directions. Cast on a number of stitches divisible by 14, or 7 if 14 becomes too wide.
1st row, k. 7, p. 1, k. 6; repeat to the end.
In the next 2 rows increase the number of purl stitches by 1 on each side of those in the previous row until there are 5 purl sts. and 9 plain. In the following row the purled lines of 3 sts. divide to the right and left with 1 plain st. between. In successive rows the 3 purled sts. move outwards 1 st. every row until they converge to a point of 1 purl st.

FURTHER PATTERN SUGGESTIONS

For those who like a horizontal pattern,
here is one made with ribbing and triangles.

I

I. Purl triangles on a plain-wise ground divided by a horizontal purled rib.

Directions. Cast on a number of stitches divisible by 9.

1st row, k. I, p. 8; repeat to the end.

Continue reducing the number of purl stitches as seen from the right side until all are plain. Knit the next row purl. Knit the next row all plain. Plain the next row for the ridge on the right side. The next row is plain and the next is purl; that finishes the pattern. As the wrong side of the work is now facing the knitter the pattern will commence with 7 plain and 2 purl.

2

2. The diagonal ridged pattern has been developed here to form a V shape at the centre. The work can be followed from the photograph.

3

3. This is a more complicated pattern which entails some counting. The pattern is made with a wide rib of garter stitch, and a purled background with blocks of stocking stitch. The stocking stitch appears to be threaded through the purled ground.

TRIANGLE PATTERNS

Triangles of purled stitches on a plain background are an easy method of forming a good pattern for many kinds of garments. Large triangles of plain knitting on a purled ground, or vice versa, stand out well and make a good geometric pattern for sports wear. For the best results the fabric should be a close one.

I. Here is an all-over pattern of triangles in purl stitch.

Directions. Cast on a multiple of 12 sts.

1st row, p. 6, k. 6; repeat to the end.

2nd row, p. 6, * k. 5, p. 7; repeat from * to the end.

3rd row, k. 8, p. 4; repeat to the end.

Continue working less purl stitches and more plainwise stitches, when seen on the right side, until all the stitches are plain. In the next band of pattern the triangles may be moved to commence 2 plain sts. to the left of those in the first band. The third band of triangles could be moved the same distance to the left of the second band.

2. This pattern is made with triangles of plain and purl in equal sizes, alternating vertically and horizontally. The stitches are so planned that the vertical plain stitches cannot form pleats as those seen on the page of pleat effects. Pattern is made with 8 sts. and 14 rows.

Directions. Cast on a number of stitches divisible by 8.

1st row, p. 7, k. 1; repeat to the end.

2nd row, p. 2, k. 6; repeat to the end.

3rd row, p. 5, k. 3; repeat to the end.

Continue lessening the purl stitches on the right side until there are 7 plain and 1 purl (when seen on the right side).

Now reverse the order of work.

8th row, k. 7, p. 1; repeat to the end.

9th row, k. 2, p. 6; repeat to the end.

Continue to decrease the number of purl stitches until there are again 7 plain and 1 purl sts. in the row.

DIAGONAL PATTERNS

Ridges running diagonally across the fabric are useful patterns for closely knitted jumpers and small jackets, when a fairly coarse texture is required.

The size of the needles should be chosen to give close knitting.

1

1. A diagonal purl ridge runs across a plain background. No. 11 needles were used for 4-ply wool. The pattern is made with 6 sts., i.e., 4 plain and 2 purl.

Directions. Cast on a number of stitches divisible by 6.

1st row, k. 4, p. 2; repeat to the end.

2nd row, p. 1, k. 2, p. 4; repeat from k. 2 to within 3 sts. of the end, p. 3.

It will be seen that the 2 ribbed stitches move 1 st. along in every row. Press the work lightly.

2

2. The reverse side of the same pattern is quite as attractive; the first purled stitch is a little more prominent than the rest.

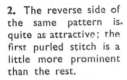

3

3. The diagonal lines in this pattern are not so sharp; the basis is a rib of 3 purl and 1 plain, the pattern being made with twisted purl stitches.

Directions. Cast on a multiple of 4.

1st row, k. 3, p. 1; repeat to the end.

2nd row, k. 1, p. 3.

3rd row, same as the 1st.

4th row, as the 2nd.

5th row, p. the second stitch, k. the first and take both stitches off the left-hand needle; k. 2; repeat to the end.

The diagonal lines are formed by the twisted purl passing over the plain stitch. Repeat these 5 rows throughout.

A LITTLE PIXIE HAT

This quaint little hat is made from 2 ozs. of tweed effect wool and it is knitted on No. 7 needles. A skein of embroidery wool is required for the thonging and the cord for fastening can be made from another ounce of the same wool as the hat, or from two more skeins of embroidery wool. A small bone crochet hook will be required for making the length of chain.

The work is so simple that a young girl could make one for herself.

Cast on 40 sts. and k. the 1st row into the backs of the stitches. Continue knitting in garter stitch until the first oz. of wool is nearly used. Cast off and leave an end long enough to sew one side of the hat. Knit up the second oz. in the same way, but leave a longer end; about 20 ins. of wool will be needed for the rest of the sewing. Press the squares lightly and lay them on top of each other, the two cast-on edges must be together. With the tweed wool oversew along the two cast-off edges and two side edges, leaving two sides open, place the stitches close together. Crochet a chain with the embroidery wool and, using a very large chenille needle, or darning needle, sew this chain over the seamed edges. For fastening the little hat, make two lengths of cord from part of another oz. of wool, or from more embroidery wool. Directions for making cords are given on another page. Join one end of each piece of cord to a free corner of the hat. The hat is worn with the cast-on edges round the neck. It will fit more closely like this; the sides of the knitting will come round the face.

PLEAT EFFECTS

Pleat effects can be obtained very easily in knitting. They are used for skirts, the skirt part of dresses, collars and cuffs, and sometimes for scarves.

1

1. The simplest method of getting pleat effects is with a ribbing. The wide purl rib is the right side of the fabric.

Directions. Cast on a multiple of 9.

1st row, k. 6, p. 1, k. 1, p. 1; repeat to the end.

2nd row, k. 1, p. 1, k. 1, p. 6; repeat to the end.

These 2 rows are worked throughout.

2. A very attractive pleat effect is gained by making triangles of plain and purl stitches. Its use is illustrated in the little girl's pleated skirt; turn to the next page for a fuller description of the working of the stitch. The ridge is made by the plain knitted stitches which run all down the length of the fabric dividing the purl blocks from the plain. A flared and pleated skating skirt can be made very quickly in thick wool. Calculate the number of stitches required at the waist. Cast on that number on a circular needle and k. 3 rounds of 3 plain, 1 purl, 1 plain and 1 purl. The skirt may be worked in two pieces on 2 needles, if preferred.

4th round, knit twice in the first stitch, k. 2, p. 1, k. 1, p. 1; repeat all round.

5th, 6th and 7th rounds, k. 4, p. 1, k. 1, p. 1.

8th round, k. 3, knit twice into the next stitch, p. 1, k. 1, p. 1; repeat to the end.

Continue in a similar manner, increasing 1 st. in every rib and at alternate sides of the rib, in every 4th and 8th round until the skirt is long enough. Mount the skirt on to petersham if it has been made in two pieces, or on to elastic if it has been knitted on a circular needle.

2

A PLEATED SKIRT FOR A SMALL GIRL

Measurements. Length from shoulder to lower edge, 22 ins.; length of bodice, 9½ ins.; width round chest, 25 ins.

Materials required. 4 ozs. of 4-ply crêpe wool; two No. 9 needles; two No. 7 needles; ⅓ yd. of white sateen; buttons or press studs for fastening at the back opening.

Directions. With No. 9 needles cast on 98 sts. Every first and last stitch is knitted plain for the seam; the pattern is worked on the other 96 sts. For the pattern use No. 9 needles.

1st row, k. 7, p. 1.
2nd row, k. 2, p. 6.
3rd row, k. 5, p. 3.
4th row, k. 4, p. 4.
5th row, k. 3, p. 5.
6th row, k. 6, p. 2.
7th row, k. 1, p. 7.
End of half the pattern.

8th row, k. 1, p. 7.
9th row, k. 6, p. 2.
10th row, k. 3, p. 5.
11th row, k. 4, p. 4.
12th row, k. 5, p. 3.
13th row, k. 2, p. 6.
14th row, k. 7, p. 1.
End of pattern.

Change to No. 7 needles. Repeat these 14 rows 6 times more (there will be 14 bands of triangles) and cast off. Make a similar piece for the other side of the skirt.

MAKING UP THE LITTLE GIRL'S SKIRT

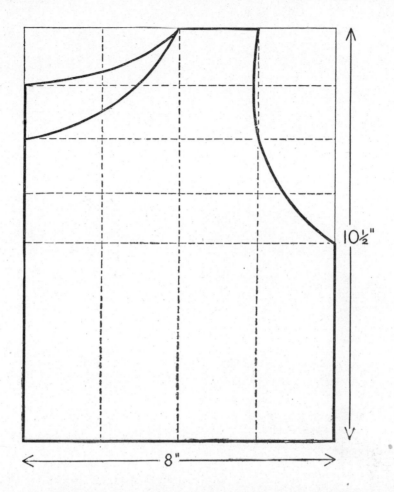

10½"

8"

Lightly press the two pieces of the skirt and tack them together wrong sides outside. The right side of the knitting has the purled triangles below the plainwise triangles. Seam the sides with the sewing machine, or back stitch by hand, using Sylko for the work. Press the seam. A diagram is given for making the very simple pattern for the sateen top. Join the shoulder and side seams with a french seam and neatly hem the neck and armholes. Make a placket down the centre back and fasten it with buttons and buttonholes, or with press studs. A ¼-in. hem neatens the bottom. Press the bodice. The cast-on edge of the skirt goes to the top. As the casting off opens out the pleats slightly, that edge is more suitable for the bottom of the skirt. Place the top of the skirt over the hem of the bodice. The side seams must be placed together, and the centre fronts and centre backs together. The remainder of the top edge of the skirt is fitted to the bodice between these points. Oversew this join by hand. It is not practicable to make a hem in this kind of knitting; if extra length is desired to allow for growing, overlap the bodice and skirt and let the skirt down the bodice as the child grows taller.

Directions for the bodice pattern. Cut a piece of paper as wide as one-third the chest measure and as long as the measure from shoulder to waist. The measurements given in the diagram are for a five to six-year-old. Fold the paper in half lengthways and into four widthways; the creases are represented by dotted lines. Fold the top half into four. Construct the pattern as shown in the diagram. The back neck is one section deep and two wide, the front neck is two sections deep and two wide, and the armhole is drawn one section wide and four deep. There need not be a seam on the shoulder. Except for the depth of the neck, the front and back patterns are alike, so only one quarter of the bodice pattern is required. Make the pattern for the back first.

Cutting out. Cut out the back, place the centre to a fold and allow turnings at the seams but not at the neck and armholes. Now cut the front neck in the paper pattern, and then cut out the front bodice in material, place the centre to a fold and allow turnings at seams only. To cut out without a shoulder seam fold the material into half lengthways and then widthways, and place the shoulder and the centre lines to these folds.

A MAN'S VEST

The drawing shows the style of this vest: it is straight, without shaping at the waist, the short sleeve is magyar and a gusset is let in at the top of the side seam. Ribbed bands are sewn round the neck and sleeve ends after the vest is made up. A placket at the front neck fastens with rubber or linen buttons, horizontal buttonholes being worked in the front band.

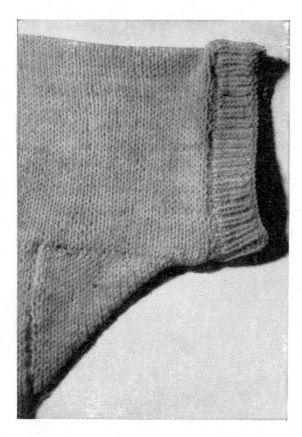

Materials required. 12 ozs. of 4-ply fingering in natural colour; a pair of No. 9 needles.

Measurements. 30 ins. from shoulder; 36 ins. under the arm; 4½ ins. for short sleeve.

Directions. The vest is knitted in stocking stitch, garter stitch and narrow ribbing.

Front. Cast on 108 sts. using method A for slack edge and knit the first row in the usual method for plain knitting. Knit for 10 rows in garter stitch and then change to stocking stitch and knit until 22 ins. have been worked. End on a purl row. Knit 54 and place the remainder of the stitches on a holder. Keeping to stocking stitch, knit the 54 sts. for 3 ins. End with the wool at the outer edge. Cast on 25 sts. for the sleeve and continue knitting for 1 more

inch. End with the wool at the inside edge. Cast off 27 sts. for the neck, and knit the remainder for 4 ins. Cast off, very loosely, for the shoulder. Take the stitches from the holder and knit the second front similar to the first.

Back. Cast on 108 sts., knit the first 10 rows in garter stitch and then continue knitting in stocking stitch for 25 ins. End on a purl row. Cast on 25 sts. for the sleeve. Knit back and cast on 25 sts. at the other end. Continue for another 3 ins. Knit 52 and put on to a holder. Cast off 54 sts. for the back neck and knit the remainder in stocking stitch for 2 ins. Cast off very loosely. Take the stitches from the holder, join the wool and knit up the second shoulder like the first. Cast off loosely.

Gusset. Cast on 22 sts. and knit 25 rows of stocking stitch. Cast off loosely.

Making up. Sew up the side seams to within 3½ ins. of the sleeve. Sew up the sleeve seam for 1 in. from the outer end. Sew up shoulder seams and press the work. Sew in the gusset and press again.

Placket strip. Cast on 8 sts. Slip all first stitches. Knit in ribbing of 1 plain and 1 purl for 2 ins., make a buttonhole (for directions see page on horizontal buttonholes). Knit 10 rows and make a buttonhole. Knit another 10 rows and make another buttonhole. Knit 5 rows, cast off, and sew to the left-hand side of the front opening. This band will extend above the opening.

Ribbed bands. For the sleeves, cast on 80 sts. and knit in ribbing of 1 plain and 1 purl for 10 rows. Join into a ring, make another band in the same way and sew them round the ends of the sleeves. For the neck, cast on 190 sts. and knit 10 rows in the same ribbing. Cast off and join the band to the neck commencing at the placket; sew the placket to the end of the ribbing. The illustration shows the gusset below the sleeve.

A SET OF COLLAR, REVERS AND POCKET TOPS

An attractive and inexpensive set of astrakhan collar, revers and pocket tops can be made in an hour or two.

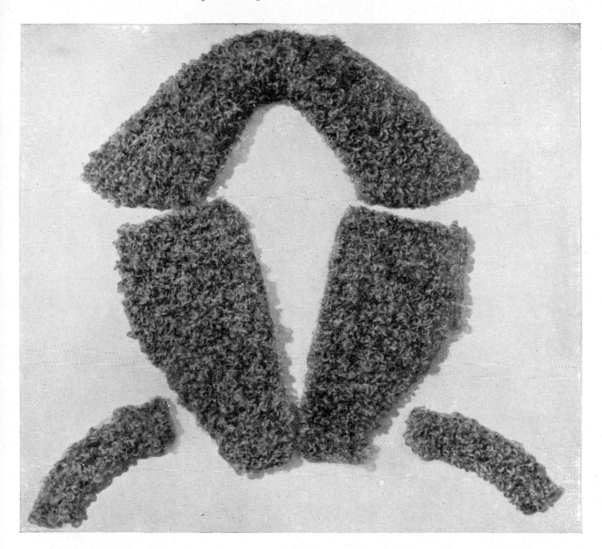

Measurements. Length o. revers, 8 ins.; width of revers at narrowest, 2 ins.; width of revers at widest, 4½ ins.; length of collar inside, 10½ ins; outside, 16½ ins.; width of collar, 3½ ins.; length of pocket top, 5 ins.; width of pocket top, 1¼ ins.

Materials required. 4 ozs. of astrakhan wool; a pair of No. 3 needles.

Directions.

Revers. Cast on 9 sts. Knit in garter stitch, increasing at the beginning of every fourth row, until there are 13 sts. Knit plain until work measures 8 ins.

Collar. Cast on 44 sts. (outer edge). Knit 6 rows plain. K. 2 together at the beginning of every row until the collar is 3½ ins. wide. Do not cast off; leave an end long enough to thread the stitches on to it. As each stitch is knitted in the next row pull the wool through. At the end draw up the wool to shape the collar in a slight curve and then fasten off the end.

Pocket tops. Cast on 15 and knit 5 rows plain. Finish off as for the collar. These tops will be sewn to the coat to extend above the pocket openings.

COLLAR AND CUFFS WITH A
FROTHY EDGE

These should be knitted up in white; the collar is suitable for a round neck.

Measurements. Length of collar, 14 ins.; width of collar, 2 ins.; length of cuffs, 6 ins. stretching to 7 ins.; cuffs are same width as collar.

Materials required. 1 oz. of 2-ply wool; a pair of No. 1 needles; a pair of No. 13 needles.

Directions.

Collar. Cast on 162 sts. on the No. 1 needles and knit 1 row. Change to No. 13 needles and k. 1, k. 2 tog., repeated to the end. 108 sts. remain. Knit a rib of 1 plain and 1 purl for 18 rows. Cast off loosely.

Cuffs. Cast on 84 sts. on No. 1 needles and knit 1 row. Change to No. 13 needles and k.1, k. 2 tog., repeated to the end. 56 sts. remain. Knit 18 rows of ribbing as for the collar. Cast off loosely. Press the ribbing but not the frill. Silk should not be used for these as the edging stitches will be too loose.

A COLLAR WITH POINTS

This collar will be suitable for a V-shaped neck.

Measurements. Width of collar at narrowest, 3¼ ins.; width of collar at widest, 4½ ins.; width across base of point, 2 ins.; length of point, 1¼ ins.

Materials required. 1 oz. of bouclé wool; a pair of No. 7 needles. A crêpe knitting silk will make up very well.

A COLLAR WITH POINTS *continued*

Directions

Cast on 15 sts. Knit the first row into the backs of the cast-on stitches. The work is done in stocking stitch. Increase 1 st. at the beginning of every knitted row 8 times. Decrease at the beginning of every knitted row 8 times. This makes the first point. Increase by knitting twice into the first stitch and decrease by knitting the first 2 sts. together. Repeat the point for as many times as will give the required length of the collar.

A MOSS STITCH COLLAR

This collar will be suitable for a V or square neck.

Measurements. Length of neck edge, 10¾ ins.; length of outer edge, 17½ ins.; width of collar, 2½ ins.

Materials required. 1 oz. of wool string; a pair of No. 11 needles.

Directions

Cast on 100 sts. and knit the first row into the backs of the cast-on stitches. Knit 6 rows in 1 plain and 1 purl ribbing. Knit 24 rows in moss stitch, increasing 1 st. at the beginning of every row. Increase by knitting twice into the first stitch. Knit 3 rows plain, still increasing. Cast off very loosely and press lightly. The side of the collar having the cast-off chained edge will be the right side. When sewing this collar into a dress the ribbing will be placed inside the neck of the dress.

A PRETTY TRIMMING WITH MANY USES

Knit these little pink petals in firm knitting silk. They have many decorative uses; these pictures show only a few. Other suggestions are that a number could be made in alternate colours and sewn, overlapping along a belt; enough separate petals could be made to go round the neck of a dress, the petals being sewn at their base to a piece of crossway binding which would be sewn just inside the neck and the petals allowed to hang loosely over the edge of the dress.

1

To make a petal. The work is done in fine ribbing of 1 plain and 1 purl. Cast on 2 sts. on fine needles. Continue in ribbing, increasing 1 st. at the beginning of each row until there are 28 sts. on the needle. Knit 6 rows without shaping. K. 1, k. 2 tog. in every row until there are only 2 sts. left, k. 2 tog., fasten off.

1. Three petals to form triangular trimming.

2. Petals arranged to trim the front of a waist.

3. Bows made with two petals.

3

2

76

DRESS TRIMMINGS

I. Here is a very useful dress trimming: it can be worn placed as a bow, or it can be let into a dress at the neck, as seen *in the drawing*. Two more will make cuffs for the same dress.

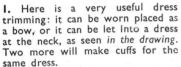

Measurements. Width of outer edges, 7½ ins. (when pressed); length, 8½ ins.

Materials required. 1 hank of art. silk crêpe; a pair of No. 11 needles.

Directions. Cast on 50 sts. and knit in fine ribbing of 1 plain and 1 purl for 8½ ins. Cast off loosely. Knit a strip in garter stitch 4 sts. wide and 4 ins. long. Gather this strip round the middle of the trimming, being careful to arrange the folds naturally, and join the ends by sewing them together. Press the outer edges only of this trimming.

2

A NET FALL

2. This will make decoration for the front of a blouse, or for the neck of a dress of fine wool cloth.

Materials required. 1 oz. of wool string; a pair of No. 1 needles; a pair of No. 11 needles.

Directions. Cast on 10 sts., k. 1, k. 2 into the next stitch. Repeat to the end (15 sts.). Repeat this row twice more (33 sts.).

4th row, knit, winding the wool twice round the needle in every stitch. Knit back, slipping the double loop as 1 st. Change to No. 1 needles. Repeat the 4th row, and knit back using No. 11 needles. Continue knitting in these last 2 rows until the work is the required length. Cast off very loosely on the No. 11 needles. Press under a damp cloth, pulling the work from under the iron in order to open out the loose rows. Mount it on to a button or a buckle and the trimming will be ready to wear.

BOWS FOR TRIMMING

I. This useful set of three stiff bows can be made from 1 oz. of 4-ply wool worked on No. 11 needles.

Directions. Cast on 20 sts. and work 2 rows in plain knitting, taking the first row into the backs of the cast-on stitches. Then knit in double knitting for 5½ ins. Always work the first 3 and last 3 sts. plainwise.

To do double knitting

1st row, k. 3, * k. 1 taking 2 loops round the needle before slipping the stitch from the left-hand needle, bring the wool forward, slip the next stitch purlwise, take wool back*; repeat from * to * until 3 sts. remain, k. 3.

2nd row, k. 3 and continue as for the first row. Every stitch that was slipped purlwise will be knitted with a double loop and the stitch which has a double loop in the previous row will be slipped purlwise, the loop being worked as 1 st. Repeat these 2 rows. Knit 3 rows plain and cast off. A strip of plain knitting gathers in the centre of the bows. Cast on 6 sts. and knit plain for 2½ ins. Cast off and sew round the bows making the join of the band come on the wrong side.

2. Here is a bow made from 5 pieces of ribbed knitting. Make the loops from 2 pieces of ribbing 22 sts. wide and 5½ ins. long. The pointed ends are made by casting on 2 sts. and then increasing in the first stitch of every other row until 22 sts. are on the needle, knit straight until the end measures 5½ ins. The middle strap is made with 16 sts. and 2½ ins. of ribbed knitting. To make up, fold the pieces for the loops in half and pleat, sew securely. Pleat the straight ends of the pointed pieces and sew to the loops. Wrap the small strip to form the knot and the bow is complete.

PART III

PATTERNED KNITTING

DECREASING AND INCREASING PROCESSES

Knitted fabric is made narrower by decreasing the number of stitches, and it is made wider by increasing the number of stitches. Both these processes are simple; but, as each has several variations, the right one must be used. The photographs on the next eight pages show the effect of each method of decreasing and increasing. By glancing at these pages the worker will be able to pick out the one best suited to her purpose; full directions are given for working the processes illustrated.

The photographs on this page show how to work the stitches required for decreasing and increasing.

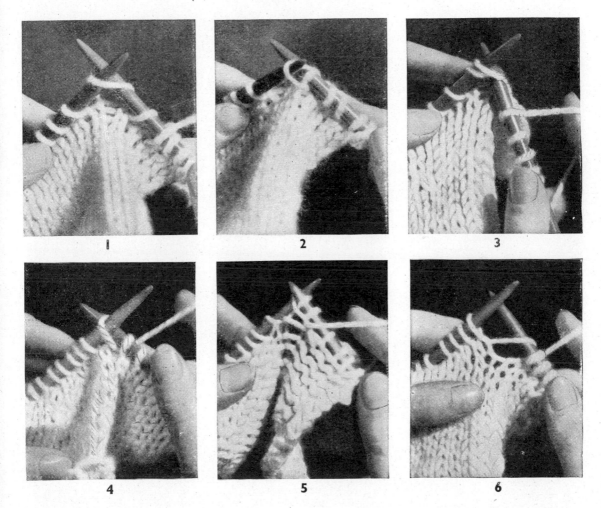

Decreasing
1. Slip 1, knit 1 (sl. 1, k. 1).
2. Pass the slipped stitch over (p.s.s.o.).
3. Knit 2 together (k. 2 tog.).

Increasing
4. Knitting twice into the same stitch. Knit the stitch as a plain stitch and before taking it off the needle, knit again into the back of it.
5. Purling twice into the same stitch. A purl stitch is worked into the front and another into the back of the stitch on the left-hand needle.
6. Knitting the strand between two stitches in the previous row.

DECREASING AT THE LEFT-HAND EDGE

Shaping at a left-hand edge by decreasing can be effected on the last two stitches of the row, or on the fourth and third stitches from the end. Each method gives a very different effect.

1. Decreasing on the last 2 sts. Knit to within 2 sts. of the end, k. 2 tog. This gives a seam edge required for outer garments where the seam join needs to be as invisible as possible; it is not good for lingerie.

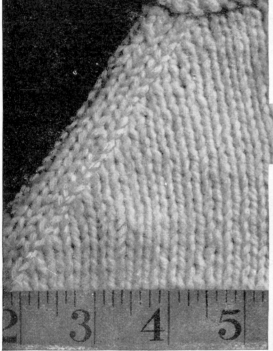

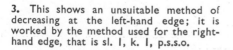

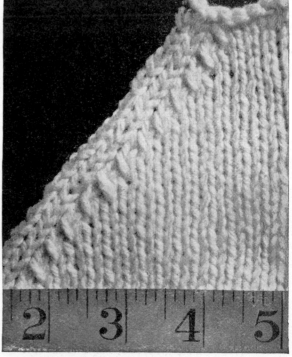

2. Decreasing on the fourth and third stitches from the end. Knit to within 4 sts. from the end of the row, k. 2 tog., k. 2. This is a stronger seam edge for lingerie. It is also a good edge for shaping scarves and edges of garments which do not come to a seam, such as neck lines which will not be covered by a collar.

3. This shows an unsuitable method of decreasing at the left-hand edge; it is worked by the method used for the right-hand edge, that is sl. 1, k. 1, p.s.s.o.

DECREASING AT THE RIGHT-HAND EDGE

At this edge too, there are two methods of shaping, and each is suitable for a different purpose. The first example, which has no margin, is used for outer garments and is worked in conjunction with the method which gives a similar effect at the left-hand edge of the work. The second method leaves a margin of two stitches and is used on lingerie in conjunction with the edge leaving a similar margin at the left-hand side.

1. Decreasing on the first 2 sts. Sl. 1, k. 1, p.s.s.o.; continue knitting in the usual way. Use this method together with the first method shown on page 80.

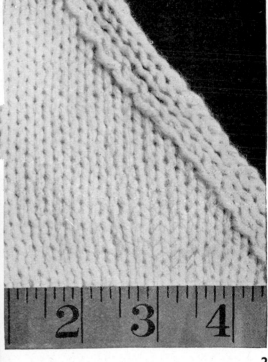

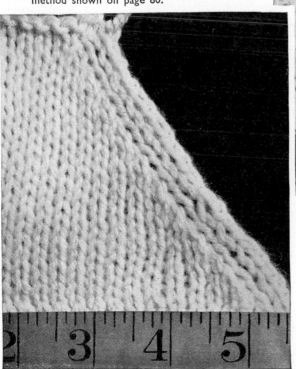

2. Decreasing on the third and fourth stitches of the row. K. 2, sl. 1, k. 1, p.s.s.o.; continuing knitting in the usual way. Work this method with the second method on the previous page.

3. This illustrates the kind of edge gained by working k. 2 tog. on the third and fourth stitches of the row; it is not such a neat edge as the one in photograph 2.

DECREASING IN THE CENTRE OR PLACES OTHER THAN EDGES

The methods of decreasing at places other than edges depend on the position of the decreasings and which row they have to be worked on. If the decreasing is to be worked towards the right-hand edge, then the same method as for shaping at a right-hand edge is used, i.e., sl. 1, k. 1, p.s.s.o. But when the shaping occurs towards the left-hand edge, then the decreasing is done by k. 2 tog., as at a left-hand edge.

These illustrations and directions show how to shape at centres, which require special planning.

2

1

1. A gradual shaping such as this, is useful for the tops of skirts and to take in the waist line of lingerie. The shaping process is always done on a plain row. First mark the centre stitch with a small safety pin. Knit to within 1 st. of the centre, sl. 1, k. 1, p.s s.o. Continue knitting to the end and purl back. Next row, knit to the centre stitch and repeat the shaping on the centre stitch and the following stitch. Continue knitting and again purl back. Repeat these 4 rows throughout the shaping. By using the stitch in front and the one after the centre stitch, alternately, the shaping is kept to the middle of the work and the stitches in each half are reduced equally.

2. For a sharper decrease, shaping is done on every row.
1st row, k. to within one of the centre, sl. 1, k. 1, p.s.s.o.; continue knitting to the end.
2nd row, p. to within one of the centre, k. 2 tog.; continue purling to the end. Repeat these 2 rows throughout. This method also uses the centre stitch with the one on either side alternately, so that the stitches are decreased equally in each half.

DECREASING AT BOTH SIDES TO MAKE A POINT

Where points with stitch margins are required, the following directions should be worked to ensure a good point that will not curl.

I. Shaping is gained by the methods used for decreasing with margins, as worked for left-hand and right-hand edges.
K. 2, sl. I, k. I, p.s.s.o.; continue knitting to within 4 sts. of the end, k. 2 tog., k. 2. P. back and repeat these 2 rows until there are 6 or 7 sts. left. Then proceed to shape the point. K. 2, sl. I, k. I (or, if there are 7 sts., k. 2 tog.) p.s.s.o., k. 2.

Next row, p. I, p. 2 tog., p. 2.

Next row, sl. I, k. I, p.s.s.o., k. I.

Last row, p. 2 tog. and fasten off.

I

DECREASING ON THREE NEEDLES

2

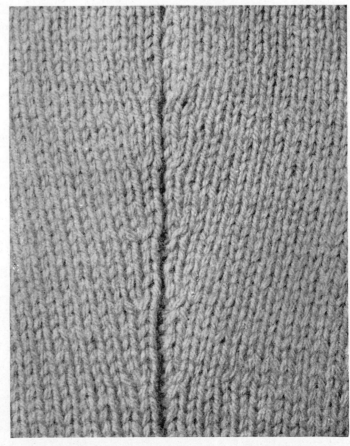

When socks are knitted in plain, or stocking stitch fabric, the legs are shaped with decreasing between the calf and the ankle so that the width gradually diminishes between these two points. It is a good plan to mark the centre stitch of the leg, i.e., the first stitch of the round, by working it as a purl stitch.

2. Leg decreasing. Work the required length of ribbing for the top and also the number of plain rounds stated in the directions before commencing the shapings; but remember to work the first stitch in every round purlwise.
Ist decreasing, p. the first stitch, k. 2 tog.; continue to within 2 sts. of the end of the round, k. 2 tog. Knit the next 5 rounds plain. Repeat these 6 rounds five times so that there are five sets of decreasings. Continue following knitting directions.

INCREASING AT LEFT-HAND AND RIGHT-HAND EDGES

It has been pointed out on previous pages that there are special ways of *decreasing* the stitches at each side of the work, and similar principles apply to *increasing* the number of stitches so that the new stitches shall radiate in the correct direction.

1

2

1. Increasing at the right-hand edge on the first stitch. Knit twice into the first stitch; this process is shown on page 79. Purl back. Repeat these 2 rows throughout. An edge worked like this will remain flat and in good shape, and makes a good seam edge for outer garments.

2. Increasing on the fourth stitch in the row. K. 3, knit twice into the fourth stitch, continue knitting to the end and purl back. Repeat these 2 rows. This method produces a margin of 3 sts. which makes a firm seam edge for lingerie.

3. Increasings at left-hand edges are also made by knitting twice into a stitch, knitting into the back of the stitch first. This illustration shows the process worked on the third stitch from the end, leaving a margin of 2 sts. which makes a good firm edge when the seam is to be joined by the sewing machine.

3

INCREASING BY PICKING UP STITCHES

The number of stitches can be increased by knitting up a strand or a stitch from the previous row. There are two ways of doing this and each method leaves holes in the fabric which can be made use of in a design.

I. A method where 2 sts. are added in every plain row.

Directions. Cast on 3 sts.

1st row, k. I, pick up the strand between the stitches and knit it, k. I, pick up strand and knit it, k. I. Purl back. Repeat these 2 rows. Picking up the strands on each side of the centre stitch in the plainwise row. A line is formed on either side of the centre stitch.

2. For a single line of holes, cast on 3 sts., knit the 1st row and purl the second.

Next row, k. I, pick up the loop below the next stitch on the left-hand needle and knit it; knit the stitch on the left-hand needle and then knit again into the loop below the stitch just knitted. Again 2 sts. are added in every plain row, the shaping being worked below the centre stitch every time.

INCREASING AT BOTH EDGES FOR POINTS

The edges of points on a yoke, or on a pointed bodice and skirt join, must be very firm and of a good shape, so that the sewing will be neat and strong. These lines will be very important, as they are part of the style or design of the garment, and any lumpiness or curve will show badly. If an edge seems stretched, run a thread along and draw it up a little to bring the fabric in.

1. Cast on 2 sts. Knit twice into the first stitch in the usual way. Knit twice into the second stitch as for the left-hand side edge, i.e., first into the back of the stitch. Purl back. Repeat these 2 rows, increasing in the first and last stitches in every plain row until the point is the required length.

2. A more rapid increase and a wider point is gained by increasing in every row. Knit twice in the first and last stitches of the plain rows and purl twice in the first and last stitches of the purl rows.

3. Knitting twice into the third stitch from each end. At the beginning of the row knit first into the front and then into the back of the stitch, but at the other end of the row, knit into the back of the stitch first.

INCREASING AT CENTRE STITCHES

Points can also be made by increasing stitches at the centre, two methods being shown on this page. Note how in each case the stitches radiate from the centre line.

1

I. This is an increase of 1 st. in every row, and the method gives an almost invisible centre line.

Directions. Cast on 2 sts.

1st row, knit twice into the first stitch, k. 1, p. 1, purl twice into next stitch, p. 1.

3rd row, k. 1, knit twice into second stitch, k. 2.

4th row, p. 2, purl twice into next stitch, p. 2.

It will be seen from the 3rd and 4th rows that in the plain rows there are an even number of stitches to be worked and the increasing is done on the last of the first half of the stitches, and that in the purl rows, there is an odd number of stitches to be worked and increasing is done on the centre stitch.

Repeat rows 3 and 4 throughout.

2. Although this point increases at the same rate as the last, the increasings only occur on the plain rows—2 sts. are made at the centre of each plain row.

Directions. Cast on 3 sts.

1st row, knit twice into both the first and second stitches, k. 1.

2nd row, p.

3rd row, k. 1, knit twice into the next 2 sts., k. 2.

4th row, p.

Continue in a similar manner, increasing in the stitch before the centre and the centre stitch, returning with a purl row.

2

A WARM KNEE-CAP FOR WINTER

Materials required. 2 ozs. of 4-ply fingering; a pair of No. 11 needles for medium-sized knee-caps, or No. 9 needles for a larger size.

Directions. Cast on 86 sts. loosely.

Knit 18 rows in 2 plain and 2 purl ribbing.

19th row, rib 40, k. 8, turn.

20th row, p. 10, turn.

Continue knitting, working 2 more stocking stitches in every row before turning, until only 18 rib sts. remain at each side. Now knit 2 rows right across, stocking stitches over stocking stitches and rib over rib.

Next row, knit 18 rib sts. Now commence to reduce the width of the stocking stitches by working 2 sts. less in each row in the reverse way to the method of increasing. Thus work to within two of the end of the stocking stitches, turn; k. 2 stocking stitches less, turn. Continue in this way, knitting 2 sts. less in every row until 8 stocking stitches remain. Knit to the end of the row in ribbing being sure to begin with the correct pair of stitches, i.e., either purl or plain. It may be necessary to count back from the 18 rib sts. Work 26 rows in ribbing and then cast off very loosely.

SHAPING SIDE SEAMS

The following facts must be known before the calculations for shaping side seams can be worked out.

1. Tension of work, i.e., the number of rows to 1 in. and the number of stitches to 1 in. of knitting.

2. Measurement from bust to waist, the bust measure and the width of the piece of knitting at the waist line, or at the top of the waist ribbing.

As a guide we will reckon that there are:—

    6 stitches to 1 in.
    8 rows to 1 in.
    Bust to waist measure = 8 ins.
    Bust measure = 34 ins.
    Waist ribbing = 30 ins.

It will be seen that the increase required in the work from waist to bust is 4 ins. That is, 1 in. at each side seam edge.

The following calculations are worked.

(*a*) Number of stitches to be increased at each edge.

(*b*) Number of rows to be worked between waist and bust.

    Divide (*a*) into (*b*). The answer will give the number of the row on which one stitch must be increased at each end.

Using the specimen measures and tensions given above we will work it out in figures.

1 in. to be increased at each side seam edge:—

    34 ins. — 30 ins. = 4 ins. (there are four side seam edges).
    ∴ 6 stitches have to be increased at each edge.
    Length between waist and bust = 8 ins. (64 rows).
    64 ÷ 6 = 11 (taken to the nearest multiple, 66).

The increasing will be done on the first, tenth and every eleventh row following four times. Nine rows will be knitted above the last increasing to finish the length from waist to bust line.

The directions given above will shape the ordinary sloping side seam. But a bloused effect is sometimes required. For this, all increasings are done in the row after the ribbing, so that the fullness begins just above the waist, and, as a rule, the ribbing is a little narrower.

Cast on ten stitches less than the directions state. Knit the rib and then increase in the next row by knitting twice into every fifth stitch

(approximately). No further shaping is worked in the side seam.

When planning the side seams of a lace stitch garment, first imagine the effect of the seams when joined. Avoid getting a wide band of plain knitting when all the rest is patterned with holes and, on the other hand, avoid having a weak line of holes on either side. Where the pattern is a striped one, try to get half of a solid stripe at each end of the knitting, so that when the seam is joined there is one plain stripe.

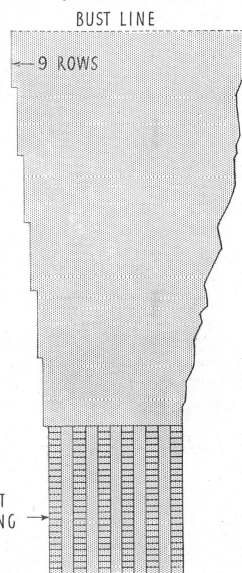

BUST LINE

← 9 ROWS

WAIST RIBBING →

This illustration shows the kind of line that is gained on a side seam worked in the method described. Note that the first increasing is done directly above the ribbing.

SHAPING ARMHOLES

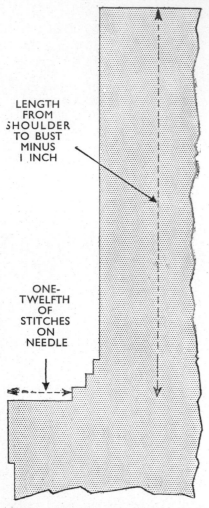

LENGTH
FROM
SHOULDER
TO BUST
MINUS
1 INCH

ONE-
TWELFTH
OF
STITCHES
ON
NEEDLE

The casting-off processes will not leave a jagged edge as the drawing shows; this was done to illustrate more clearly the positions of the two cast-off stitches and those which are knitted together. The decreasings will form a good curve.

The number of rows to 1 in. of knitting and the number of stitches on the needle at the bust line must be known in order to work out the shaping of an armhole.

How the calculations are planned.

Cast off one-twelfth of the number of stitches on the needle. Knit to the end of the row and repeat on the next row.

Cast off 2 stitches at the beginning of the next 2 rows.

Knit two together at the beginning of the next 4 rows.

Continue knitting without decreasing until the work measures 1 in. less from the beginning of the armhole than it does from the waist to the bust line. Then continue for the shoulder.

Example.

Using the same specimen tension and measures as for shaping a side seam, i.e., 6 stitches and 8 rows to 1 in. and a 34-in. bust, we should cast off 9 stitches (one-twelfth of 102 stitches on the needle taken to the next highest multiple), then two twice, and then one four times. The remainder of the armhole would be straight knitting for 56 rows, counting from the bust line (the average depth from bust to waist being 8 ins; 7 ins. will be required from the beginning to the top of the armhole).

Back and front armholes are worked alike.

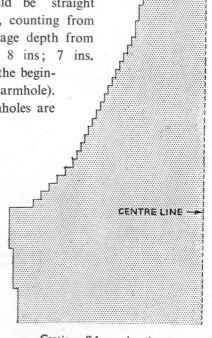

CENTRE LINE →

Casting off for raglan sleeves.

RAGLAN ARMHOLES

Here is a guide for making raglan armholes. The directions apply to 3-ply and 4-ply wool knitted with No. 9 needles. The armhole shapings will be worked at the beginning of the rows commencing at the armhole end; the neck shapings will be worked at the opposite end.

Armholes. Cast off 8 sts., cast off 2 sts. twice, k. 2 tog. at beginning of every 4th row four times, cast off 2 sts. seventeen times.

Raglan sleeve tops. To be worked at both sides of the work. Cast off 6 sts., cast off 2 sts. five times k. 2 tog. sixteen times, k. 2 tog. at beginning of every 4th row five times, cast off.

SHAPING SQUARE NECKS

The width of the neck at the shoulder and at the centre front, the depth of the neck and the tension of the stitches and rows, must be known before attempting to plan the working for a square-shaped neck.

From these can be calculated the number of stitches to be cast off and the number of rows to be worked for the side of the neck.

Directions. The next row must commence on the right side. Calculate the number of stitches to be cast off at the centre front to give the centre front edge of the neck, knit along the row to within half this number of the centre, cast off the number of stitches required and knit to the end.

Knit back as far as the cast-off stitches and place those left on the end of the needle on to a stitch holder, to be knitted up for the second shoulder later.

Returning to the stitches just knitted, cast off 2 stitches, knit to the end and return. Cast off 2 stitches again, finish the row and return. On the next 2 rows which begin at the neck edge knit two together. Thus 6 stitches have been disposed of, making the neck opening 1 in. wider.

Continue knitting straight until work measures the required depth from centre front to top of shoulder. Then work the shoulder seam.

For the second shoulder, pick up the stitches from the holder so that work will commence at the armhole end of the row, join on the wool and repeat the work as for the first shoulder, the only difference being that decreasings will be worked on the row which comes on the wrong side of the garment.

A narrow ribbed band makes a good finish to a square neck. Multiply the number of stitches in 1 in. by the length round the neck, cast on that number of stitches and knit in ribbing of k. 1, p. 1 for $\frac{1}{2}$ in. Cast off very loosely indeed and sew the band to the neck edge, stretching it at the corners.

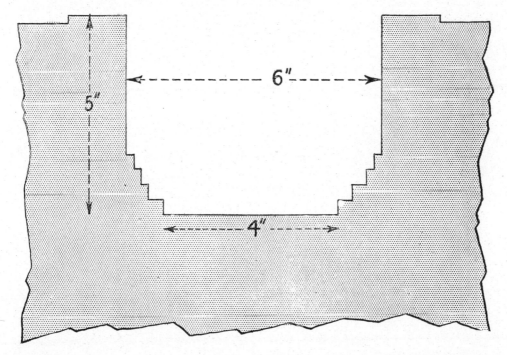

This diagram shows how the width of the neck opening is made gradually. When the garment is being worn the neck will appear quite square. If the sides of the neck rose straight up from the front line, the front line would become so stretched in wear that the neck opening would be too large. The sleeves tend to pull the front edge of the neck outwards to the side, and these extra stitches at the corner prevent the neck becoming too wide. Average measures are shown here. Knitted fabric stretches, so do not make the neck too large.

SHAPING FOR A V-SHAPED NECK

The illustration shows the plan for a V neck as it appears when drawn out on squared paper.

The depth of the neck opening, its width at the top and the tension of work must be known, from these points the working calculations can be made.

The measurements given are the average, i.e., 6 ins. deep and 6 ins. wide at the shoulder. Thus, the neck commences 2 ins. above the bust line, or at the level of the beginning of the armhole shapings.

When this point is reached continue as follows:—

The last row must end on the wrong side so that the next can be worked on the right side.

Mark the centre stitch, or the two stitches in the centre if there is an even number of stitches, and knit as far as the centre. If there is one stitch at the centre slip it and pass it over the next; but where there are two, cast these off. Knit to the end of the row and return to the centre. Slip the remaining stitches on to a holder.

The decreasings must be planned to make a gentle slope at the side of the neck, to widen the neck by 3 ins. from the beginning and to make the depth of the decreasing take up about two-thirds of the depth of the neck. To do this divide the number of rows in this two-thirds by the number of stitches in the half-neck width. As a rule it will be found that a decreasing will have to be worked on every alternate row, but much depends on the thickness of the wool and needles. For this reason it is most important to measure the tension, that is, the number of stitches and rows to 1 in. of knitting, accurately.

One-third of the depth of the neck will be knitted straight. Cast off for the shoulder.

Pick up the stitches on the holder, arranging them so that work begins at the armhole end.

Knit to the centre and knit up the second shoulder like the first, making all the decreasings at the neck edge.

In working the decreasings any of the methods described in the section on decreasing at edges may be used.

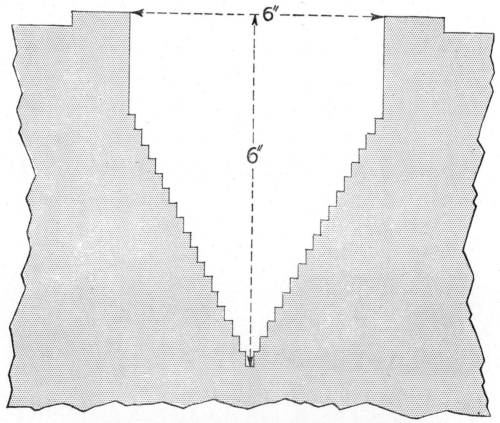

Shaping for a V-shaped neck. The effect will be the same whether there is an even number or an uneven number of stitches on the needle.

SHAPING ROUND NECKS

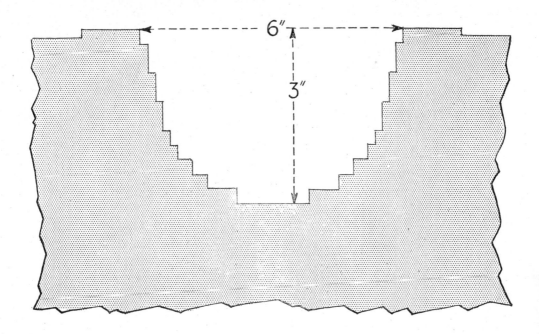

Only the general shape of a round neck can be given. These are average measures and the usual shape required for a Peter Pan collar.

The shapings required for a round neck are more difficult to work out. Only a general outline of the process can be given because much more depends on the gauge of the needles and the thickness of the wool and a rule of proportions cannot be laid down.

The drawing shows the shape of an average round neck, as is required for a Peter Pan collar, that is, a high neck line.

The shaping commences 5 ins. above the bust line.

The front edge is 1½ ins. wide. Knit to within ¾ in. of the centre, cast off 1½ ins. of stitches and knit to the end. Return to the cast-off stitches.

Cast off half the number of stitches as were cast off before, knit to the end and return.

In the next and third row cast off half as many as were cast off the second time. At the beginning of the next two rows which start at the neck, knit two together.

Knit two together at the beginning of the fourth, eighth and twelfth rows after.

Knit straight up to the shoulder line.

The above directions are good for 4-ply wool and Nos. 9 or 8 needles. Finer wool and needle, such as 2-ply and Nos. 11 or 12 needles, may require twice the number of rows and stitches for each step.

A larger neck will start lower down and more stitches will be worked in every process, perhaps doubling or trebling the number used for a high neck line.

The above directions will make an average round neck, requiring a collar to make a finish. When stitches will be picked up round the neck to make a ribbed band, the neck space will have to be much larger. For a polo neck, do not cast off any stitches. Where directions say "cast off," slip those stitches on to a spare needle, join up the shoulder seams, and pick up stitches down the sides of the front neck. Add these to the back neck stitches and arrange all on a circular needle. Knit a straight band of ribbing for the collar.

SHAPING SHOULDERS

FOR THE FRONT.

Shoulders are very easy to shape. The only calculation to make is to find one-third of the total number of stitches left on the needle after the neck shapings have been made. The work must commence at the armhole end of the row. Cast off one-third of the number of stitches, knit to the end and return.

Repeat this once more and then cast off the remainder of the stitches.

FOR THE BACK.

The back neck is not shaped.

The work must commence at the armhole end of a row.

Cast off the same number of stitches at the beginning of the next 4 rows as were cast off each time on the front shoulder.

Cast off the remainder of the stitches.

The weight of the garment will give all the shaping required to the back neck.

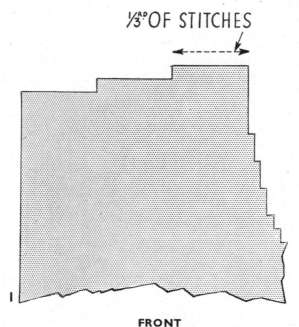

⅓ᴿᴰ OF STITCHES

FRONT

1. The shoulder shapings are very simple. If there are a few stitches left after dividing by 3, leave these to be cast off at the end.

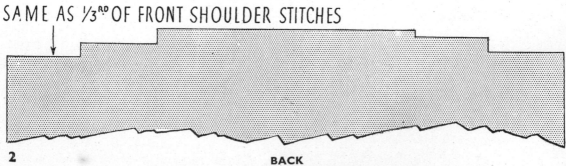

SAME AS ⅓ᴿᴰ OF FRONT SHOULDER STITCHES

BACK

2. Although the shapings on one side are a row higher this difference is not noticeable when the garment is worked.

94

SHAPING A SLEEVE SEAM

Sleeve seams are very easy to plan. The work is done in a similar manner to side seams shaping.

The tension of work and length of the sleeve seam must be found first of all. Then the length of the wrist ribbing must be measured and subtracted from the length of the sleeve seam (not the total length of the sleeve, i.e., length from top of shoulder to wrist).

The desired width of the sleeve and the number of stitches required to give that width at the beginning of the armhole, must next be found.

Subtract the number of stitches on the needle after the ribbing has been worked from the number of stitches required at the top. Halve this number to give the number of stitches to be increased at each side of the sleeve, and, when the number of rows in the sleeve from ribbing to armhole is known, the position of the increasings can be worked out.

The drawing shows the increasings required for a sleeve 17 ins. long at the seam with a ribbed band 3 ins. long. The tension of the work has been planned at 6 stitches and 8 rows to the inch of knitting. There are 42 stitches on the needle and the required width at the top of the sleeve is 12 ins.

> 3 ins. from 17 ins. = 14 ins. = 112 rows.
> 12 ins. = 72 sts.
> 42 sts. from 72 sts. = 30 sts.
> ∴ Number of stitches to be increased at each side = 30 ÷ 2 = 15.

When 15 is divided into 112 it is found that an increasing must be worked at each end of every seventh row, with the odd number left over added at the top.

Quite a well shaped sleeve seam is gained by knitting without shaping as far as the elbow and then increasing on every fourth or fifth row, according to thickness of wool.

For a sleeve with a very full top, similar to a leg-of-mutton shape, knit to the elbow without shaping, then increase by knitting twice into the first stitch of every row. For a still fuller sleeve, increase in the first and last stitches of every row. When the sleeve is long enough, follow the shaping for the average sleeve top and, when setting in the sleeve, gather the top as is done in dressmaking. These leg-of-mutton sleeves are seldom successful in thick wool, but they are suitable for 2-ply, 3-ply and 4-ply wools.

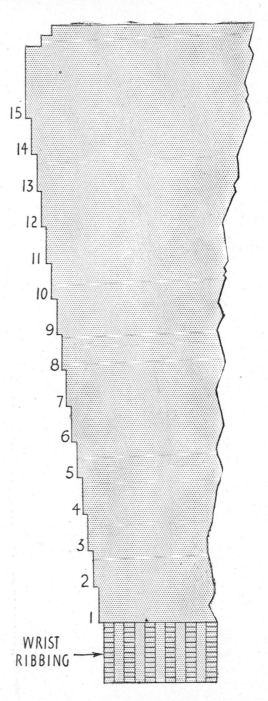

WRIST RIBBING →

The kind of shaping required for a straight sleeve. For a sleeve with a fuller top, work these increasings as far as the elbow and then double the number from the elbow to the armhole, that is, an increasing will be worked at each end of every fourth row.

SHAPING SLEEVE TOPS

This is another instance where only general hints can be given because sleeve tops can vary so much in size and shape and, providing well-shaped curves are gained, it is not important how the decreasings are worked.

The width of the sleeve at the beginning of the armhole and the depth of the top, that is, from the beginning of the armhole to the top of the shoulder, are the two measurements that must be known.

The drawing shows a sleeve top of average measures, i.e., 12 ins. wide and 5 ins. deep. The decreasings have been calculated to leave a straight line of cast-off stitches at the top about $3\frac{1}{2}$ ins. long.

The following directions describe how to do the shaping by measurements, so that it is immaterial what size of needles, thickness of wool or size of tension is being used.

Work the directions at the beginning of the rows, first at one side and then at the other side of the sleeve. Cast off $\frac{3}{4}$ in. Cast off $\frac{1}{2}$ in. three times. Cast off $\frac{1}{4}$ in. (or 1 or 2 stitches according to thickness of wool) twelve times. Cast off $\frac{1}{2}$ in. twice. Cast off remainder of stitches.

N.B.—The measurements are more important than the methods, so before following the above directions calculate roughly how your tension will work.

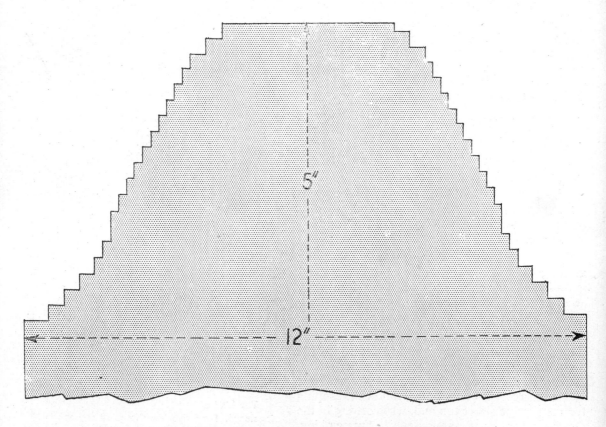

How to plan an average sleeve top 12 ins. wide at the beginning of the armhole and 5 ins. deep in the centre. Note the 4 rows worked without shaping. This is done to give a slight S-shaped curve to this part of the sleeve edge.

A PLAIN AND A SHAPED SLEEVE TOP

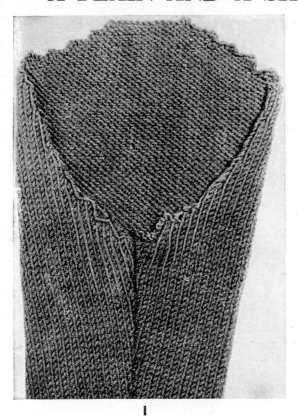

1

2

1. This is how a sleeve top, knitted in a similar way to that described for a plain sleeve top, will appear when it is made up. The steps in decreasing can be seen clearly in this thick wool.

2. Two small darts shape the top of this sleeve for a tailored jumper. A short length of petersham, or a small roll of cotton wool, should be fixed under top or a tailors' padding may be used instead.

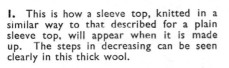

3

3. Make the sleeve at least 14 ins. wide at the beginning of the armhole. Then shape it in the ordinary way for 5 ins. Divide the number of stitches into three (approximately), and knit each third separately. First and last thirds: knit 2 together at the beginning of every row. The middle section: knit plain for 1 in., knit 2 together until there are half the number of stitches on the needle, cast off. When seaming the darts, pin the outer ends together and stretch the shorter edge to fit the longer one.

SHAPING REVERS

These are the points to be known before the shaping of revers can be planned out:—

Tension of the work, the number of rows and stitches to 1 in. of knitting.

The depth of the rever.

The width required for the top of the rever (this is measured beyond the centre front line).

The width of the wrap beyond the centre line at base of rever.

Subtract the width of the wrap from the width of the top of the rever, measured from the centre line.

Calculate the number of stitches in the measurement left; this will give the number of stitches to be increased.

Calculate the number of rows in the length of the rever.

Divide the number of stitches into the number of rows; the result will give the row on which one

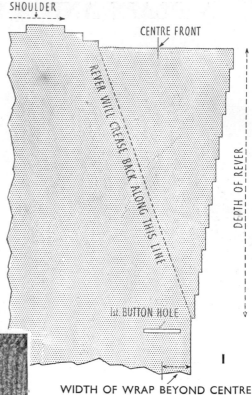

WIDTH OF WRAP BEYOND CENTRE LINE

stitch must be increased at the beginning.

At the top of the rever cast off twice the number of stitches that there are from the centre line to the edge of the rever and then finish the usual shaping for the neck.

1. A medium-sized rever will have an increasing worked on every sixth row.

2. The moss stitching of the wrap-over has been carried up into the rever. Positions of buttonholes, especially of the first one, must be taken into account when deciding on the length of the rever.

2

OPENINGS FOR FASTENINGS

When it is necessary to have an opening in a garment fastened with buttons or press studs, very careful planning is necessary to get this opening in the right place.

The width of the work is divided equally, and on to one set of stitches further stitches are added to make a wrap, just as a false piece is added to an opening in dressmaking, the only difference being that in knitting the wrap is in one piece with the rest of the garment.

Let us consider that buttons are to be used for the fastening, and that the buttons are to come at the centre front. A jumper fastens right over left, so, with the wrong side of the work towards the knitter, count to the centre of the stitches. This will be where the middle of the buttons should come. Next consider the width required for the buttonhole; as a rule this will be 4 stitches. Beyond the centre stitch, count half the number of stitches of the buttonhole, plus two for the edge (4 more stitches), and this will give the stitch at which the work will be divided.

Mark the position of the stitch with a small safety pin, knit to it and turn. Knit backwards and forwards on these stitches, making the buttonholes where they are needed, until the neck line is reached.

2. A neck opening completed.

(If the opening is to be quite short, the stitches which are not being worked may remain on the needle, but if the work is heavy, or the opening long, it will be best to put the spare stitches on to a holder.)

Work the armhole and shoulder according to the directions for the garment.

The left side of the opening is extended for the wrap which holds the buttons. Arrange the stitches so that knitting will commence at the opening end of the row, and join on the wool.

The wrap must be wide enough to go completely under the buttonholes: to calculate the number of extra stitches required, add together the stitches of the buttonholes (4), the stitches at the edge (2), and 2 stitches more for the edge of the wrap, making 8 stitches altogether.

Cast on 8 stitches at the opening end of the left front and continue knitting as for right front, but omitting the buttonholes.

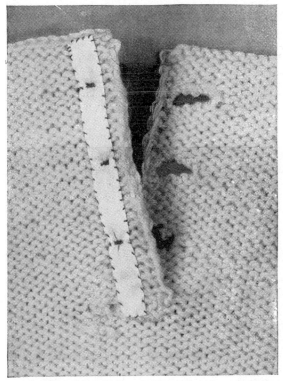

I. The lower edge of the wrap is sewn to the right front; a strip of narrow tape is sewn at the back to make the fabric strong enough to hold the buttons. The edges of the buttonholes may be oversewn for extra strength.

MAKING STITCHES

Lace or openwork patterns in knitting are made by forming holes with a "made" stitch. In order to keep the same number of stitches on the needle after one row of knitting has been completed, a number of stitches, equal to the number of "made" stitches, are disposed of in the solid part of the pattern. A new line of stitches will spring from the "made" stitch. It is possible to make this line of new stitches take a right-hand or a left-hand slope by the careful planning of the position of the decreased stitches. This is more fully dealt with a little later; the illustrations on this page show how to work the "made" stitches.

1. To make one stitch the wool is brought forward and the next stitch is knitted in the usual way. Thus a loop is formed round the right-hand needle. The decreased stitch may be worked on the left or the right of the made stitch, or it may be done two or three stitches away. It must be remembered that every made stitch must be balanced by a decreased stitch in order to keep the width of the knitting even. The majority of lace patterns are made with 1 made stitch (m. 1) and 1 decreased stitch (k. 2 tog. or sl. 1, k. 1, p.s.s.o.).

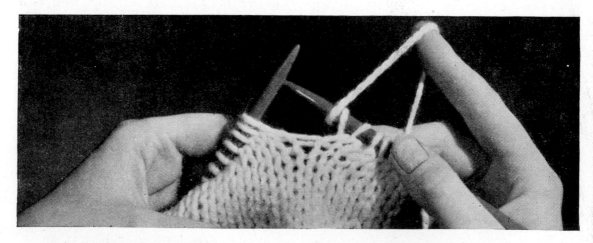

2. For very open lace patterns, such as are sometimes required for bed jackets and dressing gowns, two stitches can be made in the same place by bringing the wool forward twice, making two loops round the needle. As a rule a stitch is decreased on either side of these two made stitches, or, in the next row, the first loop is knitted and the second loop is slipped.

MAKING SHAPES WITH HOLES

By carefully planning the positions of the decreased and "made" stitches, it is possible to form shapes with either the solid parts of the knitting, or with the holes.

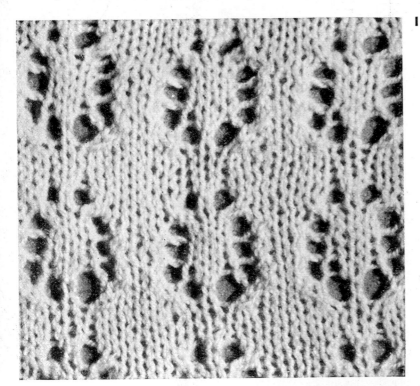

1. This illustration shows shapes made with holes; a kind of pineapple design is formed.

Directions. Cast on a number of stitches divisible by 8.
1st row, k.
2nd and alternate rows, p.
3rd row, k. 2, sl.1, k. 1, p.s.s.o., m. 1, k. 1, m. 1, k. 2 tog., k. 1; repeat to the end.
5th row, k. 1, sl. 1, k. 1, p.s.s.o., m. 1, k. 3, m. 1, k. 2 tog.; repeat to the end.
7th row, the same as the 5th.
9th row, the same as the 3rd.
11th row, k.
12th row, p.
Repeat these 12 rows throughout.

2

2. A less formal pattern is made with vertical zigzag lines of holes, leaving diamond shapes in solid knitting. The decreased stitches have been arranged so as to form ridges on the top edges of the diamonds.

Directions. Cast on a number of stitches divisible by 12.
1st row, k. 3, k. 2 tog., m. 1, k. 2, sl. 1, k. 1, p.s.s.o., k. 3; repeat to the end.
2nd and alternate rows, p.
3rd row, k. 2, k. 2 tog., m. 1, k. 4, m. 1, sl. 1, k. 1. p.s.s.o., k. 2; repeat to the end.
5th row, k. 1, k. 2 tog., m. 1, k. 6, m. 1, sl. 1, k. 1, p.s.s.o., k. 1; repeat to the end.
7th row, k. 2 tog., m. 1, k. 8, m. 1, sl. 1, k. 1, p.s.s.o.; repeat to the end.
9th row, k. 1, m. 1, sl. 1, k. 1, p.s.s.o., k. 6, k. 2 tog., m. 1, k. 1; repeat to the end.
11th row, k. 2, m. 1, sl. 1, k. 1, p.s.s.o., k. 4, k. 2 tog., m. 1, k. 2; repeat to the end.
13th row, k. 3, m. 1, sl. 1, k. 1, p.s.s.o., k. 2, k. 2 tog., m. 1, k. 3; repeat to the end.
14th row, p.
Repeat these 14 rows throughout.

LACE PATTERNS

Openwork patterns can be planned to give any kind of lacy fabric desired. Holes are formed by bringing the wool forward to make a stitch and then disposing of the extra stitch so made in one of two ways: either by knitting two together, or by slipping one, knitting one and passing the slipped stitch over the knitted stitch.

Remember that the position of the decreased stitch will govern the method of its disposal. If it comes *before* the made stitch then the work must be sl. 1, k. 1, p.s.s.o.; but when the decreasing comes *after* the made stitch, two stitches must be knitted together; the former pulls the fabric to the right and the latter pulls the work to the left, hence the importance of using the right method in the right place.

1

1. A simple all-over lace pattern.
Directions. Knit 4 rows in st.st.
5th row, k. 1, * m. 1, k. 2 tog.*; repeat from * to *; k. 1. Repeat these 5 rows throughout. The stitches which are knitted together give the fabric a very pleasant broken surface.

2

2. Picot edges are very useful for lingerie and babies' garments. Knit 4 or 5 rows in stocking stitch. Knit the next row in the same manner as the 5th row of pattern 1. Purl the next row and then continue in the stitch of the garment.

3. When making up the garment turn up the knitted rows at the holes, making the fold come across the decreased stitches to form a picot edge.

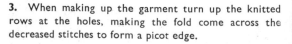

3

LACE PATTERNS

Other interesting all-over patterns can be made with groups of holes. Plan to have sufficient plain fabric between each group, otherwise the work will look very weak.

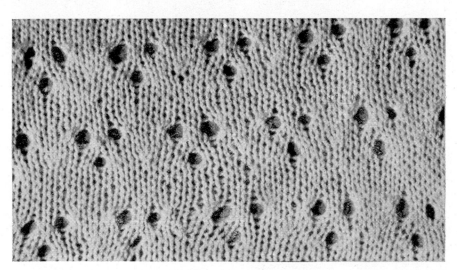

1. Groups of three holes make a pleasant pattern for summer jumpers. This pattern requires a number of stitches divisible by 8.

Directions.

1st row, k. 2, sl. 1, k. 1, p.s.s.o., m. 1, k. 2, m. 1, k. 2 tog.; repeat to the end.

2nd row, p.

3rd row, k. 2 tog., k. 3, m. 1, k. 3; repeat to the end.

4th row, p.

Knit 6 rows in stocking stitch and then repeat the 4 pattern rows, moving the working of the holes along to the right-hand side so that the 1st row will commence with k. 1, m. 1, k. 2 tog. and then follow the directions as given in the 1st row. The beginning of the 3rd row will have to be altered to k. 3, k. 2 tog., k. 3, m. 1, repeated to the end, finishing with a m. 1 in the appropriate part of the pattern so as not to decrease the number of stitches on needle by 1. Knit the 6 rows of stocking stitch, and then repeat these 20 rows as many times as will be required for the garment.

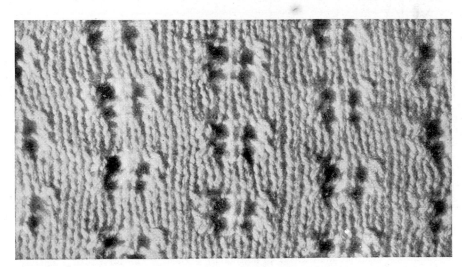

2. An all-over pattern of little flowerlets is made with four holes repeated at regular intervals.

A number of stitches divisible by 14 is required.

Directions.

1st row, k. 2, sl. 1, k. 1, p.s.s.o., m. 1, k. 1, m. 1, k. 2 tog., k. 7; repeat to the end.

2nd row, p.

3rd row, same as the 1st row.

4th row, p.

5th row, the pattern of the 1st row is moved along to the right so commence the work with: k. 7, and thence repeating the 1st row as given above.

6th row, p.

7th row, as the 5th row.

8th row, p.

Repeat these 8 rows throughout.

LACE PATTERNS *continued*

Striped lace patterns are a development from the all-over pattern.

1. Here is an all-over pattern with a slight suggestion of a stripe. To break what would otherwise be a vertical stripe, the decreased stitches are worked on different sides of the made stitch in alternate pattern rows. Three rows, purl, plain, purl, are worked between the pattern rows.

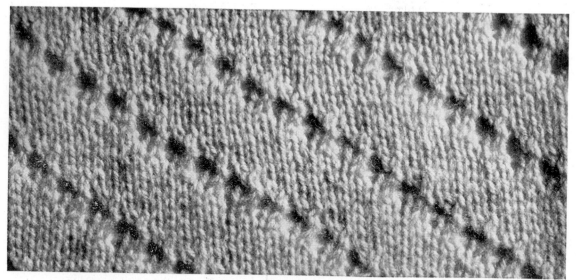

2. Diagonally striped fabric is very useful for sports wear. An open texture will be given by working only a few stitches between the pattern stitches and a close texture will be given by working at least 8 sts. between.

Directions. Plan out the number of stitches by calculating two for knitting together and the number required between, plus the made stitch.

1st row, k. the number of sts. to form the plain band, m. 1, k. 2 tog.; repeat to the end.

2nd row, p.

3rd row, move the made stitch 1 st. to the left in order to make lines sloping upward to the left. If it is desired to have the lines sloping in the opposite direction, move the made stitch 1 st. to the right.

Repeat the 3rd row throughout, returning with a purl row.

STRIPED LACE PATTERNS

1. The working of this zigzag pattern has been planned with the decreasing stitch in the centre of the plain band, which makes an interesting formation of lines.

Directions. Cast on a number of stitches divisible by 6, plus 2 extra stitches.

1st row, k. 2 tog., k. 2, m. 1, k. 2; repeat to the end, k. 2.

2nd row, p.

Repeat these 2 rows twice more.

7th row, k. 1, * k. 2, m. 1, k. 2, k. 2 tog. *; repeat from * to * to the end, k. 1.

8th row, p.

Repeat rows 7 and 8 twice more.

2. A broken horizontal zigzag stripe is useful for garments knitted in heavy wools.

Directions. Cast on 11 sts., plus 2 extra stitches.

1st row, k. 1, * m. 1, k. 2 tog., k. 9 *; repeat from * to * to the end, k. 1.

2nd row, p. Every even numbered row will be p.

3rd row, k. 2; repeat from * to * in 1st row.

5th row, k. 3, * k. 2 tog., m. 1, k. 3, m. 1, k. 2 tog., k. 4 *; repeat from * to * to the end.

7th row, k. 2, k. 2 tog., m. 1, k. 5, m. 1, k. 2 tog.; repeat to the end.

9th row, k. 1, * k. 2 tog., m. 1, k. 9 *; repeat from * to * to the end.

11th row, k. 2 tog., m. 1, k. 9; repeat to the end.

Knit as many rows as required in stocking stitch and then repeat the pattern rows.

STRIPED LACE PATTERNS *continued*

Children's jerseys and dresses seem to require a special kind of pattern. Girls of seven to eleven are too old for the light patterns worked for young children's garments and yet they are not quite old enough for the more definite patterns used for the " grown-ups' " jumpers.

The two patterns illustrated on this page combine a light treatment with the hard lines of a striped pattern to make a texture suitable for school jerseys and little boys' suits.

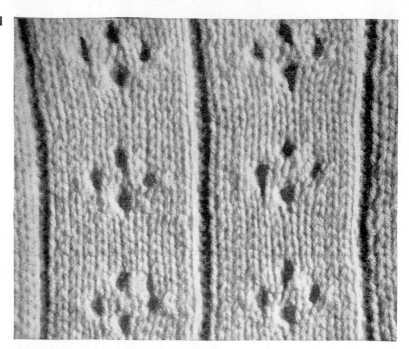

1. Horizontal bands of flowerlets are divided by stripes of two purled stitches.

Directions. Cast on a number of stitches divisible by 13.

1st row, k. 5, m. 1, k. 2 tog., k. 4, p. 2; repeat to the end.

2nd and every alternate row, p. 11, k. 2; repeat to the end.

3rd row, k. 2, sl. 1, k. 1, p.s.s.o., m. 1, k. 3, m. 1, k. 2 tog., k. 2, p. 2; repeat to the end.

5th row, the same as the 1st. Knit as many rows without holes as required, and then repeat the pattern.

2. Both stripes in this pattern are horizontal, the purl stripe stands out on the right side instead of receding to the back as in the last pattern.

Directions. Cast on a number of stitches divisible by 7, plus two extra stitches.

1st row, k. 1, * k. 3, m. 1, k. 2 tog., k. 2 *; repeat from * to * to the end, k. 1.

2nd, 4th and 6th rows, p.

3rd row, k. 1, * sl. 1, k. 1, p.s.s.o., m. 1, k. 3, m. 1, k. 2 tog.*; repeat from * to * to the end, k.1.

5th row, the same as the 1st row.

7th row, k.

8th row, k.

9th row, p.

10th row, k.

11th row, p.

Repeat these 11 rows throughout.

OPEN AND SOLID STRIPES

Underwear for autumn and spring does not need to be in solid texture, and yet a slightly clinging rib is required to make the garment fit. Patterns which combine stripe and lace are ideal for the purpose.

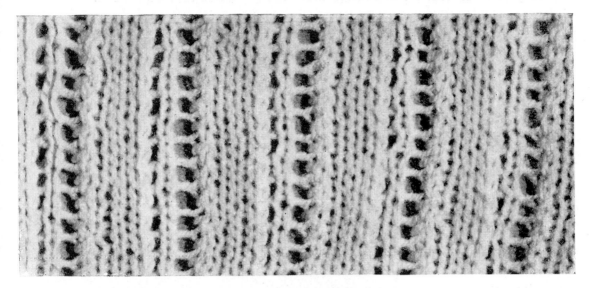

I. A very good texture for vests.
Directions. The pattern requires a number of stitches divisible by 7.
1st row, k. 1, sl. 1, k. 1, p.s.s.o., m. 1, k.1, m.1, k. 2 tog., k. 1; repeat to the end.

2nd row, p.
Repeat these 2 rows throughout. If a slightly more solid pattern is required, work a plain and a purl row between the pattern rows.

2. This is a similar pattern in thicker wool.

Directions. The pattern requires a number of stitches divisible by 8.
1st row, k. 2, m. 1, sl. 1, k. 1, p.s.s.o., k. 2 tog., m. 1, k. 2; repeat to the end.
2nd row, p.
Repeat these 2 rows throughout. A more solid texture is made by knitting 1 plain and 1 purl row between the pattern rows.

FORMING SCALLOPS

By looking at the illustrations on the pages on increasing and decreasing at centres, it will be seen that the stitches run diagonally to the centre and the side edges, pulling the lower edge diagonally too. If both the decreasings and increasings are used together, in the same proportions and in alternating positions, the lower edge will be pulled into scallop shapes. These scalloped edges cannot be hemmed. They are chiefly used on children's dresses.

1. This type of pattern is sometimes called "feather pattern."
Directions. *N.B.*—Pick up a strand to make a stitch. Cast on a number of stitches divisible by 13, plus 1.
1st row, k. 1, m. 1, k. 4, sl. 1, k. 1, p.s.s.o., k. 2 tog., k. 4, m. 1; repeat to the end, k. 1.
2nd row, p.
Repeat these 2 rows throughout.

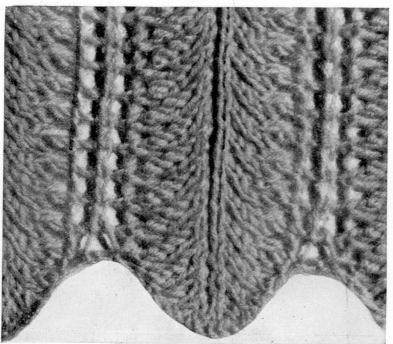

2. Here is a similar pattern with a more open texture. The same number of stitches are required on the needle, and the pattern is commenced on the 1st row.
Directions. *N.B.*—The wool is brought round the needle to make a stitch.
1st row, k. 1, m. 1, k. 4, k. 2 tog., k. 2 tog., k. 4, m. 1; repeat to the end, k. 1.
2nd row, p.
A yet different pattern will be gained if one plain and one purl row is worked between the pattern rows.

SCALLOPED EDGES

These scalloped edges are particularly suitable for babies' dresses and petticoats; a neat hem is formed and no turn up is necessary.

1

1. This is an attractive variation of the first illustration on the previous page.

Directions. First k. 2 rows as before and then repeat the 2 pattern rows 5 times.

Next row, p.

Next row, k.
Repeat these 12 rows as often as required.

3

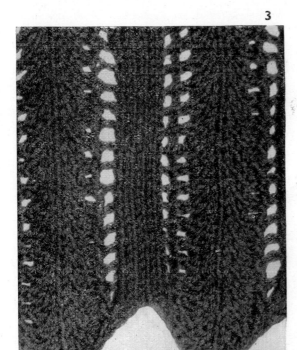

2

2. A more lacy pattern with a scalloped edge for babies' summer dresses.
Directions. Cast on a number of stitches divisible by 11. An edging of garter stitch is worked first, then the pattern is commenced.
1st row, k. 1, m. 1 by picking up a strand, k. 1, k. 2 tog., m. 1 by bringing wool forward, sl. 1, k. 1, p.s.s.o., m. 1 by bringing wool forward, k. 2 tog., k. 1, m. 1 by picking up a strand; repeat to the end.
2nd row, p.
Repeat these 2 rows throughout.

3. A further variation with a pronounced plain stripe.
Directions. Cast on a number of stitches divisible by 15. A firm edge may be made with 2 or 3 rows of garter stitch, or the pattern can begin on the 1st row, as shown here, whichever is desired.
1st row, k. 2, m. 1, k. 4, k. 3 tog., k. 4, m. 1, k. 2.
2nd row, p.
Repeat these 2 rows.

A MATRON'S JUMPER

MEASUREMENTS

To fit 38-in. bust.

Sleeve seam, 17 ins. long with cuff turned back.

MATERIALS

8 ozs. of 3-ply fingering.

A pair of No. 12 and a pair of No. 10 needles.

DIRECTIONS

THE FRONT

Using No. 12 needles, cast on 113 sts.

K. in ribbing of k. 1, p. 1 for 32 rows. Change to No. 10 needles.

The Pattern. The spots are embroidered in the centre of each diamond.

1st row, * k. 1, m. 1, sl. 1, k. 1, p.s.s.o., k. 11, k. 2 tog., m. 1 *; rep. from * to * to the end, finish with k. 2 tog., m. 1, k. 1.

2nd and all even numbered rows, p.

3rd row, k. 2, * m. 1, sl. 1, k. 1, p.s.s.o., k. 9, k. 2 tog., m. 1, k. 3 *; rep. from * to * to the end, finish with k. 2 tog., m. 1, k. 2.

5th row, k. 3, * m. 1, sl. 1, k. 1, p.s.s.o., k. 7, k. 2 tog., m. 1, k. 5 *; rep. from * to * to the end, finish with k. 2 tog., m. 1, k. 3.

7th row, k. 4, * m. 1, sl. 1, k. 1, p.s.s.o., k. 5, k. 2 tog., m. 1, k. 7 *; rep. from * to * to the end, finish with k. 2 tog., m. 1, k. 4.

9th row, k. 5, * m. 1, sl. 1, k. 1, p.s.s.o., k. 3, k. 2 tog., m. 1, k. 9 *; rep. from * to * to the end, finish with k. 2 tog., m. 1, k. 5.

11th row, k. 6, * m. 1, sl. 1, k. 1, p.s.s.o., k. 1, k. 2 tog., m. 1, k. 11 *; rep. from * to * to the end, finish with k. 2 tog., m. 1, k. 6.

13th row, k. 7, * m. 1, k. 3 tog., m. 1, k. 13 *; rep. from * to * to the end, finish with k. 3 tog., m. 1, k. 7.

15th row, k. 5, * k. 2 tog., m. 1, k. 3, m. 1, sl. 1, k. 1, p.s.s.o., k. 9 *; rep. from * to * to the end, finish with k. 5.

17th row, k. 4, * k. 2 tog., m. 1, k. 5, m. 1, sl. 1, k. 1, p.s.s.o., k. 7 *; rep. from * to * to the end, finish with k. 4.

19th row, k. 3, * k. 2 tog., m. 1, k. 7, m. 1, sl. 1, k. 1, p.s.s.o., k. 5 *; rep. from * to * to the end, finish with k. 3.

21st row, k. 2, * k. 2 tog., m. 1, k. 9, m. 1, sl. 1, k. 1, p.s.s.o., k. 3 *; rep. from * to * to the end, finish with k. 2.

23rd row, k. 1, * k. 2 tog., m. 1, k. 11, m. 1, sl. 1, k. 1, p.s.s.o., k. 1 *; rep. from * to * to the end.

25th row, k. 2 tog., * m. 1, k. 13, m. 1, k. 3 tog. *; rep. from * to * to the end, finish with k. 3 tog., m. 1, k. 2 tog. Turn and p. back.

Rep. these 26 patt. rows twice more and then once from the 1st row to the 14th. K. twice in the first and last stitch of every 13th row.

ARMHOLE SHAPING

At the beginning of the next 2 rows, cast off 12 sts.

At the beginning of the next 4 rows, cast off 2 sts.

At the beginning of the next 3 rows, k. 2 tog.

K. in patt. without shaping until 3½ patts. are complete.

NECK SHAPING

K. to within 3 sts. of the centre and cast off 7 sts.

K. in patt. to the end and return to the neck.

Cast off 4 sts. at the beginning of the next 2 rows that start at the neck.

Cast off 2 sts. at the beginning of the next 2 rows that start at the neck.

K. 2 tog. at the beginning of the next 4 rows that start at the neck.

K. in patt. without further shaping until another 1½ patts. are complete.

SHOULDER SHAPING

At the beginning of the next 3 rows that start at the armhole, cast off one-third of the number of sts. now on the needle. Work the second half of the neck in the same way.

THE BACK

Follow the directions for the front, ignore the neck shapings. When it is 5 complete patts. long, cast off at the beginning of the next 6 rows the number of sts. that were cast off each time on the front shoulder. Cast off the remainder.

THE SLEEVES

Using No. 12 needles cast on 65 sts. and k. in rib for 36 rows. Change to No. 10 needles and work in patt. for 5 complete patts., inc. on the first and last sts. every 7th, 13th, 19th and 25th patt. row.

SHAPING THE TOP

Cast off 6 sts. at the beginning of the next 2 rows.

K. 2 tog. at the beginning of the next 8 rows.

K. 2 tog. at both ends of the next 7 rows. Cast off.

THE COLLAR

With No. 12 needles, cast on 130 sts. and k. in rib for 28 rows. Cast off loosely.

TO MAKE UP

Press the patt. but not the ribbing and embroider the spots in satin stitch. Sew the side, shoulder and sleeve seams and set in the sleeves. Sew on the collar, first at one edge and then form it into a roll by sewing the opposite edge to the other side of the jumper. Make a cord 1 yard long and thread it through the collar.

A MATRON'S JUMPER

A YOKE EFFECT JUMPER

Measurements. To fit 36-in. bust; 19 ins. from top of shoulder to edge of ribbing; sleeve 18 ins. from edge of ribbing to armpit.

Tension. 7 sts. to 1 in.; 8 rows to 1 in.

Materials. 7 ozs. of 3-ply fingering; a pair of No. 11 needles; a pair of No. 9 needles.

DIRECTIONS

THE FRONT

Using No. 11 needles, cast on 108 sts.

K. in ribbing of k. 2, p. 2 for 3 ins.

Change to No. 9 needles, and begin the 1st patt. of stripe.

1st row (with No. 9 needles), k. 2, m. 1, k. 2 tog., * k. 6, m. 1, k. 2 tog.; rep. from * to within last 2 sts., k. 2.

2nd row, p. Every even numbered row will be purled. Rep. these 2 rows 11 times more, 24 rows in all.

N.B.—K. twice into the first st. of every 8th and 9th row after the ribbing.

Now commence the second patt. in the centre stripe.

25th row, k. in stripe up to the centre stripe, then, k. 2, m. 1, k. 2 tog., k. 2, m. 1, k. 2 tog.

Continue to the end in the usual stripe.

27th row, k. again to the centre stripe and then proceed, sl. 1, k. 1, p.s.s.o., m. 1, k. 1, m. 1, k. 2 tog., k. 1, m. 1, k. 2 tog.

Continue to the end in stripe.

Rep. row 27 four times more, purling return rows as usual. On the second rep. of row 27, commence a patt. in the stripes on either side of the centre and at all second repeats of row 27, begin a patt. in the stripe on each side of those already worked, until patts. are being worked in every stripe. After 5 rows of double holes have been worked in a patt., 1 hole is worked to complete the patt. in a similar way to row 25. Six rows of plain stripe are worked between each patt.

N.B.—Inc. on the 8th and 9th rows until there are 126 sts. on the needle.

THE ARMHOLE

Cast off 8 sts. at the beginning of the next 2 rows. K. 2 tog. at each end of the next 9 rows (92 sts.). Continue until the armhole measures 3 ins.

NECK SHAPING

1st row, k. 44 sts. in patt., k. 2 tog. Sl. the remainder of the sts. on to a holder and p. back on those just knitted.

On the next 8 rows, which begin at the neck edge, k. 2 tog. Continue without shaping until the armhole measures 8 ins.

SHOULDERS

At the beginning of the next 3 p. rows, cast off 12 sts. This finishes one shoulder.

2nd shoulder. Join in wool at the neck end of the row and work the second shoulder as the first, making sure that all shapings are worked at the correct ends of the rows. It is a good plan to leave the end of wool long enough to sew up the shoulder seams. This saves joining on a sewing thread.

THE BACK

Work exactly like the front until the armholes are reached.

THE ARMHOLES

Work in the same way as the front armholes. Continue working in patt. until the armholes measure 7 ins.

THE SHOULDERS

Cast off 12 sts. at the beginning of the next 6 rows and then cast off the remaining sts., which will become the back neck.

THE SLEEVES (both alike)

Cast on 48 sts. using No. 11 needles.

K. in ribbing of k. 2, p. 2 for 3 ins.

Change to No. 9 needles.

1st row, * k. 2, k. twice into the next st.; rep. from * to the end of the row (64 sts.).

2nd row, p. Every even numbered row will be p. Now commence the stripes as follows:

1st row, * k. 6, m. 1, k. 2 tog.; rep. from * to the end. Work in stripe until the work measures 11 ins. from the beginning.

Then, still keeping to the patt. and adding stripes when there are enough extra sts., inc. 1 st. at the end of the next and every following 4th row until there are 92 sts. on the needle. The work should measure 17 ins. from the beginning.

SHAPING THE TOP

K. 2 tog. at each end of every row until only 26 sts. remain. Cast off.

MAKING UP

Pin the pieces out on an ironing blanket without stretching them, lay a damp cloth over and iron with a warm iron. Do not press the ribbing. Leave each piece on the cloth to steam off, then sew the side seams, shoulder seams and sleeve seams together with the same wool. Set the sleeves in next, beginning at the underarm, putting the side seam and sleeve seam together.

THE COLLAR

Using No. 11 needles, cast on 170 sts. to go round the neck of the jumper, and knit in ribbing of k. 2, p. 2 for 16 rows. Press this collar fairly hard; it is the only part of the ribbing which should be pressed.

SEWING ON THE COLLAR

Pin the centre of the collar to the centre back neck, pin the ends of the collar to the end of the centre front V and then pin the edge of the collar evenly between these points. Oversew the edges together loosely and press the seam from the right side of the jumper.

A YOKE EFFECT JUMPER

113

A JUMPER IN STRIPES OF TWO COLOURS AND TWO THICKNESSES OF WOOL

Measurements. To fit a bust of 34 to 38 ins.; 20 ins. from shoulder to lower edge of ribbing; sleeve is 18 ins. from edge of ribbing to armpit.

Materials. 4 ozs. of double knitting wool (dark colour); 2 ozs. of 3-ply fingering (light colour); a pair of No. 5 needles; some buttons and a strong clip.

DIRECTIONS

The knitting is worked across the figure for the bodice, the ribbing at the waist is added afterwards. The sleeves are knitted from the wrist to the armhole in the usual way.

Using the thick wool cast on 20 sts.

1st row, k.
2nd row, p.
3rd row, cast on 4 sts., k.
4th row, p.
5th row, cast on 4 sts., k.
6th row, join on the thin wool and k.
7th row, cast on 4 sts., p.
8th row, join on the thick wool and k.
9th row, cast on 4 sts., k.
10th row, p. **11th row,** k. **12th row,** p.
13th row, join on thin wool, k.
14th row, p.
15th row, join on thick wool, cast on 2 sts. (neck end of row), and k.
16th row, k. **17th row,** cast on 2 sts., p.
18th row, k. **19th row,** cast on 12 sts. (for edge of armhole), and p. **20th row,** k.
21st row, join on thin wool and k.
22nd row, p.
23rd row, join on thick wool and k.
24th row, k. **25th row,** p. **26th row,** k.
27th row, p. **28th row,** k.
29th row, join on thin wool, cast on 2 sts. and k.
30th row, p.
31st row, join on thick wool and k.
32nd row, k. **33rd row,** p. **34th row,** k.
35th row, p. **36th row,** k.
37th row, join on thin wool, cast on 2 sts. and k.
38th row, p.
39th row, join on thick wool and k.
40th row, k. **41st row,** p. **42nd row,** k.
43rd row, p. **44th row,** k.
45th row, join on thin wool, cast on 2 sts. and k.
46th row, p.
47th row, join on thick wool. Make a thick stripe by repeating rows 23 to 28.

THE COWL NECK

Join on the thick wool. * K. 50, turn. K. back. P. 42, turn. K. back. P. 34, turn. K. back. Join on thin wool. K. 26, turn. P. back. Join on thick wool. K. 24, turn. K. back. P. 22, turn. K. back. P. 20, turn. K. back. Join on thin wool. * K. 18, turn. P. back. Join on thick wool.

Make a thick stripe, the length of the jumper (working along all the sts. on the needle), by repeating rows 23 to 28. Join on thin wool.

Work the other half of the cowl by following the directions from * to *, changing the wool at the beginning of the appropriate rows.

THE SECOND HALF OF THE FRONT

Follow the directions in the reverse order as given for the first half, changing the wool at the beginning of the appropriate rows and casting off sts. that are given as cast-on sts. in the first half.

Cast off the last row loosely.

THE BACK

Work as for front as far as third shoulder shaping—increasing, that is, up to rows 45 and 46. Then work in stripes without shaping until there are 8 thick stripes across the back, counting from the top edge of the armhole. Reverse the order of work from rows 45 and 46 to the beginning to complete the back, casting off those sts. which were cast on. Cast off loosely.

THE SLEEVES (both alike)

Using thick wool, cast on 36 sts. K. in ribbing of k. 2, p. 2 for 17 rows.

18th row (right side of work), * p. 2, p. twice into next st.; rep. from * to the end.

19th row, k. **20th row,** p. **21st row,** k. **22nd row,** p. **23rd row,** k.

24th row, join on thin wool and k. **25th row,** p.

Join on thick wool and rep. rows 19 to 25 ten times. Then work the first 4 rows of a thick stripe.

THE SLEEVE TOP

Still keeping to the stripe patt., cast off 4 sts. at the beginning of the next 2 rows.

K. 2 tog. at the beginning of the next 24 rows.

Cast off fairly tightly.

THE WAIST RIBBING

Two pieces are required, one for the front and one for the back.

For each piece, cast on 64 sts., using the thick wool. K. in ribbing of k. 2, p. 2 for 20 rows. Cast off very loosely.

MAKING UP

This jumper does not require pressing.

Seam the sides, shoulders and sleeves. Put in the sleeves and join the ribbed bands into a ring. Mark the centre front and centre back of the lower edge of the jumper and mark the centres of the two lengths of ribbing. Seam the band to the lower edge of the jumper; commence by pinning seams to seams and centres to centres, then stretch the band between these points until it fits. Oversew very loosely so that the stitching will stretch with the fabric.

TO ARRANGE THE COWL

Turn the top edge down inside the jumper until the two shortest thin stripes are folded in half. Sew securely in position, running this turning off to nothing at the shoulder. Gather the centre front down in pleats to suit the wearer, sew firmly and then stitch the clip over the thickest part of the fold, and sew the buttons down the centre stripe.

The edge of the back neck must be firmly oversewn and the thread pulled up until the neck fits snug'y at the back.

A JUMPER IN STRIPES OF TWO COLOURS AND TWO THICKNESSES OF WOOL

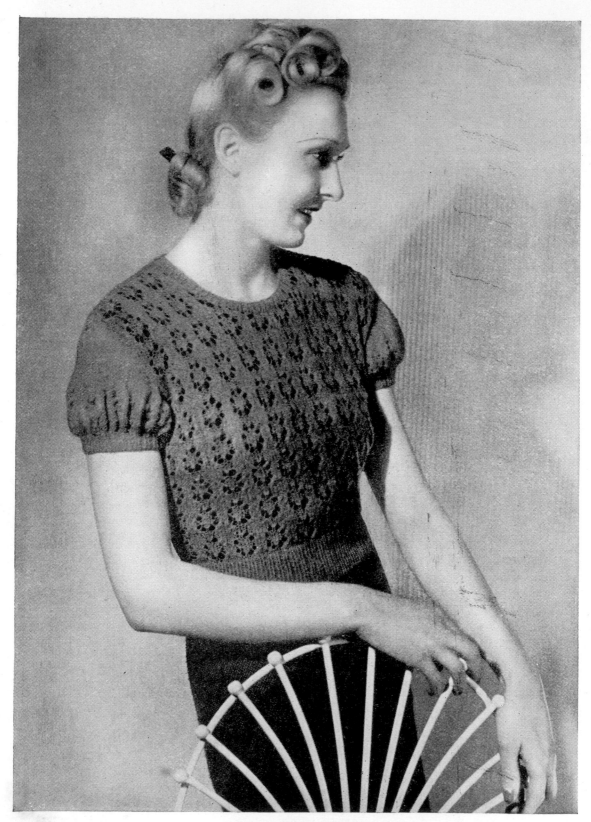

LACE PATTERN JUMPER

116

LACE PATTERN JUMPER

Measurements. To fit a 34 to 36-in. bust; 18 ins. from shoulder to lower edge; sleeves, 3 ins. at seam.

Materials. 3 ozs. of 2-ply fingering or Shetland wool; a pair of No. 10 needles; a pair of No. 8 needles; a small circular needle No. 10 for the neck band. If a circular needle is not available, knit the band on the two No. 10 needles and sew it to the neck edge with small but very loose oversewing sts.

Tension. 6½ sts. to 1 in.; 9 rows to 1 in.; both measured over the lace patt.

DIRECTIONS

THE FRONT

Cast on 94 sts. with the No. 10 needles.
K. in ribbing of k. 1, p. 1 for 26 rows.
Change to No. 8 needles.
1st row, k.
2nd and every even numbered row, p.
3rd row, k. 2, * k. 2, sl. 1 k. 1, p.s.s.o., m. 1, k. 1, m. 1, k. 2 tog., k. 1 *; rep. from * to * to within 4 sts. of the end, k. 4.
5th row, k. 2, * k. 1, sl. 1, k. 1, p.s.s.o., m. 1, k. 3, m. 1, k. 2 tog. *; rep. from * to * to within 4 sts. of the end, k. 4.
7th row, k., knitting twice into the first and last sts. for the seam shaping.
9th row, same as the 5th row (begin k. 3 and end k. 5).
11th row, same as the 3rd row (begin k. 3 and end k. 5).
13th row, k.
15th row, same as the 7th row.
These 15 rows make one patt.
Rep. these patt. rows 4½ times more, inc. on every 7th and 15th rows, and adding patts. and parts of patts. at the side as the inc. sts. allow. (The additional patts. at the side seam may be omitted by the beginner.)

ARMHOLE SHAPING

Cast off 8 sts. at the beginning of the next 2 rows.
Cast off 2 sts. at the beginning of the next 2 rows.
K. 2 tog. at the beginning of the next 4 rows.
Continue in patt. until 6½ patts. have been worked from the ribbing. Omit the inc. at rows 7 and 15.

NECK SHAPING

Continuing in patt. knit to within 5 sts. of the centre, and put these on to a holder or spare needle. (The right side of the work should be facing the knitter.) Cast off 10 sts., continue knitting to the end and p. back.
Cast off 2 sts. at the beginning of the next 6 rows.
K. 2 tog. at the beginning of the next 6 rows.
Continue knitting without shaping until 2 more patts. are complete, that is, there should be 9 complete patts. from the ribbing.

SHOULDER SHAPING

Cast off one-third the number of sts. at the beginning of the next 3 p. rows (thus, the dec. commences at the armhole end of the rows).

SECOND HALF OF THE FRONT NECK

Pick up the sts. on the holder and join on the wool at the neck edge.
Rep. the directions for the first half of the neck, remembering to make all neck shapings at the neck end of the rows.
Rep. the directions for casting off at the shoulder, remembering to begin at the armhole end of these rows.

THE BACK

This is knitted just like the front as far as the neck shaping.
Continue knitting, omitting the neck shapings, as far as the shoulder.
Then continue as follows:—
Cast off the same number of sts. at the beginning of the next 6 rows as were cast off each time on the front shoulders. Cast off the remainder of the sts. This will be the back neck edge.

THE SLEEVES (both alike)

Cast on 46 sts. with the No. 10 needles.
Knit in ribbing of k. 1, p. 1 for 12 rows. Change to No. 8 needles.
Next row, k. twice into every st.
Next row, p.
Next row, k. twice into every st.
Next row, p.
Knit the 15 rows of 1 patt., omitting the side seam, inc. on the 7th and 15th rows.

SHAPING THE TOP

1st row, cast off 16 sts., * k. 4, k. 2 tog. *; rep. from * to * to the end.
2nd row, cast off 16 sts. and p. to the end.
3rd row, k., knitting together the first and last 2 sts.
4th row, p., knitting together the first and last 2 sts.
5th row, k. 2 tog., * k. 3, k. 2 tog. *; rep. from * to * to within 2 sts. of the end, k. 2 tog.
6th and 7th rows, like the 3rd and 4th.
8th row, k. 2 tog., * k. 2, k. 2 tog. *; rep. from * to * to within 2 sts. of the end, k. 2 tog.
9th and 10th rows, like the 3rd and 4th.
11th row, k. 2 tog., * k. 1, k. 2 tog. *; rep. from * to * to within 2 sts. of the end, k. 2 tog.
Rep. rows 3 and 4, five times more (10 more rows).
Cast off remaining sts.

TO MAKE UP

Pin each piece out to shape on an ironing blanket, lay a damp cloth over it and press lightly with a warm iron. Do not press heavily with a hot iron as this would stretch the jumper too much. Do not press any of the ribbing. Oversew the seams together lightly and sew in the sleeves, putting sleeve seam to underarm seam.

THE NECK BAND

1. When a circular needle is used.
Pick up 132 sts. round the neck edge of the jumper, commencing at the centre back. It is a good plan to divide the neck edge into quarters and pick up one-fourth of the number of sts. in each quarter (33). Knit 7 rounds of k. 1, p. 1.
Cast off very loosely using No. 8 needles.

2. When two needles are being used to make a band.
Cast on 132 sts. on No. 10 needles.
Knit 7 rows of k. 1, p. 1.
Cast off very loosely using No. 8 needles and join into a ring.
To join the band to the neck, place the seam to the centre back and the half of the band to the centre front, stretch the band to fit the neck edge between these two points and sew strongly but not tightly. This method will not look quite so neat as the band which is knitted on the circular needle.

A POLO-NECKED JUMPER

MEASUREMENTS

To fit a 35-in. bust. 18 ins. from shoulder to lower edge; length of sleeve, 17 ins. at the seam.

MATERIALS

7 ozs. of 3-ply fingering; a No. 9 circular needle; a pair of No 9 and a pair of No. 7 needles.

A POLO-NECKED JUMPER *continued*

DIRECTIONS

THE FRONT

With No. 7 needles cast on 105 sts. and work in a rib of k. 3, p. 2, for 1 in.

Then change to No. 9 needles for 2 ins. of knitting. Change again to No. 7 needles and rib for 7 ins. Increase by knitting twice into the first stitch of every 12th and 13th row. There should then be 115 sts. on the needle.

When work measures 10 ins. from the beginning, commence to shape the armhole.

ARMHOLE SHAPING

Cast off 8 sts. at the beginning of the next 2 rows.

neck like the first, making all shapings come at the reverse side of the work.

THE BACK

Knit as for the front, leaving out the neck shaping. When the armhole measures 7 ins., cast off 10 sts. at the beginning of the next 6 rows. Leave the remainder of the sts. on the needle.

THE COLLAR

Slip all the front neck sts. which are on a thread on to a circular needle. Pick up 20 sts. at both sides of the front neck and transfer the back neck sts. to the circular needle.

Cast off 2 sts. at the beginning of the next 2 rows. K. 2 tog. at the beginning of the next 4 rows.

Then knit without further shaping until the armhole measures 4 ins.

NECK SHAPING

No sts. are cast off, they are slipped on to a thick piece of wool ready to be slipped on to a circular needle. Rib 40. Sl. 10 sts. on to a thread. Continue knitting to the end and return to the neck.

At the beginning of the next 2 rows that commence at the neck, sl. 3 sts. on to the thread.

At the beginning of the next 2 rows that commence at the neck, sl. 2 sts. on to the thread.

Knit without further shaping until the armhole measures 7 ins.

SHOULDER SHAPING

Cast off 10 sts. at the beginning of the next 2 rows that commence at the armhole.

Cast off the remainder.

Join on wool at the neck end of the sts., to be knitted up for the second shoulder, and knit the other half of the

The place where the end of the wool is at the back neck will become the beginning of each round.

Knit in rib of k. 2, p. 2, for 2½ or 3 ins., whichever is desired.

Cast off very loosely indeed.

THE SLEEVES

Cast on 40 sts. on the No. 9 needles. Knit in rib of k. 3, p. 2 for 2 ins.

Change to No. 7 needles and knit for 15 ins., inc. on the first st. in every 5th and 6th row.

SHAPING THE TOP

Cast off 6 sts. at the beginning of the next 2 rows. K. 2 tog. at the beginning of the next 10 rows. K. 2 tog. at both ends of the next 12 rows. Cast off.

TO MAKE UP

The jumper can be made up on either side, and it need not be pressed. Join the seams and set in the sleeves. The seams may be pressed lightly.

A SCHOOLGIRL'S JUMPER

MEASUREMENTS

To fit a 28-30 in. chest.

Length from shoulder to lower edge, 16½ ins.

Sleeve seam, 5½ ins.

MATERIALS

4 ozs. of 4-ply fingering (dark colour).

2 ozs. of 4-ply fingering (light colour).

A pair of No. 9 needles, and a pair of No. 11 needles.

DIRECTIONS

THE FRONT

Using dark wool and No. 11 needles cast on 92 sts. Knit the first row into the backs of the cast-on sts.

Then work 20 rows in ribbing of k. 2, p. 2.

Change to No. 9 needles; the rest of the jumper is in ribbing of k. 1, p. 1.

There is no shaping to be done at the side seams.

1st row, commence the narrow ribbing and at the same time inc. by knitting twice into every 10th st. in the 1st row only.

Work 15 more rows in dark colour.

Change to light colour and work 7 rows.

Work 2 rows in dark, 3 rows in light, 4 rows in dark, 3 rows in light, 2 rows in dark and 7 rows in light. This completes the first band of patt.

Work 15 rows in dark colour and then rep. the patt. band, commencing the armhole shaping on the 8th row of the band.

THE ARMHOLES

Cast off 8 sts. at the beginning of the next 2 rows.

Cast off 2 sts. at the beginning of the next 2 rows.

K. 2 tog. at the beginning of the next 4 rows.

Knit without further shaping until the armhole measures 2½ ins.

THE NECK OPENING

Knit to 2 sts. past the centre st. Turn and knit back to the armhole.

Knit on these sts. without shaping, for 2¼ ins., making a buttonhole on the 8th and 13th rows. (See Index for directions for making buttonholes.)

NECK SHAPING

Finish the last row at the neck opening. Cast off 15.

Cast off 2 sts. on the next 2 rows that begin at the neck edge.

K. 2 tog. on the next 2 rows that begin at the neck edge.

Knit without shaping until the armhole measures 6¾ ins. from the beginning. Cast off one-third of the sts. at the beginning of the next 3 rows that begin at the armhole.

THE SECOND SHOULDER

Join on the wool at the front opening end of the sts., and cast on 5 sts. These 5 sts. will be knitted plain in every row; they are the wrap for the buttons.

Knit this shoulder as for the first, omitting the buttonholes.

THE BACK

Knit in a similar way to the front, omitting the neck shapings. When the armholes have been completed, cast off 9 sts. at the beginning of the next 6 rows and then cast off the remainder.

THE SLEEVES

Using No. 11 needles, cast on 64 sts. and knit in ribbing of k. 2, p. 2 for 18 rows.

Change to No. 9 needles and to ribbing of k. 1, p. 1, inc. on every 4th st. in the first row.

Knit until the sleeve measures 5½ ins. from the beginning; inc. in the first st. of every 8th and 9th rows. The top is shaped with two darts. To work it, follow the directions given for a sleeve with a full top. (See Index.)

THE COLLAR

With the No. 11 needles, cast on 102 sts. and knit in ribbing of k. 2, p. 2 for 26 rows. Alternate rows begin with p. 2, so that both ends of the collar will look alike.

TO MAKE UP

Press the jumper very lightly indeed, avoiding the waist and elbow ribbing. The jumper should only be smoothed with a warm iron over a damp cloth, as heavier pressing will open the ribbing too much.

Sew up all the seams, set in the sleeves, sew on the collar and the buttons. As both sides of the fabric are alike, be sure that the jumper is being made up on the correct side, that is, that the side of the opening with the buttonholes comes at the right-hand side.

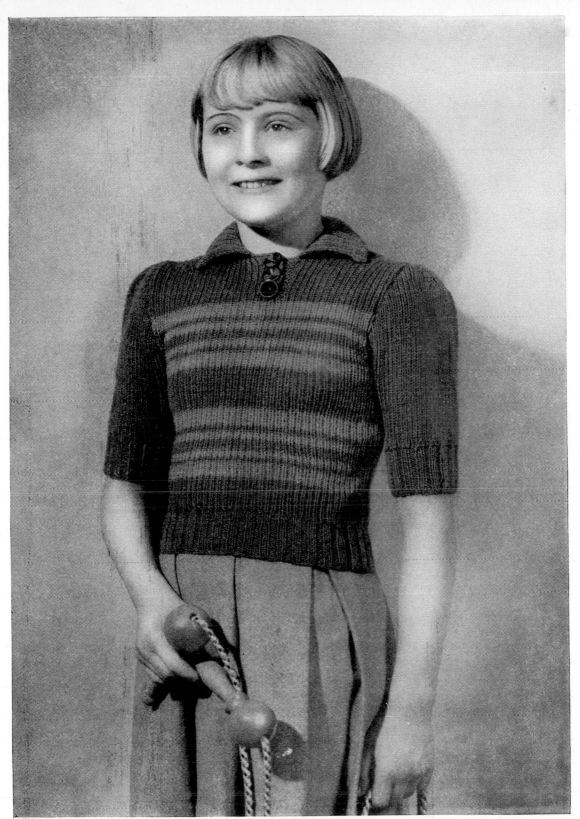

A SCHOOLGIRL'S JUMPER

A LACE-PATTERNED VEST

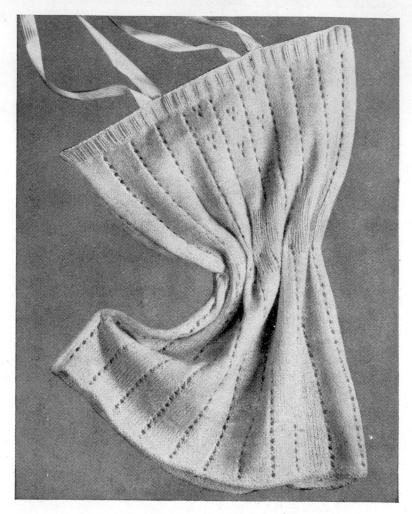

Measurements. 26 ins. round underarms, unstretched; 21½ ins. from underarm to lower edge.

Materials. 3 ozs. of 2-ply fingering; a pair of No. 10 needles; ribbon for shoulder straps.

DIRECTIONS

THE BACK

Cast on 100 sts. loosely.

Knit 3 rows in moss st.

First patt.: 1st row, k. 5, * m. 1, k. 2 tog., k. 8 *; rep. from * to * to within 5 sts. of the end, m. 1, k. 2 tog., k. 3.

2nd row, p.

3rd row, k.

4th row, p.

Rep. these patt. rows until work measures 11 ins.

Ribbing. Rib in k. 1, p. 1 for 5 sts., m. 1, k. 2 tog., p. 1, k. 1, p. 1. Rep. to the end.

Rib for 3 rows, and then rep. the ribbing with holes.

Rib without holes for 15 rows. Next row, rib with holes.

Rib for 3 rows, rib with holes and then rib for 3 more rows.

Revert to the first patt. for 6 ins.

Work in ribbing of k. 2, p. 2 for 1 in. Cast off.

THE FRONT

Work in the same manner as for the back until the work measures 16½ ins. Finish at the last row of a patt.

Next row, knit to the beginning of the middle stripe, m. 1, k. 2 tog., k. 3, m. 1, k. 2 tog., k. 3, continue in stripe patt. to the end.

Next row, p. **Next row,** k. **Next row,** p.

Next row, knit to the beginning of the middle stripe, m. 1, k. 2 tog., k. 1, sl. 1, k. 1, p.s.s.o., m. 1, k. 1, m. 1, k. 2 tog., k. 2. Continue in stripe patt. to the end.

Knit the next 3 rows as usual and then rep. the group of three holes in the stripes on either side of the centre stripe.

Knit the next 3 rows as usual, rep. the holes in the centre stripe and then again in the stripes on either side. Work the next 3 rows as usual.

Knit 1 in. in ribbing of k. 2, p. 2, then cast off.

Press the vest lightly with a warm iron on the stripe patt. only. Oversew the side seams together. Sew on the shoulder straps as desired.

A VEST WITH A BRASSIÈRE TOP

Measurements. 25 ins. round underarm, unstretched; 19 ins. from top of brassière to lower edge.

Materials. 3 ozs. of 3-ply fingering; a pair of No. 9 needles.

DIRECTIONS

THE BACK. Cast on 52 sts.

First patt.: 1st row, k. 3, p. 1. Rep. to the end.

2nd row, p. 1, k. 1, p. 2. Rep. to the end.

Rep. these 2 rows for 16½ ins.

Work in ribbing of k. 2, p. 2 for 1 in. Cast off.

THE FRONT. Cast on 52 sts. and work as for the back for 15 ins.

Second patt. (for the brassière)

1st row, k. 1, * m. 1, k. 2 tog. *; rep. from * to * to the end, k. 1.

Next row, p. **Next row,** k.

Next row, p.

Next row, k. 22, turn.

Next row, p. 8, turn.

Next row, k. 1, * m. 1, k. 2 tog. *; rep. from * to * 4 times, turn.

Next row, p. 13, turn. **Next row,** k. 15, turn.

Next row, p. 17, turn.

Next row, k. 1, * m. 1, k. 2 tog. *; rep. from * to * 8 times, turn.

Next row, p. 21, turn. **Next row,** k. 23, turn.

Next row, p. 25, turn.

Next row, k. 1, * m. 1, k. 2 tog. *; rep. from * to * 12 times, turn.

Next row, p. 29, turn. **Next row,** k. 31, turn.

Next row, p. 29, turn.

Next row, k. 1, * m. 1, k. 2 tog. *; rep. from * to * 16 times, turn.

Next row, p. 33, turn. **Next row,** k. 31, turn.

Next row, p. 29, turn.

From this point reverse the order of work, commencing with the row working 14 patts., until the last 3 rows are p. 9, turn. K. 7, turn. P. 5, turn. Break off the wool.

With the right side of the work facing, join on the wool at the beginning of the sts. that are to be knitted up for the second half of the brassière.

Rep. the directions for the first half, and end on a row that holds all the sts. on one needle.

Knit in ribbing of k. 2, p. 2 for 1 in.

Do not press the vest, sew up the side seams, pinning the top and bottom edges together first, and sew on the shoulder straps.

For a slightly larger vest use No. 8 needles, and for a smaller vest use No. 10 needles.

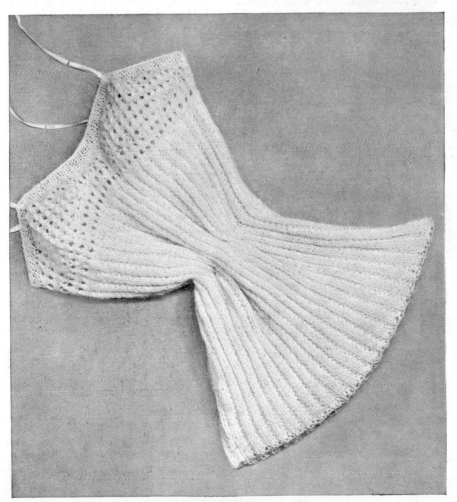

FRENCH KNICKERS IN LACE PATTERN

Measurements. To fit 38-40 in. hips; 14 ins. down centre front, unstretched.

Materials. 4 ozs. of 3-ply fingering; a pair of No. 9 needles.

DIRECTIONS

THE PATTERN (6 sts.)

K. 1, m. 1, k. 1, k. 3 tog., k. 1, m. 1.

THE FRONT. Cast on 180 sts. Knit the 1st row into the backs of the sts.

1st row, knit 12 patts., k. 1, m. 1, k. 1, k. 2 tog., k. 2 tog., k. 24 (this number will be 2 less in each successive patt. row), k. 2 tog., k. 2 tog., k. 1, m. 1, k. 12 patts., m. 1, k. 1.

2nd row, p.

3rd row, k.

4th row, p.

Rep. these 4 rows 5 times more.

Next row, knit 8 patts., k. 1, m. 1, k. 1, k. 2 tog., k. 2 tog., k. 60 (this number will be 2 less in each successive patt. row), k. 2 tog., k. 2 tog., k. 1, m. 1, knit 8 patts., m. 1, k. 1.

Work the remainder of the patt. rows and rep. the 4 patt. rows 4 times more.

Next row, knit 4 patts., k. 1, m. 1, k. 1, k. 2 tog., k. 2 tog., k. 98 (this number will be 2 less in each successive patt. row), k. 2 tog., k. 2 tog., k. 1, m. 1, knit 4 patts., m. 1, k. 1.

Work the remainder of the patt. rows and rep. the 4 patt. rows 4 times more.

Next row, k. 2, sl. 1, k. 1, p.s.s.o., knit to within 4 sts. of the end, k. 2 tog., k. 2.

Next row, p. **Next row,** k. **Next row,** p.

Rep. these 4 rows 6 times more.

Then, working the decreasings as usual, commence the rib of k. 2, p. 2 at the centre of the row, increasing the width of the ribbing by 2 purled sts. on either side in every plain row, until 3 more decreasings have been worked. Then take the ribbing right across the row. Continue ribbing for 18 rows.

SHAPING THE TOP. Rib 64 sts. Cast off 14. Rib to the end, turn.

Rib to within 12, turn and rib back. Rep. the last 2 rows 3 times. Cast off.

Rep. this shaping on the other half of the front.

THE BACK. Knit like the front as far as the commencement of the ribbing at the side seam.

Take the ribbing right across and rib for as many rows as there are at the side edge of the front.

SHAPING THE TOP. Rib to within 12, turn.

Rep. this 8 times. Cast off. Press lightly.

Oversew the side seams together and join the plain sections at the lower edges.

Round the top work a crochet edging of 1 dc., 2 ch., and thread elastic through these holes.

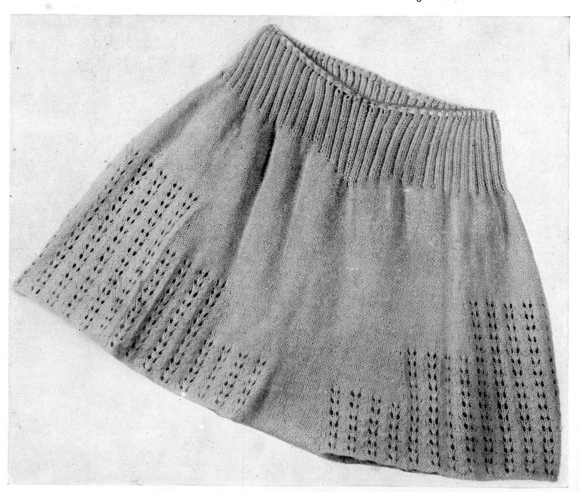

AMERICAN PANTIES

These little panties are ideal for wearing under sports clothes in winter. They are specially suitable for the schoolgirl to wear under her physical training outfit.

Measurements. To fit a 34 to 38-in. hip; 14 ins. down centre front.

Materials. 2 ozs. of 3-ply fingering; a pair of No. 9 needles; some narrow elastic for the waist; a medium-sized crochet hook.

DIRECTIONS

THE FRONT. Cast on 24 sts.

Knit 28 rows in st.st., knit twice into the first st. of every row.

Knit twice into the first and last sts. of the next 12 rows.

At the beginning of the next 6 rows cast on 3 sts.

Knit without shaping for 18 rows, ending on a p. row.

Next row, k. 2, sl. 1, k. 1, p.s.s.o., k. to within 4 sts. of the end, k. 2 tog., k. 2.

Next row, p.

Knit 4 rows in st.st.

Rep. these 6 rows, 4 times more.

Change to ribbing of k. 2, p. 2 for 15 rows, and then cast off.

THE BACK. Knit exactly the same as the front to the last row of the ribbing, ending on the wrong side.

Next row, rib 74 sts., turn. Rib 64 sts., turn.

Next row, rib 54 sts., turn. Rib 44 sts., turn. Rib 34 sts., turn.

Rib all the sts. on the needle.

Cast off loosely.

TO MAKE UP. Press the st.st. lightly and sew up the side seams and the short under-leg seam.

With the crochet hook, work an edging round the top of 1 dc. to every rib. Thread the elastic through this edging, passing over and under alternate double crochets.

THE LEG RIBBING. Cast on 144 sts. and knit in ribbing of k. 2, p. 2 for 7 rows. Join the band into a ring and sew the cast-off edge to the leg of the panties.

Directions for knickers with a longer close-fitting leg are given on page 133, " Knickers for Girls," and can be adapted for the older woman.

KNICKERS—WOMEN'S SIZE

(38, 40 and 42-in. hips)

Measurements. 38-in. hips. For larger sizes see the end of these directions; 24 ins. from waist to knee.

Materials. 5 ozs. of 3-ply fingering; a pair of No. 10 needles; some elastic for the waist.

Tension. 8 sts. to 1 in.; 10 rows to 1 in.

DIRECTIONS (with centre seams)
THE RIGHT LEG

Cast on 120 sts. Knit in rib of k. 2, p. 2 for 3 ins.

Next row, k. 7, knit twice into next st. rep. to the end. P. back.

Next row, k. 8, knit twice into next st. rep. to the end.

Work in st.st. for 18 ins., knitting twice into the first and last sts. of the 15th, 16th, 30th and 31st rows.

Change to ribbing of k. 2, p. 2 for 3 ins., finishing on the right side.

With wrong side of work towards the knitter, rib 76 sts., turn and rib back.

Rib 60 sts., turn and rib back.
Rib 44 sts., turn and rib back.
Rib 28 sts., turn and rib back.
Rib 12 sts., turn and rib back.
Cast off.

LEFT LEG

Follow the directions for the right leg as far as the last row of the 3-in. band of ribbing at the waist, but this time the last row must finish on the wrong side.

With the right side of the work facing the knitter, commence the directions for the back waist.

THE GUSSET

Cast on 24 sts. and knit in st.st. for 3 ins.
Cast off loosely.

TO MAKE UP

Press the fabric lightly over the st.st. only. Sew the centre front and centre back seams together to a point 18 ins. down from the bottom of the waist ribbing.

Place the top right-hand corner of the gusset to the top of the front leg opening and sew the side edge of it down the right front leg seam. Sew the left front leg seam down the top edge of the gusset. Place the bottom left-hand corner of the gusset to the top of the back leg opening, sew one back leg seam to the side edge of the gusset, and sew the bottom edge of the gusset to the opposite leg seam. Join up the remainder of the leg seams and work an edging of 1 dc. and 1 ch. round the top edge of the knickers through which to thread the elastic.

DIRECTIONS (with side seams)
THE FRONT

Cast on 56 sts. Rib in k. 2, p. 2 for 3 ins.
K. 7, knit twice into next st.; rep. to the end, p. back.
K. 8, knit twice into next st.
Knit in st.st. for 6 ins. Put this piece of knitting on to a holder, or spare needle, and knit another like it.

Knit the sts. of the piece on the holder so that both legs are on one needle, make sure that they both face the same way.

Now knit without shaping for 12 ins.
Change to ribbing of k. 2, p. 2 for 3 ins. and cast off.

THE BACK

Knit the back like the front as far as the last row of the 3 ins. of waist ribbing, do not cast off but add extra length in the middle, in the following manner:—

Rib 140 sts., turn.
Rib 120 sts., turn.
Rib 100 sts., turn.
Rib 80 sts., turn.
Rib 60 sts., turn.
Rib to the end. Cast off.

THE GUSSET

Knit a gusset as described before.

TO MAKE UP

Press the plain fabric lightly.

Join the side seams with oversewing and sew in the gusset as for the previous type of knickers. Sew up the leg seams as far as the gusset and crochet slots at top edge to take the elastic.

ALTERATIONS FOR OTHER SIZES

1. For a 40-in. hip measure, cast on 160 sts. and work in st.st. for 19 ins. after the ribbing.

2. For a 42-in. measure, cast on 176 sts. and knit in st.st. for 20 ins. after the ribbing.

The fabric will fit a little closer if the part described here as st.st. is worked in wide ribbing of about k. 6, p. 1, or any other number of plain and purl sts. which will divide into the number of sts. on the needle.

A CHILD'S LIBERTY BODICE

Measurements. To fit a 30 in. chest; length from top of shoulder to lower edge, 12 ins.

Materials. 3 ozs. of 3-ply fingering; a pair of No. 10 and No. 12 needles; a length of 1 in. wide tape, or strong ribbon for the shoulder straps; 4 rubber buttons, 2 large and 2 small.

DIRECTIONS

Back and front are alike.

Using the No. 12 needles, cast on 110 sts., knit into the backs of these for the 1st row.

Now change to ribbing of k. 2, p. 2 for 1½ ins.

Change to No. 10 needles and either a st.st. fabric or a finely patterned fabric like moss stitch, and knit for a further 6½ ins. without any shaping for the side seams.

SHAPING THE TOP

At the beginning of the next 2 rows cast off 8 sts.

K. 47 sts. and turn.

Now, while the first point is being made, the remainder of the sts. may be slipped on to a stitch-holder.

K. 2 tog. at the beginning and end of every row until there is only 1 st.

Break off the wool and pull this last st. through.

Pick up the sts. for the other point and knit it as the first.

Knit another piece just like the one just made

Press both pieces of knitting, avoiding the ribbing.

TO MAKE UP

Join the side seams strongly.

The shoulder straps are made from the tape or ribbon. Cut 2 pieces for the straps, as long as is required, to reach from the back point to the front point, plus 4 ins. extra. Make a narrow hem at one end of each piece and sew these strongly under the back points.

Make a hem at the other ends 1¼ ins. wide.

Into this double hem make a buttonhole large enough to fasten over the rubber button that will be sewn to the front points. This must be cut to follow the length of the tape. It must not be cut across the width, because the direction of the pull will be downwards.

Sew a large rubber button just a little way below each front point with a small one at the back; all stitches must pass through both buttons so that there is no strain on the fabric.

COMBINATIONS FOR A GIRL

(12 years)

Measurements. 34-in. hips; 32-in. bust; 31 ins. from shoulder to knee. If this is too long deduct half the difference from the measurement between leg and waist and between waist and armhole.

Materials. 11 ozs. 3-ply fingering; a pair of No. 12 and a pair of No. 10 needles; buttons for fastening the front and the back.

Tension. 8 sts. to 1 in.; 10 rows to 1 in.

DIRECTIONS

With side seams and centre seams.

THE LEFT FRONT

Cast on 54 sts. on the No. 12 needles.

Knit in ribbing of k. 1, p. 1 for 2 ins.

Next row, * k. 2, k. twice into next st.; rep. from * to the end. P. back and change to No. 10 needles.

Change to st.st.

K. for 13 ins. from the ribbing.

Next row, * k. 10, k. 2 tog.; rep. from * to the end.

Knit 5 rows in st.st.

Next row, * p. 9, p. 2 tog.; rep. from * to the end.

Knit 9 rows in st.st.

Change to No. 12 needles.

Now knit in k. 2, p. 2 for 3 ins.

Change to No. 10 needles and knit in st.st. for 2 ins.

Next row, k. 2, k. twice into the next st., k. to the end and k. 3 rows without shaping.

Rep. these 4 rows 3 times more.

Continue without shaping until work measures 3½ ins. from top of waist ribbing, finish on a k. row.

Cast on 5 sts. for the wrap which will be knitted, in every row.

K. until work measures another 2 ins.

ARMHOLE SHAPING

At the beginning of the next 2 rows cast off 10 sts.

At the beginning of the next 4 rows cast off 2 sts.

At the beginning of the next 4 rows k. 2 tog.

K. without shaping until armhole measures 2 ins.

NECK SHAPING

Commence on a p. row.

Cast off 13 sts.

Cast off 3 sts. at the beginning of the next 2 rows that commence at the neck edge.

Cast off 2 sts. at the beginning of the next 2 rows that commence at the neck edge.

K. 2 tog. at the beginning of the next 4 rows that commence at the neck edge.

Continue knitting without shaping until the armhole measures 6 ins.

Cast off.

THE RIGHT FRONT

Follow the directions for the left front, working all shapings at the opposite ends of the rows.

Buttonhole may be worked in the wrap. (See Index for directions for working buttonholes.)

THE BACK

The right half

Begin as for a half front and follow the directions as far as 10 ins. above knee ribbing, finishing on a p. row. K. 20, turn. Cast on 4 sts., these will be knitted in every row. Slip the remainder of the sts. on to a holder. Work on these 25 sts. in st.st. for 5 ins., finish on a k. row.

Cast on 32 sts. change to No. 12 needles and knit in rib of k. 2, p. 2 for 3 ins.

Change to No. 10 needles and to st.st. and knit for another 5 ins.

ARMHOLE SHAPING

Follow the directions given for the front armhole.

K. without shaping until the armhole is 3 ins. long.

NECK SHAPING

Copy the front neck shaping. Cast off.

THE BACK FLAP

Take the sts. from the holder so that work will begin on a k. row. Join on the wool.

Cast on 2 sts., these are knitted in every row, and knit in st.st. for 5 ins. Cast off.

The left half of the back

Follow the directions for the right half, but work all shapings at the opposite ends of the rows.

THE BACK BAND

Using No. 12 needles, cast on 12 sts. The entire band is worked in g.st.

Knit 4 rows, work a buttonhole, knit 5 ins., work a buttonhole, knit 5 ins., make another buttonhole, knit 4 rows and cast off.

THE GUSSET

Cast on 20 sts. on the No. 10 needles.

K. 25 rows and cast off.

TO MAKE UP

Press the plain fabric lightly.

Join the centre seams starting at a point 5 ins. above the knee ribbing, then the side seams and, lastly, the shoulder seams.

Sew the back band to the top edge of the back flap, stretching it as much as necessary and sew buttons to the lower edge of the back bodice, with smaller buttons at the back. (See Index for sewing on buttons.)

Fold the wrap on the left side of the front underneath the front and sew it firmly. This makes a good foundation to hold the buttons. Sew on the buttons to match the buttonholes, placing tape behind them. (See Index for directions for sewing buttons on to knitting.)

The neck and armhole edges should be strengthened with a facing of sateen put on to the wrong side.

Sew in the gusset (see Index) and sew up remainder of leg seams.

COMBINATIONS FOR A GIRL
(12 years)

The front, showing clearly the shaping at the waist and the three-button fastening at the neck.

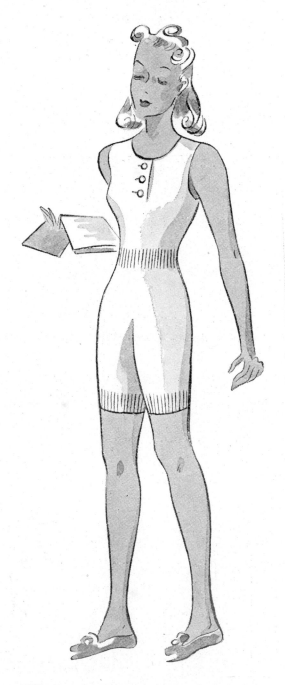

Back view, showing how back opening fastens over waist ribbing.

A QUICKLY KNITTED SPENCER

Measurements. 32 ins. round underarm (suitable for a 38 to 40-in. bust measure); 18 ins. from shoulder to lower edge of ribbing (stretching to about 20 ins. when worn).

Materials. 2 ozs. of 2-ply Shetland wool; a pair of No. 8 needles.

DIRECTIONS

THE BACK

Cast on 92 sts. loosely.

Knit in ribbing of k. 2, p. 2 for 28 rows.

Knit in g.st., every row plain, for 60 rows (30 ridges).

ARMHOLE SHAPING

Cast off 10 sts. at the beginning of the next 2 rows.

Cast off 2 sts. at the beginning of the next 2 rows.

Knit in g.st. for 60 rows.

Cast off. No shaping is required for the back neck.

THE FRONT

Work as for the back as far as the end of the armhole shaping.

Knit in g.st. for 42 rows.

NECK SHAPING

K. 22 sts. Cast off 24 sts. K. 22 sts.

Knit back to the neck. Sl. the other set of sts. on to a holder.

K. 2 tog., k. to the end. Turn and knit back.

Rep. these 2 rows 4 times more.

Knit without shaping for 14 rows. Cast off.

Pick up the sts. from the holder and knit the second shoulder, making the decreased sts. at the neck end of the rows.

It is not necessary to press this garment. Sew up the side and shoulder seams and work 3 rows of crochet round the neck and armholes. The crochet should be fairly tight; a suitable edging will be found in the crochet section of this book.

Narrow ribbon is threaded round the neck so that the neck line can be drawn up to the required size.

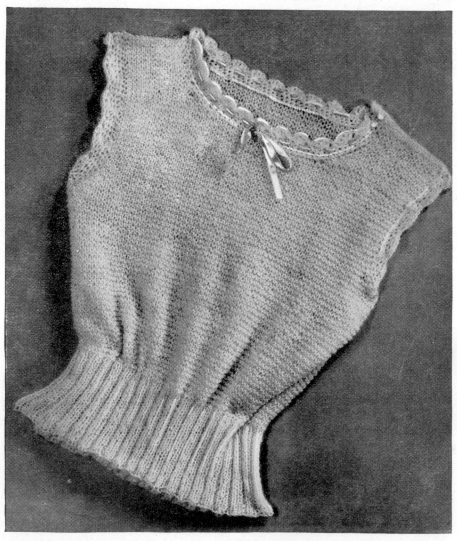

A THICKER SPENCER WITH SHORT SLEEVES

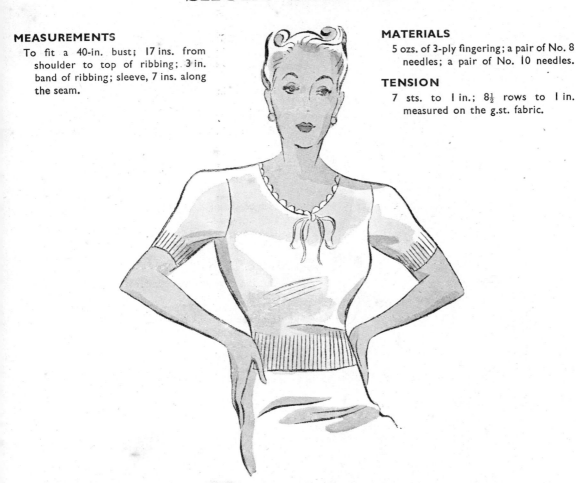

MEASUREMENTS

To fit a 40-in. bust; 17 ins. from shoulder to top of ribbing; 3 in. band of ribbing; sleeve, 7 ins. along the seam.

MATERIALS

5 ozs. of 3-ply fingering; a pair of No. 8 needles; a pair of No. 10 needles.

TENSION

7 sts. to 1 in.; 8½ rows to 1 in. measured on the g.st. fabric.

DIRECTIONS

THE FRONT

Cast on 84 sts. on the No. 10 needles.

Rib for 3 ins. in k. 2, p. 2.

Change to No. 8 needles and knit in g.st. (every row knitted plain), for 10 ins.

ARMHOLE SHAPING

Cast off 10 sts. at the beginning of the next 2 rows.

Cast off 2 sts. at the beginning of the next 2 rows.

K. 2 tog. at the beginning of the next 4 rows.

Knit until armhole measures 2 ins. from the beginning.

NECK SHAPING

Knit to within 12 sts. of the centre; cast off 24 sts. and knit to the end.

Cast off 2 sts. at the beginning of the next 4 rows that commence at the neck.

K. 2 tog. at the beginning of the next 4 rows that commence at the neck.

Knit without shaping until the armhole measures 7 ins. from the beginning.   Cast off.

Knit up the second set of sts. for the second shoulder, working all shapings at the correct ends of the rows.

THE BACK

Knit as for front as far as end of armhole shapings.

From there, k. 4 ins. without shaping and then follow the directions given for the front neck.

SLEEVES (both alike)

Cast on 76 sts. on the No. 10 needles.

Knit in rib of k. 2, p. 2 for 2 ins.

Change to No. 8 needles and knit in g.st. for 5 ins.

SHAPING THE TOP

Cast off 7 sts. at the beginning of the next 2 rows.

K. 2 tog. at both ends of every row until there are 24 sts. left.   Cast off.

TO MAKE UP

Do not press the work.

Sew up side and shoulder seams, sew up sleeve seams and set them in the bodice. Work a crocheted edging round the neck to make slots for threading the ribbon. Suitable edgings will be found in the crochet section.

PETTICOAT FOR A GIRL

(9 years)

MEASUREMENTS

30-in. hip; 25 ins. from shoulder to hem. This may drop to as much as 27 ins.

MATERIALS

11 ozs. of 4-ply fingering; a pair of No. 8 and a pair of No. 10 needles.

TENSION

6 sts. to 1 in.; 7 rows to 1 in.

DIRECTIONS

THE FRONT

Cast on 126 sts. with No. 10 needles. Knit 4 rows in st.st.

5th row, k. 1, * m. 1, k. 2 tog. ; rep. from * to * to the end, finishing k. 1. **6th row,** p. back.

Knit in st.st. for 16 rows.

23rd row, p.

24th row and 25th row, k.

26th row, p.

27th row, same as 5th row.

Knit the next 5 rows in st.st.

33rd row, * k. 3, m. 1, k. 2 tog., k. 3 *; rep. from * to * to the end.

Knit the next 5 rows in st.st.

Rep. the 5th row.

Rep. rows 26, 25, 24 and 23, in that order.

Continue in st.st. for 3 ins.

Next row, k. 2, sl. 1, k. 1, p.s.s.o., k. to within 4 sts. of the end, k. 2 tog., k. 2.

Knit 3 rows in st.st.

Rep. these last 4 rows 6 times more.

Change to No. 10 needles and knit in rib of k. 2, p. 2 for 2 ins.

Change back to No. 8 needles and knit in st.st. for 4 ins.

ARMHOLE SHAPING

At the beg. of the next 2 rows, cast off 10 sts.

At the beginning of the next 4 rows, cast off 2 sts.

At the beginning of the next 2 rows, k. 2 tog.

K. without shaping until the armhole measures 2½ ins.

NECK SHAPING

K. to within 8 sts. of the centre.

Cast off 16 sts. K. to the end and p. back to the neck.

Cast off 2 sts. at the beginning of the next 3 rows which commence at the neck edge.

K. 2 tog. at the beginning of the next 4 rows which commence at the neck edge.

K. straight until the armhole measures 6 ins. from the beginning. Cast off.

THE SECOND SHOULDER

K. up the second set of sts. for the other shoulder, working the neck shapings at the correct ends of the rows.

THE BACK

Follow the directions for the front, but begin the neck shaping 1 in. higher, that is, after shaping the armhole k. until the armhole measures 3½ ins.

TO MAKE UP

Press the work carefully and sew up the side and shoulder seams. Turn up the bottom along the first line of holes so that a picoted edge is formed. This edge will be seen in the baby's petticoat on page 137. The neck and armholes will be stronger if they are faced on the wrong side with crossway sateen.

KNICKERS FOR GIRLS

(For 6 years and 12 years)

1. AGE 6 YEARS

Measurements. 28-in. hips; 15 ins. from waist to knee.

Materials. 3 ozs. of 3-ply fingering; a pair of No. 10 needles.

Tension. 8 sts. to 1 in.; 10 rows to 1 in.

DIRECTIONS

THE RIGHT LEG

Cast on 80 sts. Knit in rib of k. 2, p. 2 for 2 ins.

Change to st.st.

K. 7, k. twice into next st. Rep. to the end. P. back.

K. 8, k. twice into next st. Rep. to the end. P. back.

For the next 20 rows k. twice in every first st.

K. without shaping for 10 ins.

Change to rib, k. 2, p. 2 for 2 ins.

With wrong side of work facing, rib 56, turn and rib back.

Rib 46, turn and rib back.

Rib 36, turn and rib back.

Rib 26, turn and rib back.

Rib 16, turn and rib back.

Cast off.

THE LEFT LEG

Knit this like the right leg as far as the top of the 2 ins. of waist ribbing. Then arrange the work so that the next row will begin on the right side of the fabric and follow the remainder of the directions (for lengthening the back).

THE GUSSET

Cast on 18 sts. and knit in st.st. for 20 rows.

TO MAKE UP

Press the plain fabric lightly. Join the centre seams down to a point 9 ins. below the bottom of the ribbing. Let in the gusset as described in the directions for women's knickers, join the remainder of the leg seams and work a crocheted edging to take the elastic.

2. 12 YEARS

Measurements. 34-in. hips; 21 ins. from waist to knee.

Materials and tension are the same as before.

DIRECTIONS

THE RIGHT LEG

Cast on 96 sts. Rib for 2½ ins.

K. 5, k. twice into next st. Rep. to the end. P. back.

K. 6, k. twice into next st. Rep. to the end. P. back.

Change to st.st.

K. twice into the first st. in every 5th row until there are 136 sts.

K. for 14 ins. Change to ribbing for 2½ ins. With wrong side of fabric facing, rib 68, turn and rib back.

Rib 58, turn and rib back.

Rib 48, turn and rib back.

Rib 38, turn and rib back.

Rib 28, turn and rib back.

Rib 18, turn and rib back. Cast off.

THE LEFT LEG

Knit just like the right leg up to the top of the 2½ ins. of waist ribbing. Then, with the right side of the work facing, work the rest of the directions.

THE GUSSET

Cast on 20 sts. and knit in st.st. for 25 rows.

TO MAKE UP

Press the plain fabric lightly.

Join the centre seams down to a point 13 ins. below the bottom of the ribbing. From now, follow the directions for making up the knickers for a 6-year-old.

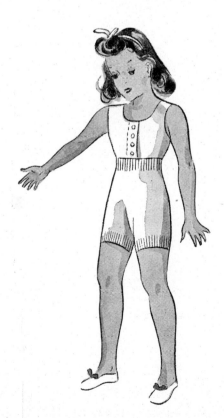

133

BOY'S PANTS

MEASUREMENTS

12 ins. down side leg seam; 10 ins. down centre front.

MATERIALS

3 ozs. of 3-ply fingering; a pair of No. 11 needles; a pair of No. 9 needles; 3 rubber buttons.

TENSION

7 sts. to 1 in.; 9 rows to 1 in.

the end of the leg increasings. Then, from this point, with the wrong side of the fabric facing, cast on 3 sts. and thereafter knit the first 5 sts. down the centre front edge plain in every row so that these will be in g.st. fabric.

Knit as far as the waist decreasings. Follow the directions for these and, at the same time, work the buttonholes in the g.st. band down the centre front. (See Index for methods of making buttonholes.)

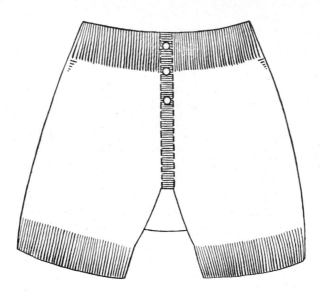

DIRECTIONS

With centre and side seams.

THE BACK RIGHT LEG

Using No. 11 needles cast on 64 sts. and knit in rib of k. 2, p. 2 for 1½ ins.

Change to No. 9 needles, and st.st.

Knit in st.st. for 2½ ins., knitting twice into the last st. in every k. row.

Knit without shaping for 4 ins., finish on a p. row.

With right side of fabric facing, k. 2, sl. 1, k. 1, p.s.s.o., k. to the end.

P. back.

Rep. these 2 rows 8 times more.

Change to No. 11 needles and rib k. 2, p. 2 for 2 ins.
Cast off.

THE BACK LEFT LEG

This is knitted in a similar manner to the back right leg; all shapings are worked at the opposite ends of the rows. Thus, after the leg ribbing, the increasings will be worked on the first st. in every plain row, and the decreasings at the top will be: k. to within 4 sts. of the end, k. 2 tog., k. 2.

THE FRONT LEFT LEG

Follow the directions for the back right leg as far as

The first buttonhole should be commenced in the same row as the first waist dec., and the remainder at intervals of 1 in. The last one will be 1 in. down from the top edge.

THE FRONT RIGHT LEG

Work this in a similar way to the front left leg, remembering to make the shapings at the opposite side of the work.

The g.st. band down the centre front edge is worked without buttonholes.

THE GUSSET

With the No. 9 needles, cast on 18 sts. and knit in st.st. for 22 rows. Cast off.

TO MAKE UP

Press the plain fabric lightly, do not touch the ribbing. Sew up the side and centre back seams.

Overlap the g.st. bands down the fronts with the buttonholes uppermost and sew them together firmly for 2 ins., starting from the bottom. Set in the gusset as described in the directions for making up women's knickers, join the remainder of the leg seams and sew on the buttons. These must be strengthened with tape at the back.

MEN'S PANTS

DIRECTIONS

THE LEFT LEG

Using the No. 11 needles, cast on 100 sts. and work in ribbing of k. 1, p. 1 for 2 ins.

Change to No. 9 needles.

Knit 10 rows in st.st.

Next row, k. twice into first and last sts. P. back.

K. 80 rows, inc. on the first and last sts. of every 4th row. Finish on a plain row.

With the wrong side of the fabric facing, cast on 4 sts.

Continue knitting without shaping for 5 ins., always working the first 7 sts. at the front edge in g.st. Commence the first buttonhole in the g.st. band on the next row, work without shaping for another 2 ins., making a buttonhole every inch.

Change to No. 11 needles and rib for 3 ins. There will be 2 buttonholes for the ribbed band, making 5 in all.

With the right side of the fabric facing, rib 60 sts., turn and rib back.

Rib 50 sts., turn and rib back.

Rib 40 sts., turn and rib back.

Rib 30 sts., turn and rib back.

Rib 20 sts., turn and rib back.

Cast off.

THE RIGHT LEG

Follow the directions for the left leg, working the g.st. band down the opposite front and omitting the buttonholes. The shaping of the waist ribbing at the back will commence with the wrong side of the fabric facing the knitter.

THE GUSSET

Cast on 21 sts. and knit 27 rows in st.st.

Cast off.

TO MAKE UP

Press the plain fabric lightly.

Join the centre back seam, overlap the g.st. bands at the centre fronts (with the buttonholes uppermost), and sew them together firmly for 2½ ins. from the bottom.

Set in the gusset (see Index for method) and join up the rest of the leg seams.

Sew on the buttons with tape at the back for strength.

MEASUREMENTS

22 ins. down outside leg; 14 ins. down centre front; the length of leg can be varied to individual measurements.

MATERIALS

6 ozs. of 3-ply fingering; a pair of No. 11 needles; a pair of No. 9 needles; 5 rubber buttons.

TENSION

7 sts. to 1 in.; 9 rows to 1 in.

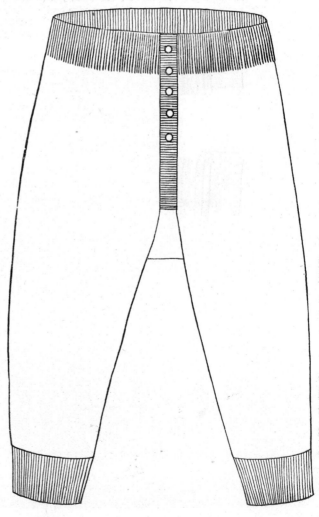

135

A BABY'S VEST

Measurements. Width all round when fastened, 18 ins.; length from shoulder to lower edge, 9 ins.

Materials. 2 ozs. of 3-ply fingering; a pair of No. 10 needles; 1 yd. of narrow washing ribbon.

DIRECTIONS

Cast on 150 sts.

Knit in g.st. (every row plain), for 6½ ins.

THE DIVISION FOR THE ARM-HOLES

K. 45 sts., turn.

K. 1½ ins. on these 45 sts., ending at the long, or front, edge.

Cast off 22 sts. Continue knitting on remaining 23 sts. for 1 in. more.

Cast off.

Arrange the sts. left on the needle so that work can begin at the front edge and join on the wool.

Rep. the directions given for the first front, remembering to cast off at the *front* edge.

On the remaining 60 sts. k. straight for 2½ ins.

Cast off.

THE SLEEVES (both alike)

Cast on 45 sts. and knit in g.st. for 2½ ins.

Cast off.

TO MAKE UP

Press the work very lightly indeed.

Join the shoulder and sleeve seams with oversewing.

Sew in the sleeves, placing the seam to the lower end of the armhole opening and the cast on edge to the vest.

Cut the length of ribbon into four pieces, sew one piece to the top corner of the upper wrap and another piece 3½ ins. lower down.

Wrap the fronts over and mark the position of the other pieces of ribbon, and sew them on strongly.

A BABY'S PETTICOAT

Measurements. Width all round at the underarm, 16 ins. unstretched; length from shoulder to lower edge, 14 ins.

Materials. 2 ozs. of 3-ply fingering; 4 small pearl buttons; ¾ yd. of narrow washing ribbon.

Tension. 7 sts. to 1 in.; 9 rows to 1 in.

DIRECTIONS

THE FRONT

Cast on 99 sts. and knit the 1st row into the backs of the cast-on sts.

Knit 3 rows in st.st.

5th row, k. 1, * m. 1, k. 2 tog. *; rep. from * to * to the end. P. back.

Knit 8 rows in st.st.

14th row, like the 5th row. P. back.

16th row, k. 1, * sl. 1, k. 1, p.s.s.o., k. 2, m. 1, k. 2 tog., k. 3 *; rep. from * to * 9 times more, sl. 1, k. 1, p.s.s.o., m. 1, k. 2, m. 1, k. 2 tog., k. 2. P. back.

18th row, k. 2, * sl. 1, k. 1, p.s.s.o., m. 1, k. 7 *; rep. from * to * 9 times more, sl. 1, k. 1, p.s.s.o., m. 1, k. 5. P. back.

20th row, k. P. back.

22nd row, same as the 5th row. P. back.

Change to a ribbing.

1st row, k. 4, * p. 1, k. 9 *; rep. from * to * to within the last 5 sts., p. 1, k. 4.

2nd row, p. 4, k. 1, * p. 9, k. 1 *; rep. from * to * to within the last 4 sts., p. 4.

Rep. these 2 rows until the ribbing measures 5¾ ins.

Next row, k. 1, k. 2 tog., continue knitting 2 tog. all along row. P. back.

Next row, like the 5th row of the first patt., this makes holes for the ribbon.

Knit in st.st., without shaping, for 2¼ ins.

SHAPING THE ARMHOLES

Cast off 4 sts. at the beginning of the next 2 rows.
Cast off 2 sts. at the beginning of the next 2 rows.
K. 2 tog. at the beginning of the next 4 rows.
Continue knitting without shaping for 1 in.

NECK SHAPING

K. 13, cast off 8 sts., k. 13.
P. back to the neck. Turn.
K. 2 tog. at the beginning of the next 2 rows that begin at the neck edge.
Continue knitting for 1 in.
Cast off for the shoulder.
Join the wool at the neck end of the second set of sts. and knit up the second shoulder like the first.

THE BACK

Knit the same as for the front as far as 5 ins. of ribbing.

THE BACK PLACKET

With the right side of the work facing, knit to the centre of the middle rib.

Continue working on this half of the sts. for ¾ in., dec. as on the front and end on the p. row after dec.

Rep. row 5 for the waist holes.

Continue knitting as for the front, omitting the neck shaping and at the shoulder cast off all the sts. Part of these will become the back neck.

SECOND HALF OF THE BACK

Join on the wool so as to commence knitting at the opening end of the row.

Cast on 5 sts. for the under wrap; these 5 sts. are k. in every row.

Continue knitting as for the first half.

MAKING UP

Press the garment carefully. Sew up the side and shoulder seams. Make the picot edge by turning up the bottom along the first row of holes. Finish edge of neck and armholes with row of double crochet and thread narrow ribbon through holes at waist. Small pearl buttons are sewn down the back for fastening. These are sewn to the wrap and buttonholed loops are worked strongly to the upper edge of the opening to fasten over the buttons. Those knitters who already know how to work buttonholes in knitting could work 4 in the right-hand half of the back.

ROMPERS

Measurements. Width all round under the arms unstretched, 22 ins.; length from shoulder to centre front of lower edge, 16 ins.; sleeves at the seam, 2 ins.

Materials. 3 ozs. of 3-ply fingering; a pair of No. 10 needles; 9 small pearl buttons.

Tension. 8 sts. to 1 in.; 10 rows to 1 in.

ARMHOLE SHAPING

At the beginning of the next 2 rows cast off 6 sts.
At the beginning of the next 2 rows cast off 2 sts.
At the beginning of the next 4 rows k. 2 tog.
Knit in patt. without shaping until work measures 14½ ins. from the beginning.

NECK SHAPING

K. to within 4 sts. of the centre, cast off 8 sts., k. to the end. P. back.
At the beginning of the next 4 rows cast off 2 sts.
At the beginning of the next 2 rows k. 2 tog.
K. without further shaping for 1 in.
Cast off.
Join on the wool at the neck edge of the remaining sts. and knit up the second shoulder like the first.

THE BACK

Knit the back like the front, ignoring the buttonholes.
Work 15 ins. before knitting the neck shaping. Knit only ½ in. beyond the neck shaping before casting off at the shoulder.

SLEEVES (both alike)

Cast on 48 sts. and knit in ribbing of k. 2, p. 2 for 10 rows. Change to patt. for 1¼ ins.

TOP SHAPING

Cast off 2 sts. at the beginning of the next 2 rows.
K. 2 tog. at each end of the next rows until 16 sts. remain.
Cast off.

THE NECK BAND

Cast on 160 sts. and knit in ribbing of k. 2, p. 2 for 2 rows.

3rd row, k. 2, p. 2, m. 1, k. 2 tog., p. 2, m. 1, k. 2 tog., p. 2, m. 1, k. 2 tog., p. 2, m. 1, k. 2 tog., continue in ribbing to the end and rib for 4 more rows.

TO MAKE UP

Press all parts of the romper except the ribbing.
Sew the side seams and the right-hand shoulder seam together. Join the sleeve seams and sew the sleeves in. The ribbed band is for the neck, the buttonholes to go along the front of the left-hand shoulder. Pin this band in position very carefully before sewing it. Start at the armhole end of the open shoulder, leave enough fullness to turn the corner, take it along the front of the neck, round the back and along the back shoulder. Sew four buttons on to this part of the ribbing to fasten the shoulder and sew three more buttons on the back of the leg opening.

THE BELT

Cast on 12 sts. and k. 2 rows.
Next row, k. 3, m. 1, k. 2 tog., k. 2, m. 1, k. 2 tog., k. 3. This makes two small buttonholes.
Knit in g.st. for 15 ins. Cast off. Sew two pearl buttons to fasten.

DIRECTIONS

THE FRONT

Cast on 28 sts. K. the 1st row into the backs of the cast on sts. **Next row,** p. **Next row,** k. into the backs of the sts. **Next row,** p.

Next row, k. twice into the 1st st., k. 2, m. 1, k. 2 tog., k. 8, m. 1, k. 2 tog., k. 8, m. 1, k. 2 tog., k. 2, k. twice into the last st. This row makes the buttonholes along the lower edge, between the legs. P. back.

Next row, k. twice into the 1st and last sts. P. back. Now commences the patt. Every 1st st. is knitted twice.

1st row, k. 4, p. 4; rep. to the end.

2nd row, p. Every even numbered row is purled.

3rd and 5th rows, k.

7th row, the order of the purl and plain sts. is reversed, work 4 p. sts. over the 4 sts. that were plain in the last patt. row, and 4 plain over the sts. that were p.

9th and 11th rows, k.

Rep. these 11 rows 5 times more, remembering to inc. on every 1st st.

Knit in patt. without shaping for 7½ ins.

A JACKET FOR A YOUNG CHILD

Measurements. 28 ins. round the underarm when fastened; 12½ ins. from shoulder to lower edge; 9½ ins. along sleeve seam. The ribbed cuff can be turned up.

Materials. 5 ozs. of 4-ply fingering; a pair of No. 8 needles; 6 buttons about 1 in. in diameter.

Tension. 6 sts. to 1 in.; 7½ rows to 1 in.

DIRECTIONS

THE BACK

Cast on 82 sts. K. into the backs of the cast-on sts. Knit 10 rows of double moss st. (See Index for directions of this stitch.)

Knit 11 rows of st.st. and then 4 rows of the double moss st.

Rep. these last 15 rows 3 times more.

Knit 8 rows in st.st.

ARMHOLE SHAPING

Cast off 8 sts. at the beginning of the next 2 rows.

Cast off 2 sts. at the beginning of the next 2 rows.

K. 2 tog. at the beginning of the next 4 rows.

Knit without shaping until two more moss st. bands have been worked.

Knit 2 more rows in st.st. and then cast off.

THE RIGHT FRONT

(With buttonholes for a girl, without buttonholes for a boy.)

Cast on 46 sts. K. into the backs of the sts.

Knit in double moss st. for 10 rows.

The banded patt. of the back is repeated, with the first 10 sts., seen from the right side of the work, always knitted in double moss st.

On every 5th st.st. row a buttonhole is made. The 3 sts., which are 3 sts. in from the edge, are cast off and in the 6th row 3 sts. are cast on in their place. If the beginner finds this too difficult to do, the coat can fasten with button and loops, or with press studs underneath the buttons.

Keeping the moss st. stripe at the front edge, follow the directions given for the back as far as the armhole.

Shape this as for one of the back armholes and then k. without shaping until the second or third row beyond the 6th buttonhole, whichever ends at the front edge.

With the right side of the work facing, cast off 10 sts.

K. the row and p. back.

K. 2 tog. at the beginning of the next 4 rows which commence at the neck edge.

Cast off for the shoulder.

THE LEFT FRONT

(Without buttonholes for a girl, with buttonholes for a boy.)

Knit the second front in a similar manner to the first.

The moss st. band will be on the opposite side, there will not be any buttonholes for the girl's pattern and the neck and armhole shapings will be on the reverse sides.

THE SLEEVES (both alike)

Cast on 38 sts. Knit into the backs of the sts. and work 10 rows of double moss st.

Rep. the banded patt. of the jacket, knitting twice into the first st. in every 5th, 6th, 10th and 11th row of the st.st. band.

Complete the fourth moss st. band and then shape the top.

THE SLEEVE TOP

Cast off 4 sts. at the beginning of the next 2 rows.

K. 2 tog. at the beginning of the next 14 rows.

Cast off 3 sts. 4 times. Cast off the remainder of the sts.

THE COLLAR

Cast on 62 sts. Knit into the backs of the sts. and work 4 rows in double moss st. For 1½ ins. knit the first 6 and the last 6 sts. in every row in double moss st. and the remainder in st.st.

TO MAKE UP

Pin the pieces on an ironing board and press lightly. Join up the side, shoulder and sleeve seams and sew in the sleeves. Sew on the buttons, and join the collar to the neck.

Pin the collar on first, before sewing it on. Place the edges of the collar 5 sts. in from both front edges of the coat, pin the centre of the collar to the centre back neck and the rest is arranged evenly between these points. If the sleeves are too long, turn the cuffs back.

139

A LITTLE MATINÉE COAT

Measurements. 19 ins. round the underarm; 9 ins. from shoulder to lower edge; 4½ ins. along the sleeve seam.

Materials. 2 ozs. of 3-ply fingering; a pair of No. 10 needles; 1 yd. of matching satin ribbon.

Tension. 7 sts. to 1 in.; 10 rows to 1 in.

DIRECTIONS

Cast on 133 sts. K. into the backs of the sts. for the first row.

Knit in moss st. for 12 rows. K. the next row and p. the next, keeping the first and last 11 sts. in moss st.

Next row, moss st. 11, * m. 1, k. 2 tog. *; rep. from * to * to within the last 11 sts. which are moss stitched.

The next 5 rows are knitted in st.st. (except those sts. which are moss stitched).

Rep. these last 6 rows 6 times more.

ARMHOLE SHAPING

K. 29 sts. in patt., cast off 8, k. 59 sts. in patt., cast off 8, k. 29. One front shoulder will be knitted up on this last set of 29 sts.

Return to the armhole. On the next row cast off 2 sts.

On the next row which begins at the armhole k. 2 tog.

K. straight until work measures 7¾ ins. from the beginning.

NECK SHAPING

Start at the front edge, cast off 11 sts.

Then cast off 2 sts. at the same edge and then k. 2 tog. at the beginning of the next 2 rows that commence at the neck end of the row.

K. until the work measures 9 ins. from the lower edge.

THE TOP OF THE BACK

Join on the wool to knit the top of the back and follow the directions for the armholes at the beginning of every row, so that both armholes are worked. Ignore the neck shapings. Cast off all the sts. when work measures 9 ins.

THE SECOND FRONT

Rep. the directions for the first front, making sure to work the decreasings at the correct ends of the rows.

THE COLLAR

Cast on 90 sts. K. into the backs of the cast-on sts. Knit in moss st. for 12 rows. Change to ribbing of k. 1, p. 1 for 5 rows, cast off.

THE SLEEVES

Cast on 45 sts. K. into the backs of the cast-on sts. Knit in moss st. for 12 rows. Change to the second patt.

Knit in the second patt. until work measures 4½ ins.

SHAPING THE TOP

Cast off 3 sts. at the beginning of the next 2 rows.

K. 2 tog. at the beginning of the next rows until there are 9 rows of holes.

Cast off 2 sts. at the beginning of the next 4 rows and then cast off the remainder.

TO MAKE UP

Press the work carefully. Sew the shoulder seams together and join the sleeve seams. Set in the sleeves and sew on the collar. The ribbon is cut in half, and one piece is sewn to the top of each front.

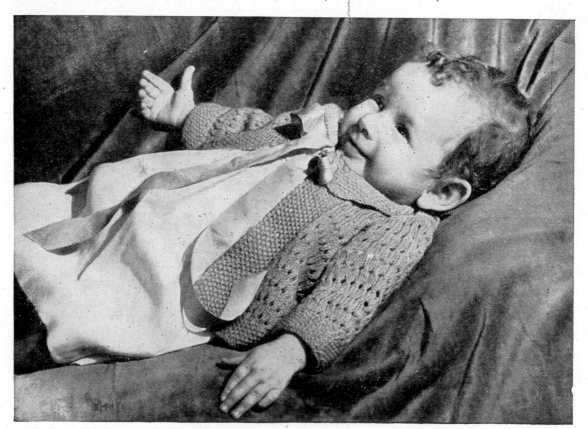

A MATINÉE COAT FOR SUMMER

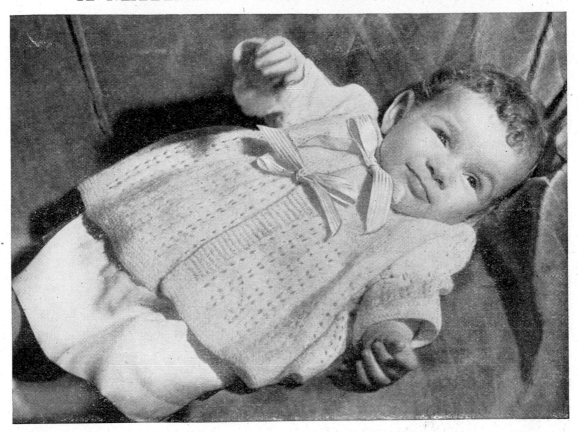

Measurements. 21 ins. round chest; 12 ins. from shoulder to lower edge; sleeve seam 5 ins.

Materials. 3 ozs. of 2-ply fingering; a pair of No. 10 needles.

DIRECTIONS

THE RIGHT FRONT

Cast on 87 sts., k. into the backs of the cast-on sts. and then knit 9 more rows in g.st.

The patt.:
The band of 9 sts. down the front edge is knitted in every row.

1st row, k. 9, * k. 1, m. 1, k. 1, k. 3 tog., k. 1, m. 1, k. 1, m. 1, k. 2 tog., k. 2 tog., m. 1 *; rep. from * to * to the end, finish with k. 1.

2nd row and every even numbered row, p., k. the last 9 sts. Rep. these 2 rows 13 times more (14 rows of holes).

Next row, k. 9, k. 2 tog. all along.

Now knit in moss st., keeping the 9 border sts. in g.st. for another 1½ ins.

ARMHOLE SHAPING

At the side seam, cast off 6 sts.

At the beginning of the next 2 rows starting at the armhole k. 2 tog.

K. without further shaping until the armhole measures 1½ ins.

SHAPING THE NECK

With right side of work facing, cast off 9 sts.

At the beginning of the next 2 rows starting at the neck cast off 2 sts.

At the beginning of the next 3 rows starting at the neck, k. 2 tog.

K. without shaping until the armhole measures 3½ ins. Cast off.

THE LEFT FRONT

Follow the directions for the right front, but the band down the front edge and all armhole and neck shapings will come at the reverse ends of the rows.

THE BACK

Cast on 144 sts., follow the directions for the front, ignoring the g.st. band down the edge. Armhole shapings will be worked at both sides and the neck shapings will be ignored.

THE SLEEVES

Cast on 56 sts. and knit the first 10 rows like the front.

Knit in patt. until the sleeve measures 5 ins.

K. 2 tog. at the beginning of every row 10 times.

K. 2 tog. at both ends of the next 10 rows. Cast off.

THE COLLAR

Before coat is made up.

Pick up 20 sts. along the neck edge of the right front, 20 sts. along the back neck edge and 20 sts. along the left front neck.

Knit in g.st. for 1¾ ins. and cast off loosely.

TO MAKE UP

Press the knitting lightly, sew the side, shoulder and sleeve seams, set in the sleeves and attach ribbons.

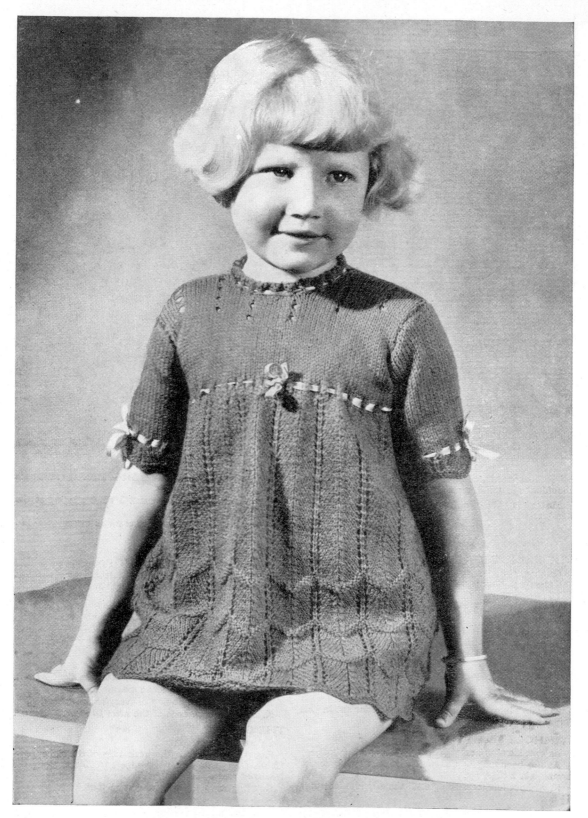

A CHILD'S DRESS

A CHILD'S DRESS

Measurements. 24 ins. round underarm; 18 ins. from the shoulder to the bottom of the points; 3 ins. at the sleeve seam from the threading holes to the armhole.

Materials. 4 ozs. of 3-ply fingering; a pair of No. 9 needles; 2½ yds. narrow ribbon; 3 small buttons.

Tension. 7 sts. to 1 in.; 8 rows to 1 in.; measured over st.sts.

DIRECTIONS

THE FRONT

Cast on 118 sts. K. into the backs of the cast-on sts.

Next row, k.

Now commence the patt.

1st row, * k. 1, m. 1, k. 4, sl. 1, k. 1, p.s.s.o., k. 2 tog., k. 4, m. 1 *; rep. to the end, finishing with k. 1.

2nd row, p.

These 2 rows make the patt., rep. them five times more (there will be 6 lines of holes).

Next row, p. **Next row,** k.

Rep. these 14 rows twice more (there will be 3 ribbed bands).

Now k. the 2 patt. rows only for 6 more ins. (there should be 22 holes from the last row of rib).

Next row, k. 1, k. 2 tog. all along. P. back.

Next row, k. 1, * m. 1, k. 2 tog. *; rep. from * to * all along the row, and p. back. This makes the threading holes. Knit in st.st. for 1½ ins.

ARMHOLE SHAPING

Cast off 5 sts. at the beginning of the next 2 rows.

Cast off 2 sts. at the beginning of the next 2 rows.

K. 2 tog. at the beginning of the next 2 rows.

K. to within 5 sts. of the centre, m. 1, k. 2 tog., k. 7, m. 1, k. 2 tog., k. to the end.

Work the next 3 rows in st.st.

K. 17, m. 1, k. 2 tog., k. 7, m. 1, k. 2 tog., k. 7, m. 1, k. 2 tog., k. 7, m. 1, k. 2 tog., k. to the end.

Knit the next 3 rows in st.st.

K. 8, m. 1, k. 2 tog., k. 7, m. 1, k. 2 tog., k. 7, cast off 10 sts., k. 8, m. 1, k. 2 tog., k. 7, m. 1, k. 2 tog., k. 6.

P. back to the cast off sts., work up the first shoulder on these sts.

Cast off 2 sts., k. to the end. P. back.

Cast off 2 sts., k. 3, m. 1, k. 2 tog., k. 7, m. 1, k. 2 tog., k. to the end. P. back.

K. 2 tog., k. to the end. P. back.

K. 2, m. 1, k. 2 tog., k. 7, m. 1, k. 2 tog., k. to the end. P. back. K. the next row and cast off.

THE SECOND SHOULDER

Knit up the second shoulder like the first, making all edge shapings come at the correct ends of the rows.

THE BACK

Knit just like the front as far as the armhole shapings.

From this point the placket is made.

Knit to the centre and place the remainder of the sts. on a holder. Knit the right half of the back on the sts. on the needle.

After shaping the armhole like the front armhole, knit straight until the back bodice measures 5 ins. from the threading holes. Cast off.

Pick up the sts. from the holder so that work will commence at the centre back.

Join on the wool and cast on 5 sts. for the wrap. These 5 sts. are k. in every row.

Knit the left half of the back like the right half, remembering to work the armhole shapings at the correct end of the rows.

SLEEVES (both alike)

Cast on 53 sts. K. into the backs of the cast on sts. Follow the direction given for the front until 3 rows of holes have been worked. P. back.

Next row, k. 1, * m. 1, k. 2 tog. *; rep. to the end. P. back. This makes the threading holes.

Work in st.st. until sleeve measures 3 ins. from the threading holes.

SHAPING THE TOP

Cast off 3 sts. at the beginning of the next 2 rows.

K. 2 tog. at the beginning of the next rows until there are 35 sts. on the needle.

Cast off 3 sts. at the beginning of the next 4 rows.

Cast off the remainder.

TO MAKE UP

Pin the pieces out on to a cloth and press lightly with a warm iron and a damp cloth.

Oversew the side, shoulder and sleeve seams and put in the sleeves.

Work a narrow crocheted edging round the neck edge, sew some small pearl buttons down the back wrap and work buttonholed loops to fasten them. Thread the narrow ribbon through the waist and wrist holes and also round the neck if desired.

BOOTEES WITH LACE TOPS

Measurements. Depth of leg, 2½ ins.; length of foot, 3½ ins.

Materials. 1 oz. of 3-ply fingering will make at least 3 pairs; a pair of No. 10 needles; 1 yd. of ribbon.

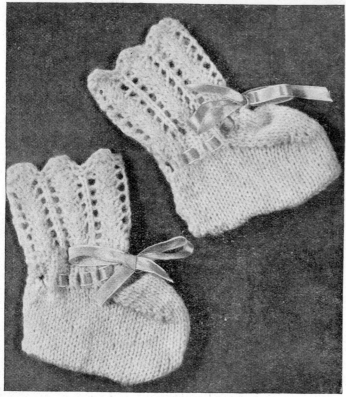

BOOTEES WITH LACE TOPS

DIRECTIONS

Cast on 37 sts., k. the 1st row.

1st row of patt., k. 1, m. 1, k. 1, k. 3 tog., k. 1, m. 1; rep. to the end.

2nd row p.

Rep. these 2 patt. rows 7 times more, k. 2 tog. at end of last row. Knit in ribbing of k. 2, p. 2, for 4 rows.

K. 1, * m. 1, k. 2 tog. *; rep. from * to * to the end. Finish with k. 1. P. back.

Next row, k. 24, turn and p. back 12 sts.

Working on these 12 sts., knit in st.st. for 12 rows.

Continuing in st.st., k. 2 tog. at the beginning and end of the next 3 plain rows.

Work will have ended at the left-hand side of the toe cap. Pick up 11 sts. down the left side of the toe cap and knit them, and continue knitting along the sts. forming the left-hand side of the leg.

Turn and p. back as far as the gap. Pick up 11 sts. down the right-hand side of the toe cap. P. these and continue purling along the sts. forming the right-hand side of the leg. There should now be 52 sts. on the needle. Knit in st.st., on these 52 sts., for 10 rows.

SHAPING THE HEEL AND TOES

K. 2 tog., k. 24, turn.

K. 2 tog., p., turn.

K. 2 tog. at the beginning of the next 6 rows.

Cast off.

Rep. these shapings on the remaining set of sts. which will form the other side of the foot.

TO MAKE UP

Join the seam running under the foot and up the back of the leg. Thread ribbon through the holes at the ankle.

A PAIR OF SLIGHTLY LARGER BOOTEES

(See illustration on page 145.)

Measurements. Depth of leg, 2½ ins.; length of foot, 4 ins.

Materials. 1 oz. of 3-ply wool will make several pairs; a pair of No. 10 needles; 1 yd. of ribbon.

DIRECTIONS

Cast on 42 sts., k. 4 rows, working the 1st row into the backs of the sts.

5th row, p.

6th row, k. 1, * m. 1, k. 2 tog. *; rep. from * to * to the end, finishing with k. 1.

7th row, p.

8th row, k.

9th row, p.

10th row, p.

11th and 12th rows, k.

13th row, p.

Rep. rows 6 to 13 twice more.

Rep. rows 6 and 7.

K. 28 sts., turn and p. 14, turn.

Working on these 14 sts., knit in st.st. for 18 rows.

K. 2 tog. at the beginning of the next 6 rows.

Pick up 11 sts. along the left-hand side of the toe cap, k. them and k. the 14 sts. on the left-hand needle. Turn and p. to the gap, pick up 11 sts. down the other side of the toe cap, p. them and p. to the end (58 sts.).

Knit 10 rows in st.st.

Next row, k. 2 tog., k. 27, turn.

Next row, k. 2 tog., p. 25, turn.

K. 2 tog. at the beginning of the next 6 rows. Cast off; leave an end long enough to sew up the foot and leg seams.

Rep. on the other half of the foot.

BABY'S OWN SOCKLET

Knitted on 4 needles.

These little socklets may be worn with the pram breechettes for extra warmth. If shoes are worn as well, make sure that the additional bulk does not make them too tight. A longer piece of ribbing can be added to the legs if required. All the principles of sock making are worked in these in miniature.

Measurements. Length of ribbed leg, 1¼ ins.; length of foot, 4¼ ins.

Materials. I oz. of 4-ply fingering will make 2 pairs; 4 No. 10 needles, pointed at both ends.

A PAIR OF SLIGHTLY LARGER BOOTEES

DIRECTIONS

Cast on 12 sts. on each of 3 needles.
Knit in rib of k. 2, p. 2, for 12 rounds.

FOR THE HEEL

Knit in st.st. on I set of 12 sts. for 10 rows.
K. 3, sl. 1, k. 1, p.s.s.o., k. 2, k. 2 tog., k. 3, turn and p. back.
K. 2, sl. 1, k. 1, p.s.s.o., k. 2, k. 2 tog., k. 2, turn and p. back.
K. 1, sl. 1, k. 1, p.s.s.o., k. 2, k. 2 tog., k. 1, turn and p. back.
Pick up 10 sts. along each side of the heel and arrange all the sts. on the 3 needles so that there are 16 on each, with one division at the centre of the heel sts., this will be the beginning of the round.

SHAPING THE INSTEP

K. 13, k. 2 tog., k. 1, k. 1, sl. 1, k. 1, p.s.s.o., k. 10, k. 2 tog., k. 1, k. 1, sl. 1, k. 1, p.s.s.o., k. 13.
2nd round, k. 12, k. 2 tog., k. 1, k. 1, sl. 1, k. 1, p.s.s.o., k. 8, k. 2 tog., k. 1, k. 1, sl. 1, k. 1, p.s.s.o., k. 12.
3rd round, k. 11, k. 2 tog., k. 1, k. 1, sl. 1, k. 1, p.s.s.o., k. 6, k. 2 tog., k. 1, k. 1, sl. 1, k. 1, p.s.s.o., k. 11.
4th round, k. 10, k. 2 tog., k. 1, k. 10, k. 1, sl. 1, k. 1, p.s.s.o., k. 10.
Knit 22 plain rounds.

SHAPING THE TOE

K. 1, sl. 1, k. 1, p.s.s.o., k. 6, k. 2 tog., k. 2, sl. 1, k. 1, p.s.s.o., k. 4, k. 2 tog., k. 2, sl. 1, k. 1, p.s.s.o., k. 6, k. 2 tog., k. 1.
2nd round, k. 1, sl. 1, k. 1, p.s.s.o., k. 4, k. 2 tog., k. 2, sl. 1, k. 1, p.s.s.o., k. 2, k. 2 tog., k. 2, sl. 1, k. 1, p.s.s.o., k. 4, k. 2 tog., k. 1.
3rd round, k. 1, sl. 1, k. 1, p.s.s.o., k. 2, k. 2 tog., k. 2, sl. 1, k. 1, p.s.s.o., k. 2, k. 2 tog., k. 2, sl. 1, k. 1, p.s.s.o., k. 2, k. 2 tog., k. 1.
Break off the wool, thread the sts. on it and fasten off securely.

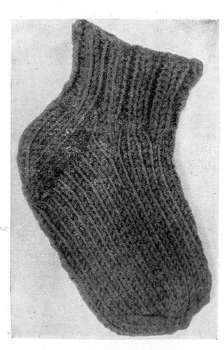

BABY'S OWN SOCKLET

BREECHETTES FOR THE PRAM

MEASUREMENTS

Depth down centre front, 8 ins.
Length down inside leg, 12½ ins. to the ankle.
30 ins. round widest part at the top.

MATERIALS

5 ozs. of 4-ply fingering.
A pair of No. 9 needles.

TENSION

6½ sts. to 1 in.
8 rows to 1 in.

DIRECTIONS

The feet are worked after the legs are made, so that it will be an easy matter for the legs to be lengthened as required. To lengthen the legs, unpick the feet, pick up the sts. round the bottom of the legs and knit in rounds until the legs measure the required length.

These breechettes are made in four pieces. There are seams at the outsides and insides of the legs.

THE RIGHT FRONT LEG

Cast on 21 sts. Knit 18 rows in st.st. End on a p. row.

With right side of fabric facing, k. 1, k. twice into next sts., k. to the end.

Rep. this in every plain row 32 times (64 rows altogether).

Now k. 33 rows without shaping.

At the end of the next 5 plain rows k. 2 tog., k. 2.

Change to ribbing of k. 2, p. 2 for 17 rows. End on a right side row.

With wrong side facing, rib 36 sts., turn and rib back.

Next row, rib 28 sts., turn and rib back.

Next row, rib 20 sts., turn and rib back.

Cast off.

THE LEFT FRONT LEG

Work the left front leg in a similar way to the right front leg, with all shapings at the reverse ends of the rows.

THE LEFT BACK LEG

Knit the left back leg like the right front leg as far as the top of the leg increasings.

Then continue: K. 43 rows, inc. by knitting twice into the first st. of every 2nd plain row.

The ribbing at the top: Rib in k. 2, p. 2 for 23 rows, or end on the wrong side of the fabric.

Next row, starting at the centre back, rib 48 sts., turn and rib back.

Next row, rib 40 sts., turn and rib back.

Next row, rib 32 sts., turn and rib back.

Next row, rib 24 sts., turn and rib back.

Cast off.

THE RIGHT BACK LEG

Knit the right back leg as for the left back leg, but work all shapings at the reverse ends of the rows.

THE BACK FOOT AND SOLE

Pick up 20 sts. across the cast-on sts. of the back leg. Arrange this so that knitting will begin on the right side of the fabric.

Knit in st.st. for 15 rows.

TURNING THE HEEL

1st row, k. 13, k. 2 tog., turn.
2nd row, p. 7, p. 2 tog., turn.
3rd row, k. 7, k. 2 tog., turn.

Rep. rows 2 and 3 until all the sts. are knitted in one row.

K. 2 rows.

On the next 3 plain rows knit twice into the first and last sts. K. without shaping for 8 rows.

K. 2 tog. at the beginning of the next 3 plain rows.

Cast off.

THE FRONT FOOT

Pick up 20 sts. along the cast-on sts. of the front leg. Arrange this so that work will begin on a right side row.

Cast on 8 sts. and then k. the first row, turn.

Cast on 8 sts. and p. the row.

Knit 22 rows in st.st.

With right side of work facing, k. 23 sts., k. 2 tog., turn. P. 11, k. 2 tog., turn. K. 11, k. 2 tog., turn.

Rep. the last 2 rows until all sts. are knitted in one row.

Break off the wool, leaving an end long enough to thread through the sts. and draw them up.

The heel and sole and top foot are alike for both feet.

TO MAKE UP

Pin the work out on an ironing blanket to the measures given, and press with a warm iron without touching the ribbing. Sew up the inside leg seams and the outside leg seams.

Join the seams down the sides of each foot and sew the top foot to the sole, pulling up the sts. at the toe to fit.

Work a crocheted edging round the top to form slots through which a cord can be threaded. Either make a twisted cord, or else use bought cord, the ends of the cord may be neatened with tassels.

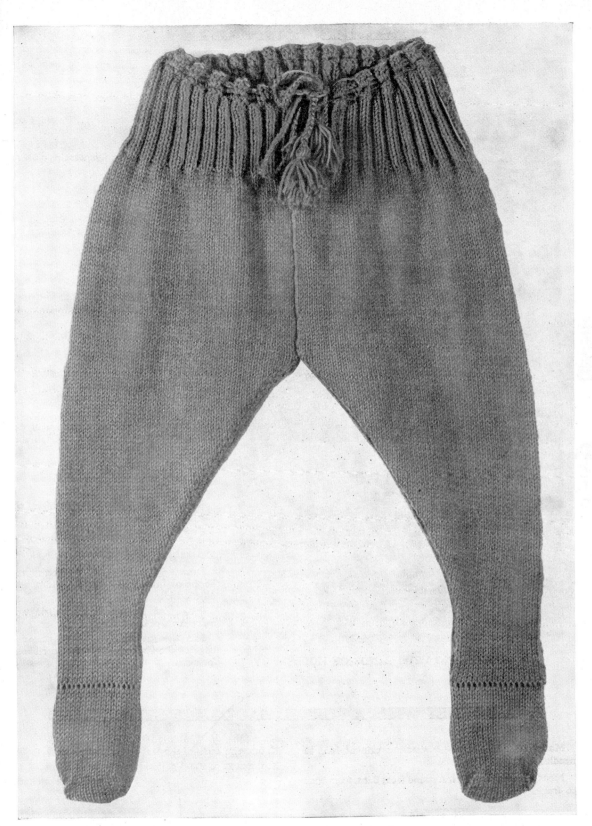

BREECHETTES FOR THE PRAM

147

BABIES' BONNETS

1. RIBBED AND WITH BANDS OF HOLES

1. RIBBED AND WITH BANDS OF HOLES

Measurements. 11 ins. round face; 7¼ ins. from centre front to back.

Materials. 1 oz. of 3-ply wool; a pair of No. 10 needles; 1 yd. of washing ribbon.

DIRECTIONS

Cast on 70 sts.

1st row, k. into backs of cast-on sts.

2nd row, k.

3rd row, k.

4th row, k.

5th row, p.

6th row, k. 1, * m. 1, k. 2 tog. *; rep. from * to * to the end, finish with k. 1.

7th row, p.

8th row, k.

9th row, p.

10th row, p.

11th row, k.

Rep. rows 4 to 11, 4 times more.

Next row, k. 2 tog. all along.

P. back, break off the wool leaving an end long enough to thread through the sts. and to draw them up.

THE BACK

Cast on 12 sts.

Knit 12 rows, k. 2 tog. at each end of the next 6 rows.

Cast off.

TO MAKE UP

Draw up the last sts. of the bonnet to fit the curved edge of the back and fasten off the end.

Press the bonnet lightly, shrinking away some of the fullness at the back.

Join the gathered sts. to the curved edge of the back and sew on the ribbon for bows.

2. A BONNET WITH A TURNED BACK LACE STITCH BAND

Materials. 1 oz. of 3-ply wool; a pair of No. 10 needles, 1 yd. of washing ribbon.

Measurements. 12½ ins. round face; 8 ins. from back to front.

DIRECTIONS

Cast on 70 sts.

K. into the backs of the cast on sts. and p. back.

K. the next row and p. back again.

The patt. is a diagonal rib of k. 6, p. 4, with 2 holes in the k. rib with 3 rows of rib between.

1st row, p. 4, k. 6 to the end.

2nd row, p. 5, * k. 4, p. 6 *; rep. from * to * to the end, finishing with k. 4, p. 1.

BABIES' BONNETS

continued

3rd row, k. 2, * p. 4, k. 2 tog., m. 1, k. 2, m. 1, k. 2 tog. *; rep. from * to * 5 times more, p. 4, k. 4.

4th row, p. 3, * k. 4, p. 6 *; rep. from * to * to the end, finishing with k. 4, p. 3.

5th row, k. 4, * p. 4, k. 6 *; rep. from * to * to the end, finishing with p. 4, k. 2.

6th row, p. 1, * k. 4, p. 6 *; rep. from * to * to the end, finishing with k. 4, p. 5.

7th row, * k. 2 tog., m. 1, k. 2, m. 1 k. 2 tog., p. 4 *; rep. from * to * to the end.

8th row, k. 3, * p. 6, k. 4 *; rep. from * to * to the end, finishing with p. 6, k. 1.

9th row, p. 4, k. 6 to the end.

P. the next 2 rows, turn.

From this point knit 3½ ins. in st.st.

The right side of the st.st. must come on the wrong side of the lace st. band, so that when the band is turned back over the crown, the right side will be uppermost.

THE BACK DECREASINGS

K. 5, k. 2 tog. to the end, turn and p. back.

K. 4, k. 2 tog. to the end, turn and p. back.

K. 3, k. 2 tog. to the end, turn and p. back.

K. 2, k. 2 tog. to the end, turn and p. back.

K. 1, k. 2 tog. to the end, turn and p. back.

K. 2 tog. all along the row.

Break off the wool, leaving an end long enough to thread through the sts. and draw them up tight.

TO MAKE UP

Press the work lightly, turn the lace back over the

2. A BONNET WITH A TURNED BACK LACE STITCH BAND

crown and sew at the sides, cut the ribbon in half and attach one piece at each side of the face.

Draw up the sts. and sew up the seam for 2 ins.

3. A BONNET WITH A LACE STITCH BAND AND A RIBBED HEAD

Measurements. 12 ins. round face; 8¾ ins. from centre front to back.

Materials. 1 oz. of 3-ply wool; a pair of No. 9 needles; 1 yd. of washing ribbon.

DIRECTIONS

Cast on 70 sts. K. into the backs of the cast-on sts., and k. the next 2 rows, turn.

Knit 4 rows in st.st.

7th row, k. 9, * m. 1, k. 2 tog., k. 8 *; rep. from * to * 4 times more, m. 1, k. 2 tog., k. 9, turn and p. back.

Next row, k. 6, * k. 2 tog., m. 1, k. 3, m. 1, k. 2 to-.,

k. 3 *; rep. from * to * 4 times more, k. 2 tog., m. 1, k. 3, m. 1, k. 2 tog., k. 7, turn and p. back.

Rep. the 7th row.

Knit 4 rows in st.st.

From this point the wrong side of the knitting becomes the right side, so that when the band, just knitted, is turned back over the crown, the right side of the lace patt. is uppermost.

With the wrong side of the band facing, k. 6, sl. 1; rep. to the end.

Next row, p.

Rep. these 2 rows for 4¾ ins.

BABIES' BONNETS *continued*

3. A BONNET WITH A LACE STITCH BAND AND A RIBBED HEAD

SHAPING THE BACK

K. 4, k. 2 tog., sl. 1, rep. to the end, turn and p. back.

K. 3, k. 2 tog., sl. 1; rep. to the end, turn and p. back.

K. 2, k. 2 tog., sl. 1, rep. to the end, turn and p. back.

K. 1, k. 2 tog., sl. 1; rep. to the end, turn and p. back.

K. 2 tog., sl. 1; rep. to the end; turn and p. back.

Break off the wool, leaving enough to thread through the sts. and to draw them up.

TO MAKE UP

Draw up the sts. tightly and sew the seam as far as the first row of dec. Turn the lace band back over the crown. Press the work lightly.

Cut the ribbon into two pieces and sew one on to each side of the face.

4. A BABY BOY'S HAT

Measurements. 12 ins. round head; 5 ins. from beginning to top of crown (with band turned back).

Materials. 1 oz. of 2-ply crêpe wool; a pair of No. 9 needles.

~~DIRECTI~~ONS

Cast on 70 sts. K. into the backs of the cast-on sts. and p. the next row. K. the next row.

Knit 7 rows in st.st.

Knit the next 3 rows.

Knit 7 rows in st.st., ending on k. row.

From this point the right and wrong sides of the knitting are reversed.

Next row, p. 1, sl. 1, k. 1; rep. to the end.

Next row, p. 2, k. 1; rep. to the end.

Work these 2 rows for 4¾ ins.

Then p. 1, * sl. 1, k. 2 tog. *; rep. from * to * to the end, turn and p. back.

K. 2 tog. all along the row. Break off the wool, leaving an end long enough to draw up the sts.

TO MAKE UP

Thread the end through the sts., pull them up tightly and join the seam right to the end.

Turn the striped band back over the ribbing and finish off the top of the crown with a pompon, or a tassel.

This little hat should not be pressed. Ribbon ties may be added if desired.

4. A BABY BOY'S HAT

This is made in a similar way to a bonnet, the only difference being that the seam is joined all the way down. It is an easy matter to make a bonnet into a hat, or a hat into a bonnet.

5. A FLUFFY BONNET WITH A FRILL

Measurements. 12 ins. round face; 8 ins. from centre front to back.

Materials. 1 ball of real angora wool. This will be enough for mittens or bootees as well; a small amount of fingering in a contrasting colour; a pair of No. 10 needles.

DIRECTIONS

Cast on 140 sts. with the fingering.

K. into the backs of the cast-on sts., and k. the next row.

Change to the angora wool and knit in st.st. for 4 rows.

Next row, k. 2 tog. all along. Knit the next 3 rows in st.st.

P. the next row and work in st.st. for 4 ins.

The right side of the work will be reversed, so that when the frill is turned back, its right side will be uppermost.

SHAPING THE TOP

Commence on a k. row.

K. 8, k. 2 tog.; rep. all along the row, turn and p. back.

K. 7, k. 2 tog.; rep. to the end, turn and p. back.

K. 6, k. 2 tog.; rep. to the end, turn and p. back.

K. 5, k. 2 tog.; rep. to the end; turn and p. back.

K. 4, k. 2 tog.; rep. to the end, turn and p. back.

K. 3, k. 2 tog.; rep. to the end, turn and p. back.

K. 2, k. 2 tog.; rep. to the end, turn and p. back.

K. 1, k. 2 tog.; rep. to the end, turn and p. back.

Break off the wool, leaving an end long enough to thread through the sts. and to draw them up.

TO MAKE UP

Press the work very lightly, draw up the sts. and sew up the seam for 2½ ins.

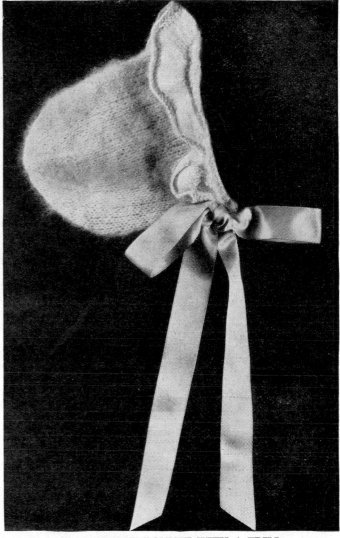

5. A FLUFFY BONNET WITH A FRILL

Brush the wool with a teasel brush, turn the frill back from the face and sew on ribbon ties.

BABIES' MITTENS

1. FLUFFED AND FRILLED TO MATCH BONNET NUMBER 5

Measurements. 3½ ins. from wrist (ribbon), to top of fingers.

Materials. 1 ball of real angora will make at least 3 pairs; a small amount of fingering in a contrasting colour; a pair of No. 10 needles.

DIRECTIONS

With the fingering, cast on 80 sts., k. into the backs of the cast-on sts. and k. the next row.

Change to angora wool and knit 6 rows in st.st.

Next row, k. 2 tog. all along, turn and p. back.

Next row, k. 1, * m. 1, k. 2 tog. *; rep. from * to * to the end, finish with k. 1.

Knit 6 rows in st.st.

1st row, k. 18, k. twice into next st., k. 2, k. twice into next st., k. 18, turn and p. back.

3rd row, k. 18, k. twice into next st., k. 4, k. twice into next st., k. 18, turn and purl back.

BABIES' MITTENS *continued*

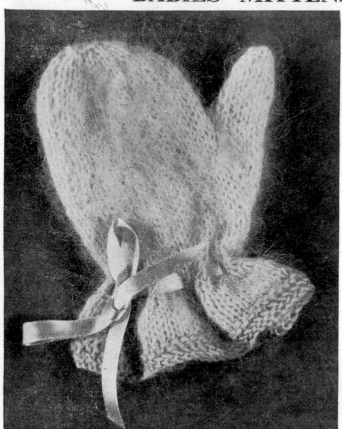

5th row, k. 18, k. twice into next st., k. 6, k. twice into next st., k. 18, turn and p. back.

7th row, k. 18, k. twice into next st., k. 8, k. twice into next st., k. 18, turn and p. back.

9th row, k. 18, k. twice into next st., k. 10, k. twice into next st., k. 18, turn and p. back.

11th row, k. 18, k. twice into next st., k. 12, k. twice into next st., turn and p. back 16 sts.

Working on these 16 sts., knit in st.st. for 10 rows.

Next row, k. 2 tog. all along, break off the wool, leaving an end long enough to draw up the sts.

Thread this end through the sts. at the top of the thumb.

THE HAND

Join on the wool at the beginning of the left-hand needle and k. the sts. on the left-hand needle. Turn.

P. right across the 2 sets of 18 sts. and work on these in st.st. for 10 rows.

Next row, k. 4, * k. 2 tog., k. 2 *; rep. from * to * all along. P. back.

Next row, k. 3, * k. 2 tog., k. 1 *; rep. from * to * all along. P. back.

Next row, k. 2 tog. all along. Cast off the remaining sts.

TO MAKE UP

Draw up the sts. at the top of the thumb and sew up the thumb seam, putting a few strong sts. at the base.

Sew up the seam across the top of the fingers and down the side of the hand. Thread ribbon through the wrist holes.

2. A LARGER MITTEN KNITTED IN FINGERING

Measurements. 5 ins. from beginning of rib to the top of the fingers.

Materials. 1 oz. of 4-ply fingering will make 3 pairs; a pair of No. 10 needles.

DIRECTIONS

Cast on 40 sts.

Knit in rib of k. 1, p. 1 for 14 rows.

Knit 6 rows in st.st.

From this point follow the directions for the base of the thumb, as given for the fluffy mittens, up to the end of row 9.

10th row, p. 12.

Working on these 12 sts., knit in st.st. for 8 rows for the thumb.

Next row, k. 2, k. 2 tog. all along, turn and p. back.

Next row, k. 2 tog. all along.

Break off the thread and thread the end through the sts.

Join on the wool at the beginning of the left-hand needle and k. along the sts. on the left-hand needle. Turn and p. back along the sts. of the 2 sets of 18 sts. (36 in all).

Knit the next 8 rows in st.st.

Next row, k. 2, sl. 1, k. 1, p.s.s.o., k. 10, k. 2 tog., k. 4, sl. 1, k. 1, p.s.s.o., k. 10, k. 2 tog., k. 2, p. back.

Next row, k. 2, sl. 1, k. 1, p.s.s.o., k. 8, k. 2 tog., k. 4, sl. 1, k. 1, p.s.s.o., k. 8, k. 2 tog., k. 2, p. back.

Next row, k. 2, sl. 1, k. 1, p.s.s.o., k. 6, k. 2 tog., k. 4, sl. 1, k. 1, p.s.s.o., k. 6, k. 2 tog., k. 2.

Cast off, leaving an end long enough to sew up the seam along the top of the fingers and down the side of the hand.

A JERSEY SUIT
FOR A SMALL BOY

Measurements (for jersey). 13 ins. from shoulder to lower edge; 22 ins. round underarm; sleeve 7 ins. at the seam.

Measurements (for trousers). Leg seam, 2½ ins.; centre front seam, 7½ ins.

Materials (for both garments). 7 ozs. of 3-ply wool; a pair of No. 10 needles; 4 small pearl buttons for the neck.

These directions tell how to make a little suit from the directions given for rompers and breechettes.

Any kind of suitable fabric, either plain or patterned, can be worked for these garments; the jersey may be the same fabric as the rompers with stocking stitch trousers, or, both garments could be worked in slipped stitch stripe. (*See* Index for this stitch.)

A small patterned fabric will be more suited to the small size of these garments than will a large pattern, like cable stitch. Ribbed bands with the rest in moss stitch will be a good fabric, or the fabric of the rompers will be suitable. The small boy will be overwhelmed in a large pattern.

Smooth wools will be more effective than rough bouclés, or tweed effects, and will knit up more quickly. A two-colour suit would be useful: the trousers in dark blue and the jersey in scarlet for everyday and a white one for best.

The suit will need frequent laundering. Therefore, if it is necessary to leave the shoulders open for the passage of the head, do sew the buttons on strongly and choose those that will not wear out the fabric. Sew a small button on the wrong side with the same stitches that sew on the fastening button, so that there is no strain on the fabric.

If it is desired to fasten the little trousers on to a shirt or bodice, make vertical buttonholes at the top edge at suitable places. Directions for working vertical buttonholes will be found elsewhere in this book; please refer to the index for the number of the page.

DIRECTIONS

FOR THE JERSEY

Cast on 80 sts. Work into the backs of the cast-on sts. in the first row.

Knit in ribbing of k. 1, p. 1, for 1½ ins.

K. without shaping for 7½ ins.

From this point follow the directions given for rompers, commencing at the armhole shapings.

THE SLEEVES

The sleeves are like those for the rompers, but knit beyond the ribbing until the sleeve measures 6 ins.

THE TROUSERS

The directions are similar to those for breechettes.

Cast on 44 sts. K. into the backs of the cast-on sts. for the first row. K. until the leg measures 2½ ins., working the same increasings as for the leg of the breechettes.

The remainder of the trousers are worked just like the breechettes after the 64th row of increasings. Elastic should be used instead of a crocheted cord.

The making up of these garments is the same as for rompers and breechettes.

TWO FABRICS AND A CORNER FOR SHAWLS

In giving instructions for the making of shawls, it is unnecessary to give complete details, because once the plan of work has been decided, the rest of the knitting is straightforward.

The average size for shawls is 63 ins. square; larger ones go up to 72 ins. and smaller ones are about 54 ins. square.

The average amount of wool required for a 72-in. square shawl will be 1½ lbs. of 2-ply wool worked with No. 8 needles. Average amounts can be worked to proportion for smaller shawls. The average amount of 3-ply wool for a 54-in. square shawl will be 1½ lbs. But much will depend on the kind of pattern worked.

Shawls with borders can be worked in two ways. The border may be knitted without a corner, the change of pattern taking place in every row, as in the illustration on this page, or the border can be knitted with the body of the shawl, at the top and bottom edges, and the side borders knitted on stitches picked up from each side. The mitred corner is made by decreasings and increasings on the appropriate edges.

Any suitable patterned fabric may be used for the body of the shawl; many of the lace stitch fabrics described earlier in the book will be very useful.

First of all, find the tension of your wool and needles by knitting a small sample and decide on the size for the shawl. Then calculate the number of stitches required for the width of the borders at either side and the total width of the shawl. From the total number of stitches subtract the number of stitches which will be taken up by the two borders at the sides.

The pattern used for the main part of the shawl must work into the remaining number of stitches.

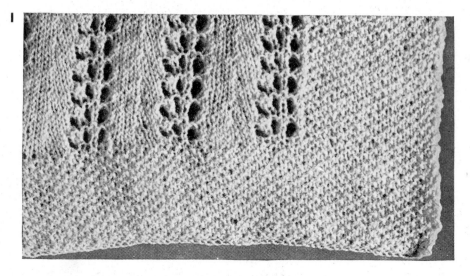

1. The pattern shown here requires 12 sts. for one pattern, so the number of stitches left in the main part of the shawl (that is, the number left after subtracting the number of stitches in the two borders), must be a multiple of 12 plus 6 sts. for a portion of one pattern at the end to make the pattern alike at both ends of the knitting. 17 sts. are moss stitched for each border, i.e., 34 sts. for the two borders. If the shawl is to be 54 ins. wide and the tension is 6 sts. to 1 in., there will be 6 x 54 = 324 sts. required on the needle. Thirty-four of these stitches will be required for the two borders, leaving 290 sts. for the main part of the shawl.

To work the pattern into the number of stitches.
First of all take away the 6 sts. required to even up the end of the pattern, 290 — 6 = 284.

The pattern requires a multiple of 12, but 12 will not go evenly into 284, so we must take it to the next nearest multiple, which is 288 sts., and on these we shall get 24 patterns across our knitting.

Directions. Cast on 328 sts. Knit in moss stitch for 18 rows.

1st pattern row, moss stitch 17, k. 2 tog., * m. 1, k. 1, m. 1, k. 1, m. 1, k. 2 tog., k. 2, k. 2 tog., k. 2, k. 2 tog. * ; repeat from * to * to within 23 sts. of the end (24 patterns), finish with m. 1, k. 1, m. 1, k. 1, m. 1, k. 2 tog., k. 2 tog., moss stitch 17.

2nd pattern row, purl, with the two borders of 17 sts. in moss stitch.

3rd pattern row, moss stitch 17, k. 1, * p. 5, k. 7 *; repeat from * to * to within 19 sts. of the end, finish with p. 2, moss stitch 17.

4th pattern row, purl, with the two borders of 17 sts. in moss stitch.

Repeat these 4 rows until the shawl measures a square, all but the width of the moss stitch border. Then proceed as follows: Work 18 rows entirely in moss stitch. Cast off fairly loosely. If liked, a fringe may be added to the shawl.

TWO FABRICS AND A CORNER FOR SHAWLS
continued

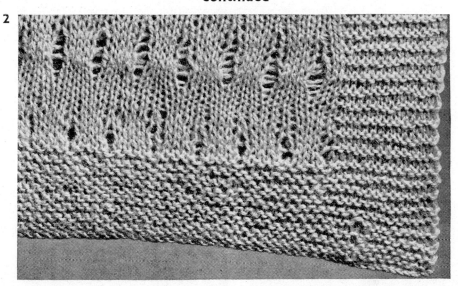

2

2. A very easy shawl pattern to be worked in Shetland wool. Work out amount required according to size of shawl from the hints given above. As the thickness of Shetland wool varies, ask at your shop whether the wool you are buying is equivalent to a 2-ply or a 3-ply fingering, and buy the quantity needed for that thickness. The border may be in any stitch desired. The one in the illustration is done in garter stitch.

The pattern. Work the border according to width required.

1st pattern row, knit the border, * m. 1, k. 4 *; repeat from * to * to within the border sts., knit the border.

2nd pattern row, p., working the borders as usual.

3rd pattern row, k., working the borders as usual.

4th pattern row, p., working the borders as usual.

5th pattern row, knit the border. * Drop 1, which was the made stitch, k. 4 *; repeat from * to * to within the border sts., knit the border. Stroke the dropped stitches down to the 1st pattern row, this makes the lace pattern. Work the next 5 rows in stocking stitch. Move the pattern along 2 sts., thus:

1st pattern row, knit the border, * k. 2, m. 1, k. 2 *; repeat from * to * to within the border stitches, knit the border.

Continue working the pattern as before.

Repeat the 5 rows of stocking stitch, and then work these two sets of patterns until the shawl measures all but the width of the border to make a square. Knit the top border. Cast off loosely.

3. This illustration shows a mitred corner to a shawl.

3

Cast on the number of stitches required to give the full width of the shawl. Remember the number of stitches. While working the lower border k. 1, k. 2 together at the beginning of every row. The main part of the shawl is knitted without shaping at the sides and no border is worked at the sides. Knit until the main part of the shawl measures a square and then change to the border pattern, and while working this top border k. 1, k. twice into the next stitch at the beginning of every row, until there is the same number of stitches as were cast on.

To make the side borders. Pick up the same number of stitches along each side as remained on the needle after the bottom border had been worked. Knit in the border pattern, increasing in the second stitches at the beginning of every row until the border measures the same width as the top and bottom borders. Cast off and sew the short seams.

FRINGES

Shawls, knitted table mats and scarves will often be improved if a fringe is added. The following directions describe a very simple way of making fringes for knitted articles.

Tools required. A piece of card about the size of a post card, some fairly closely twisted wool, a rug needle and a small pair of scissors.

1. Cut the wool into strips by winding it round the card, taking it round either the narrow way or the wide way, whichever will give the most convenient length. Cut the strands through along one edge of the card.

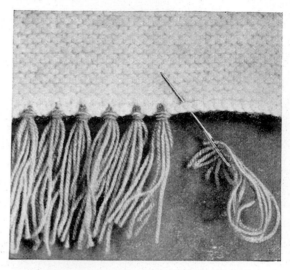

2. Thread the rug needle with four of the strands doubled in half, the cut ends going through the eye of the needle. Insert the point of the needle through the edge of the knitted fabric, from the back.

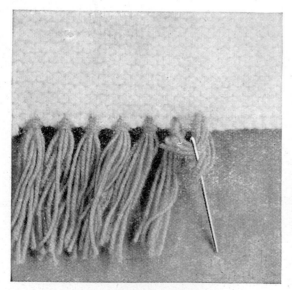

3. Pull the needle out, leaving the loops protruding from under the fabric. Pass the needle through the loops.

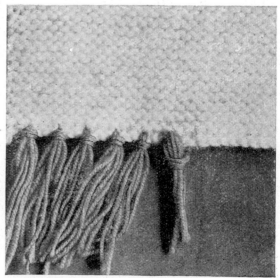

4. Remove the needle and pull the loop tightly over the strands of wool; repeat all along the edge to be fringed. The thickness of the fringe will depend on taste and type of wool.

CORDS AND TASSELS

Two of the cords shown on this page are made with a crochet hook; they are given here, instead of later in the crochet section, because many cords are required in knitting. Crocheted cords are the easiest to make as they only require a hook.

1

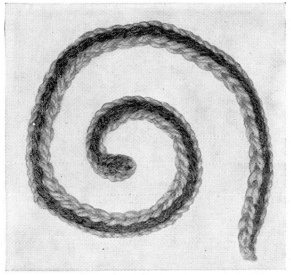

2

1. A plaited cord of three chains. Make a length of chain in each of three colours, tie the ends together and plait them. When the plait is long enough, tie the cords once or twice (as shown here) and tie a bead or button to the end of each chain. The distance from the knot to the bead may be any distance desired.

2. A magic chain cord. First of all, crochet a chain a little longer than required, then work a double crochet into every second chain. After this, work another chain in a contrasting colour through each double crochet stitch.

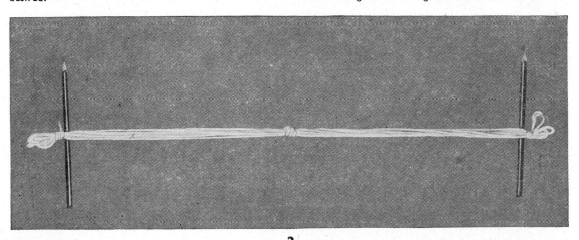

3

3. Preparations for a twisted cord. Another variety of cord used with knitting; the wool and three pencils are required. Cut the strands of wool three times as long as the required length of cord. Tie a loop exactly in the centre and tie a knot at each end. Insert one pencil through the strands at each end, and twist the pencils in opposite directions until the wool is tight. Place the third pencil through the centre loop and, keeping the twisted wool taut, double it so that the two end pencils are together. Slacken the wool just a little and notice in which direction the two twisted strands turn and spin the pencil at the centre in that direction until the wool is again tightly twisted. Remove all the pencils and tie the cord at each end, let the cord hang, stroking it if necessary, to form a good cord. Both steps in twisting must be done tightly to make a firm cord.

A SWING BACK COAT

This little swing back coat is designed to be carried out in astrakhan knitting wool. A thick silk cord finishes the neck and the buttons are made by coiling a length of the cord flat. Directions for making are given for two kinds of astrakhan, the first is for light-weight wool and the second for heavy-weight wool. The knitting is in garter stitch throughout.

Measurements. To fit a bust measure of 34 ins.; sleeve length 17 ins. at the seam; length from shoulder to lower edge, 24 ins.

Materials. Light-weight astrakhan; 3 lbs. of astrakhan knitting wool; a pair of No. 4 needles; 1½ yds. of heavy silk cord.

Tension. 3 sts. to 1 in.

DIRECTIONS

BOTH HALVES OF THE BACK (both halves are alike)

Cast on 30 sts., k. into the backs of the cast-on sts. in the 1st row.

The right-hand edge will be the centre back seam line, and the left-hand edge will be the side seam. It is a good plan to put a safety pin in the right-hand edge to mark the centre back. Continue knitting in g.st. for

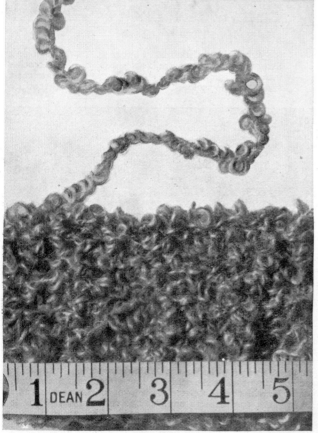

16 ins., and at the same time at the right-hand edge k. 2 tog. at the beginning of the row every 4 ins., and at the left-hand edge k. 2 tog. at the end of the row every 2 ins. These decreasings can also be marked with a safety pin as it is almost impossible to count the rows of knitting.

ARMHOLE SHAPING

Cast off 4 sts. at the beginning of the next row which commences at the side seam edge.

At the beginning of the next 2 rows that commence at the armhole, k. 2 tog.

K. without further shaping at the armhole, but continue the centre back shaping until work measures 23 ins.

Cast off one-quarter of the number of sts. at the armhole, k. the next row and then cast off all the remaining sts.

Knit the right half of the back like the left; there is no right or wrong side to the fabric, but in making up be sure that the two back pieces face.

BOTH HALVES OF THE FRONT (knitted both alike)

Cast on 30 sts. K. the first row into the backs of the cast-on sts.

The right-hand edge will be the centre front and the left-hand edge will be the side seam. Mark the centre front with a safety pin. Continue knitting in g.st. for 16 ins., repeating the directions given for the side seam decreasings of the back, but not shaping the centre front.

Shape the armhole as for the back and k. without further shaping until the armhole measures 5 ins.

FRONT NECK SHAPING

Cast off 5 sts. at the beginning of the next row which commences at the centre front.

K. 2 tog. at the beginning of the next 3 rows that commence at the neck. Knit until armhole measures 8 ins. Then cast off.

Knit the second front in the same way, there is no right or wrong side to the fabric, so when making up the coat be sure that the fronts will face.

THE SLEEVES (both alike)

Cast on 32 sts. K. into the backs of the cast-on sts. in the 1st row. Knit in g.st. without shaping for 8 ins. Now knit another 9 ins., inc. by knitting twice into the first and last sts. in the row every 2 ins.

TOP SHAPING

Cast off 4 sts. at the beginning of the next 2 rows.

K. 2 tog. at the beginning of every row until 12 sts. remain. Cast off.

A SWING BACK COAT
continued
FOR THE HEAVY ASTRAKHAN

Measurements. The same as for light-weight astrakhan.

Materials. 5¾ lbs. of heavy-weight astrakhan wool; a pair of No. 1 needles; 1½ yds. of heavy silk cord.

Tension. 2½ sts. to 1 in.

DIRECTIONS

BOTH HALVES OF THE BACK
Cast on 27 sts., continue as for the light-weight astrakhan.

BOTH HALVES OF THE FRONT
Cast on 25 sts., continue as for the light-weight astrakhan.

THE SLEEVES
Cast on 28 sts., continue as for the light-weight astrakhan.

MAKING UP (for both weights)
The work need not be pressed. Sew the centre back seam, the side seams, the shoulder seams and the sleeve seams. Set in the sleeves, sew the cord round the neck edge and make two buttons by coiling cord round, flat on the table, and sewing the coils together strongly. Leave enough cord to make two loops to sew to the right-hand front edge to fasten the buttons.

A SKATING SKIRT

This skirt, the cap and the mittens from the next two pages will make an attractive skating outfit.

MEASUREMENTS

To fit a 38-in. hip.

Length from waist to lower edge, 20 ins. (this will drop a little).

Width round lower edge, 2 yds. 12 ins.

MATERIALS

For skirt only:—

8 ozs. of dark colour 4-ply wool.

1 oz. each of two other colours in 4-ply wool.

A pair of No. 8 needles (No. 9 needles will make the skirt slightly smaller if desired).

A length of petersham for the waist and a 6-in. zipp fastener. If no opening is required, make threading holes in the second row for elastic.

DIRECTIONS

The skirt is made in four sections, all in st.st.

RIGHT FRONT

Cast on 42 sts.

K. for 7 ins., inc. on the second st. of every other plain row. Thus the centre front seam edge is straight and the side seam is shaped.

Next row, with right side of work facing, and continuing the side seam shaping as before, * k. 11, k. twice into next st.*; rep. from * to * 3 times more, k. to the end.

Rep. this row of increasings at intervals of 7 rows, inc. the number of knitted sts. between those that are knitted twice, by 1 each time until the skirt measures the required length. Change the colours as desired. In the illustration, blue, red and white were used; blue was changed for white after 13 ins. Then was worked, white for 7 rows, red for 12 rows, white for 7 rows, and blue again to the end (18 rows).

Cast off on a plain row, so that the chain-like edge makes a finish.

THE LEFT FRONT

The left front is knitted in a similar manner, with the shapings worked from opposite ends of the rows.

THE TWO BACKS

Make two more pieces like the right and left fronts for the right and left backs.

TO MAKE UP

Press the work carefully, not stretching the fabric.

Sew the pieces in pairs down the straight edges. These will become the centre front and centre back seams. Sew up the side seams, leaving one open far enough to take the zipp fastener, if required. Let in the fastener, sewing it very strongly.

In joining the seams, pin the ends together first so as to get the waist and lower edges level, and then work between these points.

MATERIALS FOR THE SET OF THREE

9 ozs. of dark colour in 3-ply wool.

2 ozs. of each of two lighter colours in 3-ply wool.

A SKATING CAP

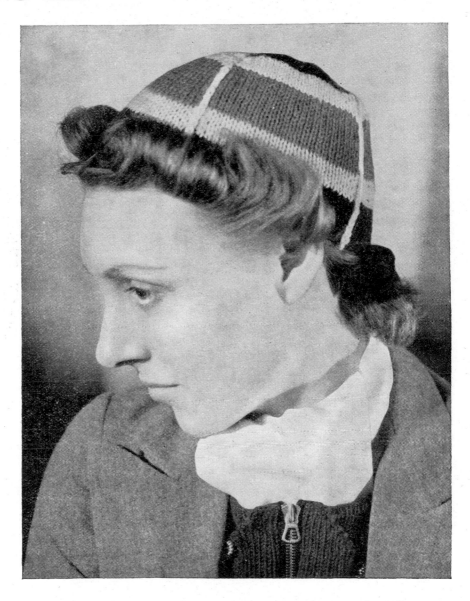

MEASUREMENTS
To fit a 22-23 in. head.

MATERIALS
If wool is being bought for the cap only:—
I oz. each of 3 colours in 4-ply wool.
A pair of No. 9 needles and a crochet hook.

DIRECTIONS
The cap is made in five sections, with a crocheted chain sewn down each seam.

Cast on 24 sts. and work into backs of the cast-on sts.

Work in st.st. for 3½ ins., changing the colours as desired. In the cap illustrated, blue is worked for 10 rows, white for 6 rows, red for 12 rows, and white again for 6 rows; blue finishes the top.

After the 3½ ins., with right side facing, k. I, k. 2 tog., k. to within 3 sts. of the end, k. 2 tog., k. I, turn and p. back.

Rep. until all sts. are disposed of.

Break off the wool, leaving an end long enough to sew the seam. Make four more sections like this one and then press lightly to flatten them.

Sew the five seams, being careful that the lower edges will be level.

With the crochet hook and one of the colours (white was used in the illustration), make two lengths of chain, each long enough to reach across the cap from one side to the other and make a shorter piece for the odd seam, to reach from lower edge to top.

Sew these chains over the seams and the cap is then complete.

SKATING MITTENS

MEASUREMENTS

To fit a 6¾ hand.

MATERIALS

If wool is being bought to make these mittens only: I oz. each of 3 colours in 4-ply wool; a pair of No. 9 needles.

DIRECTIONS

Cast on 64 sts. and knit in ribbing of k. 2, p. 2 for 3¾ ins., changing the colours as desired. Red, white and blue were used in the mitten in the illustration, blue for 8 rows, white for 6 rows, red for 8 rows and white again for 6 rows.

Continuing in blue:—

Next row, right side of work, k. 4, k. 2 tog. all along. Turn and p. back. Knit 4 more rows in st.st.

Next row, k. 23, k. twice into next st., k. 4, k. twice into next st., k. 23, turn and p. back.

Rep. these 2 rows 5 times more, knitting 6, 8, 10, 12, and 14 sts. between the 2 inc. sts. in consecutive plain rows.

THE THUMB

With right side of work facing, k. 41, turn.

P. 18, turn. K. and p. the next 2 rows, working on these 18 sts.

K. I, k. 2 tog., k. to within 3 sts. of the end, k. 2 tog., k. I, turn and p. back.

Rep. these 2 rows once more.

Knit 8 rows in st.st.

Next row, k. I, k. 2 tog. all along, turn and p. back.

Rep. the dec. row, then break off the wool, leaving an end long enough to thread through the sts., draw them up and sew the thumb seam.

THE HAND

Join on the wool at the beginning of the left-hand needle and knit the sts. on that needle. Turn and p. back across both needles. Knit in st.st. until the hand measures 3 ins. from the beginning of the thumb. This should bring the work to the base of the top joint of the first finger.

The colours may be changed, using the same order as before.

TOP SHAPINGS

With right side of work facing, k. I, k. 2 tog., k. to within 2 sts. of the centre, k. 2 tog., k. 2 tog., k. to within 3 sts. of the end, k. 2 tog., k. I. Turn and p. back.

Rep. these 2 rows 5 times more, or until the hand is long enough. Cast off and leave an end long enough to sew the hand seam.

MAKING UP

Work should not be pressed. Draw up the sts. at the top of the thumb and sew the thumb seam, making a good strong ending. Sew up the top of the hand and the side seam. For extra comfort, knit a band to fasten round the wrist. Cast on 6 sts. and knit the band as long as required. Make a buttonhole, or work a loop at one end and sew the other end to the back or the front of the wrist ribbing; sew a button on this for fastening.

A CLOSE FITTING HAT

Owing to the elasticity of the fabric, this hat will fit most head measures.

Materials. I oz. of 4-ply fingering; a pair of No. 10 needles.

DIRECTIONS

Cast on 130 sts. and k. into the backs of these for the 1st row.

Next row, p. I, * k. 3, p. 2 *; rep. from * to * to within 4 sts. of the end, finish with k. 3, p. I.

Next row, k. I, * p. 3, k. 2 *; rep. from * to * to within 4 sts. of the end, finish with p. 3, k. I.

Rep. these last 2 rows until the work measures 7 ins. Cast off loosely.

Do not press the work or the elasticity of the ribbing will be lost.

Join the seam with oversewing.

Thread the needle with a length of wool and work a row of running sts. I in. down from the cast off edge. Draw up the running thread to gather the top of the hat and fasten off strongly.

Bend back the gathered top in four places and sew the cast off edge at these points to the hat crown.

The hat may be worn with one side turned up, or a pleat can be arranged in the crown. These can be manipulated each time the hat is put on.

A CARDIGAN IN TWEED EFFECT WOOL

A CARDIGAN IN TWEED EFFECT WOOL

MEASUREMENTS

To fit a 36-37 in. bust.

Length, 18 ins. from shoulder to lower edge.

Sleeve, 17 ins. at underarm.

MATERIALS

7 ozs. of tweed effect wool.

A little 3-ply wool in a colour to match.

A pair of No. 7 needles.

A pair of No. 9 needles.

DIRECTIONS

THE RIGHT FRONT

Cast on 56 sts., k. into the backs of the cast-on sts. Knit in ribbing of k. 2, p. 2, for 2½ ins.

Change to st.st.

With right side of work facing, inc. once in the last st., this will be the side seam edge.

From the top of the ribbing to the beginning of the armhole is 8 ins. In working this, inc. in the last st. of every 6th row (side seam edge) and k. 2 tog. at the beginning of every plain row after the 12th row from the ribbing (front edge).

When work measures 8 ins. from the ribbing (10½ ins. in all), commence the armhole shaping. The front edge decreasings change, too.

ARMHOLE SHAPING

With wrong side of work facing, cast off 8 sts.

Cast off 2 sts. at the beginning of the next 2 rows, commencing at the armhole.

K. 2 tog. at the beginning of the next 2 rows, commencing at the armhole.

At the same time, k. 2 tog. at the beginning of every other plain row, only, for 7 more decreasings at the front edge. Afterwards, no more shapings are worked at this edge.

Knit the armhole straight, without further shaping at the armhole edge until it measures 7 ins.

SHOULDER SHAPING

With wrong side of work facing, cast off one-third of the sts. on the needle, turn and p. back.

Cast off the same number at the beginning of the next row, turn and p. back.

Cast off the remainder.

THE LEFT FRONT

Knit the left front like the right front, working all shapings at the opposite ends of the rows so that the fronts will face.

THE BACK

Cast on 72 sts., k. into the backs of the cast-on sts. Knit in ribbing of k. 2, p. 2, for 2½ ins.

At each side seam follow the directions for the side seam of the front.

Rep. the armhole shapings at both sides and ignore the front edge shaping.

When the back armhole measures 7 ins., shape the shoulders.

BACK SHOULDERS

At the beginning of the next 6 rows, cast off the same number of sts. that were cast off each time on the front shoulder.

THE SLEEVES (both alike)

Cast on 36 sts., k. into the backs of the cast-on sts. Knit in ribbing of k. 2, p. 2, for 2 ins.

Change to st.st.

Knit until sleeve measures 17 ins. from the beginning, inc. on the first st. of every 9th and 10th row.

SHAPING THE TOP

At the beginning of the next 2 rows, cast off 6 sts. K. 2 tog. at the beginning of the next 10 rows. K. 2 tog. at each end of the next 10 rows. Cast off.

EDGE BAND

With a small amount of wool to match the dark colour in the tweed effect wool, and using the No. 9 needles, cast on 6 sts. Knit in rib of k. 1, p. 1, until the band is long enough to go round both fronts and back neck edge a little tightly.

THE SMALL BANDS for threading the tie through.

Cast on 4 sts. and knit in the same ribbing for 3 ins.

THE TIE END

Cast on 30 sts. with the tweed effect wool and No. 7 needles. Knit in ribbing of k. 1, p. 1, for 6 ins.

TO MAKE UP

Press the st.st. parts with a warm iron and a damp cloth. Sew up the side, shoulder and sleeve seams. Sew the ribbed band round the fronts and back neck. Pleat one end of the tie and sew this end on to the edge of the ribbing of the right front. Sew the two small bands on to the ribbing of the left front in such a way that loops are formed through which the tie end can be threaded. Set in the sleeves.

A DRESS IN STOCKING STITCH AND MOSS STITCH

These directions make a flared skirt. If a narrower skirt is desired, cast on less stitches and work less decreasings. See other variations at the end.

Measurements. To fit a 34-36 in. bust and 38-in. hips; length of bodice, in front, 17 ins.; length of skirt, in front, 30 ins.; length of sleeve seam, 14½ ins.; width all round lower edge, 62 ins.

Materials. 23 ozs. of 4-ply wool; a pair of No. 7 needles; 1¼ yds. of frilling for the neck and sleeves.

Tension. 6 sts. to 1 in.; 7 rows to 1 in.

DIRECTIONS

THE CENTRE FRONT PANEL

Cast on 61 sts. Knit into the backs of the cast-on sts. for the first row.

The sides of the panel are shaped by k. 2 tog. at the beginning of every 9th and 10th rows. This dec. must also be worked and allowed for when counting sts. at each end of the rows when making the moss-stitched points.

Knit in moss stitch for 2 ins. Change to st.st. for 1¼ ins. and then change again to moss stitch for another 2¼ ins. Finish with the right side of the work facing, and 55 sts. on the needle.

SHAPING THE POINTS IN MOSS STITCH

With wrong side of work facing, moss stitch 14 sts., p. 2, moss stitch 24 sts., p. 2, moss stitch to the end, turn.

2nd row, moss stitch 12 sts., k. 4, moss stitch 22 sts., k. 4, moss stitch to the end, turn.

Continue in this way, knitting 2 sts. less in the moss stitch groups and 2 sts. less in the k. or p. groups between, until all sts. are stocking stitched.

Continue knitting in st.st. for 21 ins., dec. all the time. Cast off on a purl row.

THE FOUR SKIRT PANELS

Cast on 71 sts. Knit as for the centre front panel to the beginning of the points. Finish on a right side row.

SHAPING THE MOSS STITCH POINTS

With wrong side of fabric facing, moss stitch 24 sts., p. 2, moss stitch 24 sts., p. 2, moss stitch to the end, turn.

2nd row, moss stitch 12 sts., k. 4, moss stitch 22 sts., k. 4, moss stitch 22 sts., k. 1. Continue shaping the points, —dec. the moss stitch groups and inc. the k. and p. groups between, as on the panel, and inc. the k. and p. groups at the right-hand side by 1 st. in each successive row, until all sts. are stocking stitched.

Continue knitting in st.st. like the panel, leaving out the last 4 decreasings. Make two panels like this and two with a half moss stitch point at the opposite end of the band.

THE BODICE

THE BACK

Cast on 85 sts. Knit into the backs of the cast-on sts. for the first row.

Shape the side seam by inc. on the first and last sts. of the 17th, 34th and 51st row.

Knit in st.st. for 2½ ins., change to moss stitch for 6 rows, then st.st. for 3 ins. Moss stitch again for 6 rows.

ARMHOLE SHAPING

At the beginning of the next 2 rows, cast off 7 sts.

At the beginning of the next 4 rows, k. 2 tog.

Continue without further shaping the armhole until work measures 15 ins. from the waist. Another band of 6 rows of moss stitch is worked 3 ins. above the last.

SHOULDER SHAPING

Cast off 8 sts. at the beginning of the next 6 rows.

Cast off remainder of sts.

RIGHT HALF OF FRONT

Cast on 46 sts. Knit into the backs of the cast-on sts. in the first row.

Follow the directions of the back for the side seam shapings (which will be worked at the ends of the rows only, because the centre front is straight), and for the striped moss stitch bands. The moss stitched bands are worked as for the back.

ARMHOLE SHAPINGS

Work the armhole shapings as for the back, but remember that they will be worked at one side; that is, the side seam end of the rows only. When the armhole measures 1½ ins., start the front neck shaping.

FRONT NECK SHAPING

K. 2 tog. at the beginning of every 4th row that commences at the front edge, until there are 24 sts. left.

Knit until the armhole measures 8 ins.

SHOULDER SHAPING

Cast off 8 sts. at the beginning of the next 3 rows that commence at the armhole.

LEFT HALF OF THE FRONT

Knit the left front in a similar way to the right; make all shapings at the reverse end of the rows.

THE SLEEVES

Cast on 57 sts. Knit into the backs of the cast-on sts. for the first row.

Knit the same width bands of moss stitch and st.st. as on the panels, as far as the base of the points; finish on a right side row.

THE SLEEVE POINTS

With wrong side of fabric facing, moss stitch 28 sts., p. 2, moss stitch 27 sts., turn.

(Continued on page 168)

A DRESS IN STOCKING STITCH AND MOSS STITCH

A DRESS IN STOCKING STITCH
AND MOSS STITCH

continued

2nd row, moss stitch 26 sts., k. 4, moss stitch 26 sts., k. I, turn.

3rd row, p. 2, moss stitch 24 sts., p. 6, moss stitch 24 sts., p. I.

4th row, k. 2, moss stitch 22 sts., k. 8, moss stitch 22 sts., k. 3.

Continue in this manner, lessening the number of moss stitch sts. by 2, inc. the number of k. or p. sts. between the two groups of moss stitch by 2, and inc. the number of k. or p. sts. at the ends by I in each successive row, until all sts. are worked in st.st.

Knit in st.st. until sleeve measures 15 ins.

Knit twice into the first stitch of every 5th and 6th row, after finishing the points.

SHAPING THE TOP

Cast off 6 sts. at the beginning of the next 2 rows.
K. 2 tog. at the beginning of the next 12 rows.
K. 2 tog. at each end of the next 10 rows.
Cast off the remaining sts.

TO MAKE UP THE DRESS

Each part of the dress must be pinned out on to the ironing blanket very carefully, so that it is not stretched, and pin it in a good shape and the required measures. Lay a damp cloth over the fabric and press very lightly with an iron that is not very hot. A hot iron will flatten the texture of the knitting too much.

If time permits, leave each piece pinned down until it is dry; but when this is not possible, let the pieces hang over a line for an hour or so.

SEWING THE SKIRT SEAMS

Make up the front half of the skirt and then the back half before the side seams.

For each half, take one centre panel and two side panels. Join a side panel to each side of the centre panel. Match half points on the centre panel to half points on the side panels and join with wrong sides outside, keeping both edges flat. Pin the top edges together first, then the bottom edges; next pin the ends of the moss stitch bands together and finally work between these points, pinning the seam securely. Sew together with self wool with oversewing.

Make the back of the skirt in a similar way with the other centre panel and the two side panels. Next, join the side seams of the skirt, pinning them like the other skirt seams. Press all the seams over a padded roller.

SEWING THE BODICE SEAMS

Join the side seams first, pinning the ends of the seam and the ends of the moss stitch bands together carefully. Join the shoulder seams, pinning the neck points and

then the other end at the armhole first. Press these seams over a roller.

SEWING THE SLEEVE SEAMS

Pin the seam together at the wrist, the top, and at the ends of the moss stitch bands first, then work between these points. Oversew the seams and press them lightly over the roller.

SETTING IN THE SLEEVES

Place the top of the sleeve to the shoulder seam of the bodice. The sleeve seam should be pinned ½ in. in front of the side seam. Pin the remainder of the sleeve, placing a little fullness on each side of the top, tightening it a little at the back and it will go flat round the front of the armhole. Oversew the sleeve and armhole edges together firmly but not tightly.

The frilling is sewn in just underneath the edge of the knitting; fix it to go up the right front, round the back neck and as far down the left front as required. This can be found by trying on the bodice. Cut off the frilling and use the remainder for the edges of the sleeves.

Lap the right front over the left front for about 4 sts. Sew firmly, leaving an opening for the head below the end of the frilling on the left side, if necessary. This opening can fasten invisibly with hooks and bars, or press studs, sewn on tape and then the tape is sewn on to the dress.

TO JOIN THE SKIRT AND BODICE TOGETHER

The skirt should be on the wrong side and the bodice on the right side. Mark with pins the centres of both waist lines. Slip the bodice down inside the skirt, so that waist lines are together. Pin the waist line together at the centres, the side seams and then between these points, easing fullness, if there happens to be any, evenly. Oversew this seam very strongly, but not tightly, and turn the dress on to the right side, and if the waist seam looks a bad line, give it an edge stitching with running stitches in wool.

SUGGESTED VARIATIONS

If a less flared skirt is desired, cast on 43 sts. for the centre panels and 53 sts. for each side panel. This will give a skirt width of 52 ins. With this lesser number of sts., knit plain bands of moss stitch on the skirt and leave out the points on the moss stitched bands of the sleeves to correspond, and shape the sides by dec. on the first sts. of every 14th and 15th rows, instead of every 9th and 10th rows.

The less experienced worker may leave out the points at the top of the second moss stitch bands, making two straight bands of moss stitch round the hem.

A PINAFORE DRESS WITH FLARED SKIRT

This little pinafore dress will be very useful to wear with a knitted blouse or a blouse of printed material.

Measurements. To fit a 34-in. bust; to fit 38-in. hips; length approximately 46 ins. The actual length may be adjusted as required by altering the length of the shoulder straps.

Materials. 20 ozs. of 4-ply wool; a pair of No. 9 needles.

DIRECTIONS

The bodice and the skirt are made separately and seamed together at the waist. Both are begun at the waist line. If the skirt drops too much in the first few days of wear, it will be an easy matter to unpick a few rows to shorten it. Also, if only a flared skirt is required, without the bodice, the directions for the lower part of the dress can be followed and the work mounted on to a petersham band.

THE BODICE

Front and back are alike, but the front has shorter straps.

Cast on 84 sts. Any fairly smooth fabric may be knitted, but do not choose a ribbing.

K. for 6 ins., inc. on the 1st st. in every 7th and 8th rows.

ARMHOLE SHAPING

Cast off 6 sts. at the beginning of the next 2 rows.

K. 2 tog. at the beginning of the next 12 rows.

K. 2 tog. at the beginning of every 4th and 5th row 6 times.

When the armhole measures 3 ins., begin to make the neck.

K. to within 2 sts. of the centre.

Cast off 4 sts. and k. to the end. Turn and k. back to the neck. Work on this group of sts. for one shoulder.

Cast off 2 sts. at the beginning of the next 2 rows that commence at the neck.

K. 2 tog. at the beginning of every row that begins at the neck until the shoulder strap is as wide as required. The two straps for the front of the bodice will be shorter than those on the back. The buckle for fastening the straps may be placed either about half-way from bust line to shoulder, or on the shoulder.

Join the wool to the neck edge of the sts. to be knitted up for the opposite shoulder and follow the directions of the first shoulder, making the shapings at the appropriate ends of the rows.

Shape the ends of the back straps by k. 2 tog. at the beginning of every row until all sts. have been disposed of.

THE SKIRT

The skirt is begun at the waist, and knitted in st.st.

Cast on 84 sts. K. for 7 ins., inc. once at each end of every other right side row.

Next row, k. 9, * k. twice into next st., k. 17*; rep. from * to * to within 9 sts. of the end, finish with k. twice into the next st., k. 8.

Rep. the shaping on every following 10th row, working 1 more plain st. after the increased st. in every consecutive shaping row.

K. until the skirt, plus the length of the bodice, measures 42 ins.

Change to g.st. and k. for a further 2 ins. Cast off very loosely.

TO MAKE UP

Press the work very carefully, being careful not to open out the fabric too much.

Join the bodice seams and the skirt seams. Press them without stretching and then join the bodice to the skirt, matching centre front and centre back points and side seams.

Turn up 1 in. of the 2-in. g.st. band round the bottom and hem neatly. Press in a good line.

A facing of crossway binding can be sewn round the inside of the neck and armhole edges to keep them in good shape.

Sew on the buckles to the front shoulder straps and the dress is ready to wear.

KNITTING FROM DRESSMAKERS' PATTERNS

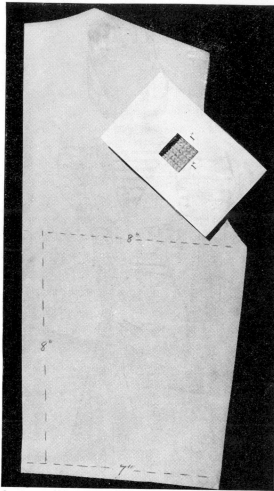

(in dressmakers' patterns the back is narrower than the front).

Now find the tension of your work, noting the number of stitches and rows to the inch in the wool and needles that will be used for the garment. On your pattern note down the measurements across the back, the waist, the bust, the depth from bust to waist and the depth from the shoulder, at the armhole end, and the bust line. From your tension find out how many stitches to cast on.

DIRECTIONS

Cast on the number of stitches for the waist line and knit the required number of rows to the bust, increasing on the appropriate rows to give the right number of stitches at the bust. Then shape the armholes and knit the required number of rows to give the depth from bust to the beginning of the shoulder. Cast off the stitches for the shoulder in 6 rows and then cast off the remainder for the back neck. Before beginning the piece of knitting for the front, mark the beginning of the front neck on your pattern. Knit the front like the back, shaping the neck according to the design.

Directions and hints on all the shapings mentioned will be found in another section of the book; refer to the Index for the page numbers. This second method is the easier to use.

I. In the pattern prepared for the second method, turnings were cut from the pattern except at the side seam. The I in. aperture in the card measures the tension, 5½ sts. to I in. and 7 rows to I in.

There are two methods of working from a paper pattern. One is to work to the measures of the pattern, without allowing turnings, and the other method is to make up both back and front to the measurements of the back pattern, allowing for turnings and making the necessary variations to the front and back neck line.

WORKING WITHOUT TURNINGS

Most bought paper patterns allow turnings, so first of all the pattern is prepared by having all the turnings cut away. From this point the process of work is the same as for the second method, except that the back and front are made to the back and front measures of the pattern, and not alike as in the second method.

WORKING WITH TURNINGS

As a rule, bought paper patterns allow ½-⅜ in. turnings on all edges, and this amount of turning left at the side seams will be just right for our purpose. Cut away the turnings from around the armhole, at the waist line, neck and shoulder seam, which will make the pattern larger at the side seam only. This will be right for working the back and the front from the back pattern

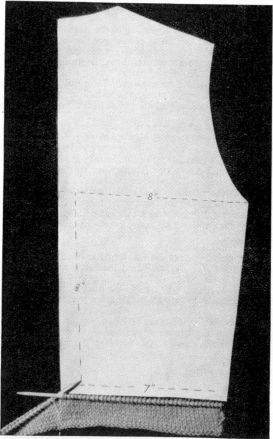

2. The knitting begun. There is an increase of I in. in the half-width of the pattern between waist and bust, therefore 6 sts. (taken to the next complete stitch) will have to be increased in 56 rows, so knit twice into the 1st st. of the 5th and 6th and then every 9th and 10th rows to the bust line.

PRESSING KNITTED FABRIC

One of the most important processes in the making of knitted garments is the pressing of the finished fabric, before it is sewn up. So many points must be borne in mind to preserve shape and condition of the work.

The texture of the fabric must be studied carefully, so that it is not flattened by too much pressure. Ribbed sections at wrists, neck, waist or knees are not pressed, in order to preserve their elasticity. Lace patterns can be spoilt by too much pressure being put on the

consider the finished sizes, width and length, of the section to be pressed. Pin the section out on the ironing cloth as near as possible to these measures; quite a lot of pins will be needed in order to make the edges a good shape. Lay the dampened muslin evenly over the work and proceed to press, rubbing the iron over the surface with a " wriggling " movement and being careful not to allow the weight of the iron to remain on any one spot and not letting the entire weight of the iron down on to the fabric.

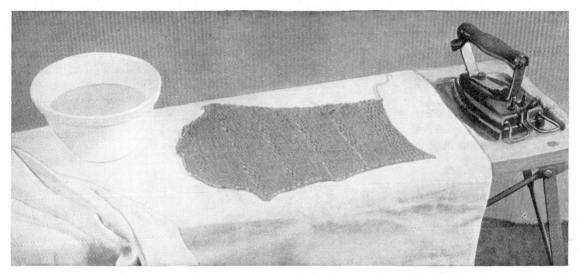

A section of a garment pinned out on the ironing cloth ready to be pressed. The muslin, wrung out in water, will be placed over it.

open stitches, pulling these too wide, or too long to the detriment of the pattern.

Another very important thing to remember is to press evenly. Never press more heavily on one part than on another; the difference will show badly when the garment is worn, the parts with more pressure will look more open and they will be of looser texture than the rest of the garment.

For pressing you will need an ironing blanket, preferably with a cotton sheet over it, a piece of muslin, a basin of water for damping the muslin as required, some pins and a very warm but not very hot iron.

Spread the blanket and sheet on the table, do not lay them too thick and soft. Next

When the whole surface of the work has been passed over, take away the muslin and leave the knitting to dry for a few minutes before removing it from the ironing cloth. Then take out the pins and hang the knitting over a line, away from heat, until it is perfectly dry.

Wring the muslin out in water again and press the next part of the garment.

Fine textured knitting needs very slight pressing, but a coarse textured fabric may need the heat of the iron to be applied until the muslin is quite dry and then iron again when the muslin is taken away.

Handle the knitting with care until it is quite dry, while it is still damp it will pull out of shape very easily.

MAKING UP KNITTED GARMENTS

There are various methods of making up knitted fabrics and it is a simple matter to choose the best one for the purpose on hand.

When the knitting has worked out to the exact measurement, the seams are joined with oversewing. Where the garment has worked out a little larger than required, the seam can be a flat one, similar to the flat seam used in dressmaking with the superfluous width taken off in the turnings and the turnings pressed open just as in a cloth seam. For sewing of this kind of seam the sewing machine may be used to get a well shaped and straight seam line. Sewing cotton or a mercerized thread should be used on the machine.

An especially good method for joining straight edges is to lay the pieces on the table with the edges to be joined side by side, and sew them together with straight stitches.

Whichever method is chosen, the first steps are the same. First the seam is pinned together, placing pins at either end of the seam and then working between these two points. The seam is then tacked to prevent one edge stretching more than the other. Do not work a back stitch anywhere when tacking, or the seam will pucker.

For working by hand, the thread for the permanent sewing should be the self wool, although sewing threads may sometimes be used. Work with a blunt wool needle so that the knitted stitches are not split.

If there is any doubt about the fit of the garment it can be tried on when tacked and any alterations made. Remember that the fabric cannot be cut, unless special provision was made for it (this process will be described in a later section). If the seam needs to be taken in, the method of working the seam will have to be altered. If an oversewn seam was intended, a flat seam will have to be worked so that more material can be taken up.

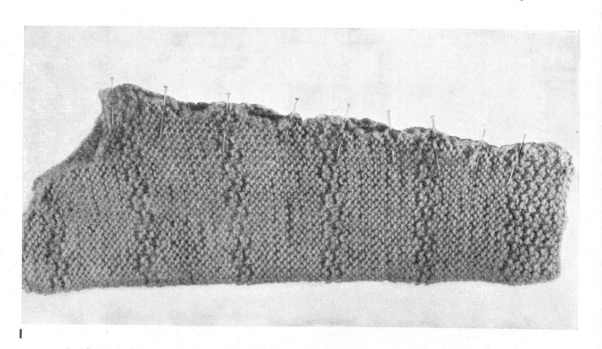

I. Preparing an oversewn seam. Both pinning and tacking should be done closely, so that the two layers of knitting will be held firmly together. Place the pins in at right angles to the edges of the seam. Tack with small evenly spaced stitches, using soft tacking cotton, and do not work any back stitches. End the thread with a knot, and when removing the tacks cut off the knot at one end and pull the thread out from the other end. It is not wise to hold the work over the fingers; a much better seam is made if the work is kept as flat as possible. Work one stitch at a time. A number of stitches pulled through will make a bad line.

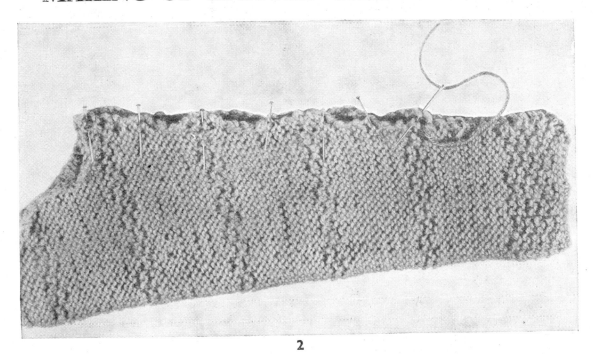

2

2. Oversewing a seam. The stitches are straight and the needle is placed slanting to the seam edge. In the case of a shoulder seam or other seam where cast off stitches are joined together, take the needle down below the cast off stitches, to prevent them standing above the seam in a ridge. Do not pull the wool tight, the stitches must give to the same tension as the knitted fabric. Also, do not leave the loops of the stitches so loose that the seam will gape. This seam may be lightly pressed with a warm iron and damp muslin.

3. A flat seam stitched by machine. The turnings are narrower than those on a cloth seam and they will not require to be neatened, neither can they be snipped, which makes this kind of seam, in knitting, unsuitable for curved edges. Press in the usual way, with the seam over a roller and a damp cloth under the iron. Be very careful not to stretch the seam in pressing.

4. Pulling the edges of a straight seam together. The stitches are made at right angles to the seam and the needle is slanting.

3

4

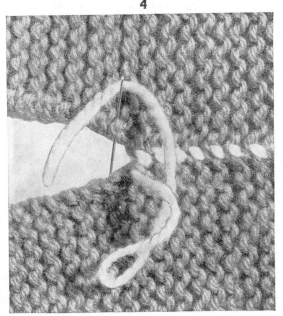

RE-KNITTING WOOL

Providing that the garment has not been too much worn, nor washed, it is possible to unpick it and knit up the wool again into something else. If the garment is soiled the wool can be washed after being unpicked.

Shake the garment well to remove all dust and then unpick the seams, taking out all the ends of the sewing wool. Then, taking each piece separately, find the last stitch of the casting off. Pull it out and proceed to unpick the knitting, being very careful not to stretch the wool by pulling hard. When the stitches catch they must be gently eased apart. Wind the wool into a ball round the fingers in the usual way.

The next step is to make the wool up into skeins. A skein holder will be useful for this. Drop the ball into a jam jar or a basin, tie the end of the wool to one arm of the holder and then turn the holder, winding the wool into a skein round its arms. If a skein holder is not available, wind the wool on the arm between the thumb and fingers and round the elbow.

The skein must be tied in several places to keep it in shape and to prevent the wool getting tangled; a long skein will need more ties than a short skein.

Now the wool can be washed, if necessary, in the usual way for washing woollens; this process will straighten the wool, too.

When the wool is not being washed it must be steamed to straighten out most of the crinkles. To do this either hang the skein in the steam from a kettle for a time, or else put it into a vegetable steamer and keep the water underneath boiling; do not place the lid on the steamer or the steam will condense and fall on to the wool. The wool must be dried thoroughly before being worked again.

I. The unpicked wool wound in skein form and ready to be washed or steamed. Note how the wool is tied.

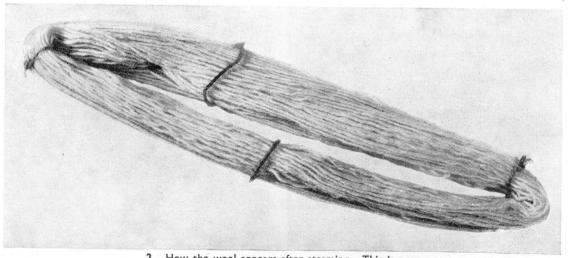

2. How the wool appears after steaming. This is now quite suitable for re-knitting; the crinkles seldom come right out.

KNITTED ROWS BETWEEN LACE ROWS AND A USEFUL SLIPPED STITCH STRIPE

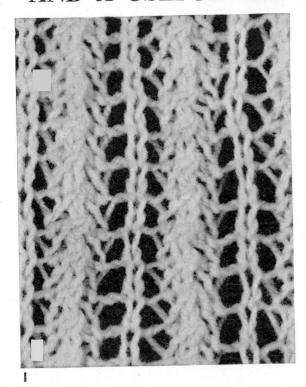

1

The two lace stitch patterns on this page show what a great difference is made in the texture when a purl, a plain and a purl row are worked between a lace stitch row. Except for the plain knitting, the working of both these patterns is the same.

I. The pattern requires a number of stitches divisible by 4.

DIRECTIONS
1st row, * k. 1, m. 1, k. 3 tog., m. 1*; repeat from * to * to the end.
2nd row, p.

3

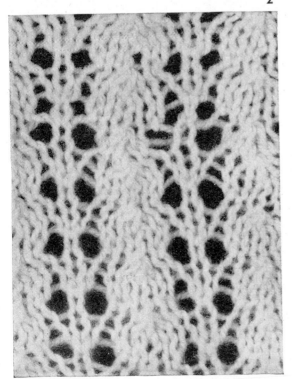

Repeat these **2** rows throughout. A very open fabric results.

2. Work rows 1 and 2 as in the previous pattern.

3rd row, k.

4th row, p.

Repeat these 4 rows throughout.

This is a much more attractive and interesting fabric.

3. A hard wearing surface with a slight stripe effect is gained by slipping an occasional stitch on a plain row. The pattern shown here is made by: k. 3, sl. 1, repeated to the end. The second row is all purl, and these two rows are worked throughout.

SOME INTERESTING TEXTURES

It is possible to design many interesting surface patterns or textures, by thickening some parts of the fabric and contrasting these with either purl or lace patterns.

1. This attractive pattern is sometimes called "blackberry" pattern, owing to its likeness to the berry. The pattern needs a number of stitches divisible by 4.

1st row, p. 3 tog., k. 1, p. 1, and k. 1 into the next stitch working all 3 sts. into the front of the loop.

2nd row, p.

3rd row, k. 1, p. 1, k. 1 into the first stitch, p. 3 tog. Repeat to the end.

4th row, p.

These 4 rows make the pattern.

2. Blackberry stripe is made by repeating the first 2 rows only.

3. An attractive leaf pattern is made quite easily with plain and purl contrast. The work is done by gradually increasing the number of plain stitches, without decreasing the purl stitches, until the required width of pattern is reached. Then the plain stitches are decreased until the original number of stitches is reached. Where the stitches are increased at the lower left-hand edge of the leaf, a row of holes is formed which gives the effect of a serrated leaf edge. The pattern requires a number of stitches divisible by 5.

1

2

3

DIRECTIONS (3 continued)

1st row, p. 4, k. twice into the next stitch; repeat to the end, finish with p. 4.

2nd row, k. 4, p. 2; repeat to the end, finish with k. 4.

3rd row, p. 4, k. 1, k. twice into next stitch; repeat to the end, finish with p. 4.

4th row, k. 4, p. 3; repeat to the end, finish with k. 4.

5th row, p. 4, k. 2, k. twice into next stitch; repeat to the end, finish with p. 4.

6th row, k. 4, p. 4; repeat to the end, finish with k. 4.

7th row, p. 4, k. 3, k. twice into next stitch; repeat to the end, finish with p. 4.

8th row, k. 4, p. 5; repeat to the end, finish with k. 4.

9th row, p. 4, k. 2 tog., k. 3; repeat to the end, finish with p. 4.

10th row, k. 4, p. 4; repeat to the end, finish with k. 4.

11th row, p. 4, k. 2 tog., k. 2; repeat to the end, finish with p. 4.

12th row, k. 4, p. 3; repeat to the end, finish with k. 4.

13th row, p. 4, k. 2 tog., k. 1; repeat to the end, finish with p. 4.

14th row, k. 4, p. 2; repeat to the end, finish with k. 4.

15th row, p. 4, k. 2 tog.; repeat to the end, finish with p. 4.

16th row, knit all plain.

These 16 rows make up one pattern. The second pattern may be moved 2 sts. to the left, like the illustration, if desired, or the pattern can be repeated in the same place at intervals of a few rows.

CLOQUE FABRICS

The quilted pattern effects of cloque materials can be made in knitted fabrics by working on the principle of the "blackberry" pattern given on the last page.

Also, the pocket weave principle of cloque materials, where the pattern is made by a second and looser layer of fabric, can be imitated as described in the directions for the third illustration on this page.

1. A slightly broken surface is given to plain fabric if, in one row, a stitch is knitted twice and in the next row these two are purled together. Two plain rows are worked and then the pattern is repeated.

2. The pocket type of cloque pattern is very simple to knit. One stitch, or a group of two or three stitches, are slipped purlwise in two or three consecutive rows, with several stocking stitch rows between.

3. A cloque fabric on the principle of " blackberry " pattern. The circular group is made in the following manner: * K. 6, then k. 1, p. 1 and k. 1 into the next stitch, and again k. 1, p. 1, k. 1 into the next stitch*. Repeat from * to *. (Any number of stitches may be worked between the groups.) In the next row, purl 3 sts. together where 3 sts. were knitted in one in the previous row. In the next row, knit three times into two more stitches, one more on each side of those that were knitted three times in the first row.

Purl the next row, working 3 sts. together four times to dispose of those that were increased in the previous row. Repeat the last 2 rows and then the first 2 rows to complete the circles. Knit several rows in stocking stitch and then, either repeat the circles again, or work one " blackberry " stitch to divide the circles, as in the illustration.

LACE AND BLOCK PATTERNS

Bands of lace and block patterns are useful when making jumpers and dresses for more formal wear. The plain bands help to strengthen the open patterns, and if they are carefully contrasted in fabric the effect will be very pleasant.

1. Quite a simple pattern for a light jumper. The lace band is made in the following way:—

K. 1, m. 1, k. 3 tog., m. 1; repeat to the end, finish with k. 1. The next 3 rows are knitted purl, plain and purl, and then the pattern row is repeated again. Make this band four or five rows of holes wide, and then work a band of equal width in either stocking stitch, or moss stitch. Similar bands can be worked vertically.

2. This illustration shows a horizontal banding of lace and moss stitch. The lace stitch pattern is made thus:—

K. 1, m. 1, k. 1, k. 3 tog., k. 1, m. 1; repeat to the end, finish with k. 1, k. 3 tog., k. 1, m. 1, k. 1. Vertical bands of this pattern are attractive, too; the narrow stripes in the lace pattern emphasizing the vertical bands.

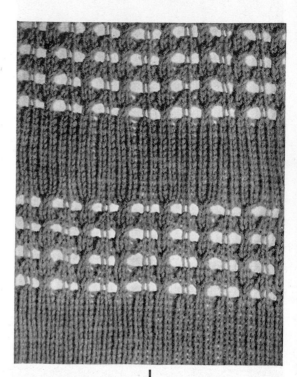

1

2

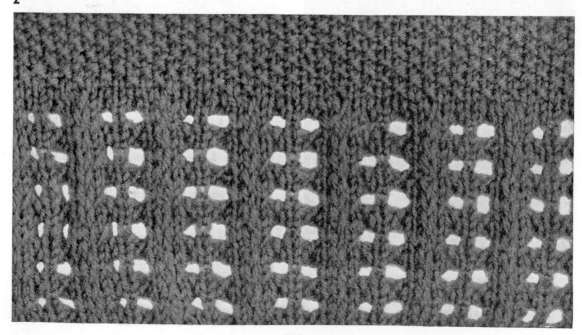

PART IV

CONSTRUCTIVE KNITTING
SHAPING LEGS OF SOCKS

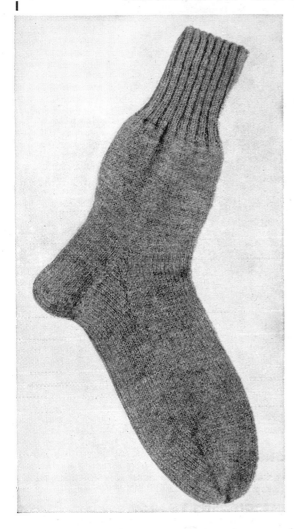

1. A plain sock leg with decreased stitches at the centre back making the shaping below the calf. To work the shapings:

Knit the top ribbing.

Knit 20 plain rounds.

1st shaping, commencing at the beginning of the round, k. 1, k. 2 tog., knit to within 3 sts. of the end of the round, sl. 1, k. 1, p.s.s.o., k. 1.

Knit the next 3 rounds without shaping.

Repeat these 4 rounds 3 times more.

Knit without further shaping until the leg measures the required length.

This picture shows a man's heavy sock, which has the leg the same length as the foot. When a longer leg is required work more plain rounds before and after the leg decreasings.

2. Leg shapings can also be made by the pattern worked into the leg. Here, an elastic fabric is made with cable stitch, the back cabling taking the place of decreasings to shape the leg. In the sock shown here, there is a plain panel at the centre front to keep that part of the sock flat; a row of cable at the side and another cable at the centre back. To help shape the sock, the side cable starts a short way down from the ribbing and the back cable begins further down still. The cable takes 8 sts., there are 3 p. sts. on each side of the cable and 2 plain bands of 6 sts. each, between the back and side cables. The remainder of the stitches are in the centre front plain panel.

2

One of the most important considerations in making socks is to obtain a shape that will keep the leg of the sock in place.

Shapings are made in two ways, by decreasing the number of stitches in that part of the leg which comes below the calf, and by ribbing. Ribbed sock legs do not require shaping with decreasings.

Socks with ribbed legs are the easiest to make. The top ribbing is done with k. 2, p. 2, and the remainder of the leg is knitted in a wider rib of k. 5, p. 1, or a similar grouping, to suit the number of stitches in the round.

A PAIR OF TENNIS SOCKLETS

MEASUREMENTS

To fit a 9½-in. foot.
Length of leg, before embroidered top is turned over, 6½ ins.

MATERIALS

2 ozs. of 3-ply wool in white or cream.
1 oz. of 3-ply wool in the desired colour for the top.
Four No. 11 needles, pointed at both ends.

DIRECTIONS

Using the coloured wool, cast on 60 sts.; that is, 20 sts. on each of three needles.

Knit in ribbing of k. 1, p. 1, for ¾ in.

Change to white wool and knit in st.st. for 1 in.

Change to coloured wool and knit in the ribbing for 1½ ins. Turn work inside out.

Change to white wool and knit plain until work measures 6½ ins. altogether.

THE HEEL

Either French or Dutch heel may be worked. For proportions for working these, see Index.

INSTEP SHAPING

After the sts. have been picked up from the sides of the heel, knit 3 plain rounds, then make 7 instep decreasings. (See Index.)

THE FOOT

K. straight until the foot measures 7¼ ins.

THE TOE

Either the round or the flat toe shapings may be worked; for their proportions, see directions on the appropriate page.

EMBROIDERING THE TOP

Using the same colour as in the top of the socklet, or else a contrasting colour, work diagonal lines of stem stitch, picking up the side of a knitted stitch each time and going 1 st. lower, or higher according to the direction of the line, for each stitch.

Press the socklets lightly, avoiding the top; turn over the top and the socklets are ready to wear.

SUGGESTIONS

These socklets, worn inside sports shoes, will be given hard wear. To strengthen them at the heel and toe, where most rub will come, knit in some coarse sewing cotton with the wool. When they have to be darned, lay a piece of cotton net under the hole and work the darning stitches through it. Cut away superfluous net close to the sock. Club colours can be used in the bands and embroidery, or a bright colour scheme can be worked in with dark bands and scarlet, green and yellow in several rows of embroidery.

FRENCH HEEL

The heel of a sock, or stocking, is knitted like a cap to fit over the heel of the foot. It is knitted as a continuation of the back of the leg, leaving the stitches across the front of the leg unknitted for the time being.

A square of knitting is made first and then the heel is turned to make the cap shape. Then a number of stitches are picked up from each side of the heel and these, together with the remaining heel stitches and the stitches left at the front of the leg are arranged into a round on the three needles and the foot is worked.

DIRECTIONS FOR A FRENCH HEEL

Presuming that there are 68 sts. on the needles at the end of the leg, proceed as follows:—

K. 17 sts. ($\frac{1}{4}$) from the first needle and sl. 17 sts. ($\frac{1}{4}$) from the third needle on to the needle which now holds the 17 sts. just knitted.

Put the remainder of the sts. ($\frac{1}{2}$) on to two needles; these are left for the foot.

Working on the 34 heel sts., knit a square in st.st.; that is, I row plain and the next row purl. All first sts. must be slipped and all last sts. in the purl rows must be knitted as plain. This will make it very easy to pick up the sts. down each side of the heel. Work must finish on a purl row.

TURNING THE HEEL

K. 20, k. 2 tog., turn.
P. 7, p. 2 tog., turn.
K. 8, k. 2 tog., turn.
P. 9, p. 2 tog., turn.

Continue in this manner, knitting and purling one more st. before the 2 sts. worked together, until all the sts. are worked in I row.

Then k. half the number of sts.; this will bring the wool to the beginning of the round again (also it will be the centre of the heel).

With the first needle of the round, k. the remainder of the heel sts. With a spare needle, pick up 18 sts. down the left-hand side of the heel and k. these on to the first needle, working into the backs of the loops.

Sl. all the instep or top-foot sts. on to one needle and k. them on to the second needle of the round.

With the spare needle, pick up 18 sts. from the opposite side of the heel and k. them, working into the backs of the loops. K. the second half of the heel sts. on to the same needle.

The sts. should now be arranged with the round commencing at the centre of the heel, with half the heel sts. and those picked up down the left-hand side on the first needle, the instep sts. on the second needle, and the sts. picked up down the right-hand side of the heel and half the heel sts. on the third needle.

Work three plain rounds and then k. the instep shapings. (See Index for directions.)

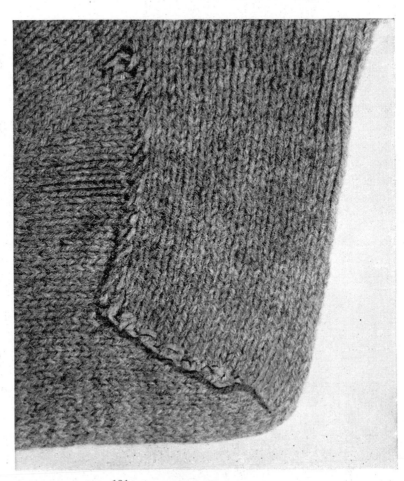

A DUTCH HEEL

The easiest heel to turn is the Dutch or square heel. One is seen on the sock illustrated on page 179. The shaping or turning stitches run at right angles to the sides of the heel and the under flap of the heel is as wide as the under part of the foot.

The first part of a Dutch heel is similar to a French heel. Divide the stitches in the same way as for a French heel, that is, one quarter of the stitches and the last quarter of the number of stitches on one needle for the heel, and the second and third quarters on two other needles to be left for the instep.

On the heel stitches knit a square in stocking stitch, that is, one row plain and the next row purl. Slip all first stitches and knit plain the last stitch in every purl row; this will simplify the picking up of the stitches down each side of the heel.

TURNING THE HEEL
The heel square must finish on a purl row.
K. 18, turn.
P. 7, p. 2 tog., turn.
K. 7, k. 2 tog., turn.
Continue in this way until all sts. have been knitted in one row.
From this point proceed as for the French heel. The sts. will be divided in the same way for the new rounds for the foot.

INSTEP SHAPINGS

In order to bring the foot down at a slight angle to the leg a number of decreasings are worked at each side of the heel. These are called instep shapings. Their effect on the direction of the foot can be seen in the illustration on page 179.

An illustration on this page shows a close up of the stitches themselves.

When the heel and instep stitches have been arranged again on to the three needles to begin the foot, knit 3 plain rounds.

1st shaping, k. to within 3 sts. of the end of the first needle, k. 2 tog., k. 1.
K. the instep sts.
On the third needle, k. 1, sl. 1, k. 1, p.s.s.o., k. to the end.
Knit 2 plain rounds.
Rep. these 3 rounds 4 times more.
Continue without shaping for the foot.

THE FLAT TOE

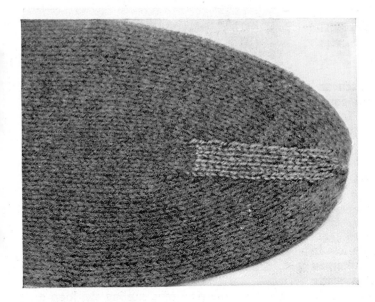

The shaping of the toe will take about 2½ ins. of knitting for a tennis sock knitted in 3-ply, and about 3 ins. of knitting in a man's sock made in 4-ply wool. Work the foot without shaping until it measures the length of the toe short of the required finished length. If the foot is to measure 11 ins. when finished and the wool is 4-ply, commence the toe shapings when work measures 8½ ins. from the back of the heel.

TO SHAPE THE TOE

Arrange the sts. on the three needles so that there is one-quarter of the number on the first needle, one-half on the second needle, and one-quarter on the third needle.

The shapings are worked at each side of the foot, and at each end of the instep or top-foot sts.

1st needle, k. to within 3 sts., k. 2 tog., k. 1.

2nd needle, k. 1, sl. 1, k. 1, p.s.s.o., k. to within 3 sts., k. 2 tog., k. 1.

3rd needle, k. 1, sl. 1, k. 1, p.s.s.o., k. to the end.

K. 2 rounds without shaping.

Rep. these 3 rounds 6 times more.

Then work 2 dec. rounds without the plain rounds between. Knit the first needle, sl. the sts. of the third needle on to the first needle. All sts. will now be on two needles; lay these side by side and k. a st. from each as 1 st. and cast off at the same time.

This row should be worked fairly tightly.

A ROUND TOE

Knit the length of the foot as described for the flat toe. Arrange the stitches on the three needles as for the flat toe. Count the number of stitches and then consider whether 9, 10 or 11 will divide into that number. If there are one or two stitches over they must be disposed of by being knitted together at the side of the foot.

1st round. For a multiple of 9, k. tog. every eighth and ninth sts.

For a multiple of 10, k. tog. every ninth and tenth sts.

For a multiple of 11, k. tog. every tenth and eleventh sts.

Knit 2 plain rounds without shaping.

Now knit four or five shaping rounds with 2 plain rounds between each, knitting 1 st. less in each successive round between the 2 sts. that are knitted together.

The last shaping round should have 3 or 4 sts. between the 2 knitted together.

Break off the wool, leaving an end long enough to thread through the remaining sts. and to draw them up. Fasten off the wool strongly.

THE AUTO HEEL

The auto heel is a less popular method of turning the heel of a sock or stocking. The heel itself is shallower than in either the French or Dutch methods, but the shaping makes a nicely rounded heel.

Arrange the stitches as for the Dutch and French heels, that is, the first and fourth quarters on one needle to be knitted for the heel, and the instep stitches, or those making the second and third quarters, on two needles, which will be left unknitted until the heel is made. The wool should come at the right-hand end of the heel stitches.

All first stitches are slipped.

Purl the heel stitches.

Now work in stocking stitch, one row plain and the next row purl, knitting 1 stitch less in every row until there are 9 stitches left unknitted on each side of the small group in the centre that have been knitted. The last row should be a purl row. Turn and knit back along the centre stitches just knitted purlwise. Pick up the strand between the last stitch, just knitted, and the first unknitted stitch, place it on the left-hand needle and knit this loop with the first unknitted stitch; turn and repeat this

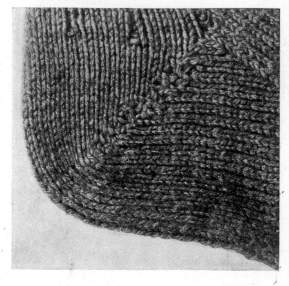

process on the purl row, purling the loop and unknitted stitch at the end of the row.

Continue in this manner until all the stitches are knitted again.

Arrange the stitches for the foot as described in the French heel, but pick up only four stitches at each side of the heel.

KNITTING SOCKS IN SECTIONS

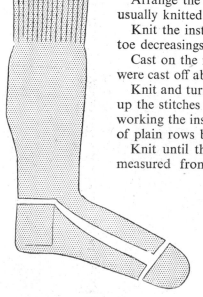

When socks wear out very quickly at the heel or the toe it is a very good plan to knit the sock in sections and join them together with oversewing, so that the heel or the toe can be replaced quickly and easily.

Knit the leg as far as the heel.

Arrange the instep stitches on one needle and cast off the stitches that are usually knitted for the heel.

Knit the instep stitches on two needles for as long as is required up to the toe decreasings. This should be measured against another sock. Cast off.

Cast on the number of stitches required for the heel (the same number that were cast off above the heel). Use two needles.

Knit and turn the heel, using either the Dutch or the French methods. Pick up the stitches at the side of the heel and continue knitting in stocking stitch, working the instep shapings at each end of the row and with the same number of plain rows between each shaping.

Knit until the sole of the foot is the same length as the top of the foot, measured from the beginning of the instep shapings. Cast off.

The toe should be knitted on four needles.

Cast on the same number of stitches that were cast off at the end of the sole and the end of the top foot, added together, and arrange them on three needles as described for either the flat or the round toe. Work two plain rounds before starting the toe decreasings.

Press each part of the sock and join together very carefully with oversewing, keeping the work as flat as possible.

TOPS FOR SOCKS AND STOCKINGS

Golf stockings and schoolboys' socks require a turnover at the top which will grip the leg sufficiently to prevent the stocking or sock slipping in wrinkles down to the ankle. The turnover can also be used to hide an elastic garter.

Club and school colours can be introduced in a pattern into the turnover, or the pattern in the turnover can contrast with the pattern used in the leg.

The turnover replaces the usual ribbed top and it is knitted half as long again as the amount that is turned back over the sock. If the turnover measures 3 ins., it will be knitted for 4½ ins. before the usual leg fabric is commenced. This is done to ensure that the top edge will grip well.

Turn the work inside out before starting the leg of the sock, to bring the top on to the right side of its fabric when it is turned over.

A ribbing of k. 1, p. 1 is usually introduced into the turnover, wider ribbing of k. 2, p. 2 is seldom used because it is not so decorative.

1

2. Another kind of turnover, which contrasts its pattern with that of the sock leg.
Cast on 4 sts. less than are required for the sock leg. Knit the first round into the backs of the stitches and then change to ribbing of k. 1, p. 1 for 11 rounds. Change to moss stitch for 6 rounds; change to ribbing for 9 rounds; change to moss stitch for 6 rounds; change again to ribbing for 30 rounds.
Knit the next round plain, increasing once at each quarter and then proceed with the leg.

2

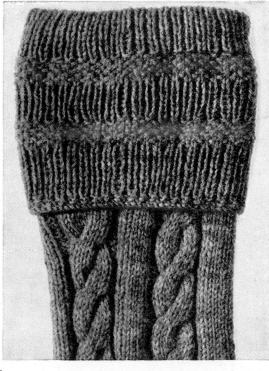

1. An easily knitted turnover, using two colours. Cast on the number of stitches required for the leg of the sock, minus 4. Thus, if the directions for the sock state " cast on 84 sts.," 80 sts. will be required for this top. Use the colour that is being introduced for decoration. K. 1 round plain, working into the backs of the stitches. Knit in ribbing of k. 1, p. 1 for 8 rounds. Break off the wool, join on the wool that is being used for the main part of the work and rib for 5 rounds. Break off the wool, join on the first colour and rib 3 rounds. Change to the second colour and rib 7 rounds; change to the first colour and rib 3 rounds; change to second colour and rib 5 rounds; change again to the first colour and rib for a further 26 rounds.
Join on the wool to be used for the remainder of the work. Knit the next round plain, increasing once at the end of every quarter of the stitches, so that there is now the required number of stitches on the needle. Continue to knit the sock, or stocking, according to directions. A wide ribbed leg, k. 6, p. 1, or a similar grouping, is more practical than a plain fabric.

DESIGNS FOR SOCK AND STOCKING TOPS

Here are the directions for knitting various types of tops, which can be added to socks or stockings.

Proportions for groups of stitches are given as well as numbers of stitches, so that the designs can be adapted to the number of stitches on the needles.

Any width of ribbing may be worked before and after the patterns, but the widths stated in the directions have been planned to suit the patterns.

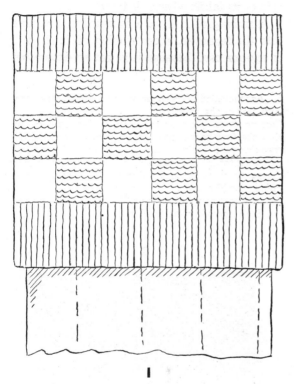

1

2. A diagonal ribbing of 12 purl and 6 plain sts. If the reverse side of the work is preferred, do not turn the knitting inside out after the second band of ribbing. Work the first inch of knitting in ribbing of k. 1, p. 1. **Next round,** p. 12, k. 6: repeat all round. **Next round,** move the pattern 1 st. farther along the needle. The work will begin k. 1, * p. 12, k. 6 *; repeat from * to * to the last 5 sts., finish with k. 5. The last 5 knitted sts. make the group of 6 with the first knitted stitch. Continue knitting, moving the pattern 1 st. along all the time, until the pattern band measures the required width. The one in the illustration measures 2¼ ins. Change to the ribbing again and knit it for 3 ins. before starting the leg of the sock.

2

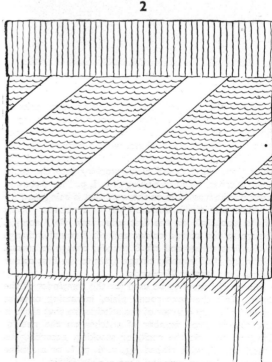

1. Knit 1 in. in ribbing of k. 1, p. 1. Divide the number of stitches into an even number of groups of a few stitches each. 72 sts. will divide into 12 groups of 6 sts. Each group will be the width of one square of the checkered pattern on this top. Work the first 6 rounds in p. 6, k. 6, continued all round. The next 6 rounds are worked k. 6, p. 6, all round. Then repeat the first 6 rounds. Knit in ribbing of k. 1, p. 1 for 3 ins. The top is folded over to show 1 in. of ribbing above the pattern.

MORE ADVANCED DESIGNS FOR TOPS

The first design on this page is based on the principle of bunching, worked with a slipped stitch.

The second design is a development of the previous patterns, where contrast of purl and plain fabric makes the pattern.

I. If preferred, there may be a third bunched band in this top.

Knit the first inch in ribbing of k. I, p. I, and then knit 3 rounds in plain knitting. Divide the number of stitches into 6, or 7, whichever is best. With 72 sts. in the round divided by 6, the result will be 12. Thus there will be 6 groups of 12 sts. in each.

Next round, p. II, sl. I; repeat all round.
Repeat this round 4 times more.
Knit 6 plain rounds.

Next round, p. 5, * sl. I, p. II *; repeat from * to * to within the last 7 sts., finish with sl. I, p. 6.
Repeat this round 4 times more.
Knit 3 plain rounds and then knit 3 ins. of the ribbing before commencing the leg of the sock.

2

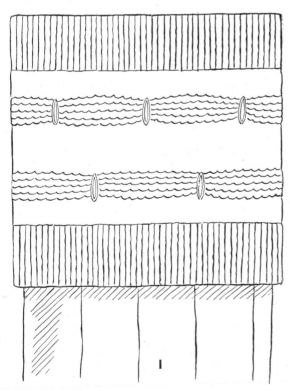

1

2. This is a much more complicated pattern and so actual numbers of stitches will be given.
The pattern requires 72 sts. in the round.
Knit I in. of ribbing in k. I, p. I.
Knit 2 rounds plain.
Now begin the pattern.
1st round, p. 5, k. 8, p. 10, k. 8, p. 10, k. 8, p. 10, k. 8, p. 5.
2nd round, p. 4, k. 4, p. 2, k. 4, p. 8, k. 4, p. 2, k. 4, p. 8, k. 4, p. 2, k. 4, p. 8, k. 4, p. 2, k. 4, p. 4.
3rd round, p. 3, k. 4, p. 4, k. 4, p. 6, k. 4, p. 4, k. 4, p. 6, k. 4, p. 4, k. 4, p. 6, k. 4, p. 4, k. 4, p. 3.
4th round, p. 2, k. 4, p. 6, k. 4, p. 4, k. 4, p. 6, k. 4, p. 4, k. 4, p. 6, k. 4, p. 4, k. 4, p. 6, k. 4, p. 2.
5th round, p. I, k. 4, p. 8, k. 4, p. 2, k. 4, p. 8, k. 4, p. 2, k. 4, p. 8, k. 4, p. 2, k. 4, p. 8, k. 4, p. I.
6th round, k. 4, p. 10, k. 8, p. 10, k. 8, p. 10, k. 8, p. 10, k. 4.
7th round, k. 3, p. 5, k. 2, p. 5, k. 6, p. 5, k. 2, p. 5, k. 6, p. 5, k. 2, p. 5, k. 6, p. 5, k. 2, p. 5, k. 3.
8th round, k. 2, p. 5, k. 4, p. 5, k. 4, p. 5, k. 4, p. 5, k. 4, p. 5, k. 4, p. 5, k. 4, p. 5, k. 4, p. 5, k. 2.
9th round, k. I, p. 5, k. 6, p. 5, k. 2, p. 5, k. 6, p. 5, k. 2, p. 5, k. 6, p. 5, k. 2, p. 5, k. 6, p. 5, k. I.
10th round, p. 5, k. 8, p. 10, k. 8, p. 10, k. 8, p. 10, k. 8, p. 5.
Working from the round before the last, knit the directions in reverse order.
Knit 2 plain rounds. Knit 3 ins. in ribbing and continue with the sock leg.

DRAFTS AND GUIDES FOR SOCKS

The knitting of socks without a set of directions is not very difficult. It is possible to make a draft or a brown paper pattern to work from, and by dividing this pattern up into the required sections and calculating the positions of all the shapings, a pair of socks to fit an individual size can be made quite easily.

Points that should be known. The size of the foot measured from the back of the heel to the end of the toes; the type of sock required, i.e., whether heavy, light or medium; the length of leg; and the style of fabric to be knitted.

The draft can be drawn on paper to quarter scale, that is, quarter size, or it can be cut from a sheet of brown paper full size. The full size pattern is the handiest.

2. Man's medium and light-weight sock. Proportions: Leg above heel, three times depth of foot; ribbing, depth of foot; width of heel and instep shaping, one section of foot; centre foot, two sections of foot; toe, one section of foot. For sizes larger than 11-in. foot, add extra length to centre foot.

For the full size pattern a piece of paper, L shape, with both arms 4 ins. wide, is needed.

Cut the lower arm as long as the foot; fold this into four equal sections. The toe shapings will take up the first section, starting from the right; the foot (centre) will take the next two sections; and the heel and instep shapings together will take the last section.

The length of the leg depends on the kind of sock to be made; a heavy sock is usually a little shorter than a light-weight sock. The legs are divided into sections, each section being equal to a section of the foot.

For a heavy sock the entire leg length, measured from the *top* of the heel is three times the width of one foot section, the ribbing taking one and the leg taking two sections. (*See* diagram.)

Medium and light-weight socks have longer legs, they are three times the depth of the foot (measured from the upper to the lower edge), with the ribbing taking up the top section.

The proportions of boys' socks are different. The legs are shorter than the feet.

Cut the L-shaped piece of brown paper with the arms 3½ ins. wide. The lower arm is the length of the foot and divided into four as before, but the leg is only twice as long as the depth of the foot and the ribbed top takes only three-quarters of one of these sections. (*See* diagram on page 189.)

2

TOP

LEG

HEEL · CENTRE FOOT · TOE

LENGTH OF FOOT
DIVIDED INTO 4 EQUAL SECTIONS

1

TOP

LEG

HEEL · CENTRE FOOT · TOE

← - - - - - - - LENGTH OF FOOT - - - - - - - →
DIVIDED IN TO 4 EQUAL SECTIONS

1. Man's heavy sock. Proportions: Leg above heel, three divisions of foot; ribbed top, one division of foot; width of heel and instep shaping, one division of foot; centre foot, two divisions of foot; Toe, one division of foot. For sizes larger than 11-in. foot, add extra length to centre foot.

Golf socks, or stockings as they are sometimes called, have different proportions for the leg. The foot is the same as an ordinary sock. The length of the leg, measured from the top of the heel, is three times the depth of the foot plus the depth of the turnover when turned down, ready for wear.

The diagrams will illustrate how to make a draft or a paper pattern.

DRAFTS AND GUIDES FOR SOCKS
continued

4. Golf stocking. Proportions: Leg, three times depth of foot; top when turned over, three-quarters of depth of foot. Foot is divided as for sock.

3. Boy's sock. Proportions: Leg, twice depth of foot; width of heel and instep shaping, quarter of foot length; centre foot, one-half of foot length; toe, one-quarter of foot length; ribbing, three-quarters of depth of foot.

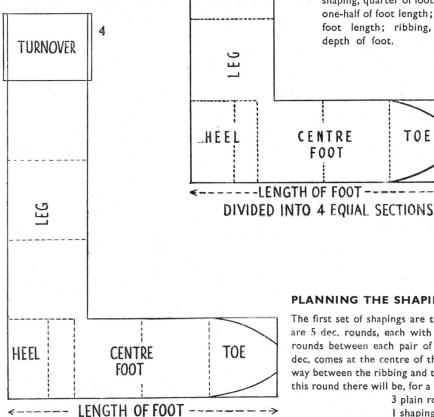

PLANNING THE SHAPINGS

The first set of shapings are the leg decreasings. There are 5 dec. rounds, each with 2 sts. dec. and with plain rounds between each pair of dec. rounds. The middle dec. comes at the centre of the leg section, that is, half-way between the ribbing and the top of the heel. Above this round there will be, for a heavy sock:—

        3 plain rounds
        1 shaping round
        3 plain rounds
        1 shaping round

altogether 8 rounds, which is about ¾ in. of knitting, calculated from the tension used before. Therefore, it is known that the first dec. round will be worked when the sock measures ¾ in. less than 2 sections. The position of this round could be marked on the pattern. The heel is commenced when the sock leg is the required number of sections long. The heel and instep shapings will take roughly one section of the foot. Knit the centre foot without shapings until it measures 2 sections long from the instep decreasings. Then commence the decreasings for the toe.

HOW TO USE THE DRAFTS AND PATTERNS

The worker's tension must be known, i.e., the knitter must know how many stitches and how many rows go to the inch of knitting. From the tension calculate the number of stitches to cast on. If the leg is to be 4 ins. wide and the worker's tension is 10 sts. to the in. then about 80 sts. will be required in the round. If 11 rows go to 1 in. of knitting and each section is 4 ins. long, then about 44 rows will be worked in the top ribbing. Of course, the depth of this top ribbing can be varied as desired. Some like it 3½ ins. wide (but it should not be much narrower than the section marked for it on the draft), and an extra ½ in. is added to the length of the leg between the ribbing and the heel, so that the total length remains the same. There will be about 88 rows in the leg section and about 88 rows in the centre foot. Crease the paper patt. to mark the various divisions and test the work against it as knitting proceeds.

DIRECTIONS FOR SOCKS

Detailed instructions are given below for ordinary types of socks. The experienced knitter will be able to adapt them to individual requirements and designs.

The shapings at the toe and heel can be changed round, Dutch heels can be used instead of French heels, and flat toes can be worked instead of round toes. The methods of working these parts will be found on the appropriate pages. Test frequently against paper pattern.

A MAN'S HEAVY SOCK

For draft of pattern see page 188. By making sock drafts these directions can be followed to make the sock any size required.

It is assumed that the knitter has made the pattern and that it is creased into the various sections for the leg and foot.

Materials required. 4 ozs. of 4-ply wool; 4 No. 11 needles with points at both ends.

Tension. 7½ sts. to 1 in.

DIRECTIONS

Cast on 60 sts. (7½ sts. by 8 ins. = 60 sts.), 20 sts. on each of three needles.

Knit in ribbing of k. 2, p. 2, for 4 ins.

Change to st.st., or a ribbing of k. 5, p. 1, until work measures ¾ in. less than the first 2 sections. Now commence the leg shapings.

1st round, k. 1, k. 2 tog., k. to within 3 sts. of the end of the round, sl. 1, k. 1, p.s.s.o., k. 1.

2nd, 3rd and 4th rounds, k. without shaping.

Rep. these 4 rounds 4 times more (10 sts. decreased altogether).

Continue knitting until work measures 3 sections deep altogether. Test against the patt.

Knit the heel, which may be Dutch, French or auto. Directions for these are given elsewhere; refer to the Index for the pages.

Work the instep decreasings. (See Index for page.)

Knit the centre foot 2 foot-sections long. If a ribbed leg has been knitted, the sts. in the second and third quarters of the round will be ribbed while those in the first and fourth quarters will be plain. The foot should now be 3 sections long. Shape the toe, using either the round toe or the flat toe method. (For directions, see Index.)

Fasten off all ends strongly and press the socks in a good and flat shape. Do not stretch the fabric when pressing and do not press the ribbing of the top section at all.

N.B.—It is not necessary to work the leg decreasings in a ribbed leg.

A MAN'S MEDIUM AND LIGHT-WEIGHT SOCKS

It is assumed that the knitter has made the paper pattern, creased into the appropriate sections, to make the sock to the correct proportions.

Materials required. 5 ozs. of 4-ply wool for medium fabric; 5 ozs. of 3-ply wool for light-weight fabric; 4 No. 13 needles, pointed at both ends.

Tension. 10 sts. to 1 in., 3-ply wool and No. 13 needles, pointed at both ends.

DIRECTIONS

Cast on 80 sts. (10 sts. by 8 ins. = 80 sts.). Rib in k. 2, p. 2, for 4 ins. (1 section).

Knit in st.st. for 3 ins.

Knit 5 sets of decreasings, as described in the previous directions, but with 5 plain rounds between the shaping rounds.

Knit until the leg measures 12 ins. from the beginning.

Knit the heel (see Index for directions of either Dutch, French or auto heel) and work the instep decreasings (also see Index for directions on how to work these).

Knit in st.st. without shaping for the centre foot, until the foot measures three-quarters of the required foot length.

Shape the toe, using either the flat toe or the round toe. (See Index for directions of these toes.)

Press the socks carefully, avoiding the ribbing.

BOYS' SOCKS

A paper pattern with the sections marked should be to hand so that the work can be tested against it.

Materials required. 3 ozs. of 3-ply wool; 4 No. 12 needles, pointed at each end.

Tension. 9 sts. to 1 in.

DIRECTIONS

Cast on 63 sts. (9 sts. by 7 ins. = 63 sts.), 21, 21 and 21. Knit in ribbing of k. 2, p. 2, for three-quarters of the depth of the top section (about 2¾ ins.).

Change to k. 7, p. 2, for 1¼ sections (about 4¼ ins.). The leg should now measure 2 sections, or 7 ins. deep from the beginning.

Turn the heel, using Dutch, French or auto methods, and work the instep decreasings. (See Index for page number of the directions for these.)

Knit the foot without shapings, working the ribbing on the second and third quarters of the number of sts. in the round while the sts. of the first and fourth quarters are all knitted plain for 2 foot-sections.

Shape the toe in either the flat or the round toe method. (See Index for directions.)

Press the socks into a good shape, avoiding the ribbing.

GOLF STOCKINGS

Make a paper pattern as described on page 189. Crease all the dividing lines.

Materials required. 8 ozs. of 4-ply wool; 4 No. 11 needles, pointed at each end.

Tension. 7½ sts. to 1 in.

DIRECTIONS

Cast on 72 sts.—24 on each of three needles. Knit the top turnover to any patt. desired, until it measures 1½ times its depth when turned over.

Change to the leg patt. and knit for half the depth of the turnover plus the depth of 1 leg section.

Leg decreasings must be worked for golf stockings, even when the leg is ribbed.

Work the 5 sets of decreasings as given for a man's heavy sock, but with 7 plain rounds between each pair of dec. rounds.

Continue knitting the leg until it measures 3 leg sections below the turnover.

Work the heel in either the Dutch, French or auto method. (See Index for directions.) Work the instep shapings.

Knit the centre foot for 2 foot-sections. The first and fourth quarters of the number of sts. in the round should be in st.st., when a patt. is worked in the top of the foot.

Shape the toe with either the flat toe or the round toe method. (See index for directions.)

DIRECTIONS FOR STOCKINGS

The principle of working to a paper pattern can be carried out successfully in the making of stockings.

These points must be known first of all: the length of the foot measured from the back of the heel to the tip of the toes; the length of leg to be worked and the knitter's tension, i.e., the number of stitches to 1 in. of knitting; and the type of fabric, i.e., light or heavy weight.

The tops of stockings pass over the knee and over a thicker part of the leg, so it is necessary to make the top of a stocking wider in comparison to the foot.

Light-weight stockings should be knitted in plain fabric for the leg, and heavy-weight stockings may be knitted in narrow ribbing of k. 1, p. 1 in the main part of the leg.

A GIRL'S HEAVY STOCKING

Have an L-shaped piece of brown paper with each arm 3½ ins. wide and with the lower arm as long as the foot and the upright arm as long as the required length of the stocking.

Divide the foot into four equal sections; from the top of the upright arm measure the depth required for the ribbed top (3-4 ins.), and then fold the leg in half (from the base of the ribbing to the top of the heel) to mark the position of the centre leg decreasing.

Materials required. 8 to 10 ozs., according to size, of 4-ply wool; 4 No. 12 needles, pointed at each end.

DIRECTIONS

Cast on 90 sts.—30 on each of three needles. Knit in rib of k. 2, p. 2, for 3 to 4 ins.

Change to either st.st. or a narrow ribbing of k. 1, p. 1, for one-third of the leg (between the ribbing and the top of the heel).

Knit the decreasings as described for a man's heavy sock, but with 8 rounds between each pair of dec. rounds.

Continue knitting the leg until the heel is reached.

Knit either a Dutch, French or auto heel (see Index for page of directions) and knit the instep shapings, too.

Now knit the centre foot until the entire foot from the back of the heel measures 3 sections.

Shape the toe in either the flat or the round toe method.

Press the stockings in a good shape, but avoid the rib at the top of the leg.

A GIRL'S FINE STOCKING

A brown paper pattern, like the one described for the previous stockings, should be made.

Materials required. 7 to 9 ozs., according to size, of 3-ply wool; 4 No. 13 needles, pointed at both ends.

DIRECTIONS

Cast on 110 sts.—36, 36 and 38 on the three needles.

Rib, as in the directions for girl's heavy stockings, for 3 to 4 ins.

Knit the rest of the stocking in plain knitting and follow the directions for the heavy stockings. Press the work as before.

HEEL AND TOE DIAGRAMS

From the diagram plans 1 to 6, choose the kind of shapings desired. The dotted lines in these diagrams show the directions in which the sts. run.

DIRECTIONS FOR SOCKS AND STOCKINGS

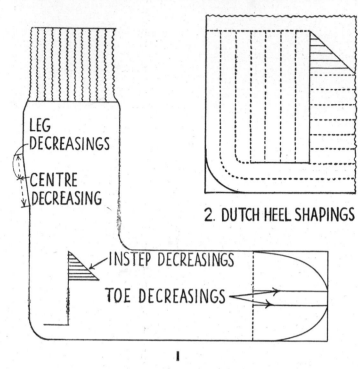

LEG DECREASINGS

CENTRE DECREASING

INSTEP DECREASINGS

TOE DECREASINGS

I

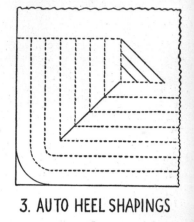

2. DUTCH HEEL SHAPINGS

3. AUTO HEEL SHAPINGS

1. A diagram of the working of a sock. It shows how the fabric expands after the ribbing, how the decreasings in the leg shape the centre back line under the calf, the relative position of the turning of the heel and the instep shapings. The toe shows a plan of the shaping of a flat toe.

2, 3 and 4. These diagrams show the plans for the three kinds of heels. It will be seen that the Dutch heel is practically square, with the line of decreasings at right angles to the picked-up stitches. The auto heel has a diagonal line of shapings, while the French heel is between the two kinds, with the decreasings running in a diagonal line and the picked-up stitch line straight.

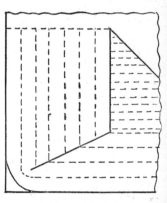

4. FRENCH HEEL SHAPING

5 and 6. Plans of the two toes, flat and round. The flat toe has two lines of decreasings on each side. The round toe has six lines of decreasings all round.

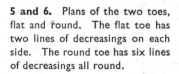

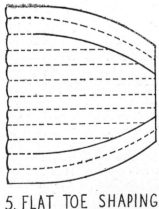

5. FLAT TOE SHAPING

6. ROUND TOE SHAPING

GARTER TOPS

Socks for summer wear can be knitted with a garter top. That is, a strap of ribbing above the leg of the sock attached to the front of the leg only. The back of the strap passes upwards over the calf of the leg and keeps the sock well in place.

A Garter Top. Cast on the required number of stitches. Knit the 1st row plain into the backs of the stitches. Rib in either k. 1, p. 1, or k. 2, p. 2 for 1½ ins.

In the last round knit for three-quarters the number of stitches.

Cast off the last quarter of the stitches.

Cast off the first quarter of the stitches.

Arrange the remaining half of the stitches on one or two needles, whichever will be easier to work.

Continue knitting the leg in plain fabric, or to a pattern, increasing once in the first stitch of every row until the original number of stitches are on the needles.

Arrange the stitches on three needles and continue knitting the leg in rounds.

As the ribbing is shorter, the depth of knitting between the ribbed top and the leg shapings must be increased by about 1½ ins. Otherwise the leg would be too short.

A PAIR OF GOLF MITTENS

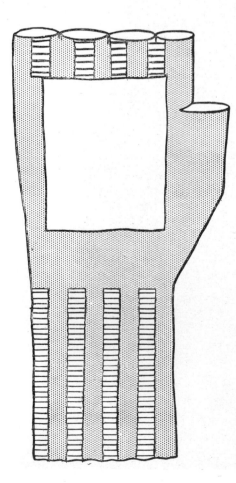

MATERIALS

2 ozs. of 4-ply wool; a set of four No. 11 needles, pointed at both ends.

DIRECTIONS

Cast on 56 sts., 16, 20 and 20 on the three needles.
Knit in ribbing of k. 2, p. 2 for 4 ins.

For the next inch follow the directions given for " A Glove Made on Three Needles," keeping to plain knitting and ignoring the patterned fabric.

After the 1 in. of knitting of the hand, continue as follows :—

Next round, k. to 3 sts. past the thumb shaping, cast off 20 sts., k. to the end of the round, and then k. the few sts. up to the cast-off sts.

From this point the work will have to continue in rows, knitting backwards and forwards in st.st.

Knit as far as the point where the thumb sts. are slipped on to a thread, and cast these off instead of threading wool through them. Continue knitting, casting on the sts. for the base of the first finger as in the other glove, for another ½ in. Then at the end of the next row, which is worked on the right side, cast on 20 sts. and knit in rounds on three needles again, for a further ½ in. and changing the fabric to k. 2, p. 2. Then cast off.

Sew the top of the glove in three places, between the fingers.

For the other hand reverse the position of the shapings to the end of the round, instead of the beginning.

Press the work lightly.

GLOVE DRAFTS

The diagram given here can be worked out to various proportions so that it is possible to knit a glove from measurements when size number is not known. The measurements required are, the width of the hand at the base of the fingers, and the depth of the hand from the tip of the middle finger to the centre back wrist.

Draw an oblong with these measurements. Fold it in half to give the division between the fingers and the hand. Now divide the top half into eight and crease at each fold. The first finger will be as long as seven of these sections, the

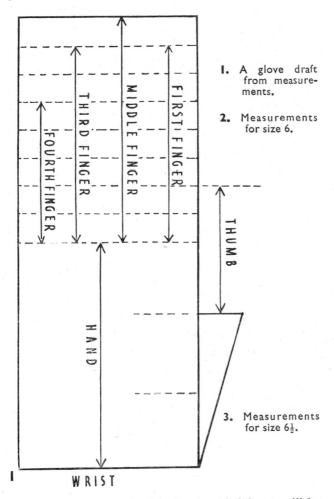

1. A glove draft from measurements.

2. Measurements for size 6.

3. Measurements for size 6½.

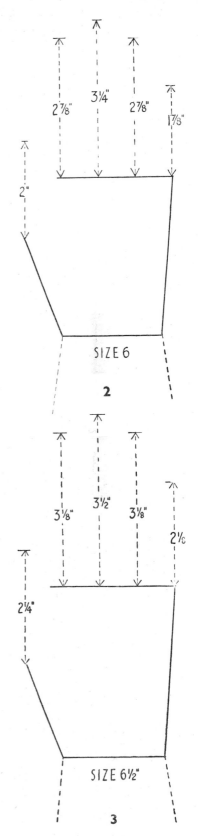

middle finger will be the entire length, the third finger will be the same as the first and the little finger will be five sections high.

To find the position of the base of the thumb, crease the diagram into three sections. The base of the thumb will be two of these sections high. On to this section add a quarter the width of the hand to give the width of the base of the thumb. The height of the thumb is up to the top of the second finger section.

GAUNTLETS FOR GLOVES

Gauntlets can serve a practical purpose as well as a decorative one. Gloves are so much warmer if they have gauntlets which can be pulled over the sleeve of the coat; or, if the coat is too thick for this, that will fill up the space between the coat sleeve and the arm. (*See* page 197 for directions for making 1 and 2.)

2

GAUNTLETS FOR GLOVES *continued*

I. A gauntlet that can be added to an existing glove pattern. Cast on 3 times the number of stitches required for the wrist of a plain glove. Use needles 2 sizes larger.

Knit the first row plain into the backs of the stitches. Work in moss stitch for 1¼ ins.

In the next row, k. 1, k. 2 tog., p. 1, k. 2 tog.; repeat to the end.

K. 2 tog. all along the next row.

Work 1 in. of ribbing in k. 2, p. 2, and then change to the size of needles stated in the glove recipe.

Continue knitting, following the directions for the glove.

2. An open gauntlet, with bands of moss stitch and a centre in blackberry stitch. (*See* directions for knitting blackberry stitch.) Needles two sizes larger than those to be used for the gloves should be used for the gauntlets. Cast on 88 sts. and knit the first row plain, working into the backs of the stitches.

Knit 8 rows in moss stitch. A band of moss stitch, taking 6 sts., is worked on each side of the blackberry pattern.

Work without shaping for 3 blackberry patterns, which will give 6 lines of blackberries. From this point decrease the number of stitches directly inside the moss stitching so that the rows of blackberries are decreased by one group at each end of every line of blackberries. Continue working and decreasing until there remains the right number of stitches to start the hand of the glove.

Next, knit 4 rows in stocking stitch, the purl side outside. Then, for the next 4 rows reverse the stocking stitch so that the plain fabric comes to the other side of the work. Change the stocking stitch to come purlside outside again, for 4 more rows. Change to the smaller needles and continue knitting the hand of the glove.

3. A plain gauntlet for a glove knitted in tweed effect wool. Use the same sized needles as required for the glove. Cast on half as many stitches again as are required for the hand of the glove. If the directions state that 50 sts. are required, then cast on 75 sts. The stitches should be arranged on the same number of needles as will be used for knitting the glove. Work the 1st row or round into the backs of the cast-on stitches.

Continue knitting in pattern or plain fabric for 1½ ins.

Shaping the gauntlet on three needles. K. 2 tog. at the end of each needle in the next round. Knit 2 rounds without shaping.

Repeat these 3 rounds until there are 51 sts. (8 sets of decreasings).

In the next round knit the first 2 sts. together. Then continue for the hand of the glove, following the directions of the recipe.

For shaping on two needles. K. 2 tog., at every third of the number of stitches. Knit 2 rows without shaping. Work these 3 rows 7 times more.

When the gloves are finished, put them on and with a needle and thread mark the wrist line.

Turn the glove inside out and sew a piece of bias binding, or narrow ribbon round the wrist line, and thread a piece of narrow elastic through it. Before sewing the ends of the elastic, try the glove on again to get the right size for the elastic.

3

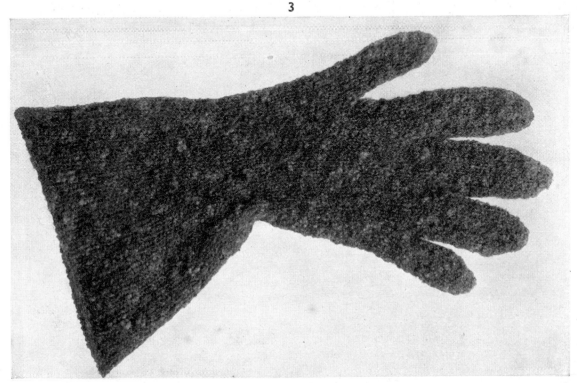

A GLOVE MADE ON THREE NEEDLES

This glove will fit a large sized woman's hand, or a medium sized man's hand. The lengths of the fingers and thumb can be altered to suit individual hands. *(See* illustration 1 on page 200.)

Materials. 3 ozs. of 4-ply wool and four No. 11 needles pointed at both ends will be required.

Cast on 56 sts. (16, 20 and 20 on three needles) and k. the first row into the backs of the stitches.

RIGHT HAND

Knit in ribbing of k. 2, p. 2 for 4 ins.

THE THUMB SHAPING

Re-arrange stitches on needles thus: 17, 21 and 18.

K. 1, k. twice into next st., k. 1, k. twice into next st. Knit the remainder of the round in patt. of p. 3, k. 3, ending with p. 3.

Knit 2 rounds in plain knitting and without shaping.

Next round, k. 1, k. twice into next st., k. 3, k. twice into next st. Knit the remainder of the round in patt. of k. 3, p. 3, ending with k. 3.

Knit 2 rounds in plain knitting and without shaping.

Knit 4 more pairs of shapings, 27 rounds altogether from the beginning of the thumb.

Next round, p. 2, sl. 21 sts. for the thumb on to a thread. In the next round, cast on 5 sts. over the sl. sts., continue in patt. for 14 rounds to finish the hand.

THE FINGERS

FIRST FINGER

At the beginning of the round k. 9 sts. Slip all the rest, except the last 7 on to a thread to be knitted up later for the second, third and fourth fingers.

Return to the 9 sts. just knitted. Cast on 2 and with the 7 sts. waiting to be knitted arrange them 6, 6 and 6 on the three needles. Knit in patt. for 2¾ ins.

TO SHAPE THE TOP

Knit the sts. together in pairs until about 3 remain. Break off the wool, leaving an end long enough to thread through the remaining sts., draw them up and fasten off strongly.

SECOND FINGER

Pick up 7 sts. from each end of the thread. Join on the wool at the beginning of the needle at the front of the hand and cast on 4 sts. Arrange the sts. 6, 6 and 6 and knit in patt. for 3 ins.

Shape the top as for the first finger.

THIRD FINGER

Pick up 7 sts. from each end of the thread. Join on the wool at the beginning of the needle at the back of the hand and cast on 4 sts. Arrange the sts. 6, 6 and 6 and knit in patt. for 2¾ ins.

Shape the top as for the first finger.

FOURTH FINGER

Pick up all the remaining sts. Join on the wool at the beginning of the needle at the front of the hand and cast on 2 sts. Arrange the sts. 6, 6 and 6, and knit in patt. for 2 ins.

THE THUMB

Pick up the sts. on the thread on to two needles. Join on the wool at the beginning of the back needle. Knit the two needles in patt., beginning with p. 3.

Cast on 6 sts. and arrange the sts. 9, 9 and 9 on the three needles. The wool will now be at the end of the round. K. the first two needles.

The third needle, k. 3, k. 2 tog., k. 2, k. 2 tog.

Next round, k. the first two needles.

The third needle, k. 4, k. 2 tog., k. 1.

Continue in patt. for 2 ins.

Shape the top like the fingers.

TO MAKE UP THE GLOVE

Sew the bases of the fingers and thumb strongly, neatening off all ends invisibly and lightly press the hand and fingers into good shape.

THE LEFT-HAND GLOVE

Thumb shapings will be worked at the ends of the rounds instead of at the beginnings. Cast-on sts. will be worked on the reverse side of the hand.

KNITTING GLOVES

Gloves to match or contrast any outfit can be made quickly and very cheaply. For plain gloves 2 ounces of 4-ply wool is the average amount required, while for gloves with gauntlets 3 to 4 ounces will be needed. Men's gloves take rather more.

For those who do not care about knitting on three needles, some directions are given here for knitting gloves on two needles.

GLOVES KNITTED ON TWO NEEDLES

To fit the average sized woman's hand.

2 ozs. of 4-ply wool and a pair of No. 11 needles will be required.

Cast on 58 sts. and knit the first row plain into the backs of the sts.

Change to ribbing of k. 1, p. 1, for 3 ins.

Change to st.st. Knit 3 rows.

SHAPING THE THUMB

K. 27, k. twice into next st., k. 2, k. twice into next st., k. 27, turn.

K. 3 rows without shaping.

Rep. these 4 rows until there are 18 sts. between the two sets of 27 sts.

The thumb is worked on these.

From the beginning of the row, k. 27 sts. and then k.

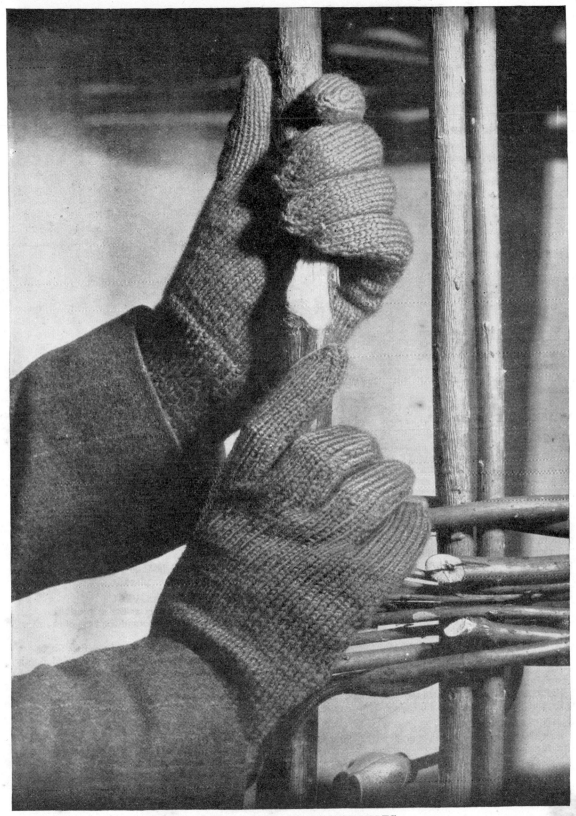

GLOVES MADE ON TWO NEEDLES

the 18 sts. for the thumb. Turn and p. back 18 sts.

Turn and k. 18 sts. Cast on 3 sts.

Work st. t. on these 21 sts. until the thumb measures 2 ins.

SHAPING THE TOP

K. 1, k. 2 tog.; rep. to the end. P. back. K. 1, k. 2 tog.; rep. to the end. P. back.

K. 2 tog. all along. Break off the wool, leaving an end long enough to thread through the sts. left on the needle and to sew up the thumb seam.

THE REMAINDER OF THE HAND

Join the wool to start working the sts. on the left-hand needle, k. these sts., turn and p. back to the thumb.

Cast on 3 sts. and continue knitting across the second set of 27 sts. There will now be 57 sts. altogether.

Knit without shaping for another 1¼ ins.

WORKING THE FINGERS

The first finger of left hand

With right side of work facing, k. 21 sts. and slip them on a thread to be picked up as required for the second, third and fourth fingers.

K. a further 15 sts. for the first finger and slip the remaining 21 sts. on another piece of thread.

To continue with the first finger. Cast on 3 sts. and p. back.

Knit in st.st. for 2½ ins., and then shape the top like the top of the thumb. Break off the wool, leaving an end long enough to thread through the sts. and sew the seam.

Second finger

Pick up 7 sts. from the thread on the right side of the first finger and knit in st.st. for 2¾ ins. Shape the top as for the thumb.

Pick up 7 sts. from the thread on the left side of the first finger.

Knit them, cast on 2 sts., turn and p. back, cast on 2 sts. Knit in st.st. for 2¾ ins. and finish off the top as usual.

Third finger

Rep. as for the second finger, but knit only 2½ ins. before dec. for the top.

Fourth finger

K. the sts. from the right-hand thread for 2 ins., and then shape the top as before.

Pick up the sts. from the left-hand thread, join on the

I

wool and cast on 2 sts. before knitting the first row.

Continue knitting in st.st. for 2 ins., and then shape the top.

When knitting the right-hand glove, add the 2 cast-on sts. to the opposite finger pieces.

TO MAKE UP THE GLOVES

Press the hand and fingers as flat as possible.

Join the seam of the thumb and the base of the thumb securely.

Join the seam down the inside of the first finger.

Join the two seams of the second and third fingers, sewing the base of each strongly to the base of the previous finger.

Join the inside seam of the fourth finger, and then the outside seam and continue down the outside of the hand to the base of the wrist.

DECORATION

A " peasant " touch can be given to these gloves by sewing over the seams with a thick wool in a brightly contrasting colour. Chain stitch may be worked round and round the tips of the fingers and thumb and three round spots down the back of each hand, all in the same bright colour.

PICKING UP STITCHES

In constructing garments in knitting it is often necessary to pick up stitches. Stitches have to be picked at the sides of heels, at the base of fingers when knitting gloves, and when grafting patch pockets. It is much neater to pick up stitches for a belt than it is to join one on with sewing. The bands round armholes and necks of pullovers set much better if the first row of stitches are picked up from the edge of the fabric of the pullover.

When picking up the stitches at the side of a heel, pick up half as many stitches as there are rows in the square of the heel, which means that the strands between the knots of the edge will be lifted.

Where the number of stitches required is equal to the number of rows, pick up the loop of the knots as well as the strands between the knots.

1. Picking up the strands as when working a Dutch, or a French heel. The 1st row of knitting will be worked into the backs of these stitches.

2. Picking up stitches on the surface of fabric, as for the 1st row in making a belt.

1

2

MARKING STITCHES

Here are some ideas for ways of marking while work is in progress.

3. If you wish to mark a row for a particular purpose, so that you can refer to the row being worked, knit in a length of cotton in a contrasting colour to the knitting thread. This thread cannot be knitted in the usual way, else it would not draw out easily. Knit the first stitch, bring the cotton forward, knit the second stitch and then pass the cotton to the back of the work, so that the cotton threads backwards and forwards between the stitches.

3

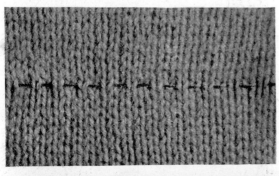

4. Where a row has to be marked after it has been knitted. Darn a thread of cotton in contrasting colour, taking the thread through every loop. This is an excellent thing to do when knitting has to be unravelled to a certain row. The cotton thread will prevent the unpicking of more rows than is necessary, and the stitches will be ready to slip on the needles.

4

PATCH POCKETS

The following few pages give directions for making different kinds of pockets.

Two kinds of pockets are made in knitting, they are: patch (of which there are two types, the separate pocket, and the pocket knitted up from the fabric of the garment), and then there are inset pockets, chiefly used for sports wear, where the fabric of the garment is opened to make the pocket opening.

The separate pocket will be described first, because it is the easiest kind to make. The following directions will make patch pockets of average size. If unusual sizes are required, alter the number of stitches or rows accordingly.

I. A triangular pocket with a flap. The one illustrated was made from 3-ply wool on No. 9 needles.

DIRECTIONS

Make I st. on the needle, k. into it twice, turn.

K. twice into the first and k. the second, turn.

K. twice into the first st.; k. the remainder.

Rep. the last row until there are 10 sts. on the needle.

Next row, k. twice into the first st., k. 3, p. I, k. 5.

Next row, k. twice into the first st., k. the remainder.

Rep. the last 2 rows, working 2 more purl sts. in each consecutive 1st row, until there are 25 purl sts.

Knit without shaping the first sts., but slipping all first sts. for the next 18 rows.

Change the st.st. to come on the reverse side of work and continue for another 8 rows. For the next 4 rows, k. 2 tog., k. 4, knit the centre as usual to within the last 6 sts., k. 4, k. 2 tog.

Knit the next 2 or 3 rows plain and cast off on a wrong side row. Pin the pocket to shape and press it, turning the flap over on the first purl row.

I

2. A fancy pocket. The upper edge is gathered together with a narrow strap. All the work is in garter stitch.

DIRECTIONS

Cast on 20 sts. Knit the first row into the backs of the cast-on sts., turn.

Cast on 3 sts., knit the row, turn.

Cast on 3 sts., knit the row, turn.

At the beginning of the next 2 rows, cast on 2 sts.

At the beginning and end of the next 4 rows, knit twice into the first and last sts. This will finish the shaping if 3-ply wool is used.

At the beginning of the next 4 rows, knit twice into the first st. only if 2-ply wool is used.

Continue knitting without shaping until the work measures 3 ins. from the beginning.

Make a vertical buttonhole 2 rows long. (See Index for directions.)

Knit until the pocket measures 5 ins. from the beginning. Cast off and make the strap on 5 sts. of a length to thread through the buttonhole.

2

MORE PATCH POCKETS

When a pocket similar to an inset pocket is required and it is not desired to open the fabric, as is necessary for an inset pocket, a patch pocket can be knitted on to the garment.

This ensures that the sides and bottom of the pocket will be nearly as invisible as an inset.

1. Mark with tacking cotton the position of the pocket and lift up the stitches in the fabric of the garment along the bottom of the pocket shape. Arrange the stitches so that knitting will begin on a right side row. It will be easy to do if a fine needle is used for the picking up and the stitches slipped on to the working needles afterwards.

2. Knit the first row, copying the fabric pattern of the garment. At the end of the row pick up the loop of the stitch in the garment fabric directly above the last stitch picked up.

Next row, knit this lifted loop together with the first knitted stitch on the needle and work to the end. Lift up the loop of the second stitch directly above the first one picked up. Repeat this last row until the depth of the pocket is reached. In this manner the pocket is knitted and grafted to the fabric of the garment at the same time. Finish the top of the pocket as desired.

INSET POCKETS

Inset pockets are often required for cardigans and sports wear. They are not difficult to do and if they are pressed and sewn carefully they will look neat and flat.

The top of the opening should have a band of contrasting patterned fabric to give a finish and the kind of pattern chosen should add a decorative touch to the garment. Moss stitch is one of the most successful patterns for pocket tops. Garter stitch may be used on the more simple types of garments. Ribbing is seldom used, because it draws the top of the pocket together too much.

The opening and the top of the pocket are knitted with the garment, therefore the position and width of the pocket must be planned before the garment is started.

Proceed to knit the garment as far as the *base* of the pocket top.

From this point there are two ways of knitting inset. One is to knit the patterned top before making the opening and the other method is to make the opening and knit the patterned band on the stitches making the front of the pocket. The latter method is the neatest if the sides of the pocket top are carefully sewn down.

1. An inset pocket with the moss stitched top knitted on the front pocket stitches and sewn at each side afterwards. Knit the garment as far as the beginning of the patterned band marking the pocket top. This band will begin the required depth below the opening of the pocket. With the right side of the work facing, knit along the row as far as the beginning of the pocket. Calculate the number of stitches required to give the width of the pocket and knit that number in k. 1, p. 1, ending with k. 1. A pocket should be about 4 ins. wide. Work backwards and forwards on these stitches in moss stitch for 9 rows. Cast off on a wrong side row. Return to the stitches on the right-hand side of the pocket. Join on the wool and cast on the same number of stitches that were used for the pocket top. Continue the row across the garment. There should now be the same number of stitches on the needle that there were before the pocket top was knitted. Proceed to knit the garment in the usual way.

To finish the pocket. Turn the work to the wrong side and pick up the cast-on stitches; pick up one stitch for every cast-on stitch and knit a square, or oblong in stocking stitch to form the back of the pocket. Cast off when the desired length is reached. Press the garment, the pocket and the pocket top in the usual way. Sew the back of the pocket to the wrong side of the garment as carefully and invisibly as possible. Sew down each side of the pocket top to the right side of the garment and the work is finished.

When it is desired to knit the band before making the opening for the pocket, knit the garment as far as the base of the pocket top. Knit along the row as far as the patterned band. Knit the number of stitches to make the pattern of the band in each consecutive row, until the position for the opening of the pocket is reached. Knit along the row as far as the patterned band. Cast off the stitches in the band and continue knitting to the end of the row. Return to the opening. Cast on the same number of stitches that were cast off and continue knitting the garment.

To finish the pocket. Turn the work to the wrong side and pick up all the cast-on stitches. Knit these stitches in stocking stitch until there is enough fabric to make the back of the pocket. Press well, sew the back of the pocket to the wrong side of the garment invisibly, and the work is finished.

HORIZONTAL BUTTONHOLES

Buttonholes cannot be cut in hand-knitted fabric and worked or bound as they are in other materials. They have to be constructed as knitting proceeds. The position of the buttonhole on the garment or the use to which it will be put determines the type of buttonhole to make.

Cardigans are fastened down the front edge with horizontal buttonholes, worked, as a rule, on a separate strip of knitting which is sewn to the edge of the cardigan after the garment has been made up.

This strip is best if knitted on fairly small needles, to give a firm fabric. Also, the buttonholes will wear better in a close fabric than they will in a looser fabric.

2

I

1. Horizontal buttonholes, such as are required for cardigans. Plan out how far apart to place the buttonholes and then calculate the number of rows to be worked between each pair of holes. Consider how far from the bottom end of the band the first buttonhole should be worked. Garter stitch will make a flatter band than will stocking stitch. Knit as far as the first buttonhole. Consider how wide to make the hole, 3 or 4 sts. are usual. These stitches will be cast off at the centre of the band. Knit to within the number of stitches to be cast off. Cast off 3 or 4 sts. Knit to the end, turn. Knit to the opening. Cast on the same number of stitches as were cast off. Knit to the end. Knit the next row, working into the backs of the cast-on stitches. Knit the number of rows to give the correct space between the buttonholes and repeat the process. Repeat until the required number of holes are made.

2. Horizontal buttonholes in stocking stitch fabric. The buttonholes have been worked round with buttonhole stitch. In order to get firm edges slip all first stitches and reverse the working of all last stitches, i.e., purl the last stitch of a plain row and vice versa

VERTICAL BUTTONHOLES

Buttonhole openings must follow the direction of the strain of the fastening. The previous page dealt with horizontal buttonholes, which run from side to side, such as are required for fastening cardigans; vertical buttonholes are those which run up and down to take the strain of a downward pull. Such buttonholes are required along the waists of small boys' trousers when they fasten on to the shirt, and they are also worked at the waists of little girls' knickers when they fasten on to liberty bodices.

The work is rather more complicated than for horizontal buttonholes, because the hole extends over several rows.

1

1. A set of vertical buttonholes, such as are required for little boys' trousers and little girls' knickers. The first step in the work is to knit the garment to the beginning of the buttonholes. With the right side of the work facing, knit along the row as far as the first hole. Turn the work backwards and forwards on these stitches for the depth of the hole. Break off the wool, leaving an end about 6 ins. long and slip the stitches on to a holder.

2

3

2. Join the wool at the first stitch at the base of the hole. Knit along the row as far as the second buttonhole, turn and knit this section as deep as the first. Break off the wool and slip these stitches on to the holder; repeat the last process for as many times as required. Do not break off the wool at the end of the last section. Slip all the stitches on to one of the needles, so arranging them that knitting will begin on a wrong side row. Knit that row linking up all the separate sections, knitting in each end of wool for 4 sts. Continue knitting as usual for the remainder of the garment.

3. Vertical buttonholes for a cardigan fastening.

FASTENINGS ON KNITTED FABRICS

After making buttonholes, the next best thing to consider is the sewing on of the buttons. The important thing to consider here is the looseness of knitted fabric compared with the close texture of cloth and the methods that can be employed to counteract the less stable foundation.

Some sort of artificial foundation must be supplied. Tape forms the handiest foundation. Attach a length of tape behind the fabric where the buttons will be sewn, and work all sewing stitches through this. There is one drawback to the use of tape, it is that tape does not stretch and it may prevent the part of the garment where it is sewn from stretching as much as the rest of the fabric. When there is that danger, it will be better to obtain some small flat buttons to be placed behind the

1. Buttons sewn through tape.

3. Press studs on tape.

2. Buttons sewn through buttons.

garment. Then, when sewing on the buttons for fastening, take the stitches through a button on the right side and one of these small buttons on the wrong side. In this way there will be no sewing stitches pulling the knitted stitches of the fabric.

Where press studs are to be used for fastening, sew the separated halves on two lengths of tape and then sew the tape in place with hemming worked down each side. Tape can be bought with these press studs already inserted.

THREADING HOLES

Children's garments and lingerie need some means of pulling in the garment to fit a smaller part of the figure. Knickers need elastic at the waist and outer garments require cords for gathering up waists and neck edges.

Where the fastening comes along an edge, a crocheted edging with holes in it can be worked over the edge of the garment. But where the fastening comes at some other place that is not an edge, the means of passing the elastic or cord must be made in the fabric of the knitting. This is done by utilizing the principle of making holes with made stitches in a similar way to making holes in a lace pattern.

I

I. This is the method of making a threading hole about ½ in. down from an edge.

Directions. Knit the garment to within ½ in. from the top.

Next row, k. 3, m. 1, k. 2 tog.; repeat to the end, making sure that the last made stitch can be balanced by a decreased stitch.

Knit the remaining ½ in. as usual.

Hat elastic, or round elastic should be used in knitted fabrics.

2

2. This illustrates a double hem above the threading.
Directions. Knit the garment to within the required depth of the hem. Make the threading holes as described above.
Knit in the usual fabric for double the depth of the hem. Repeat the threading holes, making sure that they come in the same position as the 1st row.
Knit for a further ¼ in. and then cast off. Press the hem double so that both rows of holes are together, and thread the elastic through both sets of holes.

3

3. A similar hem to the last, but with a picot edge to the top of the double fabric.
Directions. Knit to within the depth of the hem. Make the row of threading holes as described above. Knit for the depth of the hem.
Next row, k. 1, * m. 1, k. 2 tog. *; repeat from * to * all along.
Knit the depth of the hem again and then repeat the row of threading holes, making them come level with the 1st row.
Fold the hem in half, with the row of close holes at the fold and the two rows of threading holes parallel to each other. Thread the elastic or cord through the double holes.

CABLE STITCH PATTERNS

The cabled pattern is popular for thick garments and gives a very warm fabric for winter wear. The basis of cabling is a wide plain rib on a purl background. At intervals one half of the plain rib is twisted under the other half, giving the effect of a thick chain cable. The severity of these patterns is specially suited to men's garments.

How to make the twist. A spare needle is required. Knit the purl stitches, take half the plain stitches on to the spare needle, knit the second half of the stitches in the plain stripe, slip the stitches from the spare needle back on to the left-hand needle and knit them. Continue across the row, purling the purl stitches and twisting the halves of the plain stripe across each other. Variations are made by twisting half the plain stitches in different directions.

1

2

1. This illustration shows the back of the work during cabling. A few stitches have been knitted and the next 3 sts. are on the spare needle. The knitting needle is in the fourth plain stitch ready to knit it. Either 6, or 8, sts. are in the plain stripe and 3, or 4, sts. are cabled.

2. An average cable pattern, made with equal stripes of 6 plain and 6 purl sts. with a cable every 12th row. When planning a cable pattern into a garment there should be a number of purl stitches at each end of the row. Do not begin, or end, a row with a cable stripe, or it will be difficult to join the seam neatly.

FLAT CABLES

Where a cable effect is desired without the depth of the usual cable pattern, it is possible to make an imitation twist to the plain stripe. Many people prefer this flatter texture. The interest of the surface is not destroyed in any way and the work is easier to do, because a spare needle is not required.

1

2. Here is a much wider imitation cable, showing that the same principle is good for larger stripes. The stripes are made with 4 purl sts. and 6 plain sts. There are 10 rows between the twists.

Directions. Cast on a number of stitches divisible by 10, plus 4.

1st row, p. 4, k. 6; repeat to the end, finish with p. 4.

2nd row, k. 4, p. 6; repeat to the end, finish with k. 4. Repeat these 2 rows 8 times more.

9th row, p. 4, sl. 1, k. 2 tog. twice; k. 1, p.s.s.o. the last 3 sts.; repeat to the end, finish with p. 4.

10th row, k. 4, p. twice into the next 3 sts.; repeat to the end, finish with k. 4.

Repeat these 10 rows throughout.

The loose slipped stitch gives the effect of the twisted cable, without its bulk.

2

1. A fine imitation cable pattern, the cable being only 2 sts. wide.

Directions. Cast on a number of stitches divisible by 5, plus 3.

1st row, p. 3, k. 2; repeat to the end, finish with p. 3.

2nd row, k. 3, p. 2; repeat to the end, finish with k. 3.

3rd row, the same as the 1st row.

4th row, k. 3, p. the second purl st.; p. the first purl stitch and then take both purled stitches from the left-hand needle. Repeat to the end, finish with k. 3.

Repeat these 4 rows throughout.

This makes a very attractive cabled pattern suitable for most wools.

FANCY CABLES

All sorts of fancy effects can be made by treating the cabled stitches in various ways. The same group of stitches can be cabled all the time, instead of at alternate twistings, as was done on page 209. Cables can be inserted into other fabrics, but the texture of the second fabric must not compete with the interest of the cable pattern. Moss stitch can be worked in the spaces which divide the cable stripes.

1. In this piece of knitting the same group of plain stitches has been cabled each time.

Directions. Cast on a number of stitches divisible by 9, plus 3.

1st row, p. 3, k. 6; repeat to the end, finish with p. 3.

2nd row, k. 3, p. 6; repeat to the end, finish with k. 3.

Repeat these 2 rows 3 times more.

9th row, p. 3, cable the next 6 sts. in the usual way; repeat to the end, finish with p. 3.

Return on the next row as usual for the back of the work. Repeat the directions from rows 1 to 8.

Next row, p. 3, cable the next 6 sts. in the reverse direction, that is, slip the next 3 sts. on to the spare needle and bring them in front of the work while the following 3 sts. are being knitted.

Knit on the return row in the usual way.

Repeat this set of rows throughout the work.

2

1

2. Basket cable. An attractive texture with an all-over cable pattern; the twist is made in every 6th row.

Directions. Cast on a number of stitches divisible by 4. Knit 5 rows in stocking stitch, begin with a purl row (the wrong side of the work).

6th row, cable every 8 sts. (k. 4, sl. 4 on spare needle and leave at the back of the work in the usual way; k. 4, take 4 from spare needle and knit them; repeat to the end). There are no purl stitches between the cabled stitches.

Repeat rows 1 to 5.

12th row, cable all along, twisting the stitches that were not twisted in previous row and leaving the stitches on the spare needle in front of the work, instead of behind it as in the usual way. This is how the work is done: Sl. 4 on spare needle and leave in front of the work, k. 4, take 4 from spare needle and knit them; repeat all along.

Repeat these 12 rows throughout the work.

MAN'S PULLOVER WITH V-SHAPED NECK

Measurements. To fit 38-in. chest; length from shoulder, 22 ins.

Materials. 6 ozs. of 4-ply fingering; a pair of No. 11 needles; a pair of No. 9 needles.

Tension. 6½ sts. to 1 in.; 8 rows to 1 in., using No. 9 needles.

DIRECTIONS

THE FRONT

Using the No. 11 needles cast on 114 sts. Knit in ribbing of k. 1, p. 1 for 3½ ins.

Next row, k. 1, k. twice into next st., * k. 11, k. twice into next st. *; rep. from * to * to the end.

Change to No. 9 needles, and patt.

1st row, k. 3, p. 2, * k. 7, p. 2 *; rep. from * to * to within 3 sts. of the end, finish with k. 3.

2nd row, p. 3, * k. 2, p. 7 *; rep. from * to * to within 5 sts. of the end, finish with k. 2, p. 3.

Rep. these 2 rows for 10½ ins.

ARMHOLE SHAPING

Cast off 10 sts. at the beginning of the next 2 rows.

K. 2 tog. at the beginning of the next 8 rows.

Continue knitting without shaping until the armhole measures 2 ins. from the beginning.

With the right side of the work facing, knit to the 2 centre sts., k. 2 tog., turn and work on these sts. for the shoulder.

K. 2 tog. at the beginning of every row that commences at the neck, until the third purl ridge from the centre is reached. This will leave 3 p. ridges at the shoulder. Continue knitting until work measures 21½ ins. from the beginning.

SHAPING THE SHOULDER

With right side of work facing cast off 8 sts. at the beginning of the next 2 rows that commence at the armhole end.

Cast off the remainder of the sts.

Join on the wool at the beginning of the remaining sts. of the second shoulder and knit that like the first, working all shapings at the appropriate ends of the rows.

THE FRONT NECK BAND

Using No. 11 needles pick up 103 sts., that will be every knot and strand. Arrange the sts. so that work will begin on a right side row, and knit the first row into the backs of the sts.

Next row, rib in k. 1, p.1 for 50 sts., k. 3 tog., rib 50 sts.

Continue knitting in rib, always knitting the centre 3 sts. together, for ¾ in., then cast off on a wrong side row, using No. 9 needles.

THE BACK

Using No. 11 needles cast on 114 sts.

Knit like the front as far as the end of the armhole shapings. Knit straight until the armhole measures 7 ins. from the beginning.

SHOULDER SHAPING

Cast off 9 sts. at the beginning of the next 6 rows. Leave an even number of sts. on the needle. Change to No. 11 needles and knit in ribbing of k. 1, p. 1, for the same number of rows as in the front neck band. Cast off on a wrong side row.

TO MAKE UP

Press very lightly with a cool iron and a cloth that is only slightly damp, and be careful that the ribbing is not opened unevenly. Do not press waist and neck ribbing.

Oversew the shoulder seams and then make the armhole bands. Using No. 11 needles pick up 130 sts. round each armhole and knit in ribbing like the neck band.

Cast off on a wrong side row. Oversew the side seams.

MAN'S PULLOVER WITH V-SHAPED NECK

MAN'S PULLOVER WITH ROUND NECK

Measurements. To fit 38-in. chest; length 22 ins. from shoulder.

Materials. 7 ozs. of 4-ply fingering; a pair of No. 13 needles; a pair of No. 11 needles; a pair of No. 9 needles.

Tension. Working with No. 9 needles: 6 sts. to 1 in.; 7½ rows to 1 in.

DIRECTIONS

THE FRONT

Using No. 11 needles cast on 102 sts.

Work in ribbing of k. 1, p. 1 for 3½ ins. Change to No. 9 needles and patt.

1st row, k. 3, * p. 6, k. 6 *; rep. from * to * to within 3 sts. of the end, finish with p. 3.

The next 3 rows are in st.st.

5th row, p. 3, * k. 6, p. 6 *; rep. from * to * to within 3 sts. of the end, finish with k. 3.

The next 3 rows are in st.st.

Rep. these 8 rows for 11½ ins.

ARMHOLE SHAPING

Cast off 9 sts. at the beginning of the next 2 rows.

K. 2 tog. at the beginning of the next 6 rows.

Continue knitting without shaping until work measures 3¼ ins. from the beginning of the armhole.

FRONT NECK SHAPING

Knit 30 sts. in patt. Right side of work should be facing. Cast off 12 sts.

Continue to the end.

Right-hand shoulder: K. 2 tog. at the beginning of the next 6 rows that begin at the neck.

K. without shaping until the armhole measures 7 ins.

Cast off 8 sts. at the beginning of the next 3 rows that commence at the armhole side. The last set of casting off will dispose of all the remaining sts.

Left-hand shoulder: Join on the wool at the neck edge of the sts. and rep. the shapings as for the right-hand shoulder. Shapings will be worked on wrong side rows.

THE BACK

Using No. 11 needles cast on 102 sts.

Work as for the front as far as the end of the armhole shapings.

K. the back without further shaping until the armhole measures 7 ins.

SHOULDER SHAPING

Cast off 7 sts. at the beginning of the next 6 rows.

Change to No. 13 needles and knit in ribbing of k. 1, p. 1, for 1 in.

Cast off on a wrong side row. This will make the back neck band.

FRONT NECK BAND

Using No. 13 needles pick up 82 sts. with the wrong side of the work facing; thus knitting on these sts. will begin on a right side row.

Knit the first row plain into the backs of the sts.

Knit in rib of k. 1, p. 1 for the same number of rows as in the back band.

Cast off on a wrong side row. Join the shoulder seams.

THE ARMHOLE BANDS

Round each armhole pick up 126 sts. on the No. 13 needles, hold the work with the wrong side facing so that knitting will begin on the right side.

Knit the first row plain into the backs of the sts.

Knit in ribbing of k. 1, p. 1 for the same number of rows as in the neck bands.

Cast off on a wrong side row.

TO MAKE UP

Press the work very lightly with only a slightly damp cloth and a cool iron. A hot iron will flatten the fabric too much.

Oversew the side seams together, joining the ends of the bands evenly.

MAN'S PULLOVER WITH ROUND NECK

215

MAN'S CARDIGAN WITH LONG SLEEVES AND HIGH NECK

Measurements. To fit 38-in. chest; length from shoulder, 21½ ins.

Materials. 9 ozs. of 4-ply wool; a pair of No. 9 needles; a pair of No. 11 needles (optional).

DIRECTIONS

THE FRONT

Cast on 114 sts. Knit plain into the backs of the sts. Rib in k. 1, p. 1 for 32 rows.

Change to patt.

K. 1, p. 1, * k. 2, p. 4, k. 8, p. 4 *; rep. from * to * 5 more times, k. 2, p. 1, k. 1.

Next row, p. 1, k. 1, * p. 2, k. 4, p. 8, k. 4 *; rep. from * to * 5 times more, p. 2, k. 1, p. 1.

Rep. these 2 rows 7 times more (16 rows altogether). Cable the wide plain stripes in the next row.

Knit in this patt. until there are 5 cablings and 5 rows beyond the last cable.

ARMHOLE SHAPING

Cast off 10 sts. at the beginning of the next 2 rows.

K. 2 tog. at the beginning of the next 12 rows.

K. without shaping until work measures 6 ins. from the beginning of the armhole.

FRONT NECK SHAPING

With right side of work facing knit 30 sts. in patt., this will be the neck edge of the left shoulder, turn and k. back to the armhole.

K. 2 tog. at the beginning of the next 3 rows that commence at the neck.

SHOULDER SHAPING

Cast off one-third of the sts. on the next 3 rows that begin at the armhole side.

The right-hand shoulder: sl. 18 sts. on to a holder or a thread and join the wool at the beginning of the remaining sts. Knit the right-hand shoulder as for the left-hand shoulder with the shapings at the neck edge.

THE BACK

Knit the back as for the front as far as the end of the armhole shapings.

Knit without further shaping until the armhole measures 7 ins. from the beginning.

Cast off 10 sts. at the beginning of the next 2 rows.

Cast off 8 sts. at the beginning of the next 4 rows.

Leave the remaining sts. on the needle.

Change to ribbing of k. 1, p. 1, and knit for 4½ ins.

THE FRONT NECK BAND

Hold work with wrong side facing. Along the right-hand neck edge pick up 10 sts. Knit the 13 sts. from the holder or thread in k. 1, p. 1, and pick up another 10 sts. from the other side of the neck edge, making 38 sts. altogether.

Knit in ribbing for the same number of rows as in the back neck band.

An alternative method is to obtain four No. 9 needles, with points at both ends, pick up the front neck sts. as described above and arrange them, together with those left on the needle after the back shoulders have been cast off on three needles, like a stocking, and knit up the neck band in rounds. This obviates the two shoulder seams.

THE SLEEVES

Using No. 11 needles cast on 70 sts. Knit into the backs.

Knit in rib of k. 1, p. 1 for 4 ins.

Change to No. 9 needles and patt.

Begin with * k. 2, p. 4, k. 8, p. 4 *; rep. from * to * twice more, finish with k. 2, p. 4, k. 8, p. 2.

Knit in patt. for 15 ins., inc. on the 1st st. in every 9th and 10th rows.

SHAPING THE TOP

Cast off 4 sts. at the beginning of the next 2 rows.

K. 2 tog. at the beginning of the next 12 rows.

K. 2 tog. at each end of the next 12 rows.

Cast off the remaining sts.

When making up, a zipp fastener may be let into one shoulder seam.

MAN'S CARDIGAN WITH LONG SLEEVES AND HIGH NECK

A WAISTCOAT IN CLOSE FABRIC WITH REVERS

A WAISTCOAT IN CLOSE FABRIC WITH REVERS

MEASUREMENTS

To fit 34 to 36 in. bust; length from shoulder to lower edge, 18 ins.

MATERIALS

8 ozs. of 4-ply wool; a pair of No. 12 needles; a pair of No. 10 needles.

TENSION

With No. 10 needles: 7 sts. to 1 in.; 9½ rows to 1 in.

DIRECTIONS

THE LEFT FRONT

Using No. 12 needles cast on 66 sts.

Knit in ribbing of k. 1, p. 1 for 2½ ins.

Change to No. 10 needles and patt.

Moss st. 10, p. 6, k. 2, p. 6, k. 2; continue to the end in p.

Next row, knit the purled sts. of the 1st row and p. those that were knitted and moss st. the front band.

Rep. these 2 rows until work measures 10½ ins. During this, knit twice into the first st. in every 4th row which begins with plain sts.

ARMHOLE SHAPING

With the right side of the work facing, cast off 4 sts.

K. 2 tog. at the beginning of the next 12 rows that commence at the armhole.

THE REVERS

The revers begin on the same row as the first armhole shaping. At the moss st. edge k. twice into the first st. of every 6th row, thus inc. the number of moss sts. at the outside edge only. These increasings continue to the end of the front.

THE SHOULDER

After the armhole shapings, continue knitting without further shaping at the armhole edge until the armhole measures 7 ins. from the beginning.

With right side of work facing, cast off 10 sts. at the beginning of the next 3 rows that commence at the armhole end of the row.

Cast off all sts.

THE RIGHT FRONT

The right front is knitted in a similar manner, with shapings and patt. stripes at opposite ends of the rows. If buttonholes are desired, they should be worked, one in the centre of the waist ribbing, and four more at intervals of 2½ ins. (4 sts. should be cast off in each).

THE BACK

Using No. 12 needles cast on 110 sts.

Knit in ribbing like the fronts.

Change to No. 10 needles and st.st. for 1 in. From this point begin the bands of ribbing for the decoration of the back. There are five sets of 2 purl sts. with 6 plain sts. between. The centre set begins 1 in. up from the waist ribbing, and the remainder begin at intervals of ½ in.

To do the work, with right side of work facing, k. 54, p. 2, k. 54, turn.

P. 54, k. 2, p. 54, turn.

Rep. these 2 rows twice more.

Next row, k. 46, p. 2, k. 6, p. 2, k. 6, p. 2, k. 46.

Next row, p. 46, k. 2, p. 6, k. 2, p. 6, k. 2, p. 46.

Rep. these last 2 rows twice more.

Next row, k. 38, p. 2, k. 6, p. 2, k. 6, p. 2, k. 6, p. 2, k. 38.

Next row, p. 38, k. 2, p. 6, k. 2, p. 6, k. 2, p. 6, k. 2, p. 38.

Continue the centre ribbing directions throughout the back, and follow the directions of the front for the side seam and armhole shapings.

THE SHOULDERS

After the armhole shaping, continue knitting without further shaping until the armhole measures 6½ ins.

Cast off 10 sts. at the beginning of the next 6 rows.

Cast off remainder of the sts.

TO MAKE UP

Press the work lightly, omitting the waist ribbing, oversew the side and shoulder seams together and sew on the buttons.

TRIMMING

Work blanket st., or crochet an edge of one line of double crochet sts. round the armholes in a colour to match the buttons.

A WAISTCOAT IN CLOQUE PATTERN

A WAISTCOAT IN CLOQUE PATTERN

MEASUREMENTS

To fit a 36-in. bust.

Length from shoulder to lower edge, 15½ ins. down front.

MATERIALS

2 ozs. of dark colour 3-ply wool.

4 ozs. of light colour 3-ply wool.

A 12-in. zipp fastener and 10 buttons.

A pair of No. 11 needles.

A pair of No. 9 needles.

DIRECTIONS

THE FRONT BANDS

Using the No. 11 needles, cast on 38 sts. in darker wool and knit in ribbing of k. 1, p. 1 for 13 ins.

Cast off 2 sts. at the beginning of every alternate row 7 times. K. the next row and then cast off.

Make a second band like this, but cast off on the opposite side of the work.

THE RIGHT-HAND FRONT

Using No. 11 needles cast on 50 sts., and knit in ribbing of k. 1, p. 1 for 3 ins.

Change to No. 9 needles and patt.

Break off the dark wool and join on the light wool.

K. the first row, p. the second and k. the third row.

4th row, p. 4, * k. twice into the next 2 sts., p. 8 *; rep. from * to * 3 times more, k. twice into the next 2 sts., p. 4.

5th row, k. 4, * p. 4, k. 8 *; rep. from * to * 3 times more, p. 4, k. 4.

6th row, p. 4, * k. 4, p. 8 *; rep. from * to * 3 times more, k. 4, p. 4.

Rep. rows 5 and 6 once more and then row 5.

10th row, p. 4, * k. 2 tog., p. 8 *; rep. from * to * 3 times more, k. 2 tog., p. 4.

Rep. the first 3 rows.

14th row, p. 9, * k. twice into the next 2 sts., p. 8 *; rep. from * to * 3 times more, p. 1.

15th row, k. 9, * p. 4, k. 8 *; rep. from * to * 3 times more, k. 1.

16th row, p. 9, * k. 4, p. 8 *; rep. from * to * 3 times more, p. 1.

Rep. rows 15 and 16 once more and then row 15.

P. the next row, k. the next and p. the next.

Rep. from the 4th to the 21st row until the work measures 9½ ins.

ARMHOLE SHAPING

With the wrong side of the work facing cast off 8 sts., k. 2 tog. at the beginning of the next 5 rows that commence at the armhole.

Knit without further shaping until the armhole measures 5 ins. from the beginning.

NECK SHAPING

With right side of work facing k. 2 tog., k. to the end. Return to the neck. Rep. the 2 rows 7 times.

Cast off all the remaining sts.

THE LEFT-HAND FRONT

The left-hand front is knitted like the right-hand front, but with armhole and neck shapings worked on opposite ends of the rows.

THE BACK

Using No. 11 needles cast on 100 sts. and knit in ribbing like the front.

Knit in patt. on the No. 9 needles, repeating one patt. 8 times in the row where it is repeated 3 times for the front.

Follow the front armhole directions on both sides of the work and then knit without further shaping for 7 ins.

Cast off all the sts.

TO MAKE UP

Press the cloque patterned parts lightly. Sew the front bands with the long sides to the front edges of the bodice, start at the bottom and work up to the neck. Make sure that both bands end exactly opposite each other at the top. Join the side and shoulder seams.

ARMHOLE BANDS

Using No. 11 needles, cast on 114 sts. in darker wool and knit in ribbing of k. 1, p. 1 for 1 in., cast off.

Join each band into a ring and sew to the armholes, placing the seams at the side seams of the waistcoat.

TO FINISH

Fold the front dark coloured bands over for a little more than half their width, and secure with five buttons. Insert a 12-in. zipp fastener down the centre front.

A PEASANT WAISTCOAT

A PEASANT WAISTCOAT

Measurements. Length from shoulder to lower edge, 17 ins.

Materials. 4 ozs. of 3-ply wool; 1 oz. of 3-ply wool in darker shade; a pair of No. 9 needles; 5 buttons; 5 press studs.

DIRECTIONS

THE BACK

Cast on 86 sts. in the light wool. K. into the backs of these for the 1st row.

1st pattern row, * k. 1, p. 1, sl. 1 *; rep. from * to * to within 2 sts. of the end, finish with k. 1, p. 1.

2nd pattern row, p. 1, * k. 1, p. 2 *; rep. from * to * to within 2 sts. of the end, finish with p. 1, k. 1.

Rep. these 2 rows until the work measures 8 ins. from the beginning, inc. on the first st. in every 9th and 10th rows.

ARMHOLE SHAPING

Cast off 10 sts. at the beginning of the next 2 rows. K. 2 tog. at the beginning of the next 4 rows.

Continue knitting in patt. until the work measures 16 ins. from the beginning.

SHOULDER SHAPING

Cast off 6 sts. at the beginning of the next 6 rows. Cast off the remainder of the sts.

THE RIGHT FRONT

Cast on 7 sts. Return, knitting into the backs. K. 1, p. 1, sl. 1; rep. once, then k. 1, turn. Cast on 6 sts., k. 1, p. 2; rep. twice, then k. 1. Return in patt.

Rep. the last 2 rows twice more.

Cast on until there are 47 sts. on the needle.

Continue knitting, without shaping, until the side seam is the same length as the back side seam.

ARMHOLE SHAPING

Cast off 10 sts.

K. 2 tog. at the beginning of the next rows that commence at the armhole until there remain 11 patts. and 2 sts. in the row. Then begin the neck shaping.

NECK SHAPING

K. 2 tog. at the beginning of the rows that commence at the front neck edge, until 5 patts. have been disposed of. K. without further shaping until the work measures 16 ins. from the beginning.

SHOULDER SHAPING

Cast off one-third of the sts. on the next 3 rows that begin at the armhole.

THE LEFT FRONT

Knit as for the right front with all shapings worked at the opposite ends of the rows.

THE NECK BAND

With the dark wool cast on 10 sts. and knit in g.st. until the band is long enough to reach round the neck and fronts of the waistcoat. Allow enough for the ease round the points.

THE ARMHOLE BANDS

With the dark wool cast on 5 sts. and work enough in g.st. to reach round each armhole.

Press the work lightly, but not the bands.

Join the shoulder and side seams.

Join the wide band to the fronts and neck, easing it round points at the base of the front neck.

Sew the tops of 5 large press studs on to a length of tape and attach to the back of the right front band. Sew the other halves of the press studs to the left front band, with the tape at the back of the band and sew decorative buttons over the fasteners on the right-hand band.

Join each armhole band into a ring and sew to one armhole of the waistcoat.

If the lower edge of the waistcoat appears too loose, sew a facing of narrow crossway material along the wrong side, stretching it on as work proceeds.

A KNITTED BLOUSE

Measurements. To fit a 34 to 35½ in. bust; length from shoulder to lower edge, 17 ins.

Materials. 3 ozs. of mid-blue, 3-ply wool; 1 oz. of dark blue, 3-ply wool; 2 ozs. of beige, 3-ply wool; 2 ozs. of pink, 3-ply wool; a pair of No. 7 needles; 6 buttons.

Tension. 5½ sts. to 1 in.

DIRECTIONS

THE FRONT

Cast on 88 sts. K. into the backs of the sts. for the first row. Use mid-blue wool.

Knit in rib of k. 2, p. 2 for 12 rows.

Rib in k. 2, p. 2 for 12 rows.
Cast off. There is no neck shaping.

THE BACK

The back is knitted in exactly the same way as the front.

SLEEVES (both alike)

Using the mid-blue wool, cast on 52 sts. K. into the backs of the sts. for the 1st row.

Knit in ribbing of k. 2, p. 2 for 12 rows.

Change to g.st. and colour sequence until work measures 4 ins. from the beginning. This should end on the 4th

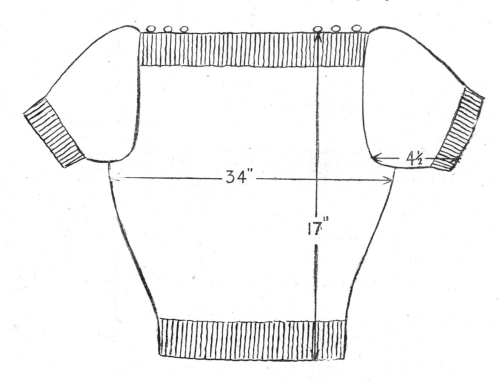

Change to g.st.

The colours are used in the following sequence: 6 rows each of mid-blue, beige and pink with 2 rows of dark blue between each colour.

Knit without shaping until work measures 11½ ins. This should be at the end of the 13th dark blue band.

ARMHOLE SHAPING

Cast off 4 sts. at the beginning of the next 2 rows.
K. 2 tog. at the beginning of the next 8 rows.
Knit without further shaping until work measures 15 ins. This should be at the end of the 7th mid-blue band, counting the one directly over the ribbing.
Do not change the colour.

dark blue band. K. twice into the first st. of every row.
Now shape the top.
K. 2 sts. tog. at the beginning of every row 20 times.
K. 2 sts. together at each end of the next 14 rows.
Cast off.

TO MAKE UP

Press the work lightly, but not the ribbing.

Oversew the side seams together and 1½ ins. of the shoulder seams, starting at the armhole.

Join the sleeve seams and set them into the armholes.

Sew buttons along the back of the shoulder seams and work buttonholed loops on the edge of the front shoulder to slip over the buttons to fasten the shoulder.

A KNITTED BLOUSE

A SIMPLE BATHING COSTUME

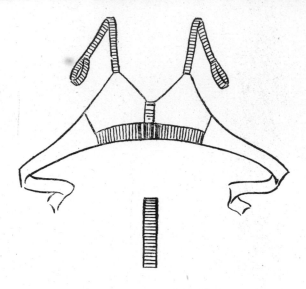

MEASUREMENTS

Brassière. To fit 32 to 33-in. bust.

Shorts. Centre front length, 14 ins.; leg seam length, 3 ins.

MATERIALS

For brassière. 2 ozs. of suitable wool; a pair of No. 11 needles.

For the shorts. 6 ozs. of suitable wool; the same needles as for brassière.

TENSION

6½ sts. to 1 in.

DIRECTIONS

THE BRASSIÈRE

The work is done from side to side and sewn to a ribbed waist band afterwards. The ties are worked separately and sewn to the side of the brassière.

Using No. 11 needles, cast on 10 sts. K. the first row into the backs of the sts. The remainder of the knitting is done in st.st., with a strip of g.st. in the centre front.

K. twice into every 4th st. in the 5th, 9th, 13th, 17th and 21st rows.

K. without shaping for 8 rows.

K. every 4th and 5th sts. together in the following 5th, 9th and 13th rows.

Knit in g.st. for 1½ ins.

For the second half of the brassière, reverse the directions. inc. where the first half was decreased and dec. where the first half was increased.

At the end, cast off on a wrong side row.

THE FRONT WAIST BAND

Using No. 11 needles, cast on 50 sts. and knit in ribbing of k. 1, p. 1, for 1½ ins.

Cast off loosely.

THE TIES (both alike)

Using No. 11 needles, cast on 14 sts. All the work is done in g.st.

Knit together the 2nd and 3rd sts. of every 4th row 4 times (10 sts. remain).

Knit in g.st. without further shaping until the ties are long enough to pass across the back and tie in the front.

Knit short straps of 5 sts. knitted in g.st., to be sewn to the front waist band.

Thread the ties through these for greater security, before tying them.

THE SHOULDER STRAPS

Pick up 7 sts. across the top of each brassière on the No. 11 needles and knit a straight strap in g.st., long enough to cross at the back and make a loop at the end through which to pass the ties.

THE SHORTS

Using the No. 11 needles, cast on 126 sts. K. into the backs of the sts. for the first row.

Knit in g.st. for 2 ins. This will be folded in half for the hem.

Continue in st.st. for another 2 ins.

A SIMPLE BATHING COSTUME

continued

THE LEFT LEG

With right side of work facing, k. twice into the 1st st.; rep. this on every alternate plain row to shape the back seam, until there are 10 more sts.

K. without shaping until work measures 17 ins. from the beginning.

Knit in ribbing of k. 1, p. 1, for 1¾ ins.

TO SHAPE THE BACK WAIST

With right side of work facing, rib 50 sts., turn, and rib back.

Rib 40 sts., turn, and rib back.

Rib 30 sts., turn, and rib back.

Cast off all the sts.

Knit the right leg with the back seam shaping and the shaping at the back waist worked at opposite ends of the rows; all the shapings will be worked on wrong side rows.

Knit a belt in g.st., to fit the waist, and 2 small straps.

TO MAKE UP

Press the work carefully.

BRASSIÈRE

Sew the front waist band to the lower edge of the brassière. Join the wide end of the ties to the side of the brassière, stretching the end of the tie to fit if necessary.

Sew the short straps to the front waist ribbing with a space of about 1 in. between them.

Sew loops at the ends of the shoulder straps through which to pass the ties.

Oversew the front and back seams of the shorts and turn up the hem round the legs. Press this hem lightly.

Sew the short straps for the belt at the top of each side seam and thread the belt through them.

Sew a buckle at one end of the belt after it has been fitted.

A variation. If a belt is not desired, connect the brassière to the shorts with a 2-in. strap of g. st. at the centre front.

The top edge of the brassière may have the first 7 sts. worked in moss stitch for decoration.

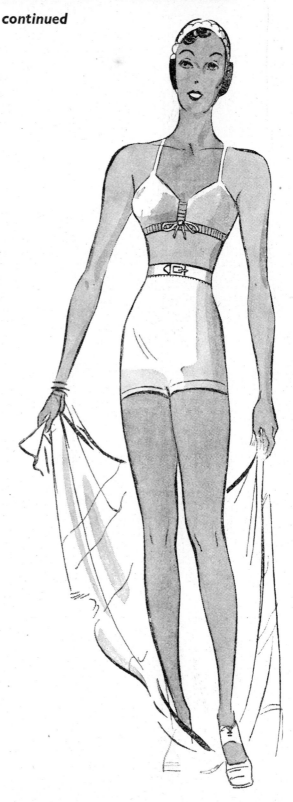

A BATHING COSTUME
FOR A 12-YEAR-OLD

Measurements. To fit 32-in. hips; length from shoulder to waist, 13 ins.

Materials. 7 ozs. of suitable wool; a pair of No. 10 needles.

DIRECTIONS

The back and the front are knitted alike as far as the chest line; the costume should be worn with the shoulder straps crossed over the shoulder blades. The front and back are joined with side seams.

THE FRONT

Cast on 57 sts. K. the first row loosely into the backs of the cast-on sts.

Knit in g.st. for 2 ins. This will be folded in half for a hem.

The remainder of the fabric, up to the ribbing, may be in any flat texture, moss st., g.st., or the same slipped st. patt. as the sun suit.

Knit without shaping for another inch. Slip this leg on to a spare needle and knit another like it.

Put both legs on to the same needle, making sure that the right sides come to the same side. Knit across one leg to bring the wool to the end of the row.

Knit without shaping for 12 ins.

Change to ribbing of k. 1, p. 1 for 2 ins.

Next row, right side of work facing, k. 2 tog. on every 10th and 11th sts.

Work in patt. for a farther 5½ ins.

ARMHOLE SHAPING

Cast off 8 sts. at the beginning of the next 2 rows.

K. 2 tog. at the beginning of the next 10 rows.

Change to g.st. and work 8 more rows, still k. 2 tog. at the beginning of every row.

Cast off on a wrong side row.

THE BACK

Knit the back like the front as far as the armholes.

Cast off on a wrong side row.

SHOULDER STRAPS

Cast on 10 sts. and knit as long as is required for the strap to reach from the top of the front, cross over at the back and sew to the top of the back at a point 1½ ins. from the centre back.

TO MAKE UP

Press the work lightly avoiding the ribbing and the straps. Join the side seams and the short leg seam, and sew on the straps. A knitted, or leather, belt may be added.

A YOUNG CHILD'S SUN SUIT

MEASUREMENTS

Length of leg from waist, 9 ins.; length from shoulder, 16 ins., this measurement can be altered as required by knitting a longer, or shorter, strap.

MATERIALS

2 ozs. of 3-ply wool; a pair of No. 10 needles.

DIRECTIONS

THE FRONT

Cast on 42 sts.

Knit in g.st., every row plain, for 12 rows.

Slip this leg band on to a holder, or spare needle.

Cast on 42 sts. again and knit another band.

At the end of the last row cast on 12 sts., and then k. up 10 sts. of the first band (64 sts. now on needle), turn.

P. 42 sts., turn.

K. 52 sts., turn.

P. 62 sts., turn.

K. 72 sts., turn.

P. all the sts. right across the two leg bands.

Change to patt.

1st row, k. 3, * sl. 2, k. 6 *; rep. from * to * to within 5 sts. of the end, finish with sl. 2, k. 3.

2nd row, p. 3, * sl. 2, p. 6 *; rep. to within 5 sts. of the end, finish with sl. 2, p. 3.

3rd row, k.

4th row, p.

5th row, k. 7, * sl. 2, k. 6 *; rep. from * to * to within 9 sts. of the end, finish with sl. 2, k. 7.

6th row, p. 7, * sl. 2, p. 6 *; rep. from * to * to within 9 sts. of the end, finish with sl. 2, p. 7.

7th row, k.

8th row, p.

Rep. these 8 rows throughout.

Work until knitting measures 9 ins. from the beginning.

Cast off 24 sts. at the beginning of the next 2 rows.

Continue knitting the bib for 3 ins.

Knit the next 8 rows in g.st.

K. 10, cast off to within 10 sts. of the end; k. 10.

G.st. these last 10 sts. for the required length of the shoulder straps, about 10 ins.

THE BACK

Rep. the directions as far as the waist and then cast off all the sts.

TO MAKE UP

Press the work lightly and sew up the side seams and the short underleg seam. Cross the straps at the back and sew them to the back waist with a gap of about 2½ ins. between.

A CHILD'S JERSEY

MEASUREMENTS

To fit a 28-in. chest measure.

Length from shoulder to lower edge, $18\frac{1}{2}$ ins.

Length of sleeve seam, $16\frac{1}{2}$ ins.

MATERIALS

5 ozs. of 3-ply wool.

A pair of No. 11 needles.

A pair of No. 9 needles.

A 6 or 7-in. zipp fastener.

TENSION

8 sts. to 1 in. measured over the main part.

DIRECTIONS

Using the No. 11 needles cast on 82 sts. K. the 1st row into the backs of the sts.

Knit in rib of k. 1, p. 1 for $2\frac{1}{2}$ ins.

Change to No. 9 needles and patt.

K. 7, k. twice into the next st. all along the next row.

THE PATTERN

1st row, p. 1, k. 4, * p. 1, k. 8 *; rep. from * to * to within 6 sts. of the end, finish with p. 1, k. 4, p. 1.

2nd row, k. 1, p. 3, * k. 3, p. 6 *; rep. from * to * to within 7 sts. of the end, finish with k. 3, p. 3, k. 1.

3rd row, p. 1, k. 2, * p. 5, k. 4 *; rep. to within 8 sts. of the end, finish with p. 5, k. 2, p. 1.

4th row, k. 1, p. 1, * k. 7, p. 2 *; rep. from * to * to within 9 sts. of the end, finish with k. 7, p. 1, k. 1.

5th row, p. all the sts.

Knit the next 3 rows like rows 4, 3 and 2 in that order, making 8 rows to a patt. altogether.

Rep. these 8 rows until the work measures $12\frac{1}{2}$ ins. from the beginning.

ARMHOLE SHAPING

Cast off 8 sts. at the beginning of the next 2 rows.

K. 2 tog. at the beginning of the next 4 rows.

K. without shaping until the armhole measures $1\frac{1}{2}$ ins. from the beginning.

FRONT NECK OPENING

With right side of work facing knit to the centre in patt., and slip the remainder of the sts. on a holder, or spare needle.

Continue working on half the sts. until the armhole measures 6 ins. from the beginning.

SHOULDER

With right side of work facing, cast off 7 sts. at the beginning of the next 3 rows that commence at the armhole end.

Knit the remainder of the sts. in rib of k. 1, p. 1 for $2\frac{1}{2}$ ins.

THE RIGHT-HAND FRONT

Join on the wool at the centre front end of the row and knit the right shoulder like the left, with the shoulder shapings at the opposite end of the row.

THE BACK

Knit the back like the front as far as the top of the armhole, omitting the opening of the centre front.

Cast off 6 sts. at the beginning of the next 6 rows.

Knit the remaining sts. in rib of k. 1, p. 1 for the back collar, for $2\frac{1}{2}$ ins.

Cast off.

THE SLEEVES

Using No. 11 needles cast on 48 sts. K. the first row into the backs of the sts.

Knit in rib of k. 1, p. 1 for $2\frac{1}{2}$ ins.

Change to No. 9 needles and patt.

Knit in patt., inc. 1 st. by knitting into the backs.

Knit in patt., inc. at both ends of every purled row, until the sleeve measures $16\frac{1}{2}$ ins. from the beginning.

SHAPING THE TOP

K. 2 tog. at the beginning of every row for 20 rows.

K. 2 tog. at each end of the next 10 rows.

Cast off.

TO MAKE UP

Press the work except the ribbing.

Oversew the side and shoulder seams together. Join the sleeve seams and set them into the armholes.

Sew the zipp fastener down the front opening.

A CHILD'S JERSEY

A MAN'S LIGHT-WEIGHT SINGLET AND SHORTS

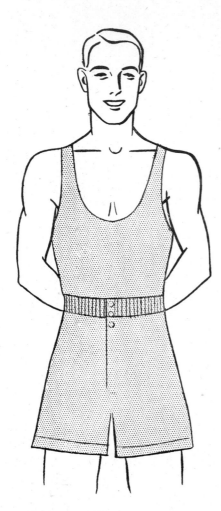

DIRECTIONS

THE SINGLET

Using the No. 12 needles, cast on 136 sts. and knit in ribbing of k. 1, p. 1, for 1½ ins.

Change to st.st. and No. 10 needles and knit for 9½ ins.

Change to No. 12 needles and knit in ribbing of k. 1, p. 1, for 2 ins.

Change again to No. 10 needles and st.st. and continue knitting for 6 ins.

SHAPING THE ARMHOLE

Cast off 12 sts. at the beginning of the next 2 rows.

K. 2 tog. at the beginning of the next 16 rows.

K. without further shaping until the armhole measures 3½ ins. from the beginning.

SHAPING THE NECK

With the right side of the work facing, k. to within 12 sts. of the centre. Cast off 24 sts. and continue knitting to the end of the row.

Continue knitting on these sts. for the shoulder, the other group of sts. may be put on to a spare needle or a holder.

At the beginning of the next 3 rows that commence at the neck, cast off 3 sts.

At the beginning of the next 12 rows that commence at the neck, k. 2 tog.

At the beginning of every 3rd row that begins at the neck, k. 2 tog. until 3 more decreasings have been made.

Continue knitting without further shaping until the vest measures the required length from the lower edge. Cast off.

Join on the wool at the beginning of the sts. to be knitted up for the other shoulder and copy the directions for the first shoulder, knitting the decreasings at the neck edge, which will be a wrong side row instead of a right side row.

THE BACK

Knit the back as for the front as far as the end of the armhole shapings. Continue knitting until the armhole measures 6½ ins.

BACK NECK SHAPING

K. to within 16 sts. of the centre. Cast off 32 sts. Continue knitting to the end of the row.

At the beginning of the next 3 rows that commence at the neck, cast off 2 sts.

At the beginning of the next 11 rows that commence at the neck, k. 2 tog.

Continue knitting without further shaping until the back measures the same as the front.

TO MAKE UP

Press the work except the ribbing and join the side and shoulder seam.

Knit an edging in g.st. for the armholes and neck. Cast on 5 sts., using No. 12 needles, and work the strips to the required length. To get the right length, these strips may be sewn to the garment as work proceeds.

THE SHORTS

Using No. 12 needles, cast on 120 sts. and knit in ribbing of k. 1, p. 1, for 1½ ins.

Change to No. 10 needles and st.st. and knit for 4½ ins.

From this point, continue shaping the leg at the back and front seams, as described in the directions for men's pants. (See Index for page.)

MEASUREMENTS

Singlet. To fit 38-in. chest; length from shoulder to lower edge, 29 ins., or as required.

Shorts-pants. Centre front depth, 13 ins.; leg seam length, 4 ins. (this may be varied according to requirements).

MATERIALS

Singlet. 6 ozs. of 3-ply vest wool.

Shorts-pants. 5 ozs. of 3-ply vest wool; a pair of No. 10 needles; a pair of No. 12 needles.

TENSION

8 sts. to 1 in.

PART V

EMBROIDERED KNITTING

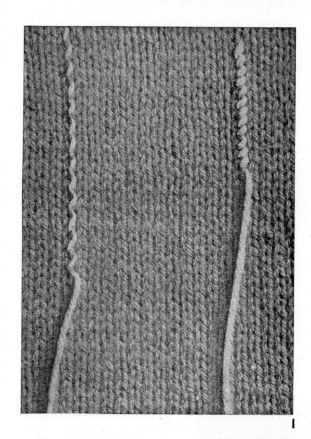

1

When the character of the knitted fabric is taken into account and the type of embroidery stitches to be used are chosen accordingly, the effect can be very attractive. But, when any kind of embroidery stitch is used, irrespective of its suitability, then, the effect can be anything but pleasant.

The working thread should be a little thicker than that used for the knitting and a blunt wool needle should be used so that the fabric threads are not split. Thin embroidery threads are seldom successful, because the stitches always tend to sink between the stitches of the knitting.

Consider the type of texture, or pattern, made by the knitting and let your embroidery stitch be consistent. Stocking stitch fabric is made up of rows of chain-like links and these can be worked with a kind of stem stitch to give suitable decoration with stitches expanding with the knitted fabric.

2

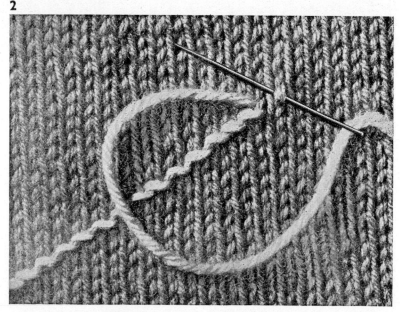

1. The thread is brought up between a link in one row of chain. Pass to the next stitch below and pick up one side of the link. Continue like this down the fabric, working one stitch into every link, and to the same side of the links.

2. The same stitch worked diagonally. Bring the thread out at the lower left-hand corner of the fabric, pass to the next stitch along and the next stitch up and pick up the far side of the link. Continue working like this, passing to the next stitch diagonally until the line of stitching is as long as required. Vandyked lines are easy to make with this type of stem stitch.

DAISY STITCH AND THREADED STITCHES

Lazy daisy stitch is a good embroidery stitch to use on stocking stitch fabric. This stitch looks like an enlarged link from the fabric itself and it seems to go with the knitted texture particularly well.

1

2

1. The stitch is worked as for ordinary embroidery. A loop is worked over a certain number of links in the fabric, the thread drawn out and a small back stitch holds the loop in place. The loop of the stitch should not be drawn as tightly as is usually done on cloth and the back stitch should be left a little slack so that the stitch can give with the knitting. The thread left at the back, to strand from 1 st. to the other, must be left loose, too.

2. The loops made by purled knitting can be used to good decorative effect by threading them with a contrasting coloured thread. Here, a single row of purl is threaded in such a way that a wavy line is formed. Pass the needle upwards under one purled stitch and downwards through the next. The thread does not pass to the back of the work.

EMBROIDERING PATTERNED FABRIC

The two illustrations on this page show how knitting can be worked to a certain pattern which is afterwards used as a basis for further decoration. In this type of work, do not make both kinds of pattern of equal importance. Either the knitted pattern must be subordinate to the embroidered design, or else, the added decoration must be less important than the knitting.

1. Here is shown a check patterned fabric made with plain and purl stripes with a horizontal row of purl at regular intervals. Three daisy loops are worked into alternate rows of plain squares, and alternate vertical stripes of purl have stem stitch worked in opposite directions on the bordering plain stitches.

2. This is a very attractive idea for jumpers and babies' dresses. Knit the fabric in diamond pattern and then work three lazy daisy loops in each diamond. The daisy stitch groups may point downwards as here, or they may be worked upwards.

SMOCKED KNITTING

Smocked knitting has many uses. It is pretty on children's frocks and on thick woolly jumpers.

First of all the fabric of the knitting is prepared for the smocking by being knitted with a purl background on to which rows of plain stitches stand out ready to be picked up for the embroidery.

1

2

1. A suitable texture is made with p. 6, k. 1 in the first row and p. 1, k. 6 in the return row. The side with the purled ground is the right side of the garment.

2. Gather up the material with tacking stitches as in ordinary smocking, picking up the plain stitch instead of transferred dots. The rows of tacking should be a little farther apart than is usual for cloth. Draw up the tacking threads and proceed to work any kind of honeycomb smocking desired. Closer types of smocking are not suitable for knitted fabrics, they take up too much width of fabric and the finished effect is too lumpy.

DESIGNS KNITTED IN

The two pictures on this page illustrate a type of decorated knitting that was very popular among the wealthy people of the seventeenth and eighteenth centuries. The pattern was marked out with a different stitch. Sometimes these stitches were worked with a double thread, one being that of the garment and the other a metal thread or one of a different colour. It is necessary to work from a chart in order to count the stitches in both right side and wrong side rows.

The work can be very tedious, because every stitch has to be counted. So do not embark on a large piece of work until you have experimented with a small specimen.

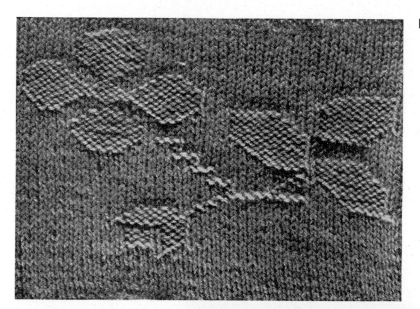

I

1. A floral design built up to the counted stitch. Purl pattern on a stocking stitch ground. Pattern stitches on the right side row are knitted purlwise, and the pattern stitches on the wrong side rows are knitted plainwise and counted from right to left of the chart. The pattern is counted in reverse on wrong side rows.

2. A leafy design in horizontal stripes with a narrower stripe of spots divided from the wide stripe with one purl row. This should not be very difficult to copy, as so much of the pattern is repeated. It would make uncommon decoration round the hem of a girl's dress.

SETTING IN ZIPP FASTENERS

Zipp fasteners are popular as a means of closing openings in knitted garments because they are easy to work and they obviate the trouble of making buttonholes during the knitting.

The addition of a light embroidery stitch to the fastener helps to make it a feature of the garment.

The chief thing to guard against is stretching the fabric of the knitting at the edge of the opening.

The most important thing is to measure the opening with the garment laid flat on the table and the opening edge as near as possible to the right tension. As a rule, the edges of openings become a little looser than the rest of the fabric. This must be allowed for when measuring for the length of fastener to buy.

1. The ends of the tape on the fastener are turned back and sewn down.

3. Lightly hem the outer edge of the tape to the knitted fabric, taking tiny stitches into the knitting.

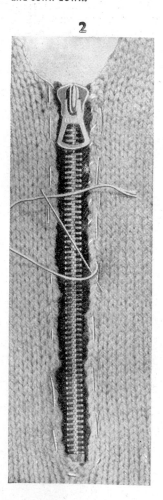

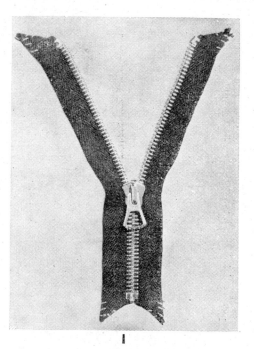

2. The edges of the opening are first tacked and then lightly hemmed down to the tape. Do not stretch the fabric in this step and make sure that the fabric is smooth at the base of the fastener. The sewing thread should match the colour of the garment. When tacked, make sure that the slider will not gather up the edge of the fabric and tear it.

EMBROIDERY ADDED TO FASTENERS

When the fastener is secure with sewing stitches, some further decoration can be added to the garment by means of stitchery round the fastener. If the garment is knitted in wool, some bright silk will give a pleasing effect, this is specially the case when a metal fastener is used as the sheen on the thread goes well with the brightness of silver, or gold.

1

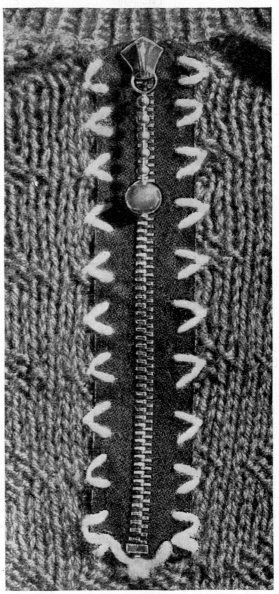

2

1. Threaded buttonhole stitch worked over the edge of the fabric. Two contrasting coloured silks are used here. A little more space will be required between the slider and the edge of the opening to allow for the thickness of the embroidery stitch.

2. This picture shows a metal fastener mounted on coloured tape, set on to the right side of the garment, so that the tape becomes part of the decorative scheme. " Y " stitch in contrasting colour softens the hard edge of the tape. The edge of the fabric was sewn invisibly to the reverse side of the tape, and a fair space left between it and the metal slider.

COLOURED KNITTING

Very attractive decoration can be evolved by using two, or more, different coloured wools in such a way that some sort of pattern is made. Prevailing fashions will decide whether colours should contrast, or whether they should be harmonious, but there are a variety of ways of gaining pattern with changes of colour.

The simplest method is with horizontal stripes, the colours being taken right across the entire width of the work. In joining the wool the old thread cannot be knitted in for a few stitches to secure it. The end will have to be darned in afterwards, otherwise the second colour line will be spoilt by the few extra stitches of the first colour.

1

2

3

1. Pattern made with three colours worked in equal quantities with a dark colour dividing each band from the other. Remember to change the colours on right side rows.

2. The colour line is diffused on the wrong side of the work, owing to the loops of the first colour coming over the beginning of the second colour.

3. Here, the point mentioned in illustration 2 has been used decoratively on the right side of the fabric.

A CUSHION IN COLOURED KNITTING

Here is an idea for using up odd lengths of wool at the end of a winter's knitting. Each side of the cushion will take about 6 ozs. of 4-ply wool and the gusset will take about 1 oz. in a single colour. The tassel can be bought ready made, or one will take ¼ oz. of wool to make. A pair of No. 9 needles will be required.

DIRECTIONS

Cast on 60 sts. and then k. one row into the backs of these cast-on sts. Knit three more rows in plain knitting. All the work is done in g.st.

Next row, k. 50 sts., turn, and k. back (right side of work).

Next row, k. 40 sts., turn, and k. back.

Next row, k. 30 sts., turn, and k. back.

Next row, k. 20 sts., turn, and k. back.

Next row, k. 10 sts., turn, and k. back.
Break off the wool and join on another colour.

K. 4 rows across the 60 sts. on the needle and then dec. the number in each right side row by 10 as before.

Change the colour after knitting back along the last set of 10 sts., until there are between 45 or 50 sections of different colour. Cast off, leaving a long end to sew the seam.

Run a gathering thread round the short edge and pull it up until the extreme end can be sewn together to close the centre of the round cushion.

Join the ends of the knitting with oversewing worked not too tightly.

THE GUSSET

Cast on 20 or 30 sts. according to whether you want a wide gusset or a narrow gusset, and knit in g.st. until the length will reach right round the circular top.

Work a second circle to match the size of the first. But the colours need not be the same. Prepare it as for the first circle, seaming it and gathering up the centre.

Press all the work lightly and then join the gusset into a ring.

Proceed to make up the cushion by seaming the gusset to the two circles with large oversewing stitches. These sts. may be in a light colour for decoration.

A large tassel may finish off the centre of the cushion top and, if liked, thick piping cord may be sewn round the outer joins.

If wool is being specially bought, the top will take 2 ozs. of each of two colours and 3 ozs. of another colour which will be used for the gusset as well as the top, and the underside of the cushion will require 2 ozs. of each of three colours.

A cheap kind of knitting wool will be quite suitable, its hard surface may be better than a soft wool. An attractive effect is given when black wool is used for the first two rows after the completion of a pattern.

A SQUARE CUSHION FROM ODDMENTS

This is a good way of using larger oddments of wool in assorted colours. Each band may be in a different colour, or, the colours can change at the corners in every band, and as many bands as desired may be made.

The work is very easy to do, first a square for the centre is knitted and then bands of straight knitting with corners are worked to fit each consecutive edge.

Each successive band should contrast with the last band, either in colour or tone. That is, two adjacent bands should be in contrasting colours, or one be a light tone of one colour and the other a dark tone of the same colour.

Work the second side of the band the same length as the first and work the second corner like the first corner.

Rep. until the band is long enough to go right round the square.

THE MITRED END

The end of the band must be the opposite slope to meet the slope of the beginning of the band. To do this, work must begin from the outer end of the row.

*Next row, k. to within I st. of the end, turn.
Next row, sl. the Ist st. and k. to the end, turn *.

Rep. from * to * knitting I st. less in alternate rows until I st. remains. Sl. this st. on to the left-hand needle and then cast off all sts. loosely.

Join the mitred seam with oversewing, press the band and the centre square lightly and join the band to the square with oversewing. This sewing can become part of the scheme of decoration by being worked in a contrasting colour.

Continue knitting bands, working each side to fit the edge to which it will be seamed, until the cushion is large enough.

The reverse side of the cushion may be of material, if no more wool is available. Four large wool tassels will make a suitable finish to the corners.

DIRECTIONS

Knit the centre square first of all, and this may be any size desired. Knit into the backs of the cast-on sts. and cast off loosely.

As each band is knitted in a strip, it has to be joined at one corner.

TO WORK A BAND

Cast on I st., k. twice into the st., turn and k. the 2 sts.
K. twice into the first st., k. the next st., turn and k. back.

*Next row, k. twice into the Ist st., k. to the end.
Next row, k. all the sts. *.

Rep. from * to * until the band is as wide as desired.

Continue knitting straight, without shaping, until the shorter side is long enough to join to one side of the square.

Next row, commence at the long side. K. to within I st. of the end, turn.

*Next row, sl. the Ist st., k. to the end.
Next row, k. to within 2 sts. of the end, turn *.

Rep. from * to *, working I st. less in alternate rows until I st. remains.

K. that st. and slip it back on to the left-hand needle.
Next row, k. 2 sts., turn.
Next row, sl. I, k. I.
*Next row, k. 3 sts., turn.
Next row, sl. I, k. to the end *.

Rep. from * to *, working I more st. in alternate rows until all sts. are knitted in one row again.

I. One band showing the mitred ends and three corners.

242

CHECKERED PATTERNS

These checkered patterns are one of the simplest of all coloured knitting patterns to work. One colour is taken over the other by means of slipped stitches. To get the best effects strongly contrasting colours should be used: the colours may be shown in equal proportions, or one may be more prominent than the other. A closely worked fabric will show the colours to better advantage than a loosely knitted fabric, so use fairly small needles for the thickness of the thread. All slipped stitches are worked purlwise.

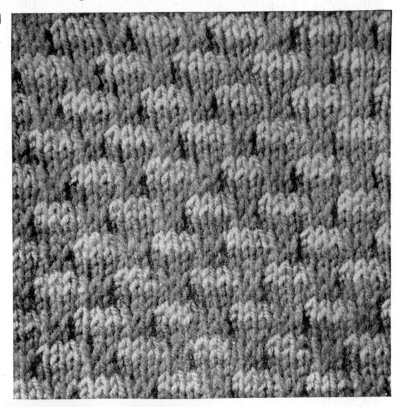

I. This is a very easy checkered pattern to knit.

Cast on the stitches in the colour that is to be more prominent than the other and knit 2 rows. All work will be in stocking stitch.

3rd row, join on the contrasting colour. * K. 4 sts., sl. 2 sts. purlwise *; repeat from * to *, ending with k. 4, if possible.

4th row, * p. 4 sts., sl. 2 sts. * (the same stitches that were slipped in the previous row); repeat from * to * to the end, finishing with p. 4.

5th row, and 6th row, are worked in the first colour, do not slip any of the stitches.

Continue knitting, repeating rows 3 to 6 inclusive.

2. Here the colours are in equal proportions. To get this effect knit the first 2 rows in one colour, change to the second colour and work like rows 3 and 4 of the previous pattern. Then change the colour of the wool again and knit the next row, slipping the 2 centre sts. of the second colour. Thus, work will begin: K. 5, * sl. 2, k. 4 *; repeat from * to * as far as possible, and the same pair of stitches will be slipped in the purl row.

MORE COMPLICATED CHECKERS

Very complicated patterns can be made up by using more than two colours in the checkered pattern method; the work is still quite easy to knit, but the effect will be that of a highly intricate design.

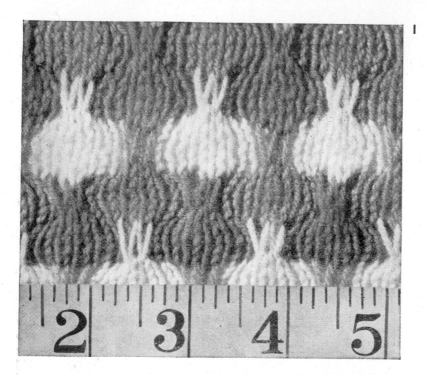

1. This illustration shows the use of three colours, with more than 2 rows of knitting in each. Work 4 rows in stocking stitch in one of the colours. Change to the next colour and k. 6, slip 2 purlwise. Repeat to the end. Purl back, slipping the slipped stitches of the previous row purlwise again.

Repeat these 2 rows, then change to the third colour and work 4 similar rows, slipping the middle pair of the stitches that were knitted in the previous colour.

Change the colour to the first used and knit 4 more rows, again changing the slipped stitches to the middle pair that were knitted in the previous colour.

Continue knitting thus, changing the colours 3 times.

2. Three colours in unequal quantities. There are 4 rows of one of the colours and this same colour is carried over the next two colours which are worked in the next 4 rows, 2 rows to each colour. The 2 centre stitches of the second colour are also slipped over the third colour. Thus, the third colour is in the smallest quantity. It will be seen that the slipped stitches of the second colour are moved along in the second pattern to come over the slipped stitches of the first colour, and the slipped stitches of the first colour are moved along to correspond.

COLOURS KNITTED INTO A DESIGN

The next step in coloured knitting is the knitting of a design into the fabric. The fabric should be stocking stitch. One colour is used for the background of the design and the other colour, or colours, are worked into a pattern. There are two ways of carrying the wool from pattern to pattern, behind the background colour, and the width of the background will determine which method should be used to give the best result.

In the easiest method, the wool is allowed to strand across the background, but this can only be done when the patterns are close together; in the other method the colour not being used is woven in with the thread being knitted. This is shown in illustration 2.

1. A very simple colour pattern in two contrasting colours. In the first row every 5th st. is worked in the dark colour; in the next row, which is the purl row, 3 sts. are knitted in dark and in the third row, the plain one again, every 5th st. is knitted dark. Then there are four rows in background colour only.

2. The wrong side of the work, showing how the threads look when they are woven in. This must be done when there are wide spaces of background between patterns.

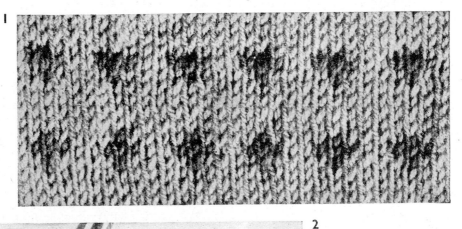

3. This shows the dark thread being woven in with the knitting of the light thread.

A DRESS WITH PLEAT EFFECTS

Measurements. Bust, 34 ins.; hips, 38 ins.; length from shoulder to hem, 46 ins.; sleeve seam length, 6 ins.

Materials. 19 ozs. of light colour 4-ply wool; 3 ozs. of dark colour 4-ply wool; a pair of No. 11 needles; a pair of No. 10 needles; a suède belt to match the colour of the dark wool and a set of 10 buttons to match the dark wool; a short zipp fastener for the front neck.

DETAILS OF THE STYLE

The main part of the garment is a st.st. ground with every 6th st. a purl st. In every 4th row the second row of purled sts. is moved along to come over the middle of the space between the purled sts. of the previous patt. row.

The front has two bands of wide ribbing running down from the shoulders and ending in finer and flared ribbing to give the effect of pleats.

Interest is given to the shoulders by the top of the ribbing being shaped to a point and a strapping of dark knitting showing around this point. The collar and cuffs are in dark wool and three bands run round the hem to emphasize the pleats. The back has only one set of ribbing running down the centre and it is wider than the bands on the front. This also ends in flared ribbing.

The sleeves are very full and they have one wide band

of ribbing. The bodice and skirt are joined at the waist, the bodice being knitted upwards and the skirt knitted downwards. With this method it is a very easy matter to alter the length of the skirt if it stretches in wear.

The ribbing of the bodice and skirt should be pressed well open. If these directions are being adapted to a larger size the ribbing should be omitted altogether, as it will not suit a larger figure. For a larger size carry the spotted pattern right across the work.

If the bust is small, but prominent, omit the ribbing on the front of the bodice.

DIRECTIONS

THE FRONT BODICE

Using No. 11 needles cast on 101 sts. Knit into the backs of these for the 1st row.

2nd row, k. 15, p. 2, k. 8, p. 2, k. 8, p. 2, k. 27, p. 2, k. 8, p. 2, k. 8, p. 2, k. 15.

3rd row, return, knitting the sts. purled in the previous row and purling the sts. that were knitted.

THE PATTERN

1st row, k. 3, p. 1, k. 5, p. 1, k. 5, p. 2, k. 8, p. 2, k. 8, p. 2, k. 1, p. 1, k. 5, p. 1, k. 5, p. 1, k. 5, p. 1, k. 1, p. 2, k. 8, p. 2, k. 5, p. 1, k. 5, p. 1, k. 3.

2nd row, p. 15, work the ribbing, p. 27, work the ribbing, p. 15.

3rd row, k. 15, rib, k. 27, rib, k. 15.

4th row, as the 2nd row.

5th row, p. 1, k. 5, p. 1, k. 5, p. 1, k. 2, rib, k. 4, p. 1, k. 5, p. 1, k. 5, p. 1, k. 5, p. 1, k. 4, rib, k. 2, p. 1, k. 5, p. 1, k. 5, p. 1.

6th row, as 2nd row.

7th row, as 3rd row.

8th row, as 4th row.

Work this patt. of 8 rows throughout. Inc. the width of the bodice by knitting twice into the 1st and last sts. of every 8th row.

Knit until the work measures 9 ins. Change to No. 10's on the 16th row.

ARMHOLE SHAPING

Cast off 7 sts. at the beginning of the next 2 rows.

K. 2 tog. at the beginning of the next 6 rows.

Knit without further shaping until the work measures 11½ ins. from the beginning.

NECK SHAPING AND SHAPING OF THE PATTERNED SHOULDER

With the right side of the work facing, knit to the beginning of the first set of ribbing.

Cast off 2 sts. (the purled sts.), k. 8, p. 2, k. 8, cast off 2 sts., knit 12 sts. (in patt. if necessary), k. 2 tog. Place the remainder of the sts. not knitted on a spare needle. Turn.

Purl back along the first set of 13 sts.

A DRESS WITH PLEAT EFFECTS

continued

on the needle and put all the rest on a holder to be knitted up in their turn.

Knit in patt. on these 13 sts. for another 26 rows.

K. 2 tog. at the beginning of the next 4 rows which commence at the neck edge, and, at the same time, knit twice into the first st. of the next 8 rows that commence on the edge away from the neck. Then continue knitting without shaping for another 10 rows. Cast off.

Now pick up the sts. that come above the band of ribbing; there will be 18 of these sts.

Knit without shaping for 22 rows, continuing the ribbing all the while.

K. 2 tog. at the beginning of every row until only 1 st. remains, break off the wool and pull the end through the last st.

Pick up the remaining set of sts. on the holder and knit these in patt. for 26 rows.

Then knit twice into the first stitch of the next 8 rows that begin at the edge opposite the armhole (the edge nearest to the point of ribbing).

Continue knitting without shaping for another 8 rows.

With the right side of work facing, cast off half the number of the sts., k. to the end and p. back. Cast off the remaining sts.

THE RIGHT SHOULDER

Pick up the sts. from the spare needle and knit along the row, casting off the 2 sets of purled sts. (as on the left shoulder just worked) and continue knitting up the strips with the shapings at the opposite ends of the rows to the shapings on the left shoulder.

THE BACK BODICE

Using No. 11 needles cast on 80 sts. Knit into the backs of these for the 1st row.

2nd row, k. 23, p. 2, k. 6, p. 2, k. 6, p. 2, k. 6, p. 2, k. 6, p. 2, k. 23.

3rd row, return, knitting the sts. that were purled and purling the sts. that were knitted in the previous row.

THE PATTERN

The speckled patt. is worked on the first and last 23 sts. and the ribbing is worked on the middle 34 sts.

1st row, k. 5, p. 1, k. 5, p. 1, k. 5, p. 1, k. 5, rib, k. 5, p. 1, k. 5, p. 1, k. 5, p. 1, k. 5.

2nd row, p. 23, rib, p. 23.

3rd row, k. 23, rib, k. 23.

4th row, as the 2nd row.

5th row, k. 2, p. 1, k. 5, p. 1, k. 5, p. 1, k. 5, p. 1, k. 2, rib, k. 2, p. 1, k. 5, p. 1, k. 5, p. 1, k. 5, p. 1, k. 2.

6th row, as the 2nd row.

7th row, as the 3rd row.

8th row, as the 4th row.

Work this patt. of 8 rows throughout.

Inc. the width of the bodice by knitting twice into the 1st and last sts. of every 8th row.

Knit until the work measures 9 ins. from the beginning changing to No. 10 needles on the 16th row.

ARMHOLE SHAPING

This is worked in the same way as on the front. Work until the back measures 15 ins.

With the right side of work facing, cast off 8 sts. at the beginning of the next 6 rows.

Cast off the remainder of the sts.

THE FRONT SKIRT

Using No. 11 needles cast on 101 sts. and knit into the backs of these for the 1st row. The sts. are divided up into patt. and ribbing like those of the front bodice, i.e., 15 sts. patt., 22 sts. for ribbing, 27 sts. for patt., 22 sts. for ribbing and 15 sts. for patt.

Copy the directions for knitting the patt. from the directions of the front bodice, increasing the 1st and last sts. of every 8th row until work measures 10½ ins. Change to No. 10 needles on the 16th row.

After the 10½ ins., inc. on the 1st and last sts. of the speckled centre front panel as well as at the side seams and on the same rows as the inc. are worked for the sides.

Knit in this way until work measures 18½ ins. End on a row on the wrong side.

The pleat effect ribbing. Continue knitting the side front and the centre front panel in speckling.

On the ribbing sts. inc. the number of sts. thus: K. to the ribbing, p. 2, k. twice into the next 20 sts., k. the centre panel (in patt. if necessary), k. twice into the next 20 sts., k. 2, k. to the end (in patt. if necessary).

In the next row, p. the sts. of the side panel, rib across the next 42 sts. in k. 2, p. 2, ending with k. 2, p. across the centre panel sts. Rep. the k. 2, p. 2 ribbing and p. across the remaining sts.

Knit in patt. and narrow ribbing for 8 more rows. Continue to inc. at the side seams and at the sides of the front panel as usual.

The width of the pleating is increased on the next and on the following 13th and 25th rows by knitting twice into the 2nd, 3rd and then the 4th plain sts. of every rib. (See illustration for this step.)

Then continue knitting until the pleats measure 6¾ ins.

Change to the dark wool and knit 4 rows in it.

Make no more incs., either at the side seams or on the centre panel.

Change again to the light colour and work the next 6 rows with it. Then work another band of dark, another light, another dark and then change again to light and knit for a further 1½ ins. Cast off loosely.

THE BACK SKIRT

Using No. 11 needles cast on 80 sts. and work the patt. and ribbing as for the back bodice. Work for 6 ins., inc. on the 1st and last sts. of every 8th row. Change to No. 10 needles on the 16th row.

Then inc. on the 1st and last sts. of both side back panels, thus there will be 4 incs. in every 8th row. Work in this manner until the skirt measures 18½ ins.

Then commence the pleated effect at the end of the centre back ribbed panel; thus, work across the speckled panel, p. 2, k. twice into the next 30 sts., p. 2, work across the speckled panel.

Return, purling across the speckled panel and knitting fine ribbing, as on the front, across the centre panel sts. and purling across the 2nd set of speckling.

Inc. the width of the pleating as on the front and knit until the pleating measures the same depth, changing the colours as in the directions for the front skirt. Cast off loosely.

THE SLEEVES (both alike)

Using No. 11 needles cast on 52 sts. in dark wool and work in ribbing of k. 2, p. 2 for 10 rows.

Change to light wool and k. 3 times into each st., first through the front, then through the back and again through the front (156 sts.).

These are divided up into 57 for speckling, 42 for ribbing and 57 again for speckling.

After inc. the number of sts., p. back.

Next row, k. 57, rib 42, k. 57.

Next row, p. 57, rib, p. 57.

THE PATTERN

The ribbing is worked with p. 2, k. 6, repeated 5 times and then p. 2, and it comes between two panels of speckling having 57 sts. in each panel.

1st row, k. 3, * p. 1, k. 5*; rep. from * to * 8 times. Rib, * k. 5, p. 1 *; rep. from * to * 8 times, k. 3.

2nd row, p. 57, rib, p. 57.

3rd row, k. 57, rib, k. 57.

4th row, as 2nd row.

5th row, * p. 1, k. 5 *; rep. from * to * 8 times. P. 1, k. 2, rib, k. 2, * p. 1, k. 5 *; rep. from * to * 8 times, p. 1.

6th row, as 2nd row.

7th row, as 3rd row.

8th row, as 4th row.

Continue these 8 rows throughout.

Knit until work measures 6 ins., change to No. 10 needles on the 16th row and inc. on the 1st and last st. of every 8th row.

SHAPING THE TOP

K. 2 tog. at the beginning of the next 32 rows (4 patts.).

K. 2 tog. at the beginning and end of the next 24 rows (3 patts.).

Cast off loosely.

THE COLLAR

Using dark wool and No. 11 needles cast on 110 sts. Work in ribbing of k. 1, p. 1 for 2½ ins., inc. at each end of every 4th row.

UNDERLAY FOR SHOULDERS

Using the dark wool and No. 11 needles cast on 30 sts. and knit in g.st. for 5½ ins. Cast off.

HOW TO MAKE UP

Darn in all ends and press with a warm iron and a damp cloth, being careful to preserve the shape of the garment. Do not press the top of the pleats, but pull out the lower ends of the pleats and press fairly hard, so that they will remain open and give fullness to the lower part of the skirt. Do not press the collar, nor the ribbing of the sleeve ends, the remainder of the ribbing should be well pressed so that it is well opened.

The square of g.st. knitting must be laid under the tops of the front shoulders and the points and side shoulders arranged on to them in good shapes. Tack the work carefully and hem all edges down with wool, placing the sts. fairly close and being careful that the edges are kept straight.

The short zipp fastener for the front neck opening should be mounted on tape to match the colour of the dark wool. A small tassel could be made and fastened to the slider to pull it up and down.

Join the side seams and the shoulder seams of the bodice. Then join the sleeve seams and set the sleeves into the armholes, putting in a running thread round the tops which can be drawn up to make the sleeves fit the armhole of the dress.

Next, join the side seams of the skirt, being careful to match the stripes around the hem and keeping both edges at the same tension.

Press the seams lightly and then set the bodice on to the skirt.

Hold the skirt on the wrong side and the bodice on the right side. Mark centre front and centre back on both, and set these corresponding points together. Then pin the side seams together and continue joining the waist between these points, matching ends of ribbings. Join this seam with running sts., which are not too tightly worked.

Now the collar must be sewn on, the ends to the top neck points of the front bodice and the centre back to the centre back neck.

A canvas pad may be slipped in underneath the fullness of the sleeve tops to hold them out.

Sew five buttons, to match the colour of the dark wool, down the middle stripe on each side of the front. A suède belt to match the buttons completes the dress.

KNITTING AND WOOL CLOTH COMBINED

Knitting and wool cloth can be combined for sports and spectator wear. Very close textured cloth should be used with knitted fabric in the manner described here. Felt is the best cloth to use because there is no pattern on its surface to compete with the pattern on the surface of the knitting.

Little felt waistcoats with knitted sleeves are useful, comfortable and very attractive. The knitted sleeves are much more comfortable to wear than sleeves made of the same felt as the body part of the waistcoat.

I

KNITTING AND WOOL CLOTH COMBINED

continued

1. A felt waistcoat with ribbed knitted sleeves. The waistcoat can be made from the pattern draft in illustration 2; this of course, gives only the shape of one-half, both sides being alike.

To knit the sleeves 3 ozs. of 4-ply wool will be required and a pair of No. 5 needles. Cast on 40 sts. Knit into the backs of these for the first row. Then change to ribbing of k. 3, p. 2, and knit without shaping for 3 ins.

On the first stitch in every following 6th and 7th rows knit twice. Do this 5 times. Then, knit twice into the first stitch of every 4th and 5th rows until work measures enough for length of underarm.

To shape the top. K. 2 tog. at the beginning of the next 10 rows.

K. 2 tog. at the beginning and end of the next 15 rows.

Cast off 10 sts. at the beginning of the next 2 rows.

Cast off the remainder of the stitches.

The sleeves are both alike. Do not press the work.

Join the sleeve seam with oversewing and set into the armhole of the waistcoat in the usual way.

If the felt is thick, the edge of the armhole should be laid over the top of the knitted sleeve and sewn down with hemming, worked closely.

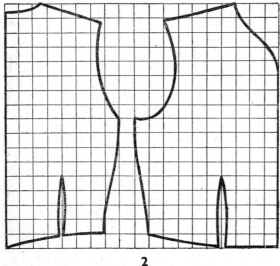

2

2. The draft for the simple little pattern of the waistcoat. This can be easily copied on to newspaper, or thin brown paper; each small square represents a 1-in. square; so to get the measures, count the number of squares and turn that number into inches.

3. Another felt waistcoat with sleeves in felt and cuffs and high-necked collar in ribbed knitting.

With 4-ply wool 2 ozs. will be needed, and a pair of No. 6 needles. The neck must have an opening, this can be along the shoulder seam, or down the centre front. A zipp fastener should close the opening.

For the collar, cast on 90 sts. and knit in ribbing until work measures the depth required for the turn down collar. Cast off very loosely.

For the cuffs, cast on 50 sts. and work in the same ribbing as the collar for 5 ins. (this allows for a turned back cuff).

To join these to the waistcoat lay the edge of the knitting against the edge of the felt and work straight stitches over the two edges.

3

KNITTING AND APPLIED FELT DECORATION

Knitted fabrics can be quickly and effectively decorated with felt shapes sewn down in a pattern.

The knitting need not be in plain (stocking stitch) fabric; quite often a slightly textured surface will be more pleasant with the smooth patternless texture of the felt.

A collection of assorted felt shapes, ready cut out in various colours, can be bought for 1s. 3d. Shapes all in one colour are a little more expensive. Some contrasting coloured embroidery threads, in either wool or silk, will be required for sewing down the little pieces of felt in a pleasing arrangement.

1

2

3

1. A useful collection of felt pieces. Circles, diamonds, leaf shapes, triangles and squares are in assorted sizes and colours.

2. The type of design that can be built up from such a collection. With care and a pair of sharp scissors these shapes can be cut at home from small squares of different coloured felts. Cut the shapes out in paper first, lay them on the felt and lightly dab some powdered chalk, or face powder, over them. Remove the paper and the shapes will be found outlined sharply in powder. Cut these out with smooth cutting lines. Lay the felt shapes in position on the knitting and sew down with embroidery stitches, if possible without previous tacking.

3. Another suggestion for felt decoration. The shapes are sewn down with hemming stitches in a fine silk thread to match.

GODETS IN KNITTING

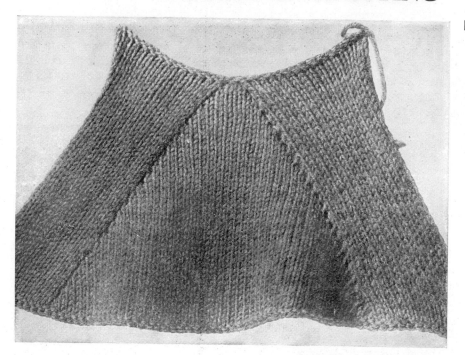

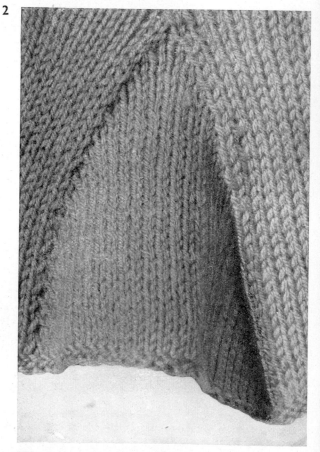

I. A godet worked from the top of the garment. A strand is picked up to make a stitch at each side of the godet in every right side row, making a decorative line of small holes to mark the area of the godet.

2. A godet worked from the hem of a garment. Two stitches are disposed of at the sides of the godet on every right side row. The first one is worked by sl. I, k. I, p.s.s.o., and the second one, at the other edge of the godet, is worked as k. 2 tog. No holes are formed by this method.

Godets in knitting give the same effect as godets in dressmaking, they are flared sections made to give extra fullness. They differ from those used in dressmaking by being in one with remainder of the garment. Knitted godets are not separate pieces of knitting let into the garment.

The direction in which the garment is being knitted will decide the method of making the godet. If the knitting begins at the lower edge, then the godet is made by decreasings, but when work starts at the top, the shaping of the godet is done with increasings. The latter method is by far the easiest, as shaping can be worked until the godet is the required width, but in the former method, the width of the godet must be worked out before knitting commences, and its height and width must be estimated too.

KNITTING FLARES

Flared sections in knitted garments are made by increasing the number of stitches on the needle. This is easier than casting on the number of stitches to make the widest part of the flare and then decreasing to the smaller part.

Therefore, the garment is commenced at the highest possible point. Skirts will start at waist lines and flared sleeves will be begun at the top of the arm.

The worker's tension must be known first so that the number of rows to be worked for that part of the garment, and the number of times that the increasing must be worked, can be estimated. The more the increasings can be spread among the stitches in the row, the better the garment will hang. The skating skirt is an example of a flared garment commenced at the top and its width increased towards the hem.

1. If the width of the garment at the hem is to be three times the width of the waist and the number of waist sts. is known and the number of rows to be worked from waist to hem is known (these can be found by measuring the tension), then the number of extra sts. to be made and the number of the row on which to work the increasings can be found easily. Decide on the number of increasings to make in each inc. row and divide that number into the number of sts. to be made altogether, the result will give the number of inc. rows. Divide this number into the total number of rows in the skirt and the answer will tell on which row to work the increasings.

Example. There are 80 sts. at the waist, therefore there will be 240 sts. at the hem (80 x 3 = 240).

Number of extra sts. = 160 (240 — 80 at waist = 160).

Number of increasings in every inc. row = 4 (this as desired). 160 ÷ 4 = 40. This is the number of inc. rows to be worked.

Number of rows between waist and hem = 168.

Therefore, increasings will be worked on every 4th row with 8 plain rows at the end (168 ÷ 40 = 4 times + 8 rows).

There will be 4 increasings in every 4th row of work, with the last 8 rows worked without shaping.

2. A flared pattern, giving the effect of sun-ray pleats. This is a very pleasant method of making a flared skirt in knitting. The method of calculating the number of times to work the increasings is found as described in the previous pattern, and the increasings are worked at either side of the plain sections of the rib. The number of ribs will, of course, give you the number of times in which to work the increasings in each row.

A BED, OR DRESSING JACKET

Measurements. Length from shoulder to lower edge 17 ins.; length of sleeve, from the neck, 25 ins.

Materials. 5 ozs. of 3-ply fingering; a pair of No. 4 needles.

DIRECTIONS

This little jacket can be knitted in a very short while. In the row where two loops are slipped off the needle, at least 1 in. of work is done at once.

Cast on 60 sts. and k. into the backs of these.

** Knit the next 2 rows plain.

3rd row, k. 1,* w.r.n. twice, k. 1 *; rep. from * to * to the end of the row.

4th row, k. 1, * sl. the two loops off the needle, k. 1 *; rep. from * to * to the end of the row.

5th row, k.

6th row, k. **

Rep. from ** to ** until there are 6 bands of slipped loops and the above patt. has been repeated 5 times more.

At the end of the next 2 rows cast on 60 sts. and continue knitting on these 180 sts. for 6 more bands of slipped loops. K. 2 rows.

TO SHAPE THE BACK NECK

K. to within 9 sts. of the centre, cast off 18 sts. and continue to the end of the row.

K. on this set of sts. until there are 3 more bands of slipped sts. At the neck end of the next row cast on 14 sts.

Continue knitting for 5 more bands of loops.

Starting at the wrist end of the sleeve cast off 60 sts., this will finish the sleeve.

K. without further shaping for another 6 patts.

Knit 3 rows plain and cast off.

Rep. the directions for the other sleeve and front, reversing the position of the casting on and off so that the shaping comes at the correct ends of the rows.

THE SLEEVE BANDS

Cast on 15 sts. and knit in g.st. for 6 ins. Gather up the end of the sleeves to the size of one of these bands and sew a band to each.

THE COLLAR

Cast on 80 sts. and knit in g.st. until the collar is as wide as desired. Cast off loosely and sew to the neck of the jacket.

Lastly sew up the underarm seam.

If liked, a crocheted edging may be worked all round the edge of the jacket including the collar and cuffs.

A thread of silk and wool will make this jacket into a very dainty Christmas present.

A LACY DRESSING CAPE

Measurements. Length from neck to lower edge, about 19 ins., this can be varied to requirements.

Materials. 2 ozs. of 3-ply white wool; 1 oz. of 3-ply coloured wool for the edging, about half this quantity will be used; a medium sized crochet hook; a pair each of No. 8, No. 4 and No. 1 needles; 1 yd. of narrow ribbon for the neck tie.

DIRECTIONS

Using No. 8 needles cast on 75 sts., k. 2 rows and then work the threading holes for the ribbon, thus: * K. 2, m. 1, k. 2 tog. *; rep. from * to * all along, finishing with m. 1, k. 2 tog., k. 1.

Continue knitting in g.st. for 2 ins.

Then change to No. 4 needles and k. another 2 rows.

K. 3, k. twice into the next st.; rep. all along.

THE PATTERN

K. 3, * k. 2 tog., k. 3, m. 1, k. 1, m. 1, k. 3, k. 2 tog., k. 3 *; rep. from * to * to the end.

Knit the next 3 rows in st.st.

Rep. these 4 rows 6 times more, changing to No. 1 needles after the 4th set of patt. rows.

Seven rows of holes completed, the patt. changes again; for the remainder of the work no more sts. are knitted together. The number of sts. being worked between the made sts. will inc. by two in each successive patt. The number of sts. in the end sections will, of course, only inc. by one.

K. until work measures about 19 ins., or until all the white wool is used and then work the crocheted edging in the other colour.

First of all work a row of double crochet into the edge of the cape, making the sts. tight enough to hold the edge into a good line. If the edge appears to curl, do not think that the stitch is becoming too tight, the pressing will straighten this out.

Into the double crochet work a row of treble scallops, thus: Turn with 3 ch., 4 tr. into the 1st d.c. from the hook, * miss 1 d.c. and work a d.c. into the next, miss 1 d.c. and work 5 tr. into the next *; rep. from * to * all along the edge.

Darn in all ends and lightly press the work, stretching the lower edge just a little.

A BED JACKET FOR A SMALL GIRL
TO BE KNITTED BY HERSELF

This extremely simple piece of knitting can be done by quite a small girl; the jacket will fit a girl up to twelve years of age.

Materials. 3 ozs. of 4-ply silk and wool mixture; a pair of No. 6 needles and a pair of No. 1 needles; some silk ribbon to sew at the neck edge to tie the fronts.

Directions. The entire jacket is knitted in one long strip, two tubes being sewn at each end for the arms to pass through. The fabric is loose enough for the remaining centre section to open out to make the back of the jacket.

Using the No. 6 needles cast on 32 sts. and knit in rib of k. 2, p. 2 for 14 rows.

Change to No. 1 needles and change the fabric to g.st., that is, knit every row plain.

In the next row, knit twice into every st., making 64 sts.

Continue knitting on these 64 sts. until work measures 40 ins. from the beginning.

K. 2 tog. all along the next row.

Change to No. 6 needles and to ribbing of k. 2, p. 2 for 14 rows. Cast off very loosely.

TO MAKE UP

This jacket must not be pressed.

Fold the strip in halves and sew up each end for 15 ins.

All sewing must be done very loosely so that the sts. stretch with the fabric. Sew two pieces of ribbon 3 ins. from each side of the centre of one of the free edges, these will make the tie at the neck.

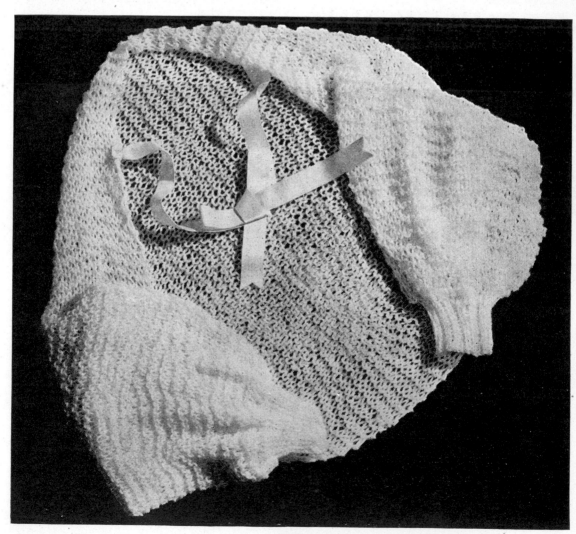

A PRAM WRAP FOR BABY

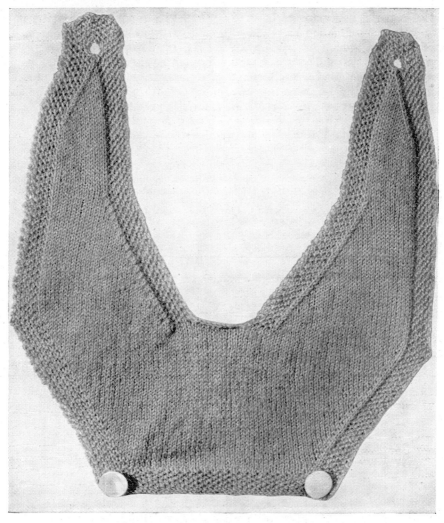

These little wraps are useful to give a
little extra warmth for the upper part of the body.

MEASUREMENT

From centre back to the buttonhole at one of the
ends, 15 ins.

MATERIALS

1 oz. of 3-ply wool for light-weight and 4-ply for heavier
weight; a pair of No. 9 needles; 2 large pearl buttons and
2 small ones.

DETAILS OF STYLE

The plain oblong may be placed across the chest, or
across the back, the two shaped ends cross over each
other, pass under the arms and fasten to the buttons.

DIRECTIONS

Cast on 49 sts. K. into the backs of these for the
1st row and then work in moss stitch for 7 rows; the first
and last 6 sts. are now worked in moss stitch, while the
remaining sts. are worked in st.st. The first and last

st.st. in every right side row is inc. by knitting twice into it.
Work 22 rows of increasings, 44 rows altogether.
K. to within 10 sts. of the centre, moss stitch 6, cast
off 8, moss stitch 6 and continue the row.

TO WORK THE STRAPS

On the first set of sts., work the first and last 6 sts.
in moss stitch and the remainder in st.st., knitting the first
2 st.sts. together on every right side row 19 times.
Continue without shaping for 20 rows.
Then knit the last 2 st.sts. together in every right side
row until all st.sts. are disposed of.
Then make a buttonhole on the middle 3 sts. and work
4 more rows in moss stitch. K. 2 together at the beginning
of the next 6 rows and cast off.
Make the other strap in the same way, but working
the shapings at the opposite ends of the rows. Press
lightly to flatten the border. The buttonhole may be
strengthened with blanket stitch being worked round it.
Sew a large pearl button, with a small button on the wrong
side, in both corners of the first border.

DESIGNING KNITTED GARMENTS

Some sort of squared paper should be used for designing garments. It may be the kind called "graph paper," which is ruled with lines $\frac{1}{4}$ in. apart each way, and on which you would make your drawing quarter size, or, the paper may be the type that dressmakers use for cutting out dress patterns. This is ruled in $\frac{1}{4}$ and 1 in. squares and on it you will be able to make your pattern, or design, full size.

Full sized drawings will be very useful, because the knitting can be laid on the paper pattern to test measurements as work proceeds. Always allowing for slight increase in size when the fabric is pressed.

Taking measures. Measurements are taken on the figure tightly, to allow for the stretch of the fabric. Quite often a figure that takes a 36-in. size in dressmaking patterns will be 34 ins. for the purpose of planning knitted garments, and a 40-in. bust figure will work to a measurement of 38 ins. Sleeve lengths, too, will be a little shorter and no extra length is allowed for the back of the arm. Bodices and skirts are not dipped 1 in. at the centre front and the length from shoulder to waist is taken a little shorter than for dressmaking. The average measures for knitted garments are: bust, 34 ins.; back length to waist, 14 ins.; and sleeve length, inside, 16 ins. The weight of the garment will stretch the lengths somewhat. Skirts are made at least 2 ins. shorter than the usual measure.

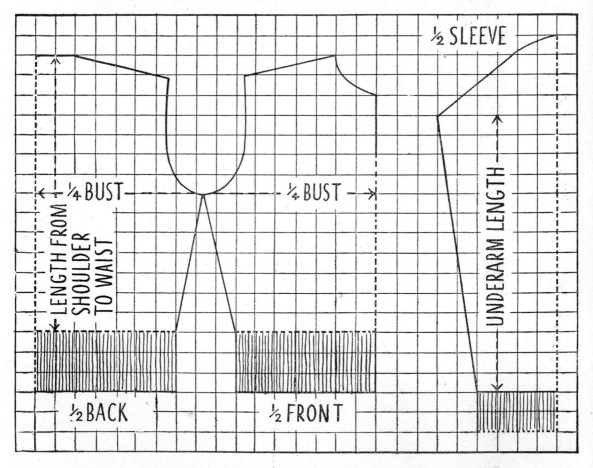

This is a draft for a simple jumper to be knitted with a 3-in. band of ribbing at the waist and a round neck, with a short opening at the centre front. The sleeve is straight and it has a wrist ribbing of 2 ins.

The draft can be used in a similar manner to a dressmaker's bodice block, it can be the basis for other and more complicated styles. Draw the pattern on to either plain paper, or squared paper; each of these small squares represents a 1-in. square. The pattern will be suitable for a 34-in. bust, as shown here, with the measure taken tightly, and the measures for an average sized figure have been used. Proportions for other sizes can be used as suggested on the draft. A loosely knitted fabric will open out during pressing more than a close fabric.

ADDING STITCH DECORATION

When the outline shape of the garment has been obtained, style and design can be added according to the type of lines in fashion. Style is given to knitted garments by the type of texture made with the knitting, and the shape of the lines taken by any change in the fabric.

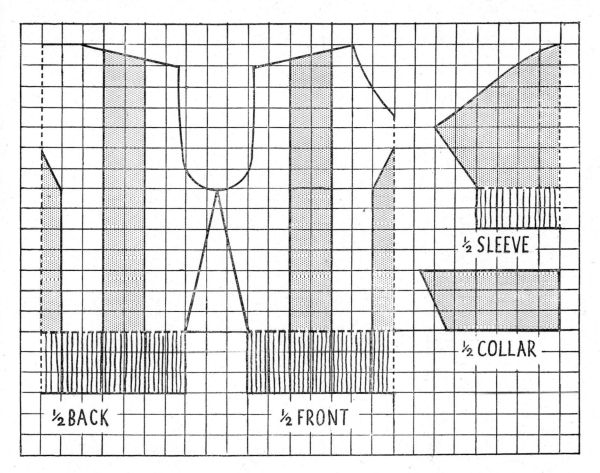

This drawing shows bands of different texture planned on the simple outline draft on the previous page. The plan is made while the garment can be seen in the flat, and if the draft has been made on squared paper, either full size, or quarter size, the work will be much simplified because the measurements and positions of these bands can be placed accurately in relation to the rest of the garment. The change in fabric can be carried out in three different ways: with ribbing; a change of texture, i.e., moss stitch on a stocking stitch ground; or with lace stitch.

To carry out this draft, or design, it will be necessary to know the tension of the work. That is, how many stitches there will be in 1-in. of width, and how many rows will be worked for 1-in. of knitting. When these are known, then the number of stitches to be cast on can be calculated, and the number of stitches and rows required to make up the various sections can be mapped out beforehand.

Supposing that there will be 7 sts. to the inch and 8 rows to the inch of knitting, we shall know that there will have to be 98 sts. at the top of the ribbing. Therefore, 98 sts. will be cast on.

From the ribbing to the beginning of the armhole, the draft measures 7 ins., so there will be 56 rows of knitting from the ribbing to the beginning of the armhole shaping. In these 56 rows the width must increase by 1½ ins. at each side. This means that there must be an increase of 10 sts. at each end, 20 sts. in the entire row.

Now, we can calculate the row upon which to increase. 10 sts. are needed at each end, so an increase must be worked on every 5th row. The increase must be worked on both side seams of the garment, therefore, we shall knit twice into the first and last stitches of every 5th row. The remainder of the shaping is worked out in a similar manner, by calculating the number of stitches, or rows, in a particular measurement.

In working out the proportion of the texture, the number of stitches on the needle after the ribbing, must be divided up to give the right proportions for each section. In this draft there are seven equal sections of two different textures. Thus there will be 14 sts. in each section (98 ÷ 7 = 14), and the depth of the centre bands, before the tops are decreased will be 56 rows (8 rows × 7 ins.).

DESIGNING KNITTED SKIRTS

Although only skirts are mentioned here, the same principles will apply to the skirt part of dresses. Many knitters commence the skirts of dresses from the waist line, knit down to the hem and make a seam at the waist to join the bodice and skirt together. This has many advantages. The work does not become so heavy as when bodice and skirt are in one piece and, when the skirt stretches in length,

which often happens, it is very easy to unpick the unwanted inch or two and cast off the stitches again. Some knitters find, too, that the skirt will hang better this way. Remember, if there is a definite way up of the pattern that it would be in reverse to that of the bodice, so consider whether this is a serious drawback before beginning the skirt at the waist line. Stitch numbers given below are for half the skirt.

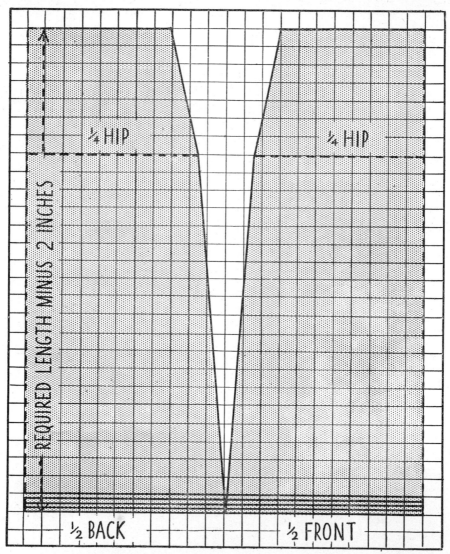

1. The draft of a plain skirt. The hip measure is taken tightly and this, with the length, is taken as the basis measures for making the draft. Skirts are made at least 2 ins. shorter than the required length to allow for the fabric stretching. If the hip measure, taken tightly, is 38 ins. and the tension of work is 6 sts. to 1 in. and 7 rows to 1 in., there must be 114 sts. on the needle by the time the hip line is reached. The top of the side seam slopes in 1½ ins. to the waist line, this is a lessening of the width by 3 ins. on both the front and the back skirt pieces. Therefore, each piece will measure 16 ins. at the top, which will require 96 sts. to be cast on. Still further reduction can be made in the width by working on needles two sizes smaller for the first 2 ins. With an increase of 1½ ins. at each side between the waist and the hip line there must be an increase of 9 sts. at each side.

DESIGNING KNITTED SKIRTS *continued*

If there are 7 rows to the inch and 7 ins. from waist to hip, there will be 49 rows between the waist and hip lines (49 ÷ 9 = 5 +), and so there must be an increase every 5 rows. The increase happens at both ends of the row; so the first and last stitches in every 5th row

will be knitted twice. The row for increasing on the remainder of the skirt can be worked out in the same way. The last inch of the skirt should be knitted in either moss stitch, or in garter stitch. This change of texture will make a good hem line.

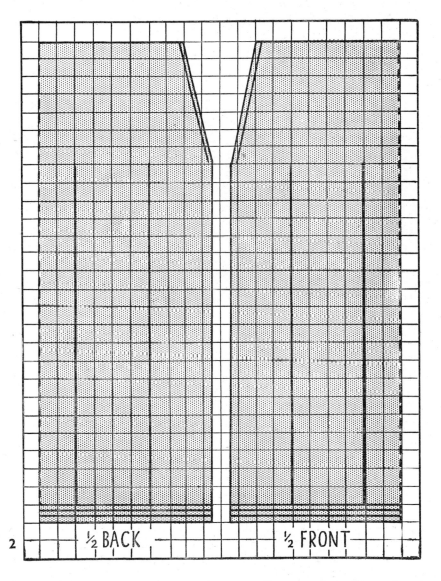

½ BACK   ½ FRONT

2. This draft shows the design and plan for a flared skirt. The shaping from waist to hip line is obtained in the same way as for the last skirt. The straight lines down the lower skirt sections show the positions of the increasing stitches, those that will be knitted twice, to give the required extra width. The amount of fullness required will determine the number of plain rows to work between each increase. It will be well to experiment on a small specimen first. The number of stitches knitted plain between the increased stitches will be increased on every shaping row. The number of stitches in the centre panels should always remain the same, in this way the two side sections will be widened while the centre sections remain the same width. An inch of knitting, without shaping and in moss stitch, or garter stitch, should finish off the hem line.

DESIGNING KNITTED FABRICS

Before beginning to plan out knitted fabrics, it is necessary to form some plan whereby stitches can be indicated with symbols. The shape of the stitches should be taken and simplified: a plain stitch can be indicated with an oval, and a purl stitch can be shown as a curved line. These symbols are shown on this page.

Squared paper, such as can be bought in an exercise book, will be needed for spacing the stitches and rows. Each square, horizontally, will represent a stitch and each row of squares, vertically, will represent a row. Diagrams and charts are used in designing stitches.

Do not confuse these diagrams with stitch charts. Diagrams show the fabric as seen from the right side, but a stitch chart shows the working of each consecutive row in the order in which it would be worked. Thus, we get a drawing showing alternate rows as they appear on the side of the fabric that they are worked; the first row as seen on the right side and the second row as seen on the wrong side of the knitting.

As knitted stitches are a little shorter than their width, the diagram will become a little deeper than the knitting will be when worked. This must be taken into consideration and the exact depth worked out from the worker's tension.

A PLAIN STITCH   A PURL STITCH

1. Suggestions for stitch symbols. A plain stitch and a purl stitch in a square.

STOCKING STITCH FABRIC

2. This is how a piece of stocking stitch fabric is indicated in a diagram, every stitch drawn as a plain stitch.

PURL STITCH FABRIC

3. Purl stitch fabric as shown in a diagram, every stitch drawn as a curve in a square.

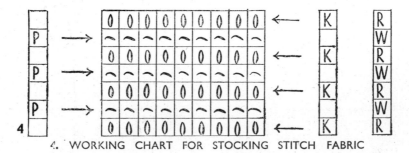

4. WORKING CHART FOR STOCKING STITCH FABRIC

4. A stitch chart for stocking stitch fabric. Each row is shown in the stitch that it is worked in. Arrows indicate the direction of the work as seen when the work is viewed from the right side, the letters in the first group tell what stitch is indicated and the letters in the second group, on the right-hand side of the chart, tell on which side of the fabric those rows of stitches are worked. From the chart we know that the first row is worked in plain knitting (k.), from right to left and that this will be on the right side of the fabric (r.). Then the arrow pointing in the opposite direction tells us that the work is turned and the next row is purl stitched (p.), and this will be the wrong side of the fabric (w.).

CHARTS FOR MOSS STITCH
AND RIBBINGS

When more than one kind of stitch is worked in one row, it is indicated by its own symbol in its right square.

A diagram for moss stitch fabric and its chart have been given here first, in order to show how different the chart can be from the diagram for even the simplest of knitting patterns.

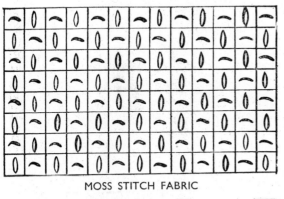

I

MOSS STITCH FABRIC

I. The fabric diagram shows plain and purl stitches alternating both ways. The number of squares used in the diagram must indicate the number of stitches that should be used for the pattern: an odd number of stitches is required for moss stitch, so an odd number of squares **must** be used in our diagram.

WORKING CHART FOR
MOSS STITCH FABRIC

2

2. Compare this chart **for** moss stitch fabric with the diagram for the same stitch and see how different this simple stitch chart can be from its diagram. The same symbols are used to tell in which direction the rows are worked and the side of the fabric on which they will appear.

3

3. The next simplest knitting pattern is a ribbing and this Is the diagram for a ribbing of k. 2, p. 2. The purled stitches are shaded to give the effect of the fabric sinking to the back on these stitches.

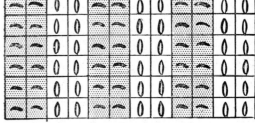

RIBBING FABRIC OF K. 2, P. 2.

4. A ribbing chart for k. 2, p. 2. Here again the number of stitches to cast on must be indicated; the number should be divisible by 4.

4 →

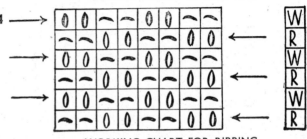

WORKING CHART FOR RIBBING
FABRIC OF K. 2, P. 2

DESIGNING LACE STITCH FABRICS

Two more symbols are required for the designing of simple lace stitch patterns. They are, one for indicating the two stitches that are knitted together and the other is for the made stitch.

Squared paper will still be required for the diagrams and charts, and on a spare piece of paper, roughly indicate the positions of the holes that are to be formed in the fabric. This rough sketch is necessary for getting an idea of the kind of shape or line that is to be formed with the lace stitch holes.

Mark off a section of squares and draw the first two rows as stocking stitch, or any other solid fabric that will form the first two rows of the knitting, then, in the next row, plan out the stitches that will be knitted together to compensate for the made stitches. The next row, being purled, will show as a plain row from the right side of the fabric and the following rows will indicate how they will be worked to form the pattern desired.

1. The symbols that can be used to indicate the 2 sts. worked in the simplest of lace patterns. They are for knitting 2 sts. together and for the made stitch coming after a knitted stitch and before the 2 sts. knitted together. When the made stitch comes after the two knitted together, the drawing is shown in reverse.

K. 2 TOG.   K. 1, M. 1, K. 2 TOG.

2. The diagram for a very simple lace stitch pattern. Every fourth row makes the holes, it is worked thus: K. 1, m. 1, k. 2 tog., repeated all along with an extra knitted stitch at the beginning and ending with a knitted stitch, to make the selvedges firm. The holes are indicated with shading.

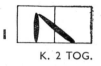

3. Here is the chart for the lace pattern shown in the previous diagram. The made stitch is shown as a straight line and alternate rows are shown worked purlwise on the wrong side of the fabric. The first group of letters to the right of the chart shows how the pattern, or lace stitch rows, are indicated by the letter O.

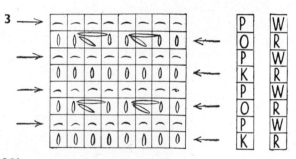

264

CHARTS AND DIAGRAMS FOR COMBINED PATTERNS

Diagrams for flat fabrics, that is, fabrics that are not lace stitch, are very easy to design on squared paper. Plan out some sort of main scheme first, putting in the most important lines and then adding the secondary detail. Let the effect of the stitch be shown in the diagram. Purl stitches will stand out on a stocking stitch background, so mark these thicker than the loops indicating plain stitches. Any vertical lines of purl stitch will sink below the plain stitches, so these will be shaded to give that effect.

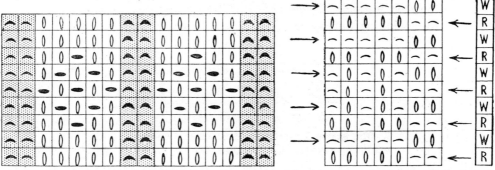

1. A combined rib and patterned fabric made entirely with plain and purl stitches. Purl stitched diamonds link up the purl stitch ribs.

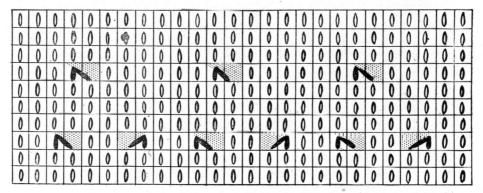

2. This diagram will make a fabric like a clover leaf lace stitch. Rows of groups of three holes will be divided by a number of stocking stitch rows. In the next row of pattern the holes can be moved along to come over the plain spaces of the first pattern.

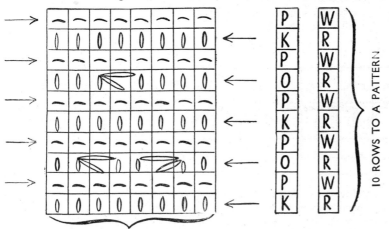

8 STITCHES TO A PATTERN

3. The chart from which the fabric would be worked. It will be seen that the first hole is formed with the made stitch beyond the two stitches that are knitted together; this is to ensure that the doubled stitches pull the fabric in opposite directions and so keep the side edges straight. The chart shows the number of rows that go to make up one pattern.

MORE ADVANCED PATTERN DIAGRAMS AND CHARTS

In an earlier section in this book there are directions for knitting fabrics that form a scalloped lower edge. The scallops are formed by bunching one part of the stitches together and compensating for this with several made stitches to send the fabric in the reverse direction. It was found that the bunching is done by knitting 3 stitches together, instead of 2 stitches. A different sort of symbol is required for indicating this process. The cast-on row is indicated by " C."

K. I, M. I, K. 3 TOG., M. I, K. I

1. The symbol for indicating three stitches knitted together and having a made stitch on either side.

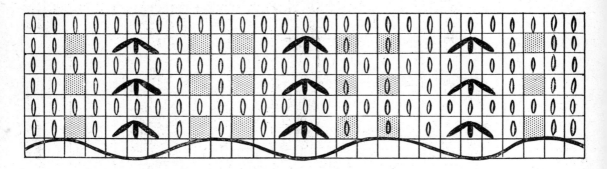

2. This is a diagram for a fabric having a scalloped edge, shown by the wavy line below the drawing. The positions of the made stitches are indicated by the shaded squares, and from this drawing it will be seen that the made stitches are not with the three stitches knitted together. In planning this kind of pattern, remember that every made stitch must be compensated for by a decreased stitch, or else the fabric will not remain the same width all down its length.

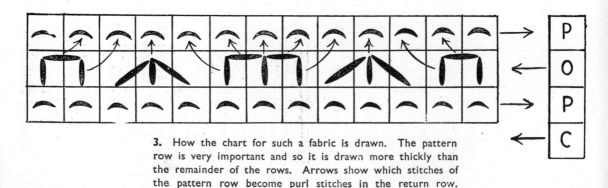

3. How the chart for such a fabric is drawn. The pattern row is very important and so it is drawn more thickly than the remainder of the rows. Arrows show which stitches of the pattern row become purl stitches in the return row.

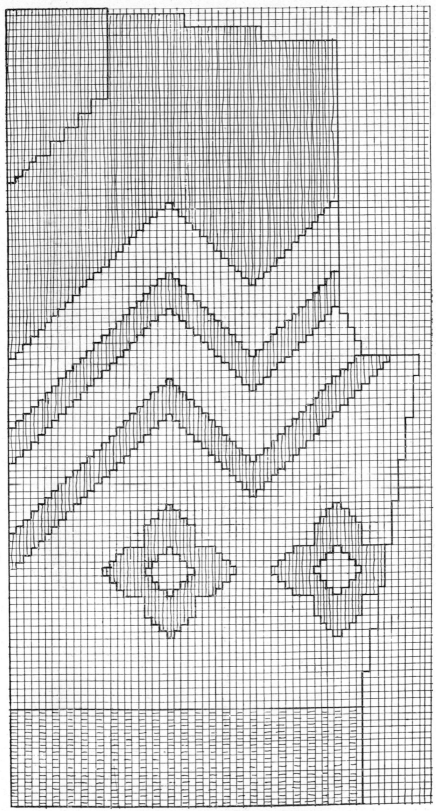

DESIGN FOR KNITTED BLOUSE

WORKING GARMENTS FROM CHARTS

When the principles of designing stitches on squared paper have been leant, it should be possible for the knitter to plan out entire garments in this method. Garments will fit so much better if they are first of all designed as described a little earlier and then the stitches designed to the size of the garment. The drawing on the previous page shows a working chart for a knitted blouse which is to be done in two contrasting fabrics: stocking stitch and purl stitch fabric would be the most suitable combination. The shaded portions being in purl stitch and the background in stocking stitch.

It will be seen that there is intended to be a yoke, which has a deep point in the centre and two smaller points at the sides. Below the yoke there are two purl stitch bands following the same shape, and then comes a flower with its centre in a line with the highest point and a portion of another by the side seam.

The squares across the garment give the number of stitches required, the centre stitch being the one at the extreme left-hand side. Each row of squares down the garment represents one row of knitting. The depth of the garment will work up a little less than the depth of the drawing because the stitches do not make an exact square. When the knitter's tension of work·is known, the correct depth of the garment can be worked out and drawn accordingly.

A blouse knitted from this chart in a thickness of wool and size of needles to make 7 stitches to 1 in. will fit a 35 to 36-in. bust measure. The depth from the shoulder to the top of the ribbing will be 13 ins., the remainder of the length is to be made up with the ribbing.

To begin work, cast on 100 stitches and knit in fine ribbing for the required depth.

For the rest of the work an odd number of stitches is required, so, at the beginning of the first stocking stitch row knit 2 together.

It will be seen that the side seams are shaped with the first stitch in every 5th and 6th rows, making increasings at both sides of the garment.

The first 10 rows are in stocking stitch and then the pattern begins on the 11th row above the ribbing. In the first pattern row the shaded stitches will be worked purlwise, but in the second pattern row the shaded stitches will be worked plainwise and the background will be purled, so that the pattern becomes purl stitch when seen from the right side.

The back and front neck shapings are shown on the same drawing. This is made possible because both the front and the back of the blouse are the same width.

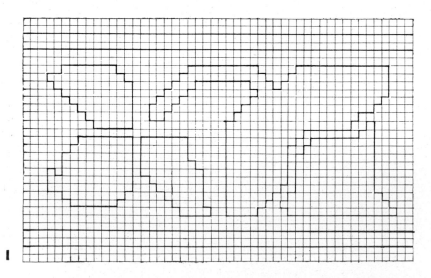

I. Here is a simple border pattern that can be worked out in two fabrics, either horizontally, or vertically, on a garment or household article. It would be particularly suitable for a knitted cushion if thick wool and needles are used. For a knitted bedspread the number of stitches could be doubled, or even multiplied by four, in order to make a very wide border.

FAIR ISLE KNITTING

Fair Isle knitting is the name given to a very attractive type of knitting which is knitted in intricate colour designs, several colours being worked into a very decorative pattern. The colours are changed along the row as the design demands and they are stranded across the back of the work (or woven in if the distance is great) until the next position for their use is reached.

1

1. A piece of simple coloured pattern. This is the right side of the work.

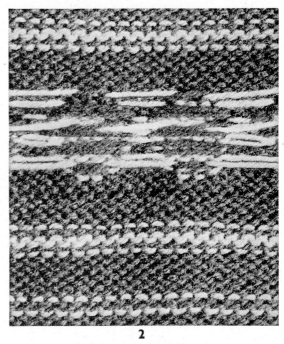

2

2. The wrong side of the same piece of work. Note the stranded method.

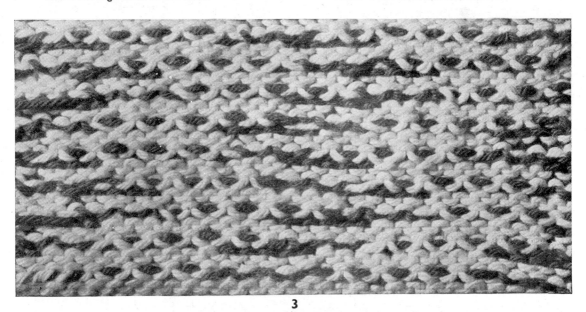

3

3. Colours should be woven into the back of the knitting when the distance between their appearance on the right side will make a strand impracticable.

DESIGNS FOR FAIR ISLE KNITTING

Fair Isle knitting should be done with bright colours in a scheme using contrasts. There may be one main colour used where there is background and this may be subdued, but the rest of the knitting should be carried out in brighter colours to be in keeping with the spirit of the work. The northern islanders who made the first of these garments probably intended them to commemorate some special occasion, or made them to be worn on ceremonial days and, therefore, they should be joyful and decorative in effect.

Colours can be indicated with symbols drawn into the squares of the paper on which the designs are built up. Work is done entirely in stocking stitch and colours are changed in every row.

Some workers find that the wools do not become tangled if each ball is kept in its own jam jar.

PURPLE
ORANGE
BLUE
BEIGE

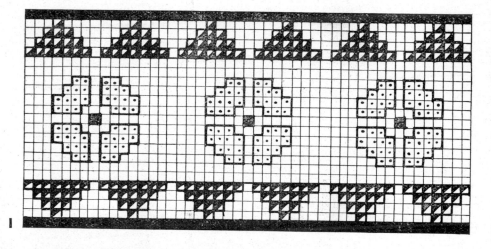

1

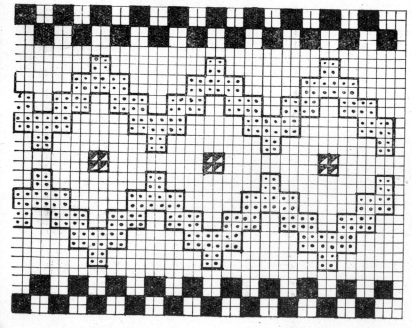

1. A flower and pyramid border to be carried out in four colours as shown. Choose bright shades of the colours named as they will look more subdued when worked. Remember that both right side and wrong side rows are shown in their order of work, that the first row worked from the drawing will be followed from right to left, but the second row will be followed from left to right.

2. This is a wider geometric border that can be combined with the previous one for a wider piece of work. The same colour symbols are used.

2

270

PART VI

CROCHET

Crochet is one of the old needlecrafts that is coming back into favour after a long period of disuse. The old style of florid designs is being replaced by a simpler and straightforward use of the various crochet stitches. Pattern is, chiefly made up with the contrast of solid blocks and open background, instead of the floral and scroll representations that were popular in the last century.

The wide laces for table-cloths and bed-spreads that were merely feats of endurance and sometimes took several years to complete are, today, replaced by the bought laces, which can be obtained in a vast variety of good designs. Patterns and methods of manufacture have so greatly improved that there is now no need to spend weeks on the making of one piece of lace. It is far better to carry out some slight piece of work that will not take a long time, and yet that will look attractive for its purpose.

Most of the crochet shown in these pages is for quickly made decoration, although there are a few design charts for those workers who still have time to make the more ambitious laces. Crochet is used generally for household linens, and trimming for lingerie and handkerchiefs, and the choice of size of hook and thickness of thread will decide the texture of the lace.

As in knitting, there are shortenings for the different names of stitches, and repeated parts are shown by asterisks.

Abbreviations in Crochet

ch. = chain.
s.c. = single crochet.
d.c. = double crochet.
tr. or trs. = treble or trebles.
d.tr. = double treble.
l.tr. = long treble.
p. = picot.
bl. = block.
sp. = space.
l. or ls. = loop or loops.
lt. = lacet.

HOW TO HOLD THE WORK

The hook should be held lightly, but firmly in the right hand, between the first finger and thumb with the weight of the hook resting on the hand, and the wrist should be relaxed so that the hand is turned to and fro quickly and easily.

The crochet is held in the left hand, also between the first finger and thumb, while the thread is held round the fingers in such a way as to give the right tension. The thread passes from the work over the second finger, which should be raised enough to form a strand which can be easily picked up on the hook. Then the thread passes under the third and fourth fingers and is held by them to give the tension required.

The direction of work depends on the type of lace being made. When working across the width, the crochet proceeds backwards and forwards from the inner to the outer edges and back again. But, when the lace is made along its length and there is to be a definite right and wrong side to the lace, work must be done in rows from right to left, breaking off the thread at the end and joining again at the beginning for each row. In decorating a handkerchief, or ready-made mat, the crochet is worked round and round in continuous rows.

CROCHET HOOKS

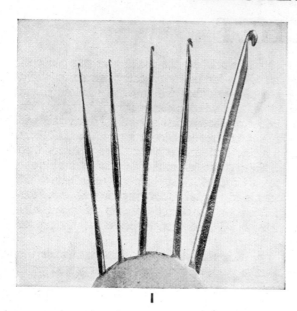

1. These are the sizes of hooks used for general lace making and they are made in metal. Their sizes run from the smallest up to No. 7.

The tool used in crochet is called a hook. Its stem is round like a knitting needle, flattened towards the working end and fashioned in a hook to pick up the thread and pull it through the loop of thread already on the hook.

Hooks vary greatly both in size and the material of which they are made. The very slender ones, for the finest lace, are made of tempered steel and they have a flattened section at about the centre of the stem which can be gripped more easily than the thin round stem. Thicker hooks are made of bone, imitation tortoiseshell, and composition. Very thick hooks can be obtained in wood. There is, also, a very large, light-weight metal hook used for making blankets and other large articles in a kind of crochet called " tricot crochet." This hook is very long and is made in sections that can be screwed together to make it the best length for the work in hand.

A soft untwisted wool is made specially to be used with this hook.

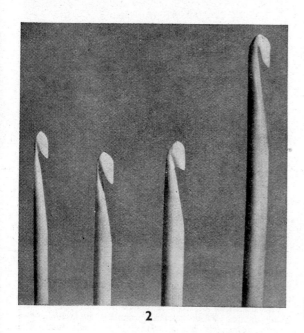

2

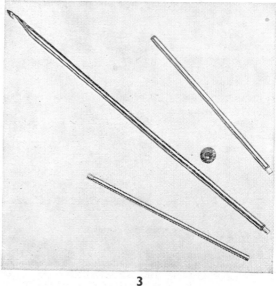

3

2. These are the larger hooks for bolder work, such as crocheted garments and cushion covers. They can be obtained in composition, bone, or wood.

3. Here is the long hook, in sections, for blanket and rug making. The knob is quite separate and can be screwed to the end of the hook at whatever length being used.

CROCHET THREADS

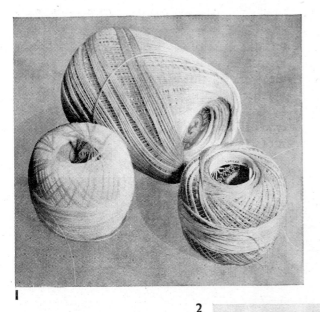

In crochet, as in knitting, there is a vast variety of threads from which to choose. Some are specially made for crochet work, while many of the knitting threads are just as suitable for crochet, too. Laces are generally made from crochet cotton, which is a specially spun strong cotton, obtainable in balls. This cotton is not very cheap because it has to be made from good quality fibres and it must be very evenly spun and given a smooth working surface. This cotton can be obtained in a range of thicknesses from one about the size of sewing cotton to one as thick as a

1. Some crochet cottons for finer types of work. These are easily obtainable in white and ecru.

2. Crochet wools, which can be bought in a range of colours. Note the purled surface.

3. Other threads for crochet: soft knitting cotton and crêpe silk, both of which can be obtained in colours as well as white.

cord. For garment making there are wools and silks. Crochet wool is spun rather differently to knitting wool, it being given a double twist or purl surface. The best silks for crochet work are the crêpe silks which have a rounder and firmer thread than the ordinary spun silks.

The soft knitting cottons are very good for cool summer garments and crochet up very well. Any loosely spun thread is not suitable for crochet, because it will split on the hook.

273

CHAIN STITCH

Where crochet is to make its own foundation, a row of chain is made first and into this the first row of pattern is worked. When work is to be done on an existing foundation, such as round the edge of a handkerchief, or mat, this chain stitching is not required, as the first row of work is done directly into the material.

The length for this chain foundation is measured tightly, as the first row of work inclines to stretch the chain. At the end of the row of chain a few more chain are added to take the place of the first stitch in the first row of pattern, and at the end of each pattern row the work is turned with a few chain. The number of chain made for this turn is decided by the kind of stitch that it replaces; a double crochet needs two chain, while a treble needs three chain.

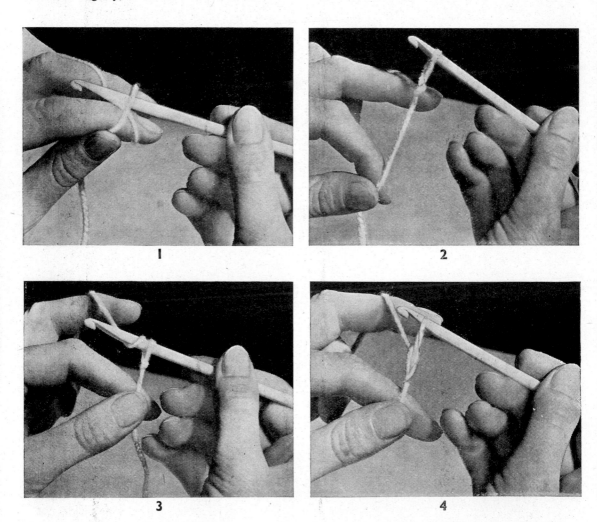

1. To make the first loop on the hook, twist the thread round the first and second fingers of the left hand twice and in such a way that the second loop crosses over and to the left of the first. Pass the hook underneath the first loop and over the second loop.

2. Withdraw the hook backwards under the first loop and at the same time it should pick up the second loop and pull it under the first. Slip the first loop from the

fingers of the left hand and pull the loop on the hook fairly tight. This is to secure the knot at its base.

3. Now hold the thread over the fingers of the left hand, ready for work. Pass the hook over the strand, under it and pick it up with the hook.

4. Pull the strand through the loop on the hook to form the new loop. Continue in this manner.

SINGLE CROCHET STITCH

This stitch is sometimes called " slip stitch," and as this name suggests, it is often used when it is desired to slip the thread along without adding materially to the depth of the work. It is seldom used as a fabric stitch because its shallowness makes it rather unpractical for that purpose. It is assumed that a length of chain has been made for the foundation of work. Single crochet needs one chain for the turn at the end of the row.

I

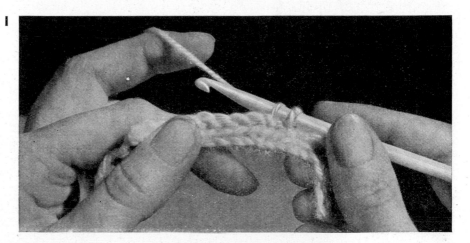

I. Insert the hook into the back of the second chain stitch. The chain is held so that the links are towards the worker, and the top loop of each chain stitch is picked at each stitch in the first row of pattern. Here the second row is being worked.

2

2. Pass the hook round the strand held in the left hand and pull it through the chain stitch as a loop over the hook. The closeness of sl. st. fabric can be seen from this illustration.

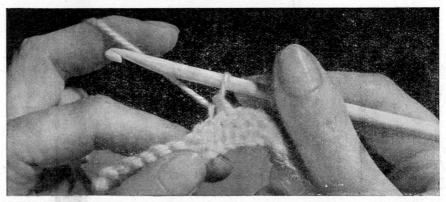

3

3. Pull this loop through the loop already on the hook. Repeat the process for each stitch.

DOUBLE CROCHET STITCH

Double crochet is used in a variety of ways in crochet work. It is used in the making of laces and for making a fine type of solid fabric. The first row will be worked into the foundation, whether it be chain or material, and the second row will be worked into the heading loops made in the first row. There are several ways of inserting the hook into the loops of the previous row and each way has its own particular effect.

First of all repeat the first and second stages of single crochet. This will result in two loops being on the hook, now proceed.

1. Pick up the strand on the hook again.

2. Pull the strand as a loop through the two loops already on the hook. This shows the sort of fabric made when the work is turned at the end of each row with 2 ch. and the 2nd row of d.c. is worked through both loops of the heading of the previous row. The hook then enters two loops of the top of the next stitch.

276

TREBLE STITCH

A variety in length of stitch can be made by twisting the strand round the hook once, twice, or three times, before pulling the strand through the foundation loop.

Treble and chain are the principal stitches used for lace patterns, the treble making blocks and the chain making spaces.

1

2

1. For an ordinary treble stitch, pass the strand round the hook once before inserting the hook into the loop of the previous row. It will be seen that treble stitch fabric is not so closely worked as double crochet fabric, and for this reason it is more quickly worked.

2. Pull the strand through the loop of the previous row, as in the last 2 sts. described, pick up the strand and pull the loop through the first two loops on the hook. Pick up the strand again and pull it through the two remaining loops on the hook.

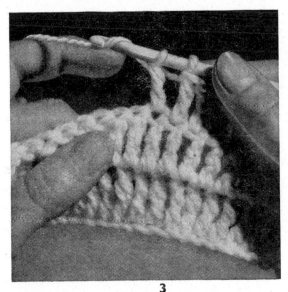

3

4

3. For a double treble, twist the strand round the hook twice before pulling a loop through the foundation loop. Then pull a loop through the loops on the hook in pairs, three times.

4. A longer treble can be made by twisting the strand round the hook three times and a loop is pulled through the loops on the hook in pairs, four times. Long trebles are used in lace patterns to make scallops and points.

CROCHETED FABRICS

Double crochet and treble crochet stitches are often used to make solid fabrics. The method of inserting the hook into the heading of the previous row can affect the texture of fabric obtained. A very ribbed effect is given when only one loop of the stitch in the previous row is picked up, and a very smooth surface is gained when both loops of the stitch are picked up. A still further effect is gained when the hook passes between the stitches of the previous row, instead of going through the loops of the stitches.

1. The fabric made with d.c. worked first on one side of the fabric and then on the other. To do the work, make the required length of ch. and 2 ch. extra. Turn and work a d.c. into the 3rd ch., continue to the end, working a stitch into every ch. At the end of the row, work 2 ch., turn and commence the d.c. again in the 2nd d.c. of the previous row (the 2 ch. take the place of the 1st d.c.). In the 2nd row the hook passes through both ls. of the stitch in the previous row.

2. This pleasant fabric is made with tr. stitches worked solidly. Work proceeds as for the d.c. fabric, first on one side, then turning and working back on the other side of the fabric.

SOLID PATTERNS

The pictures on the previous page showed solid fabrics in smooth all-over textures. The pictures on this page show other kinds of textures that can be obtained with a simple use of stitches worked in various formations.

I. SHELL PATTERN

Directions. Make the ch. foundation and 3 extra to turn. Turn the work and do 4 tr. in the 4th ch. * Miss 2 ch., 1 d.c. in the next ch., miss 2 ch., 5 tr. in the next ch. *; repeat from * to * to the end, finishing with 1 d.c.
** Make 3 ch. and turn. Work 4 tr. into the d.c., * 1 d.c. into the 3rd tr. of the block in the previous row, 5 tr. into the d.c. *; repeat from * to * to the end, finishing with 1 d.c. **.
Repeat from ** to ** throughout.

2. BRICK PATTERN

Directions. Make the ch. foundation and 3 extra ch. to turn. Work 3 tr. in the 4th ch. from the hook. * Miss 3 ch., 1 d.c., 3 ch. and 3 tr. in the next ch. *; repeat from * to * to the end, finishing with 1 d.c.
** Make 3 ch. and turn. Work 3 tr. in the d.c. of the previous row, * 1 d.c., 3 ch. and 3 tr. into the l. of 3 ch. of the previous row *; repeat from * to * to the end, finishing with 1 d.c. **.
Repeat from ** to ** throughout.

3

3. A SHAWL PATTERN

Directions. Make the required length of ch. and 3 extra to turn. Work I tr., 2 ch., 2 tr. into the 4th ch. from the hook. *Miss 3 ch; 2 tr., 2 ch. and 2 tr. into the next ch.*; repeat to the end.
Make 3 ch. and turn. I tr., 2 ch., and 2 tr. into the I. made by 2 ch. in the previous row. *2 tr., 2 ch. and 2 tr. into the next I. made by 2 ch. in the previous row*; repeat from * to * to the end.
Repeat from ** to ** throughout.

4. BULLION STITCH

Directions. Make the ch. the desired length and 3 extra ch. to turn. To make a bullion twist the strand once round the hook, bring a I. through a foundation I., repeat twice more, and draw the last I. through all but the last of the Is. on the hook and draw another I. through these two. Work one of these bullions into the 4th ch. from the hook and then in every alternate ch. to the end.
Make 3 ch. and turn. Work a bullion stitch into the space between the bullion stitches of the previous row.
Repeat from ** to ** throughout.

5

5. RAISED TREBLE STITCH

Directions. Make a ch. the required length and 3 extra ch. to turn. Work 8 tr. into the 4th ch. from the hook; *miss 4 ch. and work I d.c. into the next; miss 4 ch. and work 8 tr. into the next *; Repeat from * to * to the end, finishing with only 4 tr. Turn without making any ch.
Work 4 tr. between the second and third tr. of the next group of 8 tr.; now work 4 tr. over the 4 tr. just worked and passing the hook behind the last but one tr. of the previous group of tr. in the last row; miss 2 tr.; I d.c. in front of the next tr. All rows must end with 4 tr., like the first.

4

Repeat from ** to ** throughout.

VARYING THE TEXTURES

This page is included to point out the importance of deciding beforehand just how each stitch will be formed. The appearance of the fabric depends so much on the position of each stitch that it will be as well to explain it here. The illustrations on this page are carried out in solid double crochet and treble, and yet they are dissimilar to the fabrics on page 278. This change of texture is brought about by the varying ways of inserting the hook into the loop of the stitch in the previous row.

A glance at illustration 1 on page 278 will show the sort of texture that is gained when the hook passes through both loops of the heading of the stitch in the previous row. Contrast this with the first and second pictures on this page.

1. The ridged effect gained when only the back l. is picked up. To gain this effect on the same side of the fabric and in every row, the work must be done on one side of the fabric only. Thus the thread will be broken off at the end and joined on for the beginning of each row.

2. This is d.c. with each stitch worked between 2 sts. of the previous row. The fabric is a little more open, but the stitches are tighter.

3. The effect given to tr. fabric when the back ls. only are picked and the work is turned at the end of each row.

THE MAKING OF MESHES

The next process in crochet is the making of mesh backgrounds for lace patterns. Lace patterns are built up on the principle of blocks of solid work contrasting with a background of open fabric, and the background mesh can take several forms.

I

I. Square mesh. The horizontal lines are formed by ch. and the vertical lines are made by the trs. Here the trs. are worked into trs. forming a continuous vertical line, but, if a broken vertical line is required, the trs. would be worked into a space. The spaces are made with 3 ch. between 2 trs.

2

2. Diamond mesh. This is a more lacy mesh made with ch. and d.c. stitches. 7 ch. form the ls. and the d.c. is worked into the centre of a l., but not through a stitch. The size of this mesh may be varied by the number of ch. worked in each l.

3

3. Here is a mesh pattern that is sufficient decoration in itself

Directions. Make a ch. the required length, and 3 extra to turn. Work I tr. into the 4th ch. from the hook; 3 ch., I tr. into the top of the last tr., * miss 3 ch., I d.c. into the next, 3 ch., I tr. into the top of the d.c., 3 ch., I tr. into the top of the last tr.* Repeat from * to * to the end, finishing with I d.c.
** Turn.
* 3 ch., I tr. in the last d.c.; 3 ch., I tr. into the top of the last tr., I d.c. into the middle of the l. of the previous row*; repeat from * to * to the end.**
Repeat from ** to ** throughout.

SOME FIRST PATTERNS

After making meshes we will consider the making of blocks. For lace patterns, the best blocks are made with treble stitches worked solidly and contrasted with open spaces made with chain. The easy block and space patterns shown on this page are suitable for curtains, which may be carried out in thick knitting cotton. To get the texture desired, experiment with different sized hooks. It is difficult to give a suitable size in these directions because they vary according to their make: some manufacturers number their hooks from the smallest size, increasing the number as the thicknesses increase, while others begin numbering with the largest hook. A large steel hook, equal to a small bone one, is required.

I. One of the simplest patterns made with groups and spaces. Each group, or block, is made up of 3 tr. and each space is made with 3 ch. The trs. are worked into the space made by the ch. I. This specimen was worked in knitting cotton and a medium sized hook. It would be very suitable for short curtains. Unbleached knitting cotton would make up quite cheaply.

2. Here is the block and space taken to an easy pattern development, another pattern suitable for curtains, which could be made up cheaply in unbleached knitting cotton. There are 2 rows of spaces, then there is a block in every 4th space, made of 3 tr. worked into the space as before. In the next row there is a longer block of 9 tr. The 5th pattern row repeats the 3rd by the working of 3 tr. in the centre of the long block. Notice how the trs. of a block worked over a block are taken into the heading of the trebles in previous row.

INTRODUCING LACETS

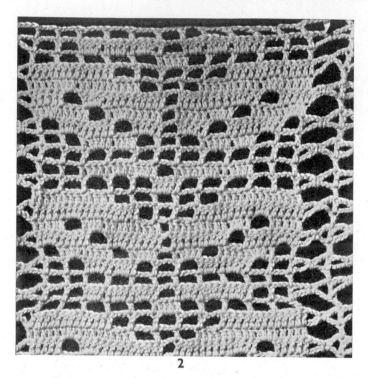

2

Lacets are the V-shaped strands across long spaces, often seen in the more complicated lace designs. The lacets themselves are quite easy to work and they give a particularly lacy effect in contrast to solid blocks.

How to work a lacet. In the first row the spaces between trebles must be made with about 7 chain, and in the second row the work proceeds as follows: work a treble into the treble of the previous row, then 3 chain, 1 double crochet into the loop of 7 chain of the previous row, 3 chain and 1 treble on the treble of the previous row. Then, the next row is a repetition of the first, and the row after that is the lacet row again.

2. This design may be adapted to many purposes, the thickness of the thread and the size of the hook can be chosen to suit the purpose of the lace. It will be useful for curtains, garments and household linens. The pattern made with blocks takes the use of trs. a step further, a simple shape being suggested with the block on a background of lt. Work can be easily followed from this picture.

1. Another curtain pattern, giving a more solid fabric than the last two. The pattern forms stripes of blocks and lt. with an ordinary space at either side of the lt. Blocks are made with 10 tr., the space with 3 ch., 1 tr. and the lt. is made as described above. The tr. in each succeeding row is worked into the tr. of the row before.

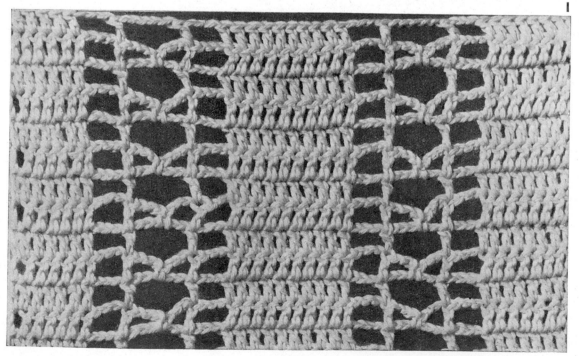

1

TURNING CORNERS

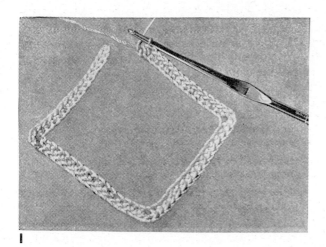

A description of the methods of turning corners will be useful here, before going on to the making of edgings.

The direction of work to be employed in making the edging will govern the method to be used in turning the corner. A corner is easier to turn when working along the length of the lace, and for this reason the first corner described will be for an edging that is worked round the article.

1. First of all make the necessary length of chain, counting the number of chain and making sure that it can be divided evenly into the number of sides that there will be on the article. If the article to be trimmed is four sided, then the number of chain must be divisible by four.

In the next row work 1 d.c. into every chain, and at the chain that will be at a corner work 3 d.c. if the corner is on a four-sided article, or 2 d.c. if there are more than four sides. Join into ring if desired.

2. The first row of work completed, continue with the pattern, working a sufficient number of stitches, or chain, to allow the lace to turn round the previous rows without making a frill and without being so tight that the edge will curl.

In this illustration, at the corner 3 tr. are worked in the 2nd row and two extra chain in the loops of the succeeding rows. The method used in any particular lace pattern must be found by trial.

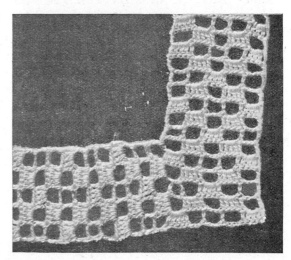

3. This shows a corner in a lace that is worked across its width, a much more difficult problem. A simple example is shown here in order to make the working clearer. The fact that the pattern is symmetrical makes the turning of the corner easier than if another type of pattern were used; also the lace has not a shaped edge to confuse the work still further.

When the length of lace has reached a measurement that will include the width of the lace as well as the length of the side of the article to be decorated and also, at a convenient point in the pattern, the work is turned and the next row worked along the side of the lace. The work will now proceed into sides of trebles instead of into tops and loops of chain. Take extra care with the tension of the work in this first row, and then continue in the usual way. Corners in more complicated patterns are turned by the same principle, though not always in a straight line.

SIMPLE EDGINGS

Here are some ideas for adding a personal touch to articles that are already made up and partly trimmed. Although handkerchiefs are shown, the same edgings can be put on to household linens, like towels and table-cloths, the texture of the thread and the size of the hook being used to suit the type of material. If there is an existing edging of hemstitching, the holes will be very useful to guide the spacing of the crochet stitches.

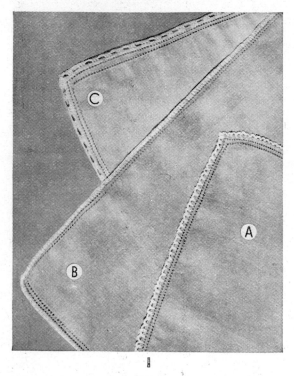

(F) Here is a very lacy edging, made with 4 rows of work.

1st row, * 1 d.c., 2 ch., miss 1 hemstitch hole; repeat from * all round.

2nd row, 1 tr. in the l. of the 1st row, 2 ch.; repeat all round, end with 5 ch.

3rd row, * 1 l.tr., 3 ch., 1 l.tr. in the same hole; miss 1 l. of the previous row; 1 l.tr., 3 ch., 1 l.tr. in the next hole, miss 1 l. Repeat from * once more; 5 ch., miss 2 ls. of the previous row. Repeat these directions all round, working the 4 middle l.tr. in the corner l., instead of missing 1 l.

4th row, * 5 ch., 1 l.tr., 3 ch., 1 l.tr. worked between the 2nd and 3rd trs. of the previous row; 5 ch., 1 d.c. worked between the 4th and 5th trs. of the previous row. Repeat from * once more, but working the d.c. into the top of the last long tr., 3 ch., 1 d.c. into the top of the next tr. Repeat these directions all round, turning the corner with an extra scallop.

2

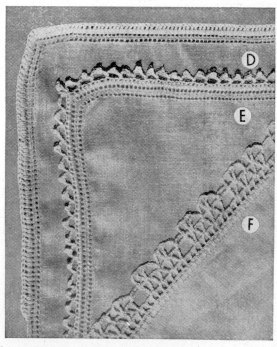

1 (A) This is a very simple semi-lace pattern worked into the outer row of hemstitching. The inner row of hemstitching adds further decoration to the crocheted edge. 1 d.c. is worked into every other hole and there are 3 ch. between. The corners are turned with 3 d.c. in the corner hole, the 3 ch. are worked between each.
(B) A useful edging with only d.c., 1 st. in each hole. This makes a strong edging for many household articles.
(C) A block and space pattern on the same principle, using the hemstitching holes as guides for spacing the tr. stitches. Groups of 3 tr. are worked all round with 3 ch. between each group. The corner is turned with 5 tr. worked into the corner hole.

2. More lacy handkerchief edgings
(D) A tr. in each hole with 3 at the corner hole to turn.
(E) An attractive p. edging. First of all, work a row of d.c., 1 st. to each hole and 3 in the corner hole. Then in the next row, work 5 ch. and make a p. with the last 3, i.e., work a slip stitch into the 3rd ch. from the hook. Then work another 2 ch., miss 2 d.c. and work a d.c. in the next. Turn the corners with 1 d.c., 5 ch., a p. with the last 3 ch. and 1 d.c. all in the corner hole.

STRAIGHT EDGINGS FOR
HOUSEHOLD PURPOSES

On the previous page some examples were given of how already neatened edges can be given crocheted trimmings, and here are shown some ways of neatening edges with the crochet itself.

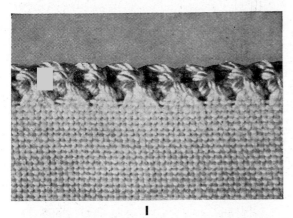

1

2. When the crocheted edging will be worked straight along the thread of the material, a guiding line for the depth of the stitches can be made by drawing out I thread of the material. This will also make the insertion of the hook more easy to do. Prepare the edge of the material by tacking the turnings to the wrong side, then consider the depth of the stitching and draw out a thread at that depth on the right side. Proceed to work d.c., which will be the best stitch for an edge with only a single turn of material, spacing the stitches to a suitable number of threads. In this illustration the next row of work is I tr. into each d.c. For the next and the last row the colour of the thread is changed, and a row of d.c., I st. to each treble, is worked. The little scalloped edging is made with I d.c., I tr., and I d.c. into every other d.c. stitch of the previous row.

3. In this edging the material has been neatened by having a very narrow hem tacked to the wrong side and then that is covered with d.c. stitches worked tightly, the spacing being done with a thick sewing needle, as described before. Into the first row is worked a row of * I d.c., 2 ch., miss 2 d.c.; repeat from * all along. For the third row another coloured thread is used. Work I tr. into each space and 2 ch. all along the row. For the very edge the colour of the thread is changed again and I d.c., I ch. is worked in each space. The lower edge is neatened with a line of embroidery ch. stitching. This is a useful device if the base of the crochet is not very neat.

3

2

I. Double crochet used as the means of neatening and decoration. Tack the turnings of the material to the wrong side, using fairly small stitches. Then, with a hook that will pass through the double thickness of material and with a fairly thick thread, work d.c. stitches all round, taking them deep enough to hold the edge firmly. It will help to space the stitches evenly if a thick sewing needle is used to pierce holes where the hook will enter the material, the spacing can be done more easily with a sharp tool. Work this crochet as tightly as possible. Crocheting finished, press the edge and cut away the superfluous turnings at the back from close to the work.

EDGINGS WITH PICOTS

A very attractive finish can be given to the edges of laces by working picots at regular intervals. A picot is a small loop of chain, making a small knot on the very edge of the crochet.

This little knot can be worked directly on a double crochet, or treble edging, or it may be at the centre of a chain loop. Both methods are illustrated on this page. Keep the picots small; large ones will look untidy.

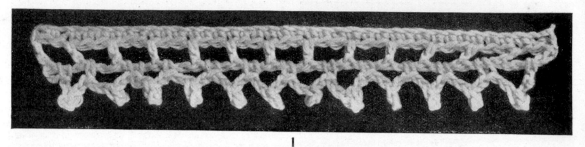

I

1. A narrow edging having the picots at the centre of a ch. loop. Make the foundation ch. as long as is required for the lace; work is done along the length of the lace. Work the first row as I d.c. into each ch. At the end, make 5 ch. and turn and work I tr. into the 3rd d.c. from the hook. Continue working spaces with 2 ch. and I tr. with a space of 2 d.c. between the trs. Turn with 3 ch. and work I d.c. into the first space from the hook. The p. edge is made in this row, with 5 ch., I slip stitch into the 3rd ch. from the hook, 2 ch. and I d.c. into the next space. Continue working thus all along the lace.

2. A different effect of p. is obtained by working the ch. loop directly on a row of d.c. The piece of frilly lace in this illustration is intended to be sewn round the neck of a child's dress. Make a length of ch. loosely and work the 1st row as I d.c. into each chain. The next row is I tr., 2 ch. worked to form spaces. Into alternate spaces, in the 3rd row, is worked a block of 3 tr. with 2 ch. The next row is made entirely of d.c., I in every stitch of the previous row and 2 in each space. The next row forms the scalloped shape at the edge. It is done in this way: work 2 d.c. in the 2 d.c. in the space, * then I tr. in the next stitch, I long tr. in the next, 2 ch. and a long tr. in the same stitch as the last, I tr. in the next stitch and 2 d.c. in the next 2 stitches; repeat from * all along. In the last row, work a d.c. in each stitch, I d.c., 3 ch. and I d.c. in each space all along the row.

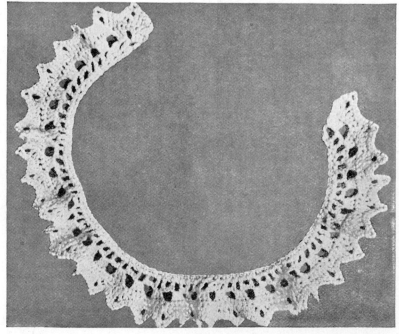

2

METHODS OF EDGING CIRCULAR MATS

There are two fairly simple methods of making edgings for round mats for table use. One method is to cut out the mat in material first and then edge it, and the other way is to make the circle of lace first and then mount it on to the linen, which is afterwards cut to shape and neatened.

1.

I. A mat, such as is used for the water jug on the dining table. Ready made round mats can be obtained, and if these are edged with hemstitching the holes will make a good guide for placing the first row of stitches. When the mat is to be cut out of a piece of material, use a saucer or small plate to mark out the circular shape. Cut out, allowing $\frac{1}{4}$ in. of turnings, and prepare the edge by tacking the turnings on to the wrong side. Then, using a hook that will pass through the double material, work the first row, generally d.c., through the double material round the edge. When the first stitch is reached, join it to the last stitch with a slip stitch and continue with the work.

The pattern is planned on the number of stitches on the mat, so, if the design requires a particular number, make sure that that number can be repeated all round the mat. The widest part of the pattern in the picture needs 5 spaces, and so the spaces of ch. and tr. in the 1st row beyond the material have to be divisible by 5.

The next row is made up of a pattern repeat made of 13 tr. worked over 3 spaces and a lt. worked over 2 spaces.

The row beyond that has 5 tr. worked over the centre of the long block of the previous row, a space on either side of it and 9 ch. between the patterns.

The next row makes the foundation for the scalloped edge, and it is made with 13 d.c. worked over the lt., a d.c. and 3 ch. worked 3 times between.

The last row is made entirely of d.c., 1 in each stitch of the previous row and 5 in each loop.

2

2. The lace edging can be worked first and then mounted on to linen; it is a little more difficult to make a perfect circle when cutting the linen, but, on the other hand, there is not the danger of stretching the material. Make the ch. the required length, trying if possible to plan the number required for each pattern and then making the length of ch. so that that number can be divided an equal number of times into it. Join the ch. into a ring. In the first row, work a d.c. into every ch. In the second row, work 1 d.c., * 5 ch., miss 1 d.c. and work 1 d.c. in the next; repeat from * all round.

The third row makes a further round of loops, thus: 7 ch. and a d.c. into the loop of the previous round. The fourth round makes a round of still larger loops, with 9 ch. and a d.c. into the loop of the previous row. The p. edging is done with 2 d.c., 5 ch. and 2 d.c. into every loop.

CROSSED TREBLE, SOLOMON'S KNOT AND A CORDED EDGE

A long treble is used for crossed treble, please refer to the page on treble stitches for directions on how to work long trebles. In working crossed treble, the cross is made in two rows of work, in the first row four diagonal stitches, two one way and two the other way, are caught together at the top, and in the second row, four more trebles are caught together to complete the cross.

For a solomon's knot, a loop is pulled through and pulled to a length of about $\frac{1}{4}$ in. and another loop is pulled through this long one.

A corded edge is easy to make. In the last but one row take strands of chain across from one group in the pattern to the next, rather tightly, the strands should be rather shorter than when the chain stitches will remain without any covering, and then, in the last row cover these strands of chain with double crochet worked tightly and closely. The closeness of these stitches will stretch the chain a little, that is the reason why they are made short.

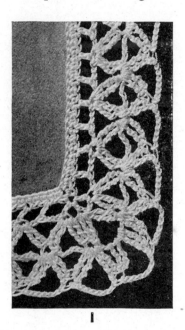

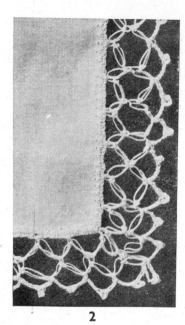

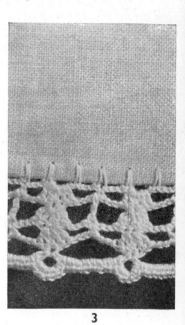

1   2   3

1. A crossed tr. edging worked into a foundation of d.c., showing a corner. The first, second and third rows of work are done as follows: ch., d.c. into each ch., with 3 at the corners, and 1 tr., * 2 ch., miss 2 d.c., 1 tr. in the next repeated from * all round, with 3 tr. and the ch. at each corner.

4th row, 5 ch., 1 l.tr. into the 1st tr. from the hook; 5 ch.; 2 l.tr., leaving the last pair of loops on the hook in each st., into the same tr. as the last l.tr.; miss 1 tr.; 2 l.tr. into the next, leaving the last pair of loops of each st. on the hook. Now take the last loop through all the loops on the hook; repeat from * all along. The illustration shows how the pattern at a corner is manipulated.

5th row, the picture shows how the groups of l.tr. and ch. are arranged to form the crosses: 2 l.tr., 5 ch. and 2 l.tr. are worked into the top of each group of 4 l.tr. in the previous row.

2. A very lacy edging is given with solomon's knot.

Here, the edging is worked into a foundation of d.c. worked into the hemmed edge of the material. Each stitch is divided from the next with a ch. The pattern is made by working a * d.c. into a loop of the first row; pull the loop of this stitch to measure $\frac{1}{4}$ in. and then bring another loop through it. Bring another loop through the last and pull it $\frac{1}{4}$ in. long; miss 4 d.c. and repeat from * into the next space. Continue all round. Work another row of similar loops with the d.c. worked into the stitch between the long loops in the previous row.

Lastly, work a row of ch. and ps., thus: 5 ch.; * 1 d.c. into the stitch between the long loops of the previous row; 8 ch., p. with the last 5 ch.; 3 ch. Repeat from * all round. The picture shows how to manipulate the corners.

3. A simple edging of tr. groups and ch. loops with a tightly worked edge of d.c. taken over the last row of ch. strands and loops.

CROCHETING BLANKETS

A special kind of crochet work is used for making blankets. It is called "tricot" work. The special long hook, illustrated on page 272, is used with a specially spun, thick, soft wool. This wool has very litt'e twist, and being very thick the work can be done very quickly. Blankets for cots and single beds can be worked in one piece, but for larger beds they are best worked in strips and afterwards joined together with crochet. Satin ribbon binding makes an attractive finish.

There are several different makes of the blanket wool, and they vary a little in thickness. Also there is a summer and a winter weight, so be guided by the saleswoman when buying the quantity for a blanket.

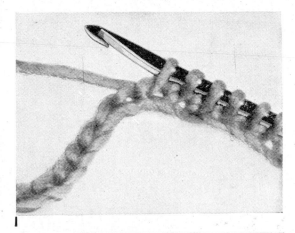

4

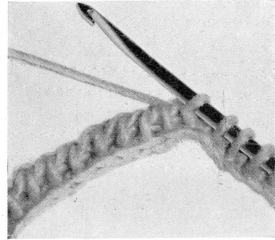

1

1. The work is always begun on a chain foundation. Make the chain the length required, plus 1 for turning at the end. Then proceed to pull a loop through each chain and leave it on the hook. At the end there should be the same number of loops on the hook as there were foundation chain.

2. The first row of work is always the same. Bring a loop through the first loop on the hook, then bring a loop through the next 2 lps. on the hook. Continue in this way, bringing a loop through the loops on the hook in pairs, until there is only 1 l. left. From this step there are several different kinds of tricot stitch, each giving quite a different texture.

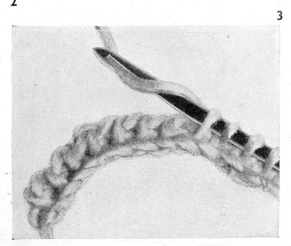

2

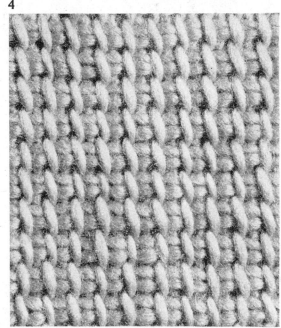

3

CROCHETING BLANKETS *continued*

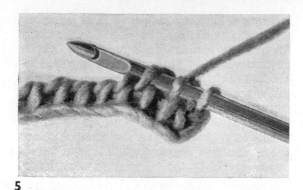

5

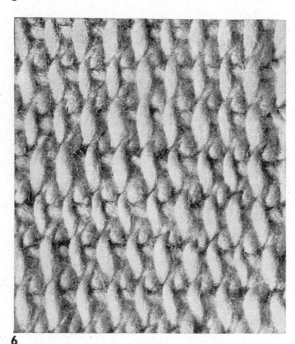

6

6. This is what the summer texture looks like. It is, of course, more economical than the heavier method of work.

7. A very strong fabric can be made by working between the stitches of the previous row. Pull a loop forwards from the back of the work, passing the hook between 2 sts. of the previous row and then dispose of the stitches as described for the two methods above.

8. The stitch between 2 sts. makes the work tighter with slightly larger holes between the rows.

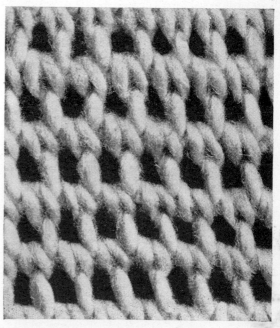

7

8

3. This tricot pattern is worked through the upright loops of the previous row. Pick up a loop on to the hook through each of the upright stitches. Work back by pulling a loop through the first stitch and then pull a loop through two at a time until only I remains on the hook. I ch. is worked to turn at the beginning of every row.

4. The kind of texture given with the stitch just described. It is very good for a thick blanket.

5. For summer blankets a lighter type of stitch can be made by working into the front of the horizontal loops of previous row. Bring a loop on to the hook through each of these horizontal stitches, and then work back as for the previous stitch, first pulling a loop through one loop on the hook and then working the remaining loops off in pairs.

CROCHETED SHAWLS

Many workers prefer crochet shawls to knitted ones, because the fabric keeps its shape better, and because the work is much more quickly done. There are several ways of commencing: work may begin with a straight foundation of chain and crochet and proceed across the width, or the shawl may be commenced in the centre. Square shawls can be started in the centre as well as along one edge, and round head shawls are begun with a ring of chain in the same way as a round table mat.

It is difficult to state exact quantities of wool to purchase for a particular size, without knowing the make of wool to be used. As a rough guide, a shawl about 60 ins. square will require about 15 ozs. of 2-ply wool when worked with a medium-sized bone crochet hook (that is to say, a hook which will make trebles ½-in. in height).

1. This centre will make a good beginning for a square shawl. The entire work can be carried out in this texture, if liked, or a more ambitious design can be worked out with blocks of trebles as well as the treble and chain spaces.

Begin by making 5 ch. and join into a ring. 3 ch., * 1 tr., 2 ch.; repeat from * 7 times more. 1 tr. into the 5 ch. loop, 2 ch., 2 tr., 2 ch., and 2 tr. into the next space; 2 ch., 2 tr. into the next space; 2 tr., 2 ch. and 2 tr. into the next space; 2 ch., 2 tr. into the next space; 2 tr., 2 ch. and 2 tr. into the next space; 2 ch., 2 tr. into the next space; 2 ch., 2 tr., 2 ch. and 2 tr. into the next space; 2 ch., 2 tr. into the next space. Continue working in rounds, working 2 tr., 2 ch. and 2 tr. into the space between the trebles at the corners of the previous row and 2 tr. into the spaces between, with 2 ch. between the groups of trebles.

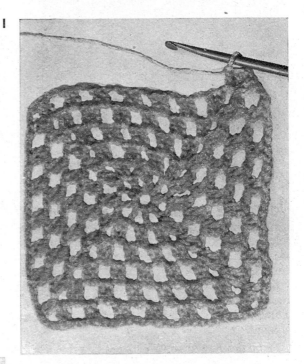

1

2

2. This is the beginning of an octagonal shawl, which is a very useful shape for a head shawl. The texture shown here, worked in a silk and wool mixture, will make a very warm fabric; if a thinner one is required use a 2-ply wool.

Commence with 5 ch. and join into a ring. 3 ch., 1 tr. into the ring, 2 ch., * 2 tr., 2 ch.; repeat from * 6 times more. Join the last chain to the top of the third chain at the beginning of the round. Then work 2 tr., 2 ch. and 2 tr. into every space. In the next round, work * 2 tr., 2 ch. and 2 tr. into the first space, 2 tr. in the next space, and repeat from * all round. Continue working in rounds, working 2 tr. 2 ch. and 2 tr. into the 8 tr. loops in previous row and 2 tr. between all the groups of 2 tr. in the previous round. Chain is only worked at the 8 turning points.

WORKING FROM A CHART

1. Measuring the height of a treble row. The inch tape is placed over the fabric vertically.

The designs are made by filling in with the soft pencil those sections that will be solidly worked; single stitches are indicated with one straight line and lengths of chain are shown by single lines, too. Lacets are indicated by two curving lines coming down to the horizontal line before.

To find out the number of foundation chain to make, count the number of stitches that would be required to make the first row of pattern solidly, add three chain to turn.

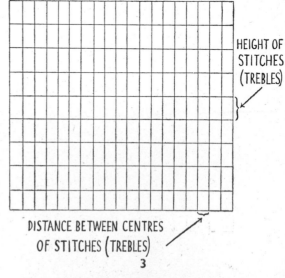

2. Measuring the distance between the centre of one treble and the centre of the next. The inch tape is placed over the fabric horizontally.

Crochet patterns are designed on paper which is previously ruled out with lines marking the height and width of the trebles or other stitches to be used. Therefore, the size of these stitches must be known first. Before commencing to design, experiment with various threads and hooks, making a 3-in. block of solid work, to arrive at the best texture of work for the purpose in hand.

From the chosen specimen, measure the height of one stitch (treble, etc.), and the distance from the centre of one stitch to the centre of the next. This will give the tension of the work.

Take a piece of paper and rule horizontal lines the height of a row apart and then rule vertical lines across the paper, the width of the stitches apart. On to this graph the design can be built up.

Graph paper can be bought ready ruled, but the measurements of the ruling are not always suitable for crochet designs and as a crochet design is seldom very large, the extra time taken in preparing the paper oneself, is well worth while, as the exact size of the finished work can be gauged fairly accurately.

Use a hard pencil for ruling the lines and a soft one or a coloured one, for drawing the design.

HEIGHT OF STITCHES (TREBLES)

DISTANCE BETWEEN CENTRES OF STITCHES (TREBLES)

3

3. A design graph prepared from the measures taken from the solid treble specimen.

THE SYMBOLS USED IN CROCHET CHARTS

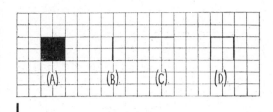

1

Simple symbols are used to indicate the kind of stitch to use when copying a design from a chart. Blocks of solid work are shown as solid blocks on the drawing and spaces are left as blanks on the paper. The shapes made by the stitches can be taken as the form of the symbol: picots may be shown as small circles and loops of chain are drawn as semicircles, as near to their relative size as possible.

Crossed trebles are shown as two V's, one up and one down. Pyramids of long trebles are shown as solid triangles.

2

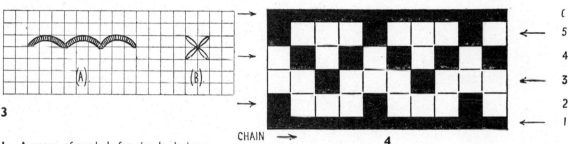

3

CHAIN →

4

1. A group of symbols for simple designs: (A) a block; (B) 1 st.; (C) length of chain; (D) a space.

2. Other symbols: (A) a lacet; (B) a picot; (C) a chain loop; (D) a long treble pyramid; (E) crossed treble.

3. How the shape of the work can suggest symbols: (A) looped and corded edge, chain loops worked with double crochet; (B) solomon's knot.

4. A simple design built up with treble, chain, blocks and spaces. The arrows at the side indicate in which direction the rows are worked and the numbers show the number of the row being worked and how many rows of work there are in the lace. The right side of the lace is indicated by the last row, the chain top of the last row of stitches should be seen from the right side.

5. A design using the less usual symbols as well as those used in the previous design chart; those for lacet, picot and chain loop are introduced.

6. A still further complicated design chart. Other symbols will be recognized from the diagrams given.

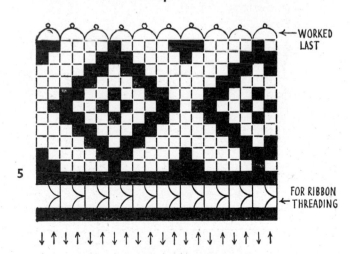

WORKED LAST

FOR RIBBON THREADING

12 11 10 9 8 7 6 5 4 3 2 1

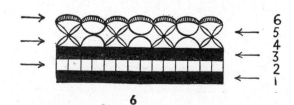

6

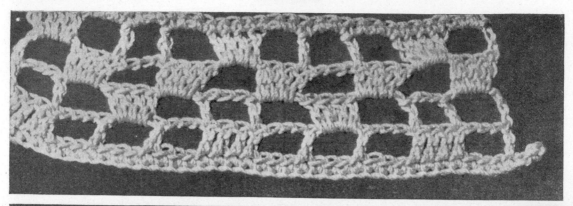

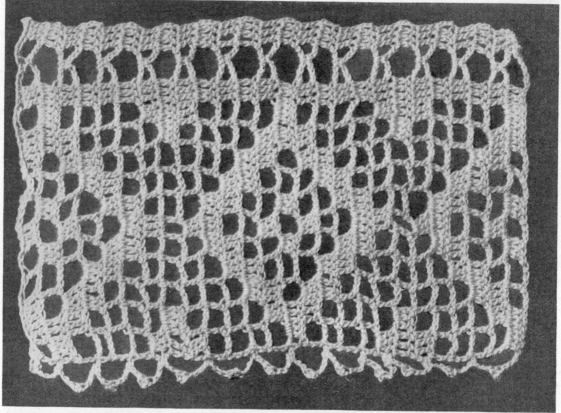

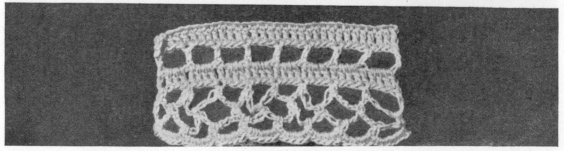

7. The three design charts made up into lace.

CROCHETED TABLE MATS

Small table mats and luncheon mats, crocheted in ecru coloured cotton, can be very effective on a dark wood table. These mats can be designed to almost any shape; but, as a rule, the simpler ones are best because they can be laundered more easily. The three mats shown here were worked in fairly thick cotton. Mats are not now made in the fine threads as formerly. The hook, also, was fairly coarse.

1

Work round again, making loops with 11 ch. and 1 slip stitch into top of each loop of the previous row.

The next row of loops requires flatter tops to be more convenient for the row beyond. Slip stitch to the top of the 1st loop as before. Make 8 ch., the first 3 of these will act as the 1st tr. Work 1 tr. into the top of the next loop, 5 ch. and another tr. into the top of the next loop. Continue all round, making loops of 5 ch. and a tr. in the top of the loops of the previous row. Join the end of the last 5 ch. into the 3rd ch. of the 1st loop.

* Make 3 ch., 3 tr. into the loop, 3 ch., 1 slip stitch into the next tr. of the previous row; repeat from * all round. To begin the next row, slip stitch the thread to the 1st tr. Make 5 chain, work 2 d.tr. into the next tr. of the previous row, 1 d.tr. into the next tr.; * 7 ch., 1 d.tr. in the next tr., 2 d.tr. in the next and 1 d.tr. in the next tr. of the previous row. Repeat from * all round, ending with 7 ch. joined to the top of the first 5 ch. with a slip stitch.

Next row, * 1 d.c. into the top of the 2nd d.tr.; 5 ch., 1 d.cr. into the top of the next d.tr., 7 d.c. into the next loop; repeat from * all round.

1. A very simple, but a very pretty mat. The thick thread makes it quite suitable for a plate mat. The points to notice are: the design is based on the 10 scallops worked directly after the centre ring, therefore the number of ch. and d.c. and the number of tr. must be divisible by 10.

Make 10 ch. and join it into a ring with a slip stitch. Into this, work 20 d.c. Make 3 ch. and work 2 tr. into the 2nd d.c. and 1 tr. into the next. Continue all round like this, working 2 tr. into the 1st d.c. and 1 tr. into the next. This will give 30 tr. Join the end of this row to the 3rd ch. at the beginning, which takes the place of the 1st tr.

Make 7 ch., 1 d.c. into the 3rd tr. from the hook, 5 ch., miss 2 tr., 1 d.c. into the next. Continue all round, making loops of 5 ch. and working 1 d.c. into every 3rd tr. This will give 10 loops.

Make 2 ch. and work 9 d.c. into every loop.

Make 7 ch., 1 slip stitch into the 5th d.c. from the hook, 7 ch., 1 slip stitch between the last d.c. in the 1st loop and the 1st in the 2nd loop. Continue all round, making 2 loops over each scallop of the previous row. This will give 20 loops.

In order to begin the loops of the next row, the thread must be taken to the top, or centre, of the 1st loop with a slip stitch worked into each of the first 3 ch. sts. Work round the circle, making loops of 9 ch. and 1 slip stitch into the top of each loop of the previous row.

Slip stitch to the top of the 1st loop of 9 ch. to bring the thread to the starting point for the next row of loops.

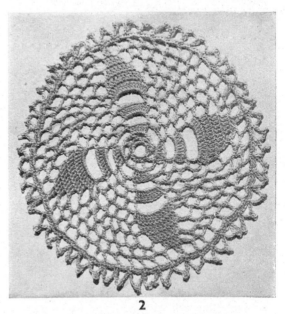

2

2. Simple shaped blocks of tr. can be worked into mats which have an otherwise plain texture. This one has 4 such blocks on an open mesh background, therefore the last row of ch. and tr. spaces which forms part of the basis of the centre must be divisible by 4.

CROCHETED TABLE MATS *continued*

Make a length of 10 ch. and join into a ring. Work 16 d.c. into this ring. Make 6 ch.; 1 tr. into the 3rd d.c. from the hook; * 3 ch., miss 1 d.c., 1 tr. into the next. Repeat from * all round, joining the last ch. into the 3rd of the 1st 6 ch. This will give 8 spaces.

The next row is made of 5 ch. and 6 tr. in alternate spaces, 3 ch. taking the place of the 1st tr. of this row.

The next row is made of long spaces of 7 ch. over the blocks and small spaces of 3 ch., 1 tr. into a space.

The next row is made of similar small spaces, and long blocks of 10 tr. into the long spaces of the previous row. The next row has small spaces and long ones of 9 ch. Then begins the pyramid pattern of trs., 14 being worked into a long space and the gaps bridged with small spaces.

In the next row the 2 trs. of the blocks in the previous row are passed over and 1 more small space is made by working 2 trs. with 3 ch. between into the centre small space of the previous row.

For the next 2 rows, decrease the number of trs. in the blocks by 2 at each end and still work small spaces between the blocks. In the next row there will be only 2 trs. worked to form the top of the pyramid and another small space is made in the middle small spaces of the previous row.

Now, a corded edge must be worked to give a firm line. Work 5 d.c. into every space.

The p. edge is made with * 6 ch., the p. being made by slip-stitching into the 3rd ch. from the hook, 3 ch., 1 d.c. over the tr.; repeat from * all round.

SHAPED MATS

The shape of the mat is determined in the very first row of work. If it is to be five, or six sided, the ring of chain is shaped to that in the first row of double crochet, or treble, whichever is to be used. In this case, the number of chain must be equally divisible into the number of sides required. If the mat is to be six sided, make a number of chain that can be divided by six.

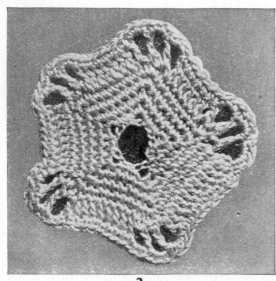

3

3. The basis of a five-sided mat. Make 15 ch. and join into a ring with a slip stitch. Work a d.c. into the 1st 2 ch. and 3 d.c. into the next ch. Repeat all round. This makes five sides.

Continue working in rounds of d.c., with 3 sts. into the centre stitch at each corner. When the solid centre is large enough, other designs can be introduced.

Tr. may be worked, putting 3 at every corner, and ch. can be worked where a lacy pattern is required. Remember to allow adequate extra stitches to turn the corners. Sharp corners will need more stitches than wide-angled corners.

4. Here is an oval mat, which needs a different type of centre foundation to any other kind of shape. The centre line is a length of 27 ch., and into this are worked blocks of tr., first on one side and then on the other in such a way that the feet of the tr. meet.

Make 27 ch., make 3 more to take the place of the 1st tr.; work 1 tr. in the 4th and 5th chs. from the hook; 3 ch., miss 3 ch. of the foundation, work 3 tr. in the next 3 ch. Work these spaces and blocks to the end, finishing with 2 trs.; 3 ch. with the last stitch joined to the 1st ch. of the foundation with a slip stitch. This makes the last stitch of the row.

Make 3 ch.; this will take the place of the 1st tr. on the opposite side of the ch. foundation. Work trs. into the feet of the tr. blocks of the 1st row and make the spaces with 3 ch. as before. End with 3 tr.

Make 6 ch., work 1 tr. round the middle of the last tr. stitch of the last block; 3 ch., 1 tr. round the 1st tr. of the opposite block; 3 ch., 3 tr. into top of the 3 tr. of the 1st block; 7 ch., 3 tr. into the next block; 5 ch., 3 tr., 5 ch., 3 tr., 7 ch., 3 tr., 3 ch., 1 tr. round the end tr. of the foundation block; 3 ch., 1 tr. round the next tr.; 3 ch., 3 tr. into the top of the block of the foundation; 7 ch., 3 tr., 5 ch., 3 tr., 5 ch., 3 tr., 7 ch., 2 tr. Join the last stitch to the 3rd ch. of the next loop.

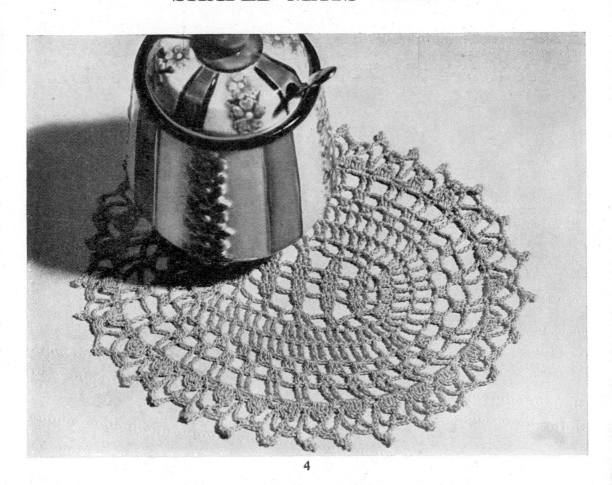

4

Make 3 ch. Work 4 tr. into each of the small spaces of the ends and along the sides work 3 ch., I tr. into the centre of each block, 3 ch. and another tr. into a loop of the previous row.

The next row is made of ch. and d.trs. At the ends the d.trs. are worked into alternate trs. of the previous row. At the sides they are worked 2 into a space with 2 ch. between. Also, 2 d.trs. are worked into the first and last trs. of the end blocks.

The next row is also of d.trs. with 2 ch. between, the d.trs. being worked into the tops of those in the previous row. 2 are worked together, as before, at the corners. 5 ch. is worked to take the place of the 1st d.tr. at the beginning of the rows.

The next row is made of blocks and spaces with tr. and ch. Work 3 tr. into alternate spaces with 3 ch. between. The next row consists of blocks of 3 tr. with 5 ch. between, 3 ch. takes the place of the 1st tr. in each of these 2 rows.

A more open row is worked next. A d.tr. is worked into the 1st and 3rd trs. of the blocks in the previous row, with 2 ch. between them; the long loops of this row are made with 5 ch.; 5 ch. will take the place of the first d.tr. The next row is made of pyramids of ch. and d.tr. Into each space work I d.c.; 3 ch., 3 d.trs., leaving the last 2 loops of each stitch on the hook until the very last stitch, which will pass through all the loops left on the hook; 3 ch., I d.c., 3 ch.

To begin the next row, slip stitch the thread to the top of the first pyramid; 7 ch., I d.c. into the strand of 3 ch. between the pyramids; 7 ch., I d.c. into the top of the next pyramid. Repeat like this all round.

The last row is made of ls. and ps., thus: slip stitch the thread to the top of a loop; this will be the loop to the left of a pyramid. * 5 ch., make a picot by working a slip stitch into the 3rd ch. from the hook; 2 ch., I d.c. into the top of the next loop; 3 ch., I d.c. into the top of the next loop. Repeat from * all round.

The size of these oval mats can be varied by the measurement of the foundation chain and the number of rows worked before the last row with picots.

Colour plays an important part in table furnishings. Make four mats to go with the china and contrast the colour of the table, or the table-cloth. If your cloths are white and your china has blue in its design, let the mats be in the same blue. If your table is dark and polished your mats may be made in silk, and if the table is of unstained wood they can be in a very dark coloured cotton. These mats do not take long to work, so make several sets in different colours.

A CROCHETED CUSHION COVER

Brightly coloured cushion covers can be very quickly made in crochet work. Thick knitting wool and a thick hook are required. The cover shown here, in the illustration, is made of double knitting wool in three colours —fawn, green and dark brown—and it measures 23 ins. by 21 ins. These are the average measures for a cushion cover. The 23 ins. is along the direction of work. 4 ozs.

of colour. Alternate stripes will be sharply defined. Work 4 rows of fawn, change to green and do 2 rows, and then change to brown and work 1 row. These 7 rows form the pattern, which is repeated 3 more times, and then 4 rows of fawn are worked to complete the background.

Before cutting out the intercover for the padding the

of fawn wool and 2 ozs. of each of the other two colours were required for this size.

Make a length of ch. loosely; this should be about 2 ins. less than the required measure for the cushion as the tr. stitches, with which the cover is made, will stretch this ch. to about another 2 ins. Turn with 3 ch. at the end of every row. For the first row, work 1 tr. into every ch. and in all succeeding rows work the stitches into the backs of the stitches at the top of the previous row; this will give the variety of width seen in the bands

crocheted cover must be lightly pressed in order to stretch the fabric. The back of the cushion may be another piece of crochet in a different colour scheme, or design, or it may be made from material. Thick wool or cotton cord may be sewn round the edge to give a neatening if one is required.

Further decoration may be added with bands of wool braid sewn on in the reverse direction to the crocheted bands of colour. Thick wool tassels can be made from the knitting wool and sewn to each corner.

PATTERNED COLOURED CROCHET

On the last page an example of coloured crochet in stripe pattern was shown. This is the simplest way of working patterned and coloured crochet; but sometimes it is desired to change the colour part of the way along a row and it will be necessary to know how this can be done to the best advantage without leaving numerous ends to be fastened off.

Treble stitch is the best stitch to use for this kind of work and the depth of the trebles will govern the outlines of the design.

There are two ways of changing the coloured wools and the method chosen will depend on the direction of work.

I. This is how colours are changed when the second colour continues in the same direction and on the same line as the previous colour. At the second step of the last treble, pick up the new colour with the old and pull it through the top of the stitch. Then, for the rest of the work, discard the old colour, leaving the thread to hang until it is picked up in the next row. When the old colour has to be picked up again it is worked into the second step of the treble as before. The strand of thread which is left at the back of the work must be left loose enough to prevent the work puckering, but not too loose so that the stitches become slack.

2

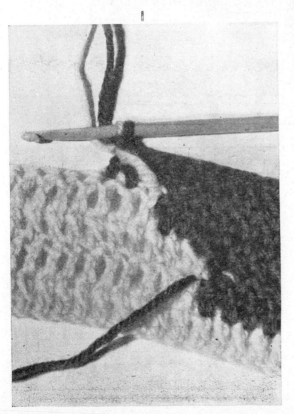

2. It is sometimes necessary to slip stitch a thread along the top of the last few trebles of the previous row, in order to leave a foundation for another colour to be worked later, or to leave a shaped edge to the work. Turn with 1 ch., slip stitch into the 2nd tr. from the hook and continue working a slip stitch into every treble that is to be left. Then make 3 ch. and work the 1st tr. of the new row into the top of the next treble of the previous row.

301

DESIGNS FOR CROCHETED CUSHION AND RUG IN COLOURED CROCHET

Before commencing one of these designs, it will be necessary to find the tension made by the wool, that is, the height of a treble row and the distance between the centre of one treble and the centre of the next. Make up a 3-in. square of solid treble for this purpose. From the measurements of the tension, it will be possible to plan the number of treble to be worked in each section of colour and the number of rows to a section.

The first design shows a pattern for a rug measuring 34 ins. by 56 ins., and the methods used to plan out the size for each section of colour. To get the exact measures, it would be necessary to use wool and a size of hook to make a stitch either 2 ins. long (a long treble in carpet yarn and a blanket hook), or else a stitch that would be 1 in. long (double knitting wool and a large size of bone hook). In the first, there would be one row to a section and in the second there would be two rows to a section, one section being the shortest step of one colour. The short step is used as a unit of design, that is, the shape of each mass of colour is built up on the measurement of one, or more, depths of this one step. A little starch paste should be brushed over the wrong side of the work to hold the strands secure.

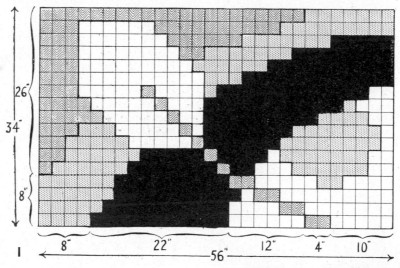

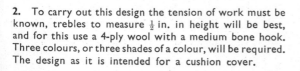

1. A geometric design for a rug to be carried out in four colours, or four shades of one colour. The shortest depth in the design measures 2 ins. and the design is built up on this unit; all edges of colour measure 2 ins., or a multiple of 2 ins. in height. If the tension of work is 1 in. to a treble row, each row in the design will be made with 2 rows of work. If a long treble in carpet yarn, or a treble in rug wool, measures 2 ins. in height, then 1 row of work will make 1 row of the design. Each square in the design is equivalent to 2 sq. ins. of work.

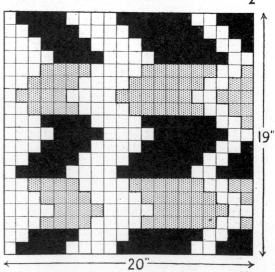

2. To carry out this design the tension of work must be known, trebles to measure ½ in. in height will be best, and for this use a 4-ply wool with a medium bone hook. Three colours, or three shades of a colour, will be required. The design as it is intended for a cushion cover.

302

A CROCHETED POCHETTE

A colourful pochette to match an outfit can be very quickly made with a few left-over oddments of wool, providing they are all the same thickness.

The entire work should be carried out with trebles in 4-ply wool and an edging of double crochet. The bag part of the pochette may be crocheted, or to save time, it may be made in felt to match one of the colours used in the crochet.

1

1. The design can be easily followed from this illustration to any size desired. This one is in 4-ply wool worked with a medium bone hook, making trebles $\frac{1}{2}$ in. high and $\frac{1}{4}$ in. from centre to centre. The measurements are 9 ins. wide and 6 ins. deep.

2. This design can be carried out to any size, when the tension of work is known. To plan out the size from the tension, follow the directions for rugs and adapt the size of the stitch to the proportion of design taken for each colour. Thus, if the trebles measure $\frac{1}{4}$ in. from centre to centre and the dark colour is to measure $3\frac{1}{2}$ ins. long, this measure will be gained by working 14 tr. sts. in a straight row. Then the colour will change for the next section.

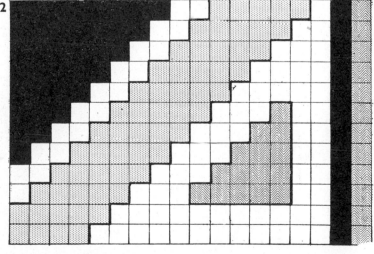

2

LACE INSETS

Small lace circles and squares, etc., can make pretty decoration for lingerie. Several designs are shown here and the thickness of thread and hook may be chosen to suit the texture of material that will be used for the garment.

The inset is made first and then applied to the garment, which should be ready made up so that the inset can be let into the correct place without any guess work. Then the material is cut away from beneath the lace and the raw edges are strongly neatened.

1

commence the next round with 5 ch., * 1 tr. into the second double crochet of the previous round, 2 ch.; repeat from * all round.

Work a row of double crochet, 3 into every space.

The next round is made of treble and chain spaces as

2

3

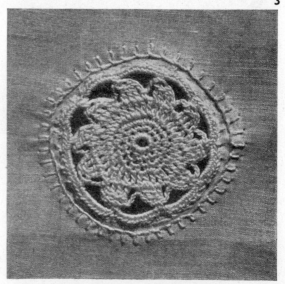

1. Here is a circular inset in the process of being made. A short length of chain has been joined into a ring with a slip stitch and into this ring there has been worked a row of close double crochet stitches. Into this row a second row has been worked and, because the ring will have to be a little longer because it is farther out from the centre, 2 d.c. sts. have been worked into alternate stitches of the first row with 1 d.c. in the other stitches between. Next, a row of treble is worked and the number of these is increased for the same reason as before. But, in order to obtain smoother spacing, a treble is worked into a stitch and the next treble is worked between the stitches of the previous row.

To give a firm edge to the treble, on which further pattern can be built, a row of double crochet is worked, with a stitch into a treble and one into a space.

The remainder of the pattern will be built up on the number of stitches in this last row, so make sure that the number of stitches can be divided equally to give the desired result.

2. A flower-like inset that will have many uses, and which can be made up into almost any size by merely repeating the double crochet and spaced rows.

Make 10 ch. and join into a ring with a slip stitch.

Work 15 d.c. into the ring.

1 d.c. into the first double crochet of the first round, 2 d.c. into the next; repeat this all round. Then

before and then neaten with 4 d.c. into every space. Round this last round work 4 d.c. and 3 ch., arranging the chain to come over the centre of the space in the previous pattern round.

3. Here is a fine inset let into linen cambric. A ring of buttonhole stitching helps to soften the hard effect of the crocheted edge. The inset is made with a small length of chain joined into a ring, into which is then worked a number of double crochet tightly. The next 3 rounds are also in double crochet, with 2 sts. worked into every other stitch of the previous round and one in the intervening stitches. Next comes a round of treble, increased in the same way. Then the number of stitches is divided into a certain number and the petals worked into each group. The picture has 1 d.c., 3 ch., 3 l.tr. with all but the last pair of loops disposed of until the last stitch and then 3 ch., 4 sts. being worked into the previous row. Thus, it would be necessary to divide the number of stitches into fours. In the next round 7 ch. is worked between each petal and a slip stitch on the top. The last round, which will hold the sewing stitches, is made with double crochet worked tightly.

When the crochet is finished, press the inset under a damp cloth and hot iron. Lay the lace in position on the garment and tack it securely. Oversew the edge of the crochet very strongly to the garment and take out the tacks.

Turn the garment to the wrong side and cut away the material from underneath the lace, leaving about ⅛ in. for turnings. Thread the needle with sewing cotton and whip the raw edge of the material to the edge of the lace.

4. Here is a useful square medallion. Of a simple design, it may be used as a unit in a large mat made up of several of these squares. The colour of the squares can be varied or alternated as desired.

Make 35 ch. loosely, miss 3 ch. and then work a treble into every other chain left. Make 3 ch. and turn. Work 3 tr. into the first 3 tr. from the hook, 2 ch., miss 2 tr., 1 tr. on the next. Continue with similar spaces until there are 3 tr. left, end with 3 tr.

Continue following the design, working spaces of 2 ch. and 1 tr. and blocks with 2 tr. worked into the chain loops of the spaces. The 2 ch. between the trebles for spaces will make the inset square. If an oblong inset of similar design is required, make the spaces with 3 ch. and 1 tr. and work 3 tr. into each chain loop.

5. An oblong inset obtained as just suggested, with 3 ch. and 1 tr. forming each space and 3 tr. worked into a space. If a square inset with the same design is required, make the spaces with 2 ch. and 1 tr. and work 2 tr. into each chain loop.

A very decorative edge is gained with a row of double crochet worked all round the inset, placing one in a stitch along the top and bottom rows and two into each treble at the sides. Where there is the chain loop at the turn of the rows, this is caught up with the treble stitch. To make the picot edge, work 4 d.c., 3 ch., 1 sl.st. into the first chain, all round except at the corners where the work is 3 d.c. on each side of the picot at the corner.

There is another method of adapting the sizes of these lace insets. To increase the depth work every row twice; this will not, of course, affect the width. The pattern for an oblong can be repeated to make a square.

4

5

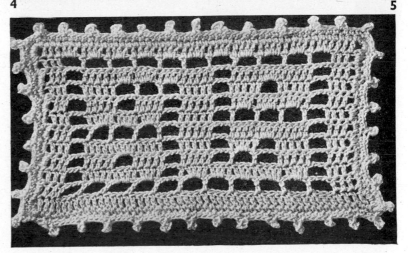

LACE PATTERNS TO BE COPIED

Many workers find that it is much easier to copy drawings of laces than it is to read directions.

Choose the size of thread and hook to give the measurements required; this can be found by measuring a square of trebles.

If the designs given in this section are required for large pieces of work, the thread must be thick and the hook correspondingly thick; while, if the piece of work is to be small, then the thread and hook will be fine.

Find out the size required and divide that measure by the number of squares shown on the drawing; this will give the size for one square of treble stitches. A square of stitches is the number required to make the width across the stitches the same as the height of one treble stitch. Choose the thread and hook to make the square of trebles that size.

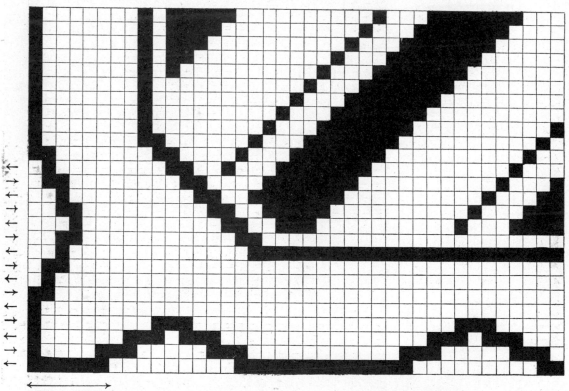

START HERE

1. Here is an extremely simple and very effective design for a mat. It may be square or oblong by making an appropriate number of sections to each edge.

The work is done entirely with treble and chain, and it is built up with squares of trebles on an open mesh ground. Work will start at one corner, making enough chain for the section marked. Then the first 3 rows will be worked and left while the first 3 rows of the next section of the edge are made. Continue in this way until there are enough edge sections for the length, and join them all together with chain. The 4th row of work will be done right across all the sections.

The diagonal lines inside the border will continue across the mat, and the border will run right round.

A DESIGN FOR A TRAY OR TROLLEY MAT

This simple design is to be carried out in treble and chain in blocks of treble and spaces of chain and 1 treble. Choose the thread and hook in a size to give a suitable measure for the finished mat. Each square marked on the design represents a square of treble stitches.

When the mat is finished, make a fringe at the two short sides with size 1 crochet cotton. (*See* page on fringe making for directions of a suitable method.)

DESIGNS FOR MOTIFS

Here are two square motifs to be used alone as mats, or to be let into material. If the same design is required but in an oblong shape, work two more trebles for each square than will make a square of trebles. Similarly work two more chain than is used for a square space.

I

1. A design made of treble blocks and chain and 1 tr. spaces only. A wider border can be made by adding another row of trebles all round, turning the corners with 5 trs.

2. This shows a geometric design using lacets as well as treble blocks and spaces. Greater care must be taken in working evenly throughout. If it is felt that a wider outer band will give a firmer finish, add a row of treble all round with 5 to turn each corner.

2

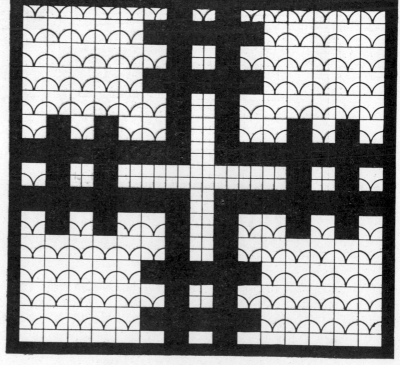

A FLORAL CORNER FOR A CLOTH

The design shown on this page is intended to be worked in very thick cotton, either size 1 or 2, with a thick steel hook, size about 4, for a cloth. The size of the cloth may be as required, the necessary number of chain for that size being made and the first row worked solidly in treble. This floral design is intended for each corner and the centre of the cloth to be dotted with blocks of treble as suggested in the drawing. A fringe added all round will make a very attractive finish. Fine coloured mercerized knitting cotton would be a pleasant change to the usual crochet cotton and, now that coloured table-cloths are fashionable the work can be quickly done in this thread. The cloth would make a very acceptable present.

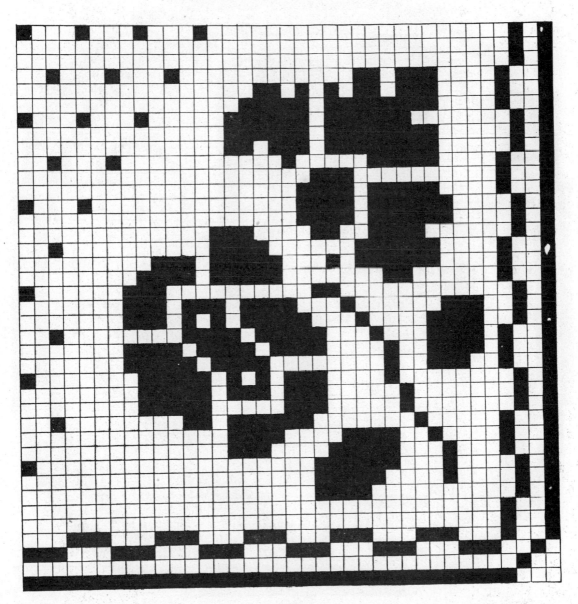

A CROCHETED CENTRE PIECE

This design can be worked for a number of purposes. If carried out in very thick thread it will be suitable for a round table cover, in medium thickness it will make a centre for a bedspread and in fine cotton it will work out to a size suitable for a table mat.

In coloured knitting cotton it will make an attractive cushion cover. The two outer rows may be worked after the rest of the mat and in two different colours. With a little ingenuity and following the directions given for working a coloured design in crochet, several colours could be introduced.

A FLUFFY BOLERO

Measurements. To fit a 34-in. bust; length from shoulder to lower front edge, 20 ins. The fronts are stretched slightly after the bolero is made up, to make the front edges hang better; sleeve seam length, 3¼ ins.

Materials. Five balls of angora (½ oz. each); a blanket hook. Only the first section of this hook will be needed; a small bone crochet hook; one small button for the neck fastening. Nothing heavy should be sewn on to the neck as it will stretch the neck edge.

DETAILS OF WORK

The fabric is made with tricot st., the hook picking up the front of the horizontal st., to make a fairly fine fabric. (See Index for page giving directions for tricot work.) Other kinds of crochet sts. are not suitable for this wool.

Work begins at the lower edge. Incs. are made at the right-hand edge by picking up the 1st loop through the 1st st. from the hook, and at the left-hand edge by making a loop through the last upright st. of the previous row, as well as the usual last st. through the end l. of the previous row. Decs. are made at the right-hand edge by picking up the 1st loop through the 3rd st. from the hook, and at the left-hand edge by omitting the last st.

Straight, unshaped fabric is made by picking up the 1st l. through the 2nd st. from the hook and working the last l. through the end st., which will seem to be at the side of the work. Make a small square in some smooth wool before starting the bolero to make sure that you can work the straight-edged fabric, and then practise the shapings. It is extremely difficult to undo angora wool, so make sure of these shapings first.

DIRECTIONS

RIGHT FRONT

Make a ch. of 32 and work the first two steps of tricot st. The directions for working the st. which picks up the loop through the front of the horizontal l. of the previous row will be found by referring to the Index.

Then inc. 5 times at the right-hand edge.

Continue with straight fabric until the work measures 8 ins. from the beginning.

ARMHOLE SHAPING

Next row, work to within 5 sts. of the end and work back.

Next row, work to within 2 sts. of the end and work back.

Continue in straight fabric until work measures 16¼ ins. Break off the wool. The neck shaping is worked when the bolero is made up by turning the fabric into the required line. A much smoother neck line is obtained in this manner.

LEFT FRONT

Make the same number of ch. and work to the same measures, but for the left-hand shapings, follow the directions given above in the details of work.

THE BACK

Make a ch. of 62 and work in straight fabric until the side seams measure the same as the front side seams. Then follow the directions for the armhole shapings and work straight fabric again until the back measures the same depth as the fronts.

THE SLEEVES (both alike)

Make a ch. of 32 and work for 3½ ins., shaping the seams by inc. 1 st. at both sides in each step of the tricot st. To shape the top, dec. the length of the next row by 2 sts. at each end. For the next 2 ins. dec. 1 st. at each end, and for the next 2½ ins. dec. 2 sts. at each end. Break off the wool.

TO MAKE UP

Join the side, shoulder and sleeve seams with over-sewing in a matching cotton. Shape the top of the fronts as desired and sew the superfluous fabric to the wrong side. Be very careful not to stretch the fabric at the seams. Work a row of d.c. down the fronts and across the lower edge of the back, using the fine bone hook. Then work two rows of tr.st., slightly tightening the edge and placing 3 sts. at the two corners of each lower front edge. If these tr.sts. are not worked so as to tighten, then the edge of the bolero will be frilly. It is unnecessary to work the edging round the sleeves.

Make a buttonholed bar to fasten the button sewn at the top of the left-hand front. Press the fabric carefully so as not to stretch the edges. The weight of the iron should not be allowed to rest on the work.

Pull the fronts downwards a little to stretch them.

COLLAR AND CUFFS

Crisp lingerie touches can be made very quickly with thick threads crocheted with loops and double crochet. There are many suitable threads, including the coarsest crochet cotton and knitting cotton, also the thick mercerized embroidery threads sold on balls.

Use a finer hook than would be used for ordinary laces, as the cuffs and collars need a certain amount of substance, to prevent them being floppy.

1. Cuffs in knitting cotton. Make a ch. foundation loosely the length required, and into every ch. work 1 d.c. Turn with 3 ch. and work 1 tr. into every d.c. stitch; repeat this row.

Then make 5 ch. and work 1 d.c. into the 3rd tr. from the hook. Work along the row with 5 ch., miss 2 tr., 1 d.c. into the next tr. End with a d.c. into the ch. at the end. Make 7 ch. and turn. Work 1 d.c. into the 1st loop of the previous row and continue working 7 ch. and 1 d.c. into the loops. At the end of the row, turn with 9 ch. and repeat the last row, working 9 ch. instead of 7. A further row with 11 ch. is worked for the last row. For extra stiffness of the edge, a row of d.c. may be worked tightly into the last row of ls.

2. Here is a collar worked on the same design as the cuffs, but showing the decorative effect of p. ls. A length of ch. is made for the foundation as long as will reach round the neck of the dress and along the ch. work 1 d.c., 1 ch., miss 1 ch., 1 d.c. into the next. Turn with 3 ch.

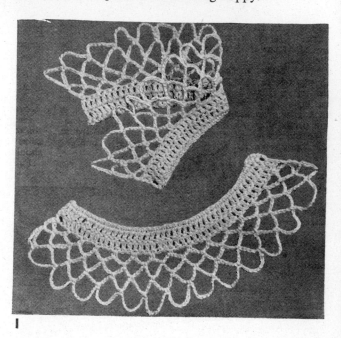

1

2

In the next row work 1 d.c. between the d.c. of the 1st row and 3 ch. between. Turn with 7 ch. and work 1 d.c. into every l. of the previous row with 7 ch. between each st. Turn with 7 ch. * Work 1 d.c. into the 1st loop; 5 ch. slip stitch into the 1st ch. to make the 1st p. l.; 5 ch.; continue working from * into every loop. Turn with 7 ch. and work 1 d.c. into every strand of 5 ch. of the previous row with 9 ch. between. Turn with 7 ch. Work 1 d.c. into the 1st l. and then make a p. as before at the middle of the ch. l. of the last row. 7 ch. are worked between each picot. Turn with 9 ch., 1 d.c. into the 1st l. of the previous row and make a p. with 5 ch.; * 11 ch., 1 d.c. into the next l. and a p. with 5 ch.; repeat from * to the end. Turn with 13 ch.

In this, the last row, the ps. are at the tops of the ls. Make a p. with the last 5 ch. of the 13 ch., 5 ch., 1 d.c. into the 1st loop of the previous row. * 10 ch., make a p. with the last 5 ch., 5 ch., 1 d.c. into the next l.; repeat from * to the end. Wider collars are made by adding further rows before the last.

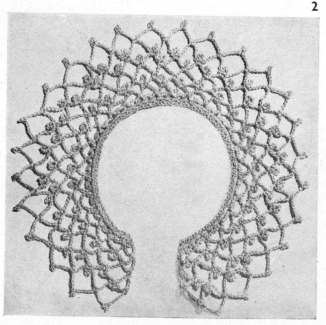

A CROCHETED JUMPER FOR SUMMER WEAR

MEASUREMENTS

Bust, 35-36 ins.; length from shoulder to lower edge, 18 ins.; length of sleeve seam, 7 ins.

MATERIALS

Two balls (4 ozs.) of dark colour; I ball (2 ozs.) of light colour; I ball (2 ozs.) of white; I small bone crochet hook.

DETAILS OF STYLE

The work is done in diagonal rows, first down the right front and then turning to work up the left front by working a group of 5 tr. into the middle tr. of the corresponding group in the previous row.

The bands around the waist and edges of the sleeves are worked after the rest of the garment.

All work is done in tr.st.

DIRECTIONS

THE FRONT

The chain for the front neck is made first. It must consist of an odd number and be long enough to reach round the front neck—that is, from the top of one shoulder to the top of the other—and it should also be long enough to make the size required. The actual number will depend on the size of the hook. The one used for the illustration made trebles $\frac{3}{8}$ in. high and $\frac{3}{16}$ in. apart on the solid fabric, and 79 ch. were made for the foundation, with 3 more to turn. The chain must be made loosely.

1st row, miss the 3 ch. made for turning and work a tr. in the next ch. Work tr. in every ch. until there are 39 tr., work 5 tr. in the next ch. and then 39 tr. in the next 39 ch., 3 ch., turn.

Next row, I tr. in the 1st tr. from the hook and then I tr. on top of every tr. of the previous row, with 5 tr. worked into the middle tr. of the group of 5 tr. in the centre of the previous row, 3 ch., turn at the end.

Work a third row of tr. with the same colour, working the 5 at the centre front.

Change to white and work another row.

Change to the light colour and work 2 more rows.

Change to dark colour and work 3 rows.

Change to white and work I row.

Change to light colour and work 2 rows.

This will finish the shoulders.

The entire patt. is made with 3 rows dark, I row white and then 2 rows light.

Join on the dark colour above the 7th tr. down and work as far as the 7th tr. from the end. Break off the thread. Join on over the 5th tr. of the previous row and work to the 5th tr. of the end. Break off the thread.

Join on over the 3rd tr. of the previous row and work round to the 3rd tr. from the end.

Join on the white over the 2nd tr. of the previous row and work round to the last but one of the end.

Join on the light colour over the 2nd tr. on the previous row and work to the 2nd from the other end, 3 ch. and turn.

Work the 1st tr. into the 2nd tr. from the hook and work as far as the end but one of the other end. Join on the dark colour, 3 ch. and turn.

Work in this way, working the 1st tr. into the 2nd tr. of the previous row and going as far as the end but one at the other end, in every row until there are 4 white bands.

After the 4th white band, the waist line is made straight. The work is not taken as far as the centre front and each row will become shorter by 3 trs. at the waist end. To

do this, at the waist end of the row, turn with 3 ch. when work reaches the 3rd tr. from the end and work the 1st tr. of the next row into the top of the 3rd tr. from the hook.

In the next 4 rows, commencing at the armhole end, begin each row with the 1st tr. worked into the 1st tr. of the previous row and going to the last tr. at the other end.

Now work is shortened by 3 tr. at both ends to make the shaping of the side seam as well. Work, reducing the number of trs. by 3 at each end of every row, until there are 6 white bands and 2 light rows beyond the 6th white row.

To make the other side of the front, join on the appropriate colour to the correct side of the work and work as for the other side of the front, shaping by inc. the armhole end of the rows and dec. the waist ends and then dec. both ends when the end of the armhole is reached.

THE BACK

As the top of the neck Is straight, make 2 ch. for the foundation and 3 more to turn.

Work 5 tr. into the 4th ch. from the hook, I tr. into the next, 3 ch., turn.

Next row, I tr. into the top of the 1st tr. from the hook, work I tr. into each tr. of the 1st row with 5 in the middle tr. of the group of the previous row; at the other end of the row, work I tr. into the last tr. and another into the ch. loop, 3 ch. and turn.

Work in this way, changing the colour as before and working the ends of the rows as just described, until the last row of the second dark band.

Now, as far as the end of the third light band, work the shoulders as for the front.

Continue working as for the front as far as the end of the second dark band, which ends at the waist.

THE SLEEVES (both alike)

Commence as for the back and work in a similar way as far as the end of the third dark band.

Now reduce at each end of the rows by 2 trs. to the end of the next dark band.

Then inc. the ends of the rows, by working to the last tr. and beginning on the first.

Work stops at the elbow after the fourth white band and the remaining rows are shortened at the elbow as at the waist of the jumper.

The sleeve finishes at the end of the fifth light band.

The straight bands across the bottom of the jumper are worked before the jumper is made up and the bands round the ends of the sleeves are worked before the seam is joined.

Work d.c. across the waist edges, working I st. to each tr. and I st. at the junction of 2 trs. This should give the right tension. Use the dark colour for this.

On these d.c., work 2 rows of tr., still in dark colour. Work I row of white, 2 rows of light colour, and then 3 rows of dark.

Around the sleeves, work the row of d.c. and 2 rows of tr., all in dark colour, I row of white and 2 rows of light colour.

TO MAKE UP

Press the work very lightly under a damp cloth and dry it with the iron. Join the seams with oversewing, pinning them together to make the stripes fit well. The sleeves are large enough to be pleated, one small pleat being made at each white stripe across the top.

A CROCHETED JUMPER FOR SUMMER WEAR

A BABY'S DRESS IN CROCHET

This little dress can be crocheted in cotton for summer and in wool for winter. The dress in the illustration was worked with crêpe cotton which is equivalent to 3-ply wool.

Measurements. Round the chest, 17 ins.; length of bodice, from shoulder, 6 ins.; length from shoulder to lower edge, 18 ins. when pressed; length of sleeve seam, 3½ ins.

Materials. 7 ozs. of crêpe cotton; a small bone hook (about size 10); some ribbon for the waist, neck and sleeves, and a few buttons for the back opening.

DETAILS OF STYLE

The bodice is worked first, from the waist to the shoulders, then the skirt is worked on to the bottom of the bodice and downwards to the hem. It will be very easy to alter the length of the skirt as required. The bodice is in d.c. and the skirt is in tr. and ch. A narrow scalloped edging is worked around the hem, sleeves and neck. The bodice and top of the skirt opens down the centre back.

DIRECTIONS

THE FRONT BODICE

Make 43 ch., then 2 more ch. to turn.

1st row, I d.c. into the 3rd ch. from the hook and then a d.c. into every ch. (43 d.c.), 2 ch., turn.

Work backwards and forwards on these 43 sts. for 2 ins.

ARMHOLE SHAPING

Work to within 2 sts. of the end of the next 2 rows. Work to within I st. of the end of the next 2 rows. Continue without shaping for another 2 ins.

FRONT NECK SHAPING

Work 18 d.c., turn, sl.st. along 2 d.c., 2 ch., then I d.c. into every remaining st. to the end, 2 ch., turn.

Work d.c. back to the neck, turn, sl.st. along 2 d.c., 2 ch., work d.c. to the armhole.

Continue working on these sts. until the bodice measures 6 ins. from the beginning.

THE BACK BODICE

Two pieces, both alike.

Make 25 ch. and 2 more to turn.

1st row, I d.c. into the 3rd ch. from the hook and a d.c. in every ch. to the end.

Work on these 25 d.c. for 2 ins.

Work the armhole shapings at one end of the rows, leaving the other end straight for the back opening, copying the directions for the front armhole shapings. Then work without further shaping until the back bodice measures the same length as the front. Rep. for the other side of the back bodice.

A BABY'S DRESS IN CROCHET *continued*

THE FRONT SKIRT

Join on the thread to the end of the lower edge of the front bodice. The 1st row will be worked into the footing of the bodice.

1st row, 2 ch., 1 d.c. into the 1st d.c. of the bodice, then work 2 d.c. into every d.c. of the bodice (85 d.c.) 2 ch., turn.

2nd row, 2 d.c. into every d.c. of previous row (170 d.c.), 3 ch., turn.

The remainder of the skirt is worked on these 170 sts.

1st row, * 10 tr., 3 ch., miss 3 d.c., 1 tr., 2 ch., miss 2 d.c., 1 tr., 3 ch., miss 3 d.c.; rep. from * to the end, finishing with 10 tr., 3 ch., turn.

2nd row, * 10 tr., 3 ch., miss 3 ch., 1 tr., 2 tr. into the space, 1 tr., 3 ch., miss 3 ch.*; rep. from * to the end, finishing with 10 tr., 3 ch., turn.

Rep. these 2 rows throughout until the skirt measures 10 ins., or other required measure.

SKIRT EDGING

The little edging is made with 4 tr. worked into every 3rd st. of the previous row.

THE BACK SKIRT

1st row, work 2 d.c. into every st. of the bodice (50 d.c.), 2 ch., turn.

2nd row, work 2 d.c. into every d.c. of the previous row (100 d.c.), 3 ch., turn.

On these 100 d.c., work the patt. as given for the front skirt, but commencing with the set of spaces instead of 10 tr., thus, * 3 more ch., miss 3 d.c., 1 tr., 2 ch., miss 2 d.c., 1 tr., 3 ch., miss 3 d.c., 10 tr.; rep. from * to the end.

The next row will correspond to the next patt. row on the front, working the long tr. blocks over those of the 1st row and a small block over the middle space.

Continue until the skirt measures about 2½ ins., break off the wool and work the same on the other half of the back bodice. Now overlap the two centre back solid tr. blocks and in the next row work the headings of these two blocks tog., picking up the 1st st. of one with

the last st. of the other, so that in the working of the row these two blocks are joined to make the wrap of the back opening.

Continue working right across the skirt until it measures the same length as the front. Then work the same narrow scalloped edging.

THE SLEEVES (both alike)

Make 43 ch. and 2 more to turn.

Work 1 d.c. into the 3rd ch. from the hook and 1 d.c. in all other ch. Work on these 43 sts. for 3 ins.

SHAPING THE TOP

Make the next 6 pairs of rows shorter at each end by 2 sts. (4 sts. altogether for each pair of rows).

Work the same small scalloped edging across the bottom of the sleeves.

TO MAKE UP

Press the work lightly, smoothing the iron down the skirt, not across it.

Join the shoulder and side seams of the dress and the sleeves seams. Set the sleeves into the armholes and work the narrow scalloped edging round the neck.

Thread narrow ribbon through the holes made by the 1st row of increased sts. round the waist and through the holes made in the scalloped edging of the neck and wrists. Sew buttons down the back opening and make button-holed bars for fastening them.

SUGGESTED DECORATION

The plain bodice with its smooth d.c. texture will give scope for adding embroidery to the fabric. Lazy daisy stitches will be the best because, as in knitting, these stitches give with the expansion of the fabric when the dress passes over the head. Little flowers may be worked over the bodice and sleeves, either in rows, with the colours gradating in tone, or scattered here and there. Use either embroidery wool or stranded embroidery cotton. If embroidery silk is used it should be a thick one.

A CROCHETED MATINÉE COAT

MEASUREMENTS

Length from shoulder to lower edge, 12½ ins.; width round underarm, 17 ins.

MATERIALS

Four ozs. of 3-ply wool, or wool and silk mixture; a small bone crochet hook, No. 8; 1½ yds. of narrow satin ribbon.

DETAILS OF STYLE

The work is commenced at the lower edge and worked up to the shoulder. The patt. is worked in tr. and ch. entirely.

DIRECTIONS

THE FRONTS (both alike)

Make 48 ch.

Into the 4th ch. from the hook, work 2 tr., 2 ch. and 2 tr., * miss 3 ch., 2 tr., 2 ch. and 2 tr. in the next ch. repeat from * to the end, making 12 groups, 3 ch. and turn.

In the next and succeeding rows, work 2 tr., 2 ch. and 2 tr. into every l. of 2 ch. of the previous row. Always turn with 3 ch. Repeat these rows until the work measures 7½ ins.

Next row, 1 d.c. into every l. of ch. and 2 ch. between. This will pull up the top edge of the skirt to the size required for the bodice.

Now work 1 d.c. into the d.c. of the last row and 2 d.c. into the spaces. Then into these sts. work trs. for 6 rows.

TO SHAPE THE ARMHOLES

Work trs. to within 6 of the end, turn, slip st. along 3 tr., 3 ch., 1 tr. into the next st. of the previous row and continue to the end, working tr. sts. as before Work 3 more rows of trs. and then shape the front neck. Work to within 6 tr. of the neck edge and turn; work to the armhole and turn; work to within 3 tr. of the neck edge and turn. Work on these sts. for another 3 rows and fasten off.

THE BACK

Make 96 ch. and work the skirt in the same st. and for the same length as the front skirt.

Treat the top of the skirt as for the front and work the bodice in solid tr. in the same way, making the armhole shapings at both sides of the work. There is no neck shaping: make the bodice the same length as the front and finish off with a straight line of trs.

THE SLEEVES

Make 48 ch. and work as for the front skirt for 3½ ins.

SHAPING THE TOP

Shorten each row at the end, by one group until the sleeve measures 6 ins., then fasten off.

TO MAKE UP

Lightly press the work and join the seams by catching the tops of the scallops together. Set in the sleeves with slight fullness at the tops and then work a simple edging of 1 row of the skirt patt. round the hem and sleeve edges, putting a group opposite a group, and also a row round the neck edge.

To fasten the coat, thread ribbon through the holes made by the groups of tr. and ch. round the neck and waist.

INDEX